THE DIRECTORY
OF THE WORLD'S
WEAPONS

THE DIRECTORY OF THE WORLD'S WEAPONS

BARNES
&NOBLE
BOOKS
NEW YORK

This edition published by Barnes & Noble, Inc.
by arrangement with Brown Packaging Ltd

1996 Barnes & Noble Books

ISBN 0-7607-0264-0

M 10 9 8 7 6 5 4 3 2 1

Material previously published in 1993 as part of the partwork *In Combat*

Editorial and design: Brown Packaging Ltd
255-257 Liverpool Road, London N1 1LX

Printed in The Slovak Republic

CONTENTS

MAIN BATTLE TANKS No. 1

Main Battle Tanks remain the most important single weapon system in the land battle. New tank armour has made the latest Western tanks all but immune to most hand-held infantry anti-tank weapons. Computerised fire control systems make tank gunnery faster and more accurate than ever before.

M1 Abrams

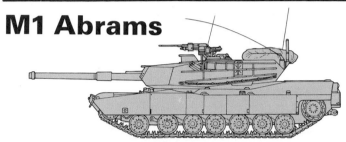

The first tank in the world to have Chobham armour – a combination of ceramic blocks and steel plate – the M1 Abrams achieves a high standard of protection without sacrificing mobility. The M1's gas turbine has a tremendous reserve of power, enabling it to travel cross-country at over 60 km/h. Most M1s deployed to the Gulf were the M1A1 version, which has since been superseded by the M1A2. The M1A1 has depleted uranium in its armour plate which is an incredibly dense metal and, though increasing its weight to nearly 65 tonnes, makes it the most heavily armoured tank in the world.

Specification
Crew: 4
Combat weight: 54.5 tonnes (53 tons 1433 lb)
Road speed: 72 km/h (45 mph)
Power-to-weight ratio: 27 hp/tonne
Length of hull: 7.9 m (26 ft)
Height: 2.37 m (7 ft 9 in)
Armament: 1×120-mm gun; 1×50-cal machine-gun; 1×7.62-mm machine-gun

Assessment
Firepower ★★★★★
Protection ★★★★★
Age ★★★
Worldwide users ★

The M1 Abrams series is the best tank in service today. Its gas turbine engine and advanced suspension allow unprecedented cross-country speed, while its armour protection and firepower are equal or superior to any tank it might meet in combat.

Challenger

The British Challenger tank was developed from an upgraded Chieftain design ordered by the Shah of Iran. Much faster than the ageing Chieftain tank, Challenger is powered by a diesel engine and protected by Chobham armour. Its 120-mm rifled gun is the same as the one fitted to the Chieftain, but although the weapon is extremely powerful the Challenger performed badly in NATO tank gunnery competitions because of serious problems with its modernised fire-control system. The British Army actually ceased to enter the annual NATO tank shoot because Challenger kept coming last! Its frontal armour is 500 mm thick, making it almost as well protected as the M1. Many Challengers in the Gulf War were fitted with extra armour to protect them from the Iraqi infantry's extensive range of Soviet-made missiles and the 125-mm main armament of their T-72 MBTs.

Specification
Crew: 4
Combat weight: 62 tonnes (61 tons)
Road speed: 56 km/h (35 mph)
Power-to-weight ratio: 19 hp/tonne
Length of hull: 8.3 m (27 ft 3 in)
Height: 2.9 m (9 ft 6 in)
Armament: 1×120-mm gun; 2×7.62-mm machine-guns

Assessment
Firepower ★★★★★
Protection ★★★★★
Age ★
Worldwide users ★

The British Challenger is well-protected and has a good cross-country performance. Its only real weakness was the fire control system that reduced the accuracy of its 120-mm gun, which cannot effectively be fired on the move.

T-72

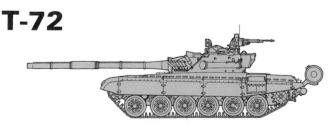

The T-72 is the latest type of Russian tank to be widely exported, but is no match for the latest Western tanks. Its 125-mm smoothbore gun has a much shorter effective range than the 120-mm gun of the M1A1 Abrams and the Leopard 2. To get a 125-mm gun into a low 41-tonne tank, it has a crew of only three and an automatic loader. Eary T-72s have only 250 mm of frontal armour, but the T-72G and T-72M have 350 mm and 400 mm respectively. The T-72M also has two prominent bulges of extra armour on its turret front, causing US tank crews to nickname it the 'Dolly Parton'.

Specification
Crew: 3
Combat weight: 41 tonnes (40 tons 784 lb)
Road speed: 60 km/h (37 mph)
Power-to-weight ratio: 19 hp/tonne
Length of hull: 6.95 m (22 ft 10 in)
Height: 2.37 m (7 ft 9 in)
Armament: 1×125-mm smoothbore gun; 2×7.62-mm machine-guns

Assessment
Firepower ★★★★
Protection ★★★
Age ★★★
Worldwide users ★★★

The Russian T-72 is lighter than the latest NATO tanks and cannot take much punishment, but its 125-mm gun is capable of knocking out all but the latest NATO armour.

OF-40

Closely resembling the German Leopard 1, the Italian OF-40 was designed by OTO-Melara and FIAT for the export market, and actually uses many component parts of the Leopard. It is armed with the 105-mm rifled gun widely used in 1960s-generation NATO tanks, but its modern fire control system enables it to shoot very accurately. Israeli tanks armed with 105-mm guns destroyed Syrian army T-72s without difficulty during the 1982 war in Lebanon, so the 105-mm remains an effective weapon. The OF-40 is a fast tank, almost able to match the road speeds of the Challenger or M1, but it lacks the same reserve of power for cross-country manoeuvre. But the OF-40 is not equipped with advanced Chobham-type armour, and its manoeuvrability is achieved by sacrificing armour protection. Its relatively light armour is insufficient to stop a large-calibre armour-piercing shell, and most infantry anti-tank missiles would knock it out.

Specification
Crew: 4
Combat weight: 45.5 tonnes (44 tons 1747 lb)
Road speed: 60 km/h (37 mph)
Power-to-weight ratio: 18 hp/tonne
Length of hull: 6.8 m (22 ft 4 in)
Height: 2.45 m (8 ft)
Armament: 1×105-mm gun; 2×7.62-mm machine-guns

Assessment
Firepower ★★★
Protection ★★
Age ★★
Worldwide users ★

The OF-40 is typical of the tank designs offered by Western industries for export. Lightly protected, it would be lucky to survive a hit from a main tank gun or anti-tank missile. On the other hand it is far cheaper than vehicles like the M1 Abrams, and its 105-mm gun will deal with all Soviet export tanks.

T-62

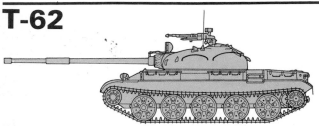

Designed during the 1950s, the T-62 was the standard MBT of the Soviet army until the late 1970s. It was a disappointment from the start, and most Warsaw Pact armies retained the earlier T-54/55-series tanks. The T-62 was the first Soviet tank to carry a smoothbore main armament: its 115-mm gun was judged an effective weapon by the Israelis, who tested captured T-62s after the 1973 Yom Kippur war. But its rate of fire was lower than comparable Western tanks, and it offered little improvement in mobility or protection over the T-54/55. At ranges greater than 1200 metres, the 115-mm gun loses its accuracy, so a shooting match with modern NATO tanks in open terrain is a recipe for disaster. The Syrians lost hundreds of T-62s in the 1973 war. Iraq is another major user of T-62s, concentrating them in the Republican Guard units with a smaller number of T-72s.

Specification
Crew: 4
Combat weight: 40 tonnes (39 tons 828 lb)
Road speed: 50 km/h (31 mph)
Power-to-weight ratio: 14.5 hp/tonne
Length of hull: 6.63 m (21 ft 9 in)
Height: 2.39 m (7 ft 10 in)
Armament: 1×115-mm smoothbore gun; 1×12.7-mm and 1×7.62-mm machine-guns

Assessment
Firepower ★★★
Protection ★★
Age ★★★★★
Worldwide users ★★★★★

The T-62 proved unsatisfactory during the 1973 Arab-Israeli war, but it still forms the bulk of Arab armies' tank forces. Cramped, uncomfortable and not well protected, it is designed to overwhelm opposition by use of superior numbers.

Type 69-II

The Chinese Type 69 is an improved version of the Type 59, a copy of the Russian T-54. Lightly armoured, it carries a Chinese-designed 100-mm smoothbore gun that requires different ammunition from the 100-mm rifled gun used by the Type 59 or T-54. Its armament is stabilised, and the tank includes an NBC (Nuclear Biological & Chemical) defence system. Iraq bought between 100 and 200 Type 69s via Saudi Arabia in 1983. They were used against Iran during the Iran-Iraq war, and many more were lost during Operation 'Desert Storm'.

Specification
Crew: 4
Combat weight: 37 tonnes (36 tons 940 lb)
Road speed: 50 km/h (31 mph)
Power-to-weight ratio: 16 hp/tonne
Length of hull: 6.2 m (20 ft 4 in)
Height: 2.8 m (9 ft 2 in)
Armament: 1×100-mm smoothbore gun; 1×12.7-mm and 2×7.62-mm machine-guns

Assessment
Firepower ★★★
Protection ★★
Age ★★
Worldwide users ★★

Chinese tanks remain inferior to Russian vehicles, which they are copies of. The Type 69-II looks like a Russian tank and is built to Russian productions standards.

M60

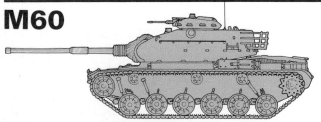

The M60 was the standard US Army Main Battle Tank from the 1960s until the late 1980s, and has been replaced by the M1 Abrams. The US Marine Corps still have some but they are now all in store. In Israeli hands it performed well against T-54/55s and T-62s. With 250 mm of frontal armour it is not significantly better protected, but its 105-mm gun is longer-ranged and more accurate, and its powerplant is more reliable. However, it is outclassed by the T-64s and T-80s, though the US Army rate it as equal to the early T-72s. M60s are also in service with Saudi Arabia, Bahrain and Egypt.

Specification
(M60A3)
Crew: 4
Combat weight: 52.5 tonnes (51 tons 1500 lb)
Road speed: 48 km/h (30 mph)
Power-to-weight ratio: 14 hp/tonne
Length of hull: 6.9 m (22 ft 8 in)
Height: 3.27 m (10 ft 9 in)
Armament: 1×105-mm gun; 1× .50-cal machine-gun and; 1×7.62-mm machine-gun

Assessment
Firepower ★★★★
Protection ★★★
Age ★★★★
Worldwide users ★★★

The M60 was the last in a long tradition of big American medium tanks. They were highly successful in Israeli hands during the 1973 Yom Kippur war.

MAIN BATTLE TANKS No. 2

These tanks all appeared during the 1950s and 1960s, replacing tanks designed during World War II. The old distinctions between light, medium and heavy tanks no longer made sense and the term 'Main Battle Tank' was coined to describe them. Despite their age, four of these tanks were used in the Gulf War.

Chieftain

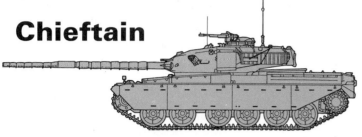

Specification
Crew: 4
Combat weight: 55 tonnes (54 tons 291 lb)
Road speed: 48 km/h (30 mph)
Power-to-weight ratio: 13.6 hp/tonne
Length of hull: 7.5 m (24 ft 7 in)
Height: 2.89 m (9 ft 6 in)
Armament: 1×120-mm gun; 2×7.62-mm machine-guns

Assessment
Firepower ★★★★★
Protection ★★★★★
Age ★★★★★
Worldwide users ★★

The Chieftain was the most powerful tank in any NATO army for many years. Its design emphasised armour and firepower at the expense of speed. The 120-mm gun was capable of knocking out any potential enemy.

Now completing its third decade in service, most British Army Chieftains are in store. When introduced in the 1960s, it had the most powerful gun and the heaviest armour in the world. The L11 120-mm rifled gun was the first weapon of its calibre deployed by a NATO army, and could easily shatter any Soviet tank then in service. The Chieftain's multi-fuel engine was always a weakness, however, being unreliable and producing a great deal of smoke from the exhaust. By 1990s standards it is very underpowered, with half the power-to-weight ratio of tanks like the M1 Abrams.

Centurion

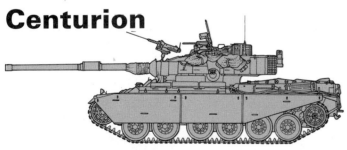

Specification
Crew: 4
Combat weight: 52 tonnes (51 tons 403 lb)
Road speed: 35 km/h (22 mph)
Power-to-weight ratio: 12.5 hp/tonne
Length of hull: 7.8 m (25 ft 6 in)
Height: 3 m (9 ft 11 in)
Armament: 1×105-mm gun; 1×12.7-mm and 2×7.62-mm machine-guns

Assessment
Firepower ★★★★
Protection ★★★★
Age ★★★★★
Worldwide users ★★★

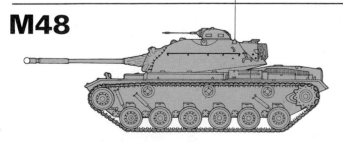

Designed in World War II, the British Centurion saw action as recently as 1989 during the South African operations in Angola. For many years it formed the backbone of the elite Israeli tank forces.

This long-serving tank arrived with British forces fighting in Germany during the last days of World War II. Of the 4,500 manufactured over the next 10 years, over half were exported. The British forces used Centurions during the Korean War, and the Israelis made extensive use of Centurions in the 1967 Six-Day War. Extensively modernised, they served again in the 1973 and 1982 Arab-Israeli wars. Although replaced in the British Army by the Chieftain, Centurions are still operational in several armies. In 1989 the South African tank units, equipped with their own version of the Centurion known as the 'Olifant', saw their first tank-versus-tank action since World War II when they engaged T-55s in Angola.

M48

Specification
Crew: 4
Combat weight: 45 tonnes (44 tons 650 lb)
Road speed: 42 km/h (26 mph)
Power-to-weight ratio: 18 hp/tonne
Length of hull: 6.7 m (22 ft)
Height: 3.1 m (10 ft)
Armament: 1×90-mm gun; 1×12.7-mm and 1×7.62-mm machine-guns

Assessment
Firepower ★★★
Protection ★★
Age ★★★★★
Worldwide users ★★★★★

An American M48 of the US Marine Corps lands in South Vietnam. US forces deployed few of their tank units to Vietnam, believing they would be useless in the jungle.

The M48 has seen combat all over the world, from the deserts of the Middle East to the steaming jungles of Asia. Rushed into production during the Korean War, it was supplied to many American allies during the 1960s. The small US armoured contingent deployed to Vietnam used M48s, and the US-trained South Vietnamese tank force soon adopted M48s as well. The Israelis used M48s very successfully in 1967, progressively upgrading them by fitting 105-mm guns and better powerplants. Various German and American companies are offering modernisation schemes to armies that still use the M48, almost 40 years after its introduction.

T-54/55

Russian tank design dates back to the massive construction programmes of World War II. Smaller and lighter than Western counterparts, the T-54/55 series of medium tanks are at least as powerfully armed and have much lower profiles, which is a major tactical advantage. On the other hand, its small size creates a number of problems, in particular poor crew comfort, limited main armament depression and primitive fire-control systems. At least 50,000 T-54/55s have been built in Russia since the end of World War II, more than any other tank, and they are still in service in nearly 50 countries.

Specification
(T-55)
Crew: 4
Combat weight: 36 tonnes (35 tons 963 lb)
Road speed: 50 km/h (31 mph)
Power-to-weight ratio: 16 hp/tonne
Length of hull: 6.45 m (21 ft 2 in)
Height: 2.4 m (7 ft 11 in)
Armament: 1×100-mm gun; 1×7.62-mm machine-gun plus optional 12.7-mm AA machine-gun

Assessment
Firepower ★★★
Protection ★★★★
Age ★★★★★
Worldwide users ★★★★★

More T-54/55s have been produced than all NATO tanks put together. Used throughout Eastern Europe, Africa and the Middle East, it is likely to remain an important weapon in the Third World.

Leopard 1

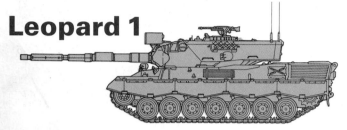

The Leopard tank was the first major armoured fighting vehicle developed in West Germany following the country's post-war re-armament. The Leopard adopts a radically different approach to tanks like the British Chieftain. The lesson that the West German army drew from World War II was that mobility was all-important, and as a result the Leopard has relatively thin armour and low weight, making it very fast across country. Armed with the British-designed 105-mm gun, it packs an adequate punch but its lack of protection makes it horribly vulnerable to the infantry anti-tank weapons it would meet on a 1990s battlefield. It is nevertheless a popular and reliable vehicle, in service with several armies around the world.

Specification
Crew: 4
Combat weight: 40 tonnes (39 tons 828 lb)
Road speed: 65 km/h (40 mph)
Power-to-weight ratio: 20.75 hp/tonne
Length of hull: 7.09 m (23 ft 3 in)
Height: 2.61 m (8 ft 7 in)
Armament: 1×105-mm gun; 2×7.62-mm machine-guns

Assessment
Firepower ★★★
Protection ★
Age ★★★★★
Worldwide users ★★★

The Leopard 1 was the first German-designed tank after World War II, and its design emphasised speed over protection. Although well armed, its weak armour puts it at a disadvantage.

AMX-30

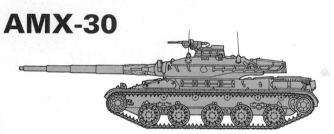

Similar in concept to the German Leopard 1, the French AMX-30 was built after a German/French collaborative tank project of the 1950s failed to progress. Like the Leopard, the AMX-30 is lightly armoured and has good mobility. It is armed with a French-built 105-mm gun, which can use the same ammunition as the Leopard and the American M60. The AMX-30 is really too lightly protected for the modern battlefield, and it lacks a number of characteristics thought essential by other armies, such as a gun stabilisation system. It was cheap, however, which explains its purchase by a dozen countries. The AMX-30 is to be replaced in the French army in the 1990s by the vastly more capable Leclerc MBT.

Specification
Crew: 4
Combat weight: 36 tonnes (35 tons 963 lb)
Road speed: 60 km/h (37 mph)
Power-to-weight ratio: 20 hp/tonne
Length of hull: 6.59 m (21 ft 7 in)
Height: 2.29 m (7 ft 6 in)
Armament: 1×105-mm gun; 1×20-mm cannon; 1×7.62-mm machine-gun

Assessment
Firepower ★★★
Protection ★★
Age ★★★★★
Worldwide users ★★★

The AMX-30 has been widely exported, but this lightly armoured tank is very vulnerable on a 1990s battlefield. French and Saudi forces used AMX-30s during the Gulf War.

Stridsvagn S-103

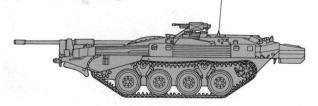

Sweden's advanced and innovative arms industry has often produced unique solutions to military problems. The Stridsvagn S-103 tank, introduced in 1966, is one example of such a non-standard approach. Its 105-mm gun, a variant of the ubiquitous British L7, is mounted direct in the hull, doing away with the need for a turret. The low profile this creates presents the enemy with a very small target, and the tank's well-sloped frontal armour also provides a good measure of protection. It was one of the first tanks equipped with an auto-loader, and it also introduced gas-turbine power more than a decade before the American M1 Abrams made its debut.

Specification
Crew: 3
Combat weight: 40 tonnes (39 tons 828 lb)
Road speed: 50 km/h (31 mph)
Power-to-weight ratio: 18 hp/tonne
Length of hull: 7.04 m (23 ft 1 in)
Height: 2.14 m (7 ft)
Armament: 1×105-mm gun; 3×7.62-mm machine-guns

Assessment
Firepower ★★★
Protection ★★★★
Age ★★★★
Worldwide users ★

Sweden's unique 'S' tank was designed as a defensive vehicle, able to dig itself in and present the smallest possible target to an advancing enemy.

MAIN BATTLE TANKS No. 3

The trend in Main Battle Tank design is for tanks to get heavier protection and more powerful armament. Modern tanks are very costly, however, so a number of designers are producing lighter, simpler vehicles with MBT levels of armament.

T-64

Specification
Crew: 3
Combat weight: 38 tonnes (37 tons 896 lb)
Road speed: 70 km/h (43 mph)
Power-to-weight ratio: 18 hp/tonne
Length of hull: 6.4 m (21 ft)
Height: 2.3 m (7 ft 7 in)
Armament: 1×125-mm smoothbore gun; 1×7.62-mm machine-gun

Assessment
Firepower ★★★★★
Protection ★★★
Age ★★★
Worldwide users ★

Although the T-64 initially had a reputation for unreliability, it could not have been a design failure since it forms about a quarter of front-line Russian tank units.

The T-64 first appeared in the early 1970s, preceding the T-72. It was never exported and was thought to have been an unsuccessful design. But it became clear that the T-64 was a much more sophisticated tank than the T-72. Although problems with the new engine, hydropneumatic suspension, fire-control systems and automatic loader have never been satisfactorily resolved, nearly 10,000 were built and it equipped the most important Russian formations, such as the Group of Soviet Forces in Germany. The T-64B variant can fire the AT-8 'Songster' guided missile from its gun.

T-80

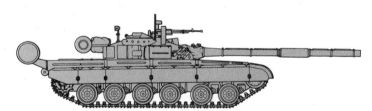

Specification
Crew: 3
Combat weight: 40 tonnes (39 tons 828 lb) (estimate)
Road speed: probably over 60 km/h (37 mph)
Power-to-weight ratio: probably over 20 hp/tonne
Length of hull: 6.9 m (22 ft 8 in)
Height: 2.2 m (7 ft 3 in)
Armament: 1×125-mm gun/missile launcher; 1×12.7-mm machine-gun; 1×7.62-mm machine-gun

Assessment
Firepower ★★★★★
Protection ★★★★
Age ★
Worldwide users ★

The T-80 is a development of the T-64. Although far smaller than Western tanks, it is nevertheless armed with an extremely powerful 125-mm smoothbore cannon.

When the T-80 emerged from the shadow of classification in the 1980s, it proved to be a development of the T-64. The overall layout is similar to that of the earlier tank, but it has a very low silhouette, even by Russian standards. The T-80 is powered by a new gas turbine, considerably increasing its mobility, and it is reported to be fitted with advanced armour, over which it regularly carries explosive reactive armour blocks. Like the T-64 and T-72 it has a three-man crew and an automatic loader, and like the T-64B it can fire the 'Kobra' anti-tank missile, known to NATO as the AT-8 'Songster'.

Leopard 2

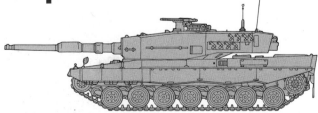

Specification
Crew: 4
Combat weight: 55 tonnes (54 tons 291 lb)
Road speed: 72 km/h (45 mph)
Power-to-weight ratio: 27 hp/tonne
Length of hull: 7.7 m (25 ft 3 in)
Height: 2.48 m (8 ft 2 in)
Armament: 1×120-mm smoothbore gun; 2×7.62-mm machine-guns

Assessment
Firepower ★★★★★
Protection ★★★★
Age ★★★
Worldwide users ★★

Leopard 2's flat planes indicate that it is fitted with laminated armour, since this is extremely difficult to produce in curved form. The Leopard's 120-mm smoothbore gun is the most powerful currently in service in the West, and when used with the tank's advanced sights and fire-control system, it is very accurate.

The German Leopard 2 Main Battle Tank emerged out of the abortive US/German MBT-70 project that was cancelled in the early 1970s. Originally intended to be an upgraded Leopard 1, the new tank was in fact a vastly more capable vehicle, strong in all three of the classic areas of armoured performance. Its powerful engine and advanced suspension give the Leopard 2 the mobility German armoured tactics call for, and 'Chobham' type armour adds considerably to the crew's protection. The main armament is a potent Rheinmetall 120-mm smoothbore gun, which has also been adopted by the Americans to arm later versions of their own M1 Abrams tank. An upgraded Leopard 2 was one of the contenders in the British Army's tank competition won by the Challenger 2, and was rumoured to have been favoured by the Generals.

Merkava

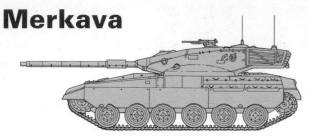

The Israeli army has more armoured combat experience than any other force, and this is reflected in its tanks. The Merkava puts protection before mobility. Lessons in combat also mean that it carries twice as many shells as NATO and Russian tanks. The early Merkavas were slow and heavy, equipped with the battle-tested British-designed 105-mm gun, which could deal with any potential enemy tanks. The Merkava Mk 3, which entered service in 1987, has increased armour protection, a hard-hitting 120-mm smoothbore gun, and a much more powerful engine. The latest version is the Mk 4.

Specification
Crew: 4
Combat weight: 60 tonnes (59 tons 112 lb)
Road speed: 46 km/h (28 mph)
Power-to-weight ratio: 15 hp/tonne
Length of hull: 7.45 m (24 ft 6 in)
Height: 2.64 m (8 ft 8 in)
Armament: 1×105-mm rifled gun; 3×7.62-mm machine-guns; 1×.50-cal machine-gun; 1×60-mm mortar

Assessment
Firepower	★★★★
Protection	★★★★
Age	★★
Worldwide users	★

Unlike other modern tanks, Israel's Merkava has its engine mounted at the front. This is to add protection to the crew: tanks are most often hit in the front, and the bulk of the engine gives the crew added security.

EE-T1 Osorio

The increasing cost of state-of-the-art Western tanks and armoured vehicles has helped to spur other nations into developing their own arms industries. Brazil's arms industry has grown rapidly, and the EE-T1 Osorio Main Battle Tank is one of the most advanced products of that industry. It uses as many existing components as possible, and can be tailored to the requirements of the customer. The Osorio can be fitted with the well-proven NATO 105-mm gun or a French-developed 120-mm smoothbore. The Osorio was trialled in Saudi Arabia, but although a very capable vehicle it could not match the latest American, British or German designs. It is nevertheless an attractive prospect for Third World armies.

Specification
Crew: 4
Combat weight: 41 tonnes (40 tons) 784 lb)
Road speed: 70 km/h (43 mph)
Power-to-weight ratio: 25 hp/tonne
Length of hull: 7.13 m (23 ft 5 in)
Height: 2.37 m (7 ft 9 in)
Armament: 1×105-mm rifled or 120-mm smoothbore gun; 2×7.62-mm machine-guns

Assessment
Firepower	★★★★
Protection	★★★
Age	★
Worldwide users	★

Brazil's EE-T1 Osorio is a capable modern fighting vehicle. It is less complex than the latest Western designs, but by the same token it is cheaper for Third World armies to acquire and operate.

Stingray

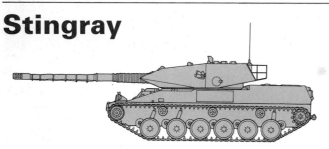

The Commando Stingray was developed as a private venture by the American firm of Cadillac Gage. Weighing in at 19.3 tonnes, it is a light tank, but is equipped with a soft-recoil version of the well-proven Royal Ordnance 105-mm gun. The Stingray has the fighting power of a Main Battle Tank, but with much greater tactical and strategic mobility. The first export order was placed by Thailand, whose army had found that its M48 and Type 69 Main Battle Tanks were too heavy for the swampy and jungle-covered terrain which is found through much of the country.

Specification
Crew: 4
Combat weight: 19.3 tonnes (19 tons)
Road speed: 67 km/h (42 mph)
Power-to-weight ratio: 27.75 hp/tonne
Length of hull: 6.2 m (20 ft 4 in)
Height: 2.55 m (8 ft 4 in)
Armament: 1×105-mm gun; 1×7.62-mm machine-gun; 1×.50-cal machine-gun

Assessment
Firepower	★★★★
Protection	★★
Age	★
Worldwide users	★

The Cadillac Gage Stingray is not a Main Battle Tank, although it has MBT firepower. At less than 20 tonnes, it is air-portable in a C-130 Hercules, and can be shipped anywhere in the world within a couple of days.

FMC CCVL

The Close Combat Vehicle Light is another private venture, developed by FMC in anticipation of a US Army requirement for an air-portable light tank. Designed to be transportable in a Lockheed C-130 Hercules, the CCVL can bolt on extra armour protection if required. It is equipped with a modified M68 105-mm gun, which is a variant of the highly successful British L7 105-mm rifled gun. To this has been added a digital fire-control system and a German-developed low-recoil system. The CCVL chassis has also been fitted with a sophisticated three-man turret developed by Vickers Defence Systems, the resulting vehicle being more appropriately described as a medium tank if not an MBT.

Specification
Crew: 3
Combat weight: 19.4 tonnes (19 tons 206 lb)
Road speed: 70 km/h (43 mph)
Power-to-weight ratio: 26 hp/tonne
Length of hull: 6.1 m (20 ft)
Height: 2.69 m (8 ft 10 in)
Armament: 1×105-mm gun; 1×7.62-mm machine-gun

Assessment
Firepower	★★★★
Protection	★★
Age	★
Worldwide users	★

Like the Stingray, the FMC CCVL is a private venture light tank with MBT fighting power. It cannot take on modern Main Battle Tanks head-on, but is capable of destroying any other armoured vehicle.

The tank really became the queen of the battlefield during World War II, and in the post-war years a whole generation of tanks was developed incorporating the lessons learned on the battlefield. Many remain in service today.

M51 Sherman

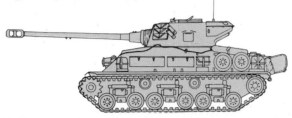

The M4 Sherman medium tank was one of the classic armoured vehicles of World War II. Some 50,000 examples were produced, and after the war the USA supplied surplus M4s to a number of armies. Israel acquired the vehicles via France in the 1950s. Fitted with 76.2-mm guns, they were renamed M1 Super Shermans and were used in both the 1956 and 1967 wars. A new turret, new engines and improved suspensions were to lead to the M50 Super Sherman, which proved capable of dealing with the Soviet-built T-34/85s and T-54/55s equipping Arab armies, but faced problems against the IS-3 heavy tank. The M51 was the result. Designed in collaboration with the French, the M51 incorporated all of the improvements of the M50, together with a long 105-mm gun. In the 1973 Yom Kippur War the M51 successfully engaged T-62 tanks used by Egypt and Syria. Some M51s remain in use with militia forces in South Lebanon, and in reserve with armies such as those of Paraguay and Chile.

Specification
Crew: 4
Combat weight: 39 tonnes (38 tons 851 lb)
Road speed: 45 km/h (28 mph)
Power-to-weight ratio: 11.8 hp/tonne
Length of hull: 6.3 m (20 ft 9 in)
Height: 3.4 m (11 ft 2 in)
Armament: 1×105-mm gun; 1×12.7-mm machine-gun

Assessment
Firepower ★★★
Protection ★★
Age ★★★★★
Worldwide users ★★★

An Israeli 'Super Sherman' during the battle for the Golan Heights. Up-gunned and up-engined, this World War II American tank proved a fair match for the Soviet armour supplied to Arab forces during the 1950s. The poor training of Syrian and Egyptian tank crew helped too.

Panzer 61

Switzerland has always tried to build its own weapons, and in the post-war years a project to develop a Main Battle Tank got under way. The Swiss army acquired 300 British-built Centurion tanks in the 1950s, before the Federal Construction Works at Thun was ready to go into production with a new tank. The first prototypes were armed with a Swiss-designed 90-mm gun, but production examples of the Panzer 61 carried the British 105-mm L7 gun. Layout is conventional, with the driver at the front, a cast-steel turret in the centre and the engine at the rear. The Panzer 61 was followed by the Panzer 68, which has a gun stabilisation system, wider tracks and a co-axial machine-gun instead of a co-axial 20-mm cannon. Unusually for Swiss-designed weapons, the Pz 61 and Pz 68 have not been a success; a 1979 report declared that there were some 50 design faults, including a short track life, an unstable gun and cracking fuel tanks.

Specification
Crew: 4
Combat weight: 39.7 tonnes (39 tons 157 lb)
Road speed: 55 km/h (34 mph)
Power-to-weight ratio: 16.6 hp/tonne
Length of hull: 6.98 m (22 ft 11 in)
Height: 2.75 m (9 ft)
Armament: 1×105-mm gun; 2×7.5-mm machine-guns

Assessment
Firepower ★★★
Protection ★★★
Age ★★★★
Worldwide users ★

An uninspired medium tank armed with a 105-mm gun, Switzerland's Panzer 61 was not a great success and it was roundly condemned in 1979. Switzerland now builds the German Leopard 2 under licence.

Vickers Mk 3

Vickers realised that the Chieftain would be too large and powerful for most armies. The private venture Vickers Main Battle Tank used the successful L7 105-mm gun as well as some of the components of the Chieftain, which was about to go into production at the Vickers Elswick works. The improved Vickers Mk 3 tank had a Detroit diesel engine and a new cast turret. Vickers MBTs are in service in India, Kenya and Nigeria, but no longer in Kuwait. More than 2,400 have been built, with production continuing at the Avadi factory near Madras into the 1980s.

Specification
Crew: 4
Combat weight: 40 tonnes (39 tons 828 lb)
Road speed: 50 km/h (31 mph)
Power-to-weight ratio: 18 hp/tonne
Length of hull: 7.56 m (24 ft 10 in)
Height: 3.1 m (10 ft)
Armament: 1×105-mm gun; 1×12.7-mm ranging machine-gun; 2×7.62-mm machine-guns

Assessment
Firepower ★★★★
Protection ★★★
Age ★★★★
Worldwide users ★★

The Vickers medium tank was developed for sale to foreign powers not able to afford the Chieftain tank. Supplied to India and East Africa, it was also acquired by the Kuwaiti forces that were so memorably steamrollered in August 1991.

Type 61

The Type 61 was Japan's first post-war Main Battle Tank. Design began in 1954 at the technical research and development headquarters of the Japanese Self-Defence Force. The first production tanks were completed in 1962. Some 560 tanks had been completed by the late 1970s, when the more Modern Type 74 entered service. The Type 61 has a conventional welded steel hull, onto which is mounted a turret similar to that on the American M47, which is fitted with a Japanese-manufactured 90-mm rifled gun. The Type 61 is more compact than the American tank and is powered by a turbo-charged air-cooled diesel. Variants of the Type 61 include an armoured bridgelayer, an armoured engineer vehicle and an armoured recovery vehicle.

Specification
Crew: 4
Combat weight: 35 tonnes (34 tons 1000 lb)
Road speed: 45 km/h (28 mph)
Power-to-weight ratio: 17.1 hp/tonne
Length of hull: 6.3 m (20 ft 8 in)
Height: 3.16 m (10 ft 4 in)
Armament: 1×90-mm gun; 1×7.62-mm machine-gun; 1×12.7-mm machine-gun

Assessment
Firepower   ★★
Protection   ★★
Age   ★★★★
Worldwide users ★

Japan's first post-war tank was a major improvement on the mediocre vehicles it fielded during the conflict. Very similar to the US M47, it equipped the 'Self-Defence Force' until the end of the 1970s.

M47

As the US Army adopted the M48 it discarded the M47s built during the early 1950s, and many of these were supplied to US allies. The armour protection is similar to that of the M48 – rather weaker than that of the T-54/55. The 90-mm gun is broadly equivalent in hitting power to the Soviet 100-mm rifled gun, but M47s have no NBC defence. Variously modified versions of the M47 continue to serve in the south-east of Europe including Turkey.

Specification
Crew: 5
Combat weight: 46 tonnes (45 tons 605 lb)
Road speed: 48 km/h (30 mph)
Power-to-weight ratio: 17.5 hp/tonne
Length of hull: 6.35 m (20 ft 10 in)
Height: 3 m (9 ft 11 in)
Armament: 1×90-mm gun; 1×12.7-mm and 1×7.62-mm machine-guns

Assessment
Firepower   ★★★
Protection   ★★★
Age   ★★★★★
Worldwide users ★★★

The M47 was the US Army's post-war medium tank and successor to the famous M4 Sherman. Although better engineered, it was out-gunned by the better protected T-54 being introduced by the Soviets.

T-10

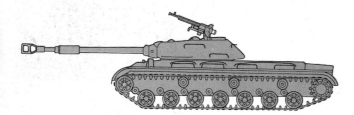

In the 1950s the major powers continued to produce heavy tanks: the British produced the 65-tonne Conqueror and the Americans deployed the M103, which they perversely gave to the Marines. The Soviets introduced the T-10 to replace their World War II JS IIs and JS IIIs. T-10s were never exported and served in independent heavy tank battalions attached to tank armies. They went out of service sometime during the 1970s and no new heavy tanks were built.

Specification
Crew: 4
Combat weight: 52 tonnes (51 tons 403 lb)
Road speed: 42 km/h (26 mph)
Power-to-weight ratio: unknown
Length of hull: 7 m (23 ft)
Height: 2.25 m (7 ft 5 in)
Armament: 1×122-mm gun; 1×12.7-mm or 14.5-mm AA machine-gun; 1×7.62-mm machine-gun

Assessment
Firepower   ★★★
Protection   ★★★★★
Age   ★★★★★
Worldwide users ★

The T-10 was the last in a line of Soviet heavy tanks that proved their worth during World War II. They were issued to independent heavy tank battalions at front and army level.

T-34

Widely rated as the finest tank ever produced during World War II, the T-34's career continues. The Soviets still manufacture 85-mm tank gun ammunition and maintain T-34s in mothballs for export to African allies like Angola. Unlike the 1939-45 models, the T-34s encountered by South African troops in Angola often have T-55-style road wheels, better engines and infra-red night vision devices. The T-34 was the ultimate soldier-proof tank and its use as a bush tank makes a great deal of sense (unless your enemy is equipped with modern armour). European mercenaries found it difficult to knock out T-34s with 66-mm LAWs during the Angolan civil war of 1976. .

Specification
Crew: 4 (5 if bow machine-gun retained)
Combat weight: 32 tonnes (31 tons 1097 lb)
Road speed: 55 km/h (34 mph)
Power-to-weight ratio: 15.6 hp/tonne
Length of hull: 6.19 m (20 ft 4 in)
Height: 2.7 m (8 ft 10 in)
Armament: 1×85-mm gun; 2×7.62-mm machine-guns

Assessment
Firepower   ★★
Protection   ★★★
Age   ★★★★★
Worldwide users ★★★

A parking lot full of T-34s captured from the Angolan communist forces by South African troops during 1982. The T-34 was the most important tank fielded by the USSR during World War II and a key factor in defeating the German invaders.

Reconnaissance vehicles, whether light tanks or armoured cars, are the cavalry mounts of modern armies. Like the cavalry in the days of the horse, one of their major tasks is to seek out the enemy and relay the information back to higher command.

Scorpion

The Scorpion is one of a series of light armoured vehicles developed for the British Army in the 1960s. Given the designation CVR(T), or Combat Vehicle Reconnaissance (Tracked), the Scorpion is basically a very light tank whose low ground pressure confers significant cross-country mobility upon the vehicle. It has been successfully exported: in addition to British Army examples, a variant armed with a 90-mm gun has been sold to Malaysia, and many other armies operate Scorpions modified to suit local requirements. Scorpions have been used by Iran during the 10-year war with Iraq, and in the Falklands they proved to be the only armour capable of handling the boggy terrain. Scorpions also armed reconnaissance units of the British 1st Armoured Division during the 1991 Gulf War against Saddam Hussein's Iraq.

Specification
Crew: 3
Combat weight: 8 tonnes (7 tons 1949 lb)
Maximum road speed: 80 km/h (50 mph)
Power-to-weight ratio 23.5 hp/tonne
Length: 4.7 m (15 ft 5 in)
Height: 2.1 m (6 ft 11 in)
Armament: 1×76-mm gun; 1×7.62-mm machine-gun

Assessment
Firepower   ★★★
Protection   ★★
Age   ★★★
Worldwide users   ★★★★

Developed during the 1960s, the Alvis Scorpion is a very light tank armed with a 76-mm low-pressure gun and possesses exceptional mobility.

ENGESA EE-9 Cascavel

The EE-9 Cascavel, named after a snake found in the South American jungles, is one of the most important products of Brazil's rapidly-growing armaments industry. Developed in the early 1970s, the Cascavel drew upon the ENGESA company's experience in the conversion of trucks from the 6×4 to 6×6 format, and shares many components with the EE-11 Urutu APC. Wheeled vehicles are much cheaper to manufacture and operate than tracked vehicles, and with careful design, their cross-country performance is not too inferior. The Cascavel's 90-mm gun gives the vehicle respectable anti-armour and direct fire-support capability.

Specification
Crew: 3
Combat weight: 13.7 tonnes (13 tons 1075 lb)
Maximum road speed: 100 km/h (62 mph)
Power-to-weight ratio: 15.5 hp/tonne
Length: 5.2 m (17 ft 1 in)
Height: 2.6 m (8 ft 6 in)
Armament: 1×90-mm gun; 1×7.62-mm and 1×.50 Browning machine-gun

Assessment
Firepower   ★★★★
Protection   ★★
Age   ★★
Worldwide users   ★★★

Sturdy, powerfully-armed, with a good cross-country performance, and simple to maintain, the ENGESA EE-9 Cascavel reconnaissance vehicle is one of those designs which proved to be a foundation stone in Brazil's rapidly-growing arms industry.

AMX-13

The AMX-13 was designed by the Atelier de Construction d'Issy-les-Moulineaux, the numeral 13 being the vehicle's designed weight in tonnes. The first prototype was completed in 1948, and production was under way by 1952. The AMX-13 is fitted with an oscillating turret, in which the gun is fixed in the upper part, which in turn pivots on the lower part. The original vehicle was armed with a 75-mm gun, but most vehicles have been equipped with 90-mm weapons, and export models are offered with 105-mm guns. All versions are fed by semi-automatic magazines in the turret bustle. In service with more than a dozen countries, the AMX-13 was used in combat by Israel in the 1967 Six Day War. Unfortunately, the light tank was seriously outmatched by Soviet-built T-54/55 tanks, and Israel has long since removed the vehicle from its inventory.

Specification
Crew: 3
Combat weight: 17 tonnes (16 tons 1680 lb)
Maximum road speed: 60 km/h (37 mph)
Power-to-weight ratio: 16.6 hp/tonne
Length: 4.9 m (16 ft 1 in)
Height: 2.3 m (7 ft 7 in)
Armament: 1×105-mm gun; 1×7.62-mm machine-gun

Assessment
Firepower   ★★★★★
Protection   ★★★
Age   ★★★★★
Worldwide users   ★★★★

The AMX-13 formed the basis for a whole family of armoured fighting vehicles, but it is as a light tank that it achieved most export success. Originally equipped with a 75-mm gun, it has been progressively upgunned to 90 mm and 105 mm.

AMX-10RC

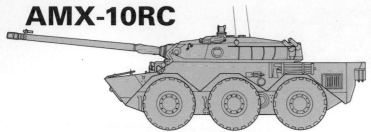

Specification
Crew: 4
Combat weight: 15.8 tonnes (15 tons 1232 lb)
Maximum road speed: 85 km/h (53 mph)
Power-to-weight ratio: 16.45 hp/tonne
Length: 6.3 m (20 ft 8 in)
Height: 2.7 m (8 ft 10 in)
Armament: 1×105-mm gun; 1×7.62-mm machine-gun

Assessment
Firepower   ★★★★★
Protection   ★★
Age   ★★
Worldwide users ★★

The AMX-10RC is one of the most powerful and sophisticated reconnaissance vehicles in service. They were used by French troops in the Gulf, where they provided flank guard to the coalition's 'Hail Mary' sweep through Kuwait and Iraq.

The AMX-10RC reconnaissance vehicle entered French service in 1979. Developed to replace the eight-wheeled Panhard EBR heavy armoured car, the AMX-10RC is powerfully armed with a semi-automatic 105-mm gun, and is equipped with advanced fire-control systems and an NBC defensive system. The AMX-10RC has extremely good cross-country mobility, and is fully amphibious, propelled in water by a pair of water-jets at the rear of the hull. Unfortunately, such sophistication comes at a considerable cost, and the French army has had to reduce its buy from 525 to 284 vehicles. Currently under consideration as an off-the-shelf buy to provide an Armored Gun System for the US Army, the AMX-10RC has seen successful combat service in Chad and with the French forces involved in the Gulf War.

BRDM-2

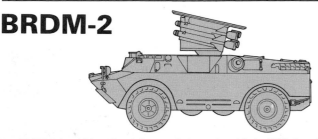

Specification
Crew: 2–4
Combat weight: 7 tonnes (6 tons 1994 lb)
Maximum road speed: 100 km/h (62 mph)
Power-to-weight ratio: 20 hp/tonne
Length: 5.75 m (18 ft 10 in)
Height: 2.3 m (7 ft 7 in) with turret; 2.0 m (6 ft 7 in) without
Armament: 1×14.5-mm and 1×7.62-mm machine-guns or 6 'Sagger' ATGMs

Assessment
Firepower   ★
Protection   ★
Age   ★★★
Worldwide users ★★★★

The BRDM-2 lacks the firepower and protection of recent Western reconnaissance vehicles, but it is nevertheless highly mobile, and is used in the reconnaissance units of more than 50 armies around the world.

The BRDM-2 Amphibious Scout Car was first seen in public in 1966, though it had entered service some years earlier. It has two belly wheels on each side of the hull that can be lowered to improve cross-country capability. One version has a turret with a 14.7-mm heavy machine-gun, but anti-armour versions exist equipped with wire-guided anti-tank missiles. The welded steel hull ranges in thickness from 14 mm on the nose to less than 3 mm under the belly, making it horribly vulnerable to mines. Russian and Russian-style reconnaissance battalions have relied heavily on the BRDM-2 for many years.

Spähpanzer Luchs

Specification
Crew: 4
Combat weight: 19.5 tonnes (19 tons 426 lb)
Maximum road speed: 90 km/h (56 mph)
Power-to-weight ratio: 20 hp/tonne
Length: 7.74 m (25 ft 5 in)
Height: 2.1 m (6 ft 11 in)
Armament: 1×20-mm cannon; 1×7.62-mm machine-gun

Assessment
Firepower   ★★
Protection   ★★
Age   ★★★
Worldwide users ★

The Spähpanzer Luchs is a large eight-wheeled vehicle with exceptional cross-country manoeuvrability. Unlike many contemporaries, the Luchs is not armed with a powerful gun. Its 20-mm cannon has remained unchanged since the Luchs' introduction in 1975.

The Luchs, or Lynx, is a product of the same West German armoured vehicle programme which produced the six-wheeled Transportpanzer. It continues the German wartime tradition of producing 8×8 reconnaissance vehicles with exceptional operational range and outstanding cross-country mobility. The Luchs is equally fast in forward and reverse gear, and the radio operator seated in the rear of the hull has a duplicate set of controls, enabling the vehicle to be driven out of danger without needing to turn around. The Luchs is a very large vehicle, but with selectable eight-wheel steering it is surprisingly manoeuvrable. Luchs is armed with a 20-mm cannon, primarily for self-defence, since the aim of reconnaissance vehicles is to see but not be seen.

PT-76

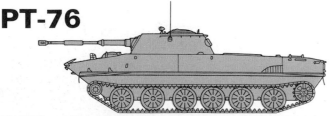

Specification
Crew: 3
Combat weight: 14 tonnes (13 tons 1747 lb)
Maximum road speed: 44 km/h (27 mph)
Power-to-weight ratio: 17 hp/tonne
Length: 6.91 m (22 ft 8 in)
Height: 2.26 m (7 ft 5 in)
Armament: 1×76.2-mm gun; 1×7.62-mm machine-gun

Assessment
Firepower   ★★★
Protection   ★
Age   ★★★★★
Worldwide users ★★★★★

The PT-76 has had to sacrifice a number of vital qualities in order to be able to float. It is as large as a Main Battle Tank but far less heavily armoured.

The PT-76 amphibious tank's design was heavily influenced by Soviet experience during World War II, especially the many river crossings encountered by the Red Army. Unfortunately, the PT-76 has purchased its amphibious capability at the expense of large size and thin armour. The lack of an NBC system in a reconnaissance vehicle is just as serious a drawback in a vehicle with one strength and many weaknesses. Although production was completed many years ago, the PT-76 is still in service with a dozen or more countries. It has seen action with the Egyptians in 1967, with the Indian Army against Pakistan in 1971, in Vietnam in 1972, and most recently in Angola during the recently concluded civil war and confrontation with South Africa.

RECONNAISSANCE VEHICLES No. 2

Modern reconnaissance vehicles face many dangers, protected by armour that is too thin to stop anti-tank missiles or tank guns. Yet they must probe the enemy front line to provide the best intelligence for their commander.

Type 63 amphibious light tank

The Type 63 is a Chinese development of the Russian PT-76 amphibious light tank. It is equally large and nearly five tonnes heavier, but has a more powerful engine which gives it better mobility and a greater top speed. North Vietnamese armoured units were equipped with both vehicles; the Chinese light tank can be distinguished from the Russian original by its larger turret, which looks similar to that of the T-54 series Main Battle Tanks. The Type 63 carries fractionally thicker armour protection than the PT-76: the hull rear has 10 mm of armour in place of 7 mm. The overall protection remains very light.

Specification
Crew: 4
Combat weight: 18.7 tonnes (18 tons 896 lb)
Maximum road speed: 64 km/h (40 mph)
Power-to-weight ratio: 21.39 hp/tonne
Length: 7.15 m (23 ft 6 in)
Height: 2.52 m (8 ft 3 in)
Armament: 1×85-mm gun; 1×7.62-mm co-axial machine-gun; 1×12.7-mm AA gun

Assessment
Firepower ★★★
Protection ★★
Age ★★★★★
Worldwide users ★★

Developed from the Russian PT-76, the Type 63 tank is more mobile than its Russian progenitor. Like all armoured amphibious vehicles, it is poorly protected for its size.

RAM

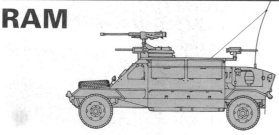

Developed by a subsidiary of Israeli Aircraft Industries, the RAM series of light recce vehicles is a comprehensive range of 4×4 vehicles offered for export. Moroccan forces bought an undisclosed number during their struggle against Polisario guerrillas. Anti-tank armament can be either a 106-mm recoilless rifle or TOW missile launcher. A self-propelled AA gun version using twin 20-mm cannon is also available.

Specification
(V-2L long)
Crew: 2+6
Combat weight: 6 tonnes (5 tons 2016 lb)
Maximum road speed: 96 km/h (60 mph)
Power-to-weight ratio: undisclosed
Length: 5.5 m (18 ft 1 in)
Height: 2 m (6 ft 7 in)
Armament: 1×.50-cal and 2×7.62-mm machine-guns

Assessment
Firepower ★★
Protection ★
Age ★
Worldwide users ★★

Israel was forced from its earliest days to make up for its lack of firepower with mobility. Successful mobile warfare needs intelligence, which is why the RAM range of reconnaissance vehicles was developed.

AML 90

Since 1961 nearly 5,000 AML 90s have been built, making it one of the most successful post-war recce vehicles. Not amphibious, the basic AML 90 also lacks NBC protection and night fighting kit, although all these features are available as optional extras. The Argentines took a few of their AML 90s to the Falklands but they could not cope with the boggy ground and did not see action.

Specification
Crew: 3
Combat weight: 5.5 tonnes (5 tons 918 lb)
Maximum road speed: 90 km/h (56 mph)
Power-to-weight ratio: 16.36 hp/tonne
Length: 3.79 m (12 ft 5 in)
Height: 2.07 m (6 ft 10 in)
Armament: 1×90-mm gun; 1×7.62-mm machine-gun

Assessment
Firepower ★★★
Protection ★★
Age ★★★★
Worldwide users ★★★★★

The AML series forms the basis of the Eland armoured car built by the South African Armscor concern. Armed with a 90-mm gun, the Eland has seen combat use in the Bush War.

FIAT-OTO Melara 6616

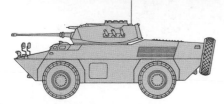

Specification
(90-mm version)
Crew: 3
Combat weight: 8.2 tonnes (8 tons 157 lb)
Maximum road speed: 100 km/h (62 mph)
Power-to-weight ratio: 29.5 hp/tonne
Length: 5.37 m (17 ft 7 in)
Height: 2 m (6 ft 7 in)
Armament: 1×90-mm Mk III Cockerill gun; 1×7.62-mm machine-gun

Assessment
Firepower ★★★★
Protection ★★
Age ★★
Worldwide users ★★

This useful armoured car is a collaborative venture between two Italian companies. FIAT provide the hull and automotive parts, while OTO Melara manufacture the turret and main armament. The 6616 is used by Italy's paramilitary *Carabinieri* organisation, and has been exported to Peru, Somalia and several other undisclosed countries. The 6616 is fully amphibious and can be supplied in many different versions. Optional extras include an NBC system, air-conditioning and/or a 106-mm recoilless rifle mounted on the roof of the turret.

As with most modern armoured vehicle developments, the FIAT-OTO Melara Model 6616 can be fitted with a variety of weapons and turrets. This example is armed with a 20-mm cannon.

VEC cavalry vehicle

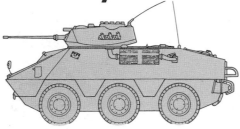

Specification
Crew: 5
Combat weight: 13.75 tonnes (13 tons 1187 lb)
Maximum road speed: 106 km/h (66 mph)
Power-to-weight ratio: 22.25 hp/tonne
Length: 6.25 m (20 ft 6 in)
Height: 2 m (6 ft 7 in)
Armament: 90-mm gun or 20/25-mm cannon plus 7.62-mm machine-gun

Assessment
Firepower ★★★★
Protection ★★
Age ★★
Worldwide users ★

Using many components of the BMR-600 armoured personnel carrier, the VEC is the Spanish army's standard reconnaissance vehicle. In Spanish service, it is fitted with an OTO Melara T25 turret mounting a 25-mm cannon and co-axial 7.62-mm machine-gun. However, the hull is designed to be compatible with other OTO Melara turrets, including that fitted to the FIAT-OTO Melara 6616. The full spectrum of machine-guns, cannon or 90-mm Cockerill gun is offered on the export versions of the VEC.

The VEC cavalry vehicle shares many components with the BMR-600 armoured personnel carrier. When possible, the designers of an armoured fighting vehicle will use common parts to limit the cost of manufacture.

Commando Scout

Specification
Crew: 2 or 3
Combat weight: 7.2 tonnes (7 tons 202 lb)
Maximum road speed: 96 km/h (60 mph)
Power-to-weight ratio: 20.5 hp/tonne
Length: 4.69 m (15 ft 5 in)
Height: 2.23 m (7 ft 4 in)
Armament: 1 or 2×7.62-mm machine-guns and/or TOW missile launcher

Assessment
Firepower ★★★
Protection ★
Age ★
Worldwide users ★

The Scout is a radical alternative to the sort of large armoured cars or light tanks used by most armoured reconnaissance formations. Smaller and more agile cross-country, the Scout carries a larger fuel load to give it much greater range – 1287 kilometres as compared with 750 kilometres for the ENGESA EE-9 Cascavel. The tiny size of the Scout precludes a powerful gun or cannon armament, but it can mount TOW anti-tank guided missiles which have no recoil problems. The tyres are 'Commando Special' run-flat combat tubeless tyres, and it has a four-speed automatic transmission.

The Commando Scout is a classic light cavalry vehicle. It is not intended to slug it out with larger enemies: its main use is in finding a foe and getting that information back to higher command levels.

MOWAG SPY

Specification
Crew: 3
Combat weight: 7.5 tonnes (7 tons 851 lb)
Maximum road speed: 110 km/h (68 mph)
Power-to-weight ratio: 27 hp/tonne
Length: 4.5 m (14 ft 9 in)
Height: 1.66 m (5 ft 3 in)
Armament: 1×12.7-mm and 1×7.62-mm machine-guns

Assessment
Firepower ★★
Protection ★
Age ★
Worldwide users ★

Sharing many key components with the MOWAG 'Piranha' range of armoured vehicles, the SPY was developed for export and has been sold to several Middle Eastern armies. The hull is shaped to deflect the blast from an anti-tank mine so the crew will hopefully survive, even if the vehicle is knocked out. The SPY is lightly protected, its armour being proof against 7.62-mm ball. The SPY is an uncomplicated design with manual turret elevation and traverse and machine-gun armament.

Like the Commando Scout, the MOWAG SPY is a reconnaissance vehicle, pure and simple. It is small, fast and mobile, but too lightly armed and armoured to take on an enemy.

RECONNAISSANCE VEHICLES No. 3

Reconnaissance vehicles are in use around the world. Many are highly sophisticated with advanced weapons and fighting systems, but there is equally a place for simple, rugged, but reliable machines originally designed in the 1940s and 1950s.

Saladin

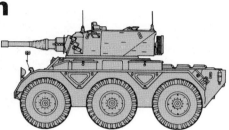

Entering production 30 years ago, the Saladin served the British Army very well in the counter-insurgency campaigns of the 1960s. Replaced in British service by the CVR(T) series, it remains in widespread use in Africa and Asia. Some war reserve stocks are reportedly maintained in the UK, so if the balloon goes up the Saladin might be trundled out once more. It is not amphibious, has no NBC system and no night vision aids. The 76-mm gun fires HE, canister and a useful HESH round.

Specification
Crew: 3
Combat weight: 11.59 tonnes (11 tons 918 lb)
Maximum road speed: 72 km/h (45 mph)
Power-to-weight ratio: 14.66 hp/tonne
Length: 4.93 m (16 ft 2 in)
Height: 2.19 m (7 ft 2 in)
Armament: 1×76-mm gun; 2×7.62-mm machine-guns

Assessment
Firepower   ★★★★
Protection   ★★★
Age   ★★★★★
Worldwide users   ★★★

Although now well into its fourth decade of service, the sturdy and reliable Saladin is still a useful fighting machine, and its lack of advanced fire-control systems is no handicap in low-intensity conflict.

Ferret

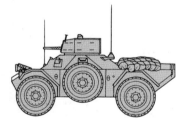

The Ferret is a light scout car introduced in the early 1950s which served alongside the Saladin in the British Army. Although manufacture ceased in 1971 many of the 4,000 Ferrets produced remain in service, particularly in Africa. Alvis in the UK offer modernised versions of reconditioned original Ferrets which still make a very cost-effective armoured scout car. Basic Ferrets have no NBC system, night vision kit or amphibious capability.

Specification
(Ferret Mk 1)
Crew: 2
Combat weight: 4.2 tonnes (4 tons 291 lb)
Maximum road speed: 93 km/h (58 mph)
Power-to-weight ratio: 30.6 hp/tonne
Length: 3.8 m (12 ft 6 in)
Height: 1.9 m (6 ft 3 in)
Armament: 1×7.62-mm machine-gun

Assessment
Firepower   ★
Protection   ★★
Age   ★★★★★
Worldwide users   ★★★★

The Ferret replaced the World War II vintage Daimler Dingo. It is most effectively used as a pure scouting vehicle, being too lightly armed and armoured to get into serious combat.

Fox

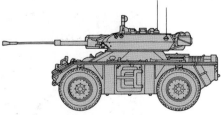

The Fox is a development of the late-production Ferret. With an aluminium hull and turret, and a 30-mm RARDEN cannon, it offers better protection and superior firepower. It can ford up to one metre and can swim with a flotation screen erected. It is air-transportable; three Foxes fit in a Lockheed C-130 Hercules which is to land them, or two if they are paradropped. The British Army's Foxes had NBC detection kit and ZB 298 surveillance radar, but they are no longer in service.

Specification
Crew: 3
Combat weight: 6.1 tonnes (6 tons)
Maximum road speed: 104+ km/h (65+ mph)
Power-to-weight ratio: 30 hp/tonne
Length: 4.2 m (13 ft 10 in)
Height: 2.2 m (7 ft 3 in)
Armament: 1×30-mm cannon; 1×7.62-mm machine-gun

Assessment
Firepower   ★★★
Protection   ★★
Age   ★★
Worldwide users   ★

Larger and heavier than the Ferret it replaced, the Fox's 30-mm cannon is much more effective armament, and the car's powerful Jaguar engine gives it excellent performance.

Panhard VBL

Adopted by the French army in 1985, the VBL (*Véhicule Blindé Léger*) has two roles: anti-tank and reconnaissance. For the former role it is fitted with MILAN anti-tank missiles, and for recce missions carries either a .50-cal or 7.62-mm machine-gun. It is fully amphibious, powered in the water by a propeller in the hull rear. The Michelin tyres are run-flats which allow it to travel 50 km at 30 km/h after a puncture. NBC and/or air-conditioning systems are optional.

Specification
Crew: 2 (recce); 3 (anti-tank)
Combat weight: 3.59 tonnes (3 tons 1187 lb)
Maximum road speed: 100+ km/h (62+ mph)
Power-to-weight ratio: 29.58 hp/tonne
Length: 3.7 m (12 ft 2 in)
Height: 1.7 m (to hull top) (5 ft 8 in)
Armament: MILAN or 1×.50-cal or 7.62-mm machine-gun

Assessment
Firepower ★★★
Protection ★
Age ★
Worldwide users ★

Small, light and highly mobile, the Panhard VBL is used by the French army as a tank hunter, using its MILAN missiles, and as an intelligence-gathering vehicle.

Panhard EBR

The EBR is a 'heavy armoured car' adopted by the French army in 1950 and only replaced by the AMX-10RC during 1987. It soldiers on in North Africa and Portugal and may turn up elsewhere if the French sell off their surviving vehicles. It has a driver at both ends, the rear one doubling as radio operator, and the two pairs of wheels in the middle are lowered when crossing rough ground. It has an oscillating turret similar to that of the AMX-13 but no automatic loading system, which was tried but proved too heavy.

Specification
Crew: 4
Combat weight: 13.5 tonnes (13 tons 650 lb)
Maximum road speed: 105 km/h (65 mph)
Power-to-weight ratio: 14.81 hp/tonne
Length: 5.56 m (18 ft 3 in)
Height: 2.32 m (on 8 wheels); 2.24 m (on 4)
Armament: 1×90-mm gun; 1×7.5-mm machine-gun

Assessment
Firepower ★★★★
Protection ★★★
Age ★★★★★
Worldwide users ★★

Large and fast, with a powerful gun armament, the Panhard EBR was one of the first products of the French armaments industry as it pulled itself together following World War II.

M551 Sheridan

Once the great white hope of US airborne forces, the M551 Sheridan light tank has not been a success. Its 152-mm gun/missile launcher produces too much recoil for the sighting equipment and the chassis to survive. Used in Vietnam, it aroused mixed reaction: some units reported favourably, citing its cross-country capability and powerful armament. Others rejected it as mechanically unreliable and poorly protected. Only 54 M551s remain in operational service, all with the 82nd Airborne.

Specification
Crew: 4
Combat weight: 15.8 tonnes (15 tons 1232 lb)
Maximum road speed: 70 km/h (43 mph)
Power-to-weight ratio: 18.95 hp/tonne
Length: 6.29 m (20 ft 8 in)
Height: 2.27 m (7 ft 6 in)
Armament: 1×152-mm gun/missile launcher; 1×12.7-mm and 1×7.62-mm machine-guns

Assessment
Firepower ★★★★★
Protection ★★
Age ★★★
Worldwide users ★

Although the Sheridan is potentially an immensely powerful vehicle, its faults have outweighed its merits, and it only remains in US Airborne service because of its air-portability.

Wiesel

Developed by Porsche, the Wiesel is a multi-purpose air-droppable vehicle produced for the German airborne forces. It can be slung beneath a Puma helicopter and is easily air-portable; a C-130 can carry three of them. It can carry a variety of armament fits; the German airborne units will use one version fitted with a 20-mm cannon as a recce vehicle and another, armed with TOW ATGW, as a tank destroyer. Other weapons fits available include HOT ATGW, Stinger SAMs or 25-mm cannon.

Specification
Crew: 2 (20-mm gun); 3 (TOW)
Combat weight: 2.75 tonnes (2 tons 1568 lb)
Maximum road speed: 80 km/h (50 mph)
Power-to-weight ratio: 30.72 hp/tonne
Length: 3.26 m (10 ft 9 in)
Height: 1.99 m (6 ft 6 in); 1.87 m (6 ft 2 in) TOW
Armament: 20-mm cannon or TOW missiles

Assessment
Firepower ★★★★
Protection ★
Age ★
Worldwide users ★

The Wiesel is in service with German airborne units. Two can be carried internally by heavy-lift helicopters such as the Sikorsky CH-53 Stallion or the Boeing CH-47 Chinook.

RECONNAISSANCE VEHICLES

Reconnaissance vehicles come in all shapes and sizes. Some are heavily armed, but they are rarely heavily armoured. Wheels allow for great on-road and good surface mobility, whereas tracks are slower but confer unmatched off-road capability.

Renault VBC 90

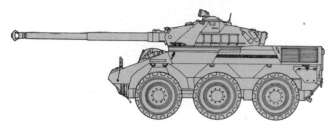

This is one of several French 6×6 armoured cars which are notable for their heavy firepower. Substantially lighter than vehicles like the German Luchs, the VBC 90 is faster but not amphibious. Oman operates a handful of VBC 90s and the French Gendarmerie bought 28 vehicles in the early 1980s, but it has not achieved major export sales. As with most light armour, the VBC is not heavily protected. Its thin armour protects the crew from small-arms fire and shell splinters.

Specification
Crew: 3
Combat weight: 12.8 tonnes (12 tons 1344 lb)
Maximum road speed: 92 km/h (57 mph)
Power-to-weight ratio: 17.96 hp/tonne
Length: 5.63 m (18 ft 6 in)
Height: 2.52 m (8 ft 3 in) (turret top)
Armament: 1×90-mm gun; 2×7.62-mm machine-guns

Assessment
Firepower   ★ ★ ★ ★
Protection   ★
Age   ★ ★
Worldwide users ★

France is probably the major manufacturer of heavily-armed wheeled reconnaissance vehicles. French companies fit 90-mm or even 105-mm guns onto wheeled armoured cars like the VBC, which contrasts strongly with German practice.

Panhard ERC

The ERC replaced the Panhard AML 60 and AML 90 in the recce formations of the French Rapid Deployment Force Divisions as a cheaper alternative to the sophisticated AMX-IORC. The 90-mm gun fires HE, HEAT and APFSDS, as well as smoke and canister. Alternative weapon fits include 25-mm cannon, twin 20-mm AA guns, six SATCP surface-to-air missiles or a 60-mm mortar. Many French units serving overseas have received ERCs, including troops in Djibouti, Gabon and the Ivory Coast.

Specification
Crew: 3
Combat weight: 10 tonnes (9 tons 1881 lb)
Maximum road speed: 110 km/h (68 mph)
Power-to-weight ratio: 19.6 hp/tonne
Length: 5.57 m (18 ft 3 in)
Height: 2.32 m (7 ft 7 in)
Armament: 1×90-mm gun; 2×7.62-mm machine-guns

Assessment
Firepower   ★ ★ ★ ★
Protection   ★
Age   ★
Worldwide users ★ ★

Nearly 200 Panhard ERC 90s have been acquired by the French army for its light formations. Although it is less sophisticated than vehicles like the AMX-10RC, it still packs a considerable punch, and is also cheaper.

AAI RDF light tank

The Rapid Deployment Force light tank is another private venture developed to prototype stage originally for a US Army programme. Rather than experiment with low recoil systems for existing 105-mm guns, the AAI vehicle carries an automatic 75-mm cannon able to fire APFSDS shells with long rod, high density penetrators at a rate of 70 shells per minute.

Specification
Crew: 3
Combat weight: 13.4 tonnes (13 tons 426 lb)
Maximum road speed: 64 km/h (40 mph)
Power-to-weight ratio: 26 hp/tonne
Length: 5.5 m (18 ft 1 in)
Height: 2.28 m (7 ft 6 in)
Armament: 1×75-mm ARES cannon; 1×7.62-mm machine-gun

Assessment
Firepower   ★ ★ ★
Protection   ★ ★
Age   ★
Worldwide users ★

The advanced automatic cannon and notably low profile of the private venture RDF light tank point in the direction that armoured vehicles might develop in the 21st century.

Light Armored Vehicle

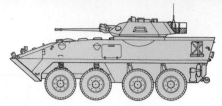

Specification
Crew: 3+6
Combat weight: 13 tonnes (12 tons 1770 lb)
Maximum road speed: 100 km/h (62 mph)
Power-to-weight ratio: 23.4 hp/tonne
Length: 6.39 m (21 ft)
Height: 2.69 m (8 ft 10 in)
Armament: various

Assessment
Firepower ★★
Protection ★★
Age ★★
Worldwide users ★★

The US Marine Corps is the largest user of the Swiss-designed MOWAG Piranha family, its Light Armored Vehicles being used for a variety of tasks including reconnaissance.

The Canadian version of the Swiss MOWAG Piranha is used by the US Marines and is air-portable beneath a CH-53 helicopter, and also amphibious. Of the 149 LAVs in a USMC LAV battalion, 56 are armed with 25-mm Chain Guns and there are assault gun, anti-tank missile, anti-aircraft missile and mortar-carrying versions. The 8×8 vehicle has excellent cross-country mobility, and allows Marine recon units to range far ahead of the main force in its tracked vehicles.

M41 Walker Bulldog

Specification
Crew: 4
Combat weight: 23.49 tonnes (23 tons 268 lb)
Maximum road speed: 72 km/h (45 mph)
Power-to-weight ratio: 21.26 hp/tonne
Length: 5.8 m (19 ft)
Height: 2.7 m (8 ft 10 in)
Armament: 1×76-mm gun; 1×7.62-mm machine-gun; 1×.50-cal machine-gun

Assessment
Firepower ★★
Protection ★★★
Age ★★★★★
Worldwide users ★★

The M41 has been in service for many years. Introduced during the Korean War, it has seen action in Vietnam and in countless small wars around the world. Although obsolete, it can still be found in many armies.

The advances in low-recoil systems for large-calibre tank guns rendered the M41 obsolete by the late 1970s. Its 76-mm gun is unable to deal with Main Battle Tanks, and those countries still using the M41 are either buying improved APFSDS ammunition from AAI or retro-fitting 90-mm Cockerill or even low-recoil 105-mm weapons.

Bernadini MB-3 Tamoyo

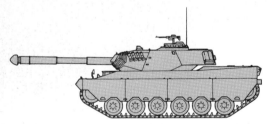

Specification
Crew: 4
Combat weight: 30 tonnes (29 tons 1187 lb)
Maximum road speed: 67 km/h (42 mph)
Power-to-weight ratio: 24.5 hp/tonne
Length: 7.4 m (24 ft 3 in)
Height: 2.45 m (8 ft)
Armament: 1×90-mm or 105-mm gun; co-axial 12.7-mm machine-gun; 7.62-mm machine-gun on commander's cupola

Assessment
Firepower ★★★★
Protection ★★★
Age ★
Worldwide users ★★

The MB-3 Tamoyo is a Brazilian medium tank, remotely descended from the M41, which is not quite a Main Battle Tank but which would make a powerful reconnaissance vehicle.

The Brazilian army's M41s have been modified almost beyond recognition by Bernadini to produce a modern light tank with much improved performance. Alloy steel armour and extra equipment increase combat weight by almost seven tonnes, and the main armament can be either 90-mm or 105-mm calibre. The most important improvement is the increased range (550 km instead of 161 km), which is essential for a recce vehicle.

Steyr SK 105 Kurassier

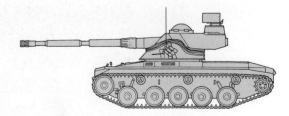

Specification
Crew: 3
Combat weight: 17.5 tonnes (17 tons 493 lb)
Maximum road speed: 65 km/h (40 mph)
Power-to-weight ratio: 18.2 hp/tonne
Length: 5.58 m (18 ft 4 in)
Height: 2.52 m (8 ft 3 in)
Armament: 1×105-mm gun; 1×7.62-mm machine-gun

Assessment
Firepower ★★★★
Protection ★★
Age ★★★★
Worldwide users ★

There are no hard and fast divisions when it comes to armoured vehicles: the Steyr Kurassier is a tank-destroyer which could just as well be used as a light tank or heavy reconnaissance vehicle.

The Austrian army uses the Kurassier as a tank destroyer rather than as a proper light tank. The oscillating turret, protected by 40 mm of armour, is similar to that on the French AMX-13, and is similarly fed by two revolver-type magazines. It mounts a 105-mm gun firing spin-stabilised HEAT or a more effective APFSDS round developed by GIAT in France.

Many modern reconnaissance vehicles are part of 'families' of armoured fighting vehicles that include APCs, command and control vehicles, and other specialist versions. However, purpose-built armoured cars are still widely used, some of them many years after their introduction.

BRDM-1

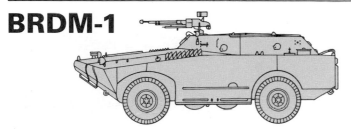

Introduced in 1959 and in front-line service with the Soviet army until the 1980s, the BRDM-1 has a boat-shaped hull to help its amphibious performance. Its front-mounted petrol engine made it vulnerable to fire, but its cross-country performance was good; in particularly bad terrain four 'belly wheels' can be lowered to improve traction. Standard armament was a DShK 12.7-mm machine-gun, but some were modified for use by anti-tank companies and carried AT-1 'Snapper' missiles. A specialist NBC recce vehicle was also built on the BRDM-1 chassis. Supplied to most Warsaw Pact forces, the BRDM-1 was also used in the Middle East, Israel putting some captured ones into service.

Specification
Crew: 5
Combat weight: 5.6 tonnes (5 tons 1142 lb)
Maximum road speed: 80 km/h (50 mph)
Length: 5.7 m (18 ft 9 in)
Height: 2.25 m (7 ft 5 in)
Armament: 1×12.7-mm machine-gun plus six firing ports for personal weapons

Assessment
Firepower ★★
Protection ★
Age ★★★★★
Worldwide users ★★★★★

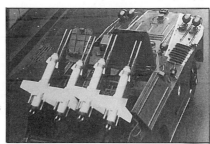

The BRDM-1 was used as a self-propelled anti-tank system as well as for reconnaissance. This BRDM carries four AT-1 'Swatter' missiles.

FUG

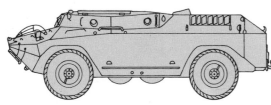

The FUG (Felderito Úszó Gépkocsi) is a Hungarian version of the BRDM-1 used by Hungarian, Polish and Czech forces since the 1960s. It is noted for a good cross-country performance and a reasonable standard of manufacture. Powered by a diesel engine in the rear of the vehicle, it is preferable to the BRDM-1. The roof hatches can be locked in the vertical position to give some protection to a crew member firing the machine-gun, and six firing ports allow troops inside to fire small arms without exposing themselves to enemy fire. From 1990 the FUG and the PSZH-IV APC have been offered for export at very low prices, but no substantial orders appear to have been forthcoming.

Specification
Crew: 2+4
Combat weight: 7 tonnes (6 tons 1994 lb)
Maximum road speed: 85 km/h (53 mph)
Length: 5.79 m (19 ft)
Height: 2.52 m (8 ft 3 in)
Armament: 1×7.62-mm machine-gun

Assessment
Firepower ★
Protection ★★
Age ★★★★
Worldwide users ★★

The Hungarian FUG is very similar to the BRDM, but it is less vulnerable to fire thanks to its diesel engine. It was adopted by several other Warsaw Pact armies.

M8

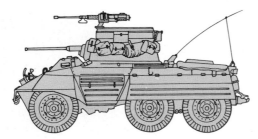

Supplied to the armies of nearly 30 nations after World War II, the M8 light armoured car was known to the British Army as the Greyhound. Built by the Ford Motor Company at its plant in Minnesota, some 8,500 M8s were completed by 1945. The turret housed a 37-mm gun, which could penetrate 46 mm of armour at 900 metres: enough to destroy any hostile armoured car but not enough to threaten tanks. HE and canister rounds were available for attacking soft vehicles and personnel. A further 3,791 M20s were built from 1943-45 – these were basically M8s with higher hull sides and no turret. A ring mount for a .50-cal machine-gun was provided instead.

Specification
Crew: 4
Combat weight: 7.8 tonnes (7 tons 1523 lb)
Maximum road speed: 90 km/h (56 mph)
Length: 5 m (16 ft 5 in)
Height: 2.24 m (7 ft 4 in)
Armament: 1×37-mm gun; 1×.50-cal machine-gun; 1×.30-cal Browning machine-gun

Assessment
Firepower ★★★★
Protection ★★★
Age ★★★★★
Worldwide users ★★★★★

M8 armoured cars of the US Army in Germany during 1945. The M8 was supplied to countries all over the world after the end of World War II; it has had one of the longest careers of any armoured fighting vehicle.

AEC armoured cars

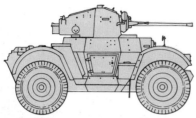

Specification
(Mk III)
Crew: 4
Combat weight: 12.7 tonnes (12 tons 1120 lb)
Maximum road speed: 60 km/h (37 mph)
Length: 5.1 m (16 ft 9 in)
Height: 2.7 m (8 ft 10 in)
Armament: 1×75-mm gun; 1×7.92-mm machine-gun

Assessment
Firepower   ★★★★
Protection   ★★★★
Age   ★★★★★
Worldwide users ★

An AEC armoured car of the British Army drives through Tripoli in 1943. After World War II some AECs were supplied to Yugoslavia and Belgium.

The AEC (Associated Engineering Company) in Southall was known for making London buses, but in 1940 the company designed an armoured car for the British Army. Tested in 1941, it entered production that year and was soon used by British forces in North Africa. Three versions were manufactured: the Mk 1 had a 40-mm gun, the Mk II a 57-mm gun and the Mk III used the American 75-mm gun normally fitted to Sherman tanks. For an armoured car, the AEC design was heavy, trading armour protection for speed. Total production of AEC armoured cars was only 629, but they were supplied to Belgium after the war and others, shipped to Tito's partisans in Yugoslavia, were also used after 1945.

Daimler armoured cars

Specification
Crew: 3
Combat weight: 7.5 tonnes (7 tons 851 lb)
Maximum road speed: 80 km/h (50 mph)
Length: 3.9 m (12 ft 10 in)
Height: 2.2 m (7 ft 3 in)
Armament: 1×40-mm gun; 1×7.92-mm machine-gun

Assessment
Firepower   ★★★★
Protection   ★★
Age   ★★★★★
Worldwide users ★

A Daimler armoured car in action against Communist guerrillas in Malaya during 1949. Daimlers were supplied to many Commonwealth armies after World War II.

Daimler designed an armoured car for the British Army on the eve of World War II and it entered service in 1941. Using the same turret as the Tetrarch light tank and fitted with a 40-mm gun, the Daimler went through the war virtually unchanged. The Mk II introduced few changes, although drivers were grateful for a new escape hatch through the engine compartment. The 40-mm gun was limited in value since it could only fire solid armour-piercing shot; for anti-personnel work the 7.92-mm machine-gun was the car's only weapon. Total production was 2,694 and many of these robust and reliable vehicles were supplied to Commonwealth armies after the war. In 1949 Daimler went on to design a new armoured car – the Ferret, still in service in limited numbers with the British Army over 40 years later.

ENGESA EE-3

Specification
Crew: 3
Combat weight: 5.8 tonnes (5 tons 1,590 lb)
Maximum road speed: 100 km/h (62 mph)
Length: 4.1 m (13 ft 6 in)
Height: 1.56 m (5 ft 2 in)
Armament: 1×.50-cal machine-gun

Assessment
Firepower   ★★
Protection   ★
Age   ★★
Worldwide users ★★

The ENGESA EE-3 has been widely exported in South America and Africa. It can be fitted with many different weapons.

Built by the Brazilian ENGESA company, the EE-3 Jararaca was designed for export and has been sold to several armies in South America and Africa. The crew of three enter and exit the EE-3 via a door in the right of the hull. Standard armament is a Browning M2 .50-cal machine-gun fitted on a pintle mount. It cannot be fired from inside the vehicle: one of the crew must stand up to operate it. Its Mercedes-Benz turbo-charged diesel develops 120 hp and gives the EE-3 a useful power-to-weight ratio. Other weapons fits offered include MILAN anti-tank missiles, 20-mm cannon or 60-mm breech-loading mortar. While not fitted as standard, an NBC system can be added. The EE-3 is not amphibious.

MOWAG Grenadier

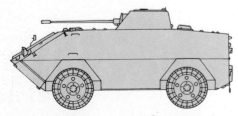

Specification
Crew: 1+8
Combat weight: 6.1 tonnes (6 tons)
Maximum road speed: 100 km/h (62 mph)
Length: 4.8 m (15 ft 9 in)
Height: 2.3 m (7 ft 7 in)
Armament: 1×20-mm cannon

Assessment
Firepower   ★★★★
Protection   ★
Age   ★★★
Worldwide users ★★★

The MR8 is one of a series of 1960s Swiss-built APCs and reconnaissance vehicles of which the Grenadier was the most successful. Both types are used by paramilitary forces as well as armies.

Developed for export by the Swiss armoured vehicle manufacturer MOWAG, the Grenadier entered production during the 1960s. MOWAG has never made public the exact number of sales, but this versatile APC/reconnaissance vehicle is in service with several armies in Africa and South America. The Grenadier is amphibious and can be fitted with a wide range of optional extras. These include air-conditioning, passive night-vision equipment and alternative armament such as anti-tank guided missiles or 25-mm cannon. The turret is offset to the left of the hull behind the driver's position. Up to eight infantrymen can be carried in the troop compartment, entering and exiting via twin doors in the hull rear.

TANK DESTROYERS

Tank destroyers first appeared during World War II. By fitting a large anti-tank gun on to an old tank chassis — and dispensing with the turret — several nations created effective tank-killers that were cheaper than a proper tank. The introduction of guided anti-tank missiles gave the tank destroyer a new lease of life, and new vehicles continue to appear.

Jagdpanzer Jaguar 1

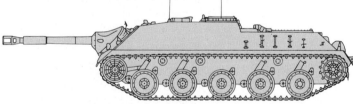

During the 1950s the West German army developed a lightly armoured tracked chassis that was to be the basis for several different vehicles. Not all of the designs entered service, but among those that did were the Jaguar tank destroyer, the Marder MICV and the Jagdpanzer Kanone. Hanomag and Henschel each manufactured 185 Jaguar 1s during 1968, and they still serve exclusively with the German army. Initially fitted with twin SS-11 launchers, they were re-armed between 1978-83 with the more modern HOT missile system.

Specification
Crew: 4
Combat weight: 25.5 tonnes (25 tons 224 lb)
Road speed: 70 km/h (43 mph)
Length: 6.61 m (21 ft 8 in)
Armament: 1×HOT launcher with 20 missiles; 1×bow 7.62-mm machine-gun, plus another one on the roof
Armour: 50 mm (2 in) (maximum)

Assessment
Firepower	★★★★★
Protection	★★
Age	★★★★
Worldwide users	★

Based on the chassis of the Marder APC, the Jagdpanzer Jaguar is available in both HOT and TOW versions. The HOT-armed variant carries 20 missiles.

Jagdpanzer Kanone

This was another vehicle developed from the same basic chassis as the Jaguar. Between 1965-67 Hanomag and Henschel produced 375 Jagdpanzer Kanones each. Apart from its armament, the Kanone is almost identical to the Jaguar. It is armed with a 90-mm gun that fires the same ammunition as the 90-mm main armament of the US M47 and M48 tanks also used by the German army during the 1960s. With its low silhouette, larger ammunition supply and relatively low cost, the Kanone was similar to the German wartime tank destroyers. However, the arrival of more heavily-armoured tanks during the 1980s made the 90 mm obsolete and 162 were converted to carry TOW missiles instead.

Specification
Crew: 4
Combat weight: 27.5 tonnes (27 tons 135 lb)
Road speed: 70 km/h (43 mph)
Length: 6.28 m (20 ft 8 in)
Armament: 1×90-mm gun with 51 rounds; 1×co-axial 7.62-mm machine-gun
Armour: 50 mm (2 in) (maximum)

Assessment
Firepower	★★★
Protection	★★
Age	★★★★
Worldwide users	★

The Jagdpanzer Kanone's 90-mm gun is not powerful enough to destroy the latest Main Battle Tanks, and many have been converted into TOW missile carriers.

Infanterikanonvagn 91

The Ikv-91 looks more like a conventional tank than the Swedish army's real MBT, the turretless S-tank. However, the Ikv-91 is light, thinly armoured and not designed to serve as a Main Battle Tank. Built for Arctic operations, its engine has a built-in blow torch to get it started in temperatures as low as −35°C. It is amphibious and exerts a ground pressure of 0.53 kg/cm^2 – little over half as much as typical MBTs. Manufactured between 1975-78, the Ikv-91 has a 90-mm gun that relies on fin-stabilised HEAT rounds to deal with enemy tanks. Since this is only marginally effective against the T-64 and later Soviet tanks, the Ikv-91 has been tested with a low-pressure Bofors 105-mm gun.

Specification
Crew: 4
Combat weight: 16.3 tonnes (16 tons)
Road speed: 65 km/h (40 mph)
Length: 6.41 m (21 ft)
Armament: 1×90-mm gun with 59 rounds; 2×7.62-mm machine-guns
Armour: undisclosed

Assessment
Firepower	★★★
Protection	★
Age	★★★
Worldwide users	★

Like the German Jagdpanzer Kanone, the Ikv-91's 90-mm gun is only marginally effective against modern tank armour. The vehicle has an advanced laser rangefinder and fire-control computer.

ASU-85

Specification
Crew: 4
Combat weight: 15.5 tonnes (15 tons 560 lb)
Road speed: 45 km/h (28 mph)
Length: 6 m (19 ft 9 in)
Armament: 1×85-mm gun; 1×12.7-mm machine-gun; 1×7.62-mm co-axial machine-gun
Armour: 40 mm (2 in) (maximum)

Assessment
Firepower   ★★
Protection   ★★★
Age   ★★★★★
Worldwide users   ★

In this age of laminated armour MBTs and man-portable missiles with ranges of three kilometres, the lightly armoured ASU-85, with its relatively puny 85-mm gun, has no place.

In service with the Russian airborne forces since 1960, the ASU-85 is armed with a version of the World War II 85-mm gun fitted to the T-34 tank. By the 1970s, each Russian air assault division had a 31-vehicle battalion of these tank destroyers. The ASU-85's armament is practically ineffective against modern tanks, so Russian paratroopers soon relied on their 'Sagger' anti-tank missiles to defend themselves against armoured attack. However, these air-portable vehicles did enhance the mobility of Russian paras. Although used in the seizure of Kabul in 1979, these 30-year old vehicles are now obsolete.

Spartan MCT

Specification
Crew: 3
Combat weight: 8.3 tonnes (8 tons 380 lb)
Road speed: 80 km/h (50 mph)
Length: 4.8 m (15 ft 9 in)
Armament: 2×MILAN missiles with 8 reloads; 1×7.62-mm machine-gun
Armour: undisclosed

Assessment
Firepower   ★★★★
Protection   ★
Age   ★★
Worldwide users   ★

The Spartan armoured personnel carrier is very agile, and when equipped with the highly effective MILAN anti-tank guided weapon the vehicle becomes a reasonable tank destroyer.

The FV103 Spartan is one of the many versions of the Alvis Scorpion recce vehicle in service with the British Army. In 1985, the Army ordered 75 Spartans fitted with the MILAN Compact Turret (MCT). Issued on a scale of four to each mechanised infantry battalion, the MCT version has a small turret fitted with two ready-to-launch MILAN missiles. As a tank destroyer it is handicapped by the difficulty of reloading – the commander/gunner cannot stay on the radio while reloading. By comparison with the Warrior MICV and the Challenger tank, the Spartan is slow and MILAN is primarily a man-portable system. Its maximum range of 2000 metres is only half that of heavier systems like HOT or TOW that are specifically designed for vehicle use.

SK 105

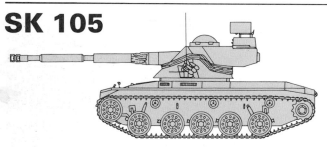

Specification
Crew: 3
Combat weight: 17.7 tonnes (17 tons 940 lb)
Road speed: 70 km/h (43 mph)
Length: 5.58 m (18 ft 4 in)
Armament: 1×105-mm gun; 2×7.62-mm machine-guns
Armour: 20 mm (1 in) (maximum)

Assessment
Firepower   ★★★★
Protection   ★★
Age   ★★★★
Worldwide users   ★★★

The Steyr SK 105 'Kürassier' is equipped with a powerful 105-mm gun, derived from the standard French tank gun. The SK 105 can be used as a tank destroyer or as a reconnaissance vehicle/light tank.

The Steyr SK 105 bears an obvious similarity to the French AMX-13 light tank. Nicknamed, for some curious reason, the 'Kürassier', this lightly armoured vehicle has an oscillating turret mounting a 105-mm gun, for which APFSDS rounds are available. One of the military curiosities arising from Austria's post-war neutral status was a constitutional ban on the use of guided missiles. Thus the Austrian army was forced to rely on conventional anti-tank guns and tank destroyers rather than adopting ATGMs like the NATO and Warsaw Pact forces. Exported to South America and North Africa, the SK 105 can be used as a light tank but its protection will only keep out heavy machine-gun fire.

M901A1

[illustration]

Specification
Crew: 3
Combat weight: 11 tonnes (10 tons 1860 lb)
Road speed: 66 km/h (41 mph)
Length: 4.8 m (15 ft 9 in)
Armament: 2×TOW launch tubes with 10 reloads; 1×7.62-mm machine-gun
Armour: 44 mm (2 in) (maximum)

Assessment
Firepower   ★★★★★
Protection   ★★
Age   ★★
Worldwide users   ★

[photograph]

The M901 is an M113 armoured personnel carrier on to which is mounted an Emerson twin TOW turret. This enables the vehicle's crew to aim and sight their weapons from the safety of the APC's interior.

In 1979, the US Army ordered 2,992 M113 armoured personnel carriers fitted with improved TOW anti-tank guided missiles. Some 1,100 of these vehicles were deployed to Europe in the 1980s, providing US infantry battalions with powerful, long-range anti-tank capability. Designated M901A1, this tank destroyer has one of the most accurate and effective missile systems available. The launcher retracts for travelling and there is a cupola-mounted 7.62-mm machine-gun fitted for emergencies.

BATTLEFIELD MISSILES

No. 1

In the early 1950s the Soviet and US armies both introduced surface-to-surface missiles similar to those used by the Germans in 1944-45. New and better missiles have appeared at regular intervals since then, and large SSMs are in use throughout the world today.

Pluton

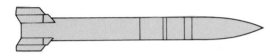

France's decision to leave NATO and develop its own nuclear weapons led to the French army adopting the Pluton surface-to-surface missile in 1974. A total of 42 launchers were built, based on converted AMX-30 tank chassis. By the early 1980s a replacement, Hades, was developed, offering a much longer range of 450 kilometres. However, only 20 or so were delivered before President Mitterand halted production in 1992. After the collapse of the Warsaw Pact and re-unification of Germany, French tactical nuclear missiles were left without a role and were scrapped.

Specification
Launcher vehicle: AMX-30 tank chassis
Weight: 2350 kg (2 tons 701 lb)
Warhead weight: 350–500 kg (772–1102 lb)
Maximum range: 120 km (75 miles)
CEP: 330 m (1082 ft)

Assessment
Age   ★★★
Range   ★★
Accuracy   ★★★
Worldwide users ★

A French army Pluton tactical nuclear missile is launched during an exercise in the 1980s. Its very short range makes it obsolete in post-Warsaw Pact Europe.

FROG

FROG (Free Rocket Over Ground) is the NATO name for a series of crude rockets introduced by the Soviets in 1957, and later delivered to most Warsaw Pact armies and many Arab forces as well. Designed to carry conventional HE, chemical or nuclear warheads, the FROG is a single-stage rocket that takes about 30 minutes to prepare for firing. In the 1960s the Soviet army seriously planned to fight and win a nuclear war in Europe, and most first-line tank and motor rifle divisions received a FROG battalion of four missile launchers and a dozen reloads. Nuclear-tipped FROGs made up for their lack of accuracy with 50-200-kiloton warheads.

Specification
(FROG-7)
Launcher vehicle: ZIL-135 truck
Weight: 2300 kg (2 tons 590 lb)
Warhead weight: 550 kg (1212 lb)
Maximum range: 11 km (7 miles)
CEP: 700 m (2296 ft)

Assessment
Age   ★★★★
Range   ★
Accuracy   ★
Worldwide users ★★★★

The Soviet army made extensive use of FROG-type short-range tactical rockets. Nuclear warheads were designed to compensate for the poor accuracy of these crude weapons.

SS-1 'Scud'

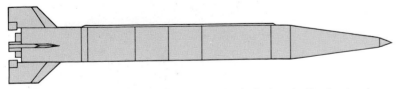

Classed as operational/tactical weapons by the Soviets, the 'Scud' series of missiles was introduced in 1957 and the first weapons were carried on converted JS-III heavy tank chassis. Later 'Scuds' were fitted to more mobile MAZ-543 wheeled launcher vehicles. Deployed in brigades of nine launchers and associated support vehicles – with a total strength of over 1,000 officers and men – 'Scud' missiles were controlled by Soviet armies or fronts. Supplied to Warsaw Pact and Arab armies, a few 'Scuds' were fired in the 1973 Arab-Israeli war and nearly 2,000 were fired in Afghanistan at rebel positions. The weapon only became a household name in the West when Saddam Hussein started launching them at Israel and Saudi Arabia during the Gulf War.

Specification
Launcher vehicle: MAZ-543 wheeled launcher
Weight: 6370 kg (6 tons 603 lb)
Warhead weight: 1000 kg (2205 lb)
Maximum range: 280 km (174 miles) (HE) or 180 km (112 miles) (nuclear)
CEP: 1000 m (3280 ft)

Assessment
Age   ★★★★★
Range   ★★★
Accuracy   ★
Worldwide users ★★★★★

Similar to the German V-2 rockets fired on London during 1944-45, the Soviet 'Scud' became world famous during the Gulf War. Most of the Iraqi mobile launchers evaded allied air strikes and commando raids.

SS-12 'Scaleboard'

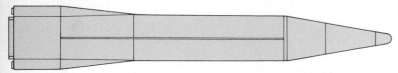

Specification
Launcher vehicle:
MAZ-543 wheeled
launcher
Weight: 8800 kg
(8 tons 1480 lb)
Warhead weight:
1250 kg (2756 lb)
Maximum range: 800 km
(500 miles)
CEP: circa 300 m (985 ft)

Assessment
Age   ★★★★
Range   ★★★★
Accuracy   ★★★
Worldwide users ★

The SS-12 'Scaleboard' enabled the Soviet army to attack targets throughout western Europe without recourse to the ballistic missiles of the Strategic Rocket Forces.

The Soviet army deployed the SS-12 in 1969. The largest missile under army control – ICBMs were controlled by the 'Strategic Rocket Forces' – the 'Scaleboard' could strike targets throughout western Europe. Grouped into brigades attached at army or front level, the 'Scaleboards' were never exported, and the precise performance of these missiles is uncertain. Although the 'Scaleboard' offers much longer range than a 'Scud' and is credited with much greater accuracy, it is still liquid-fuelled and takes over an hour to prepare for launch.

BGM-109 Tomahawk

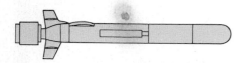

Specification
Launcher vehicle:
wheeled transporter
Weight: 1200 kg
(1 ton 405 lb)
Warhead weight: 123 kg
(271 lb)
Maximum range: 2780
km (1730 miles)
CEP: circa 20 m (65 ft)

Assessment
Age   ★★
Range   ★★★★★
Accuracy   ★★★★★
Worldwide users ★

A Tomahawk cruise missile is launched from one of the transporter-launchers that briefly operated in the UK during the 1980s.

Popularly known as the cruise missile, this long-range subsonic missile was the great bugbear of the European anti-nuclear movement during the 1980s. The deployment of these US missiles on their mobile launchers was held to be a terrible danger, while the vast numbers of Soviet nuclear missiles pointing the other way was strangely ignored. Recent revelations about KGB funding of such activities may account for this lop-sided attitude. The cruise missile alarmed the Soviets not because it carried an enormous nuclear warhead like their rockets, and not because it travelled so fast they could not react to a surprise attack: they feared it because it is formidably accurate. The subsequent performance of Tomahawk in the Gulf War showed that they were right.

MGM-52 Lance

Specification
Launcher vehicle:
M572 tracked vehicle
Weight: 1530 kg
(1 ton 1133 lb)
Warhead weight: 454 kg
(1000 lb) (HE) or 212 kg
(467 lb) (nuclear)
Maximum range: 121 km
(75 miles)
CEP: 450 m (1476 ft)

Assessment
Age   ★★★
Range   ★★★
Accuracy   ★★★
Worldwide users ★★★

A Lance missile of the US Army dangles from a crane as it is lowered onto its M572 tracked transporter-launcher vehicle.

Developed during the 1960s for the US Army, the Lance missile was introduced in 1971 and replaced the earlier Honest John battlefield missiles. It was soon adopted by other NATO armies, although in small numbers by comparison with the Soviets' vast rocket arsenal. The British Army acquired 18 launchers, the Germans 24, and the Italian, Belgian and Dutch forces each bought nine. Lance can carry a conventional warhead, but this is a very expensive way to deliver 454 kilograms of high explosive. Several armies, including Israel, use a cluster bomb warhead ideally suited to attacking enemy SAM sites and their vulnerable radars.

MGM-31 Pershing

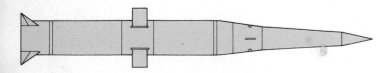

Specification
(Pershing Ia)
Launcher vehicle:
M656 towed launcher
Weight: 4600 kg
(4 tons 1160 lb)
Warhead weight: 748 kg
(1649 lb)
Maximum range: 740 km
(460 miles)
CEP: 350 m (1148 ft)

Assessment
Age.   ★★★★
Range   ★★★★
Accuracy   ★★★
Worldwide users ★★★

Named after the commander of the US expeditionary force to Europe at the end of World War I, the Pershing missile provided NATO with a tactical nuclear weapon able to reach into eastern Europe.

First fielded by the US Army stationed in West Germany in 1964, the Pershing was a long-range nuclear missile able to reach key Soviet rail and communications centres in eastern Europe. From 1969 Pershing Ia was introduced; this was more mobile and was able to come into action far quicker. In the 1980s the US Army and West German army controlled 164 Pershings between them, all ready to reply in kind to a Soviet first use of tactical nuclear weapons. Pershing II was even more dangerous to the Soviets – very fast, very accurate and able to reach targets 2500 kilometres away, this even had an earth penetrator warhead to knock out the heavily-protected underground bunkers from which the Soviet high command planned to fight World War III.

TOWED ARTILLERY

Although towed artillery has largely been superseded in front-line use by self-propelled equipment, it still has a place in the inventories of modern armies. It is cheaper to procure, maintain and operate, and towed weapons can often be heli-borne into locations inaccessible to heavier vehicles.

155-mm FH-70

The Anglo/German/Italian FH-70 entered service in 1978, replacing the British 5.5-inch gun and the American-built M114 six-inch gun. The main requirement was for a high rate of fire, good range and accuracy, and increased lethality with a new matching range of ammunition. The 39-calibre barrel of the FH-70 is 6.022 m long, with a double baffle muzzle brake and a semi-automatic wedge-type breech. An auxiliary power unit is fitted which enables the FH-70 to travel under its own power at up to 16 km/h. The loading system operates at all angles of elevation, with a loading tray that presents the projectile to the chamber. The FH-70 normally fires three types of ammunition: high explosive, smoke and illumination. It can also fire Copperhead cannon-launched laser-guided projectiles as well as extended-range RAP and base-bleed rounds.

Specification
Crew: 7 or 8
Calibre: 155 mm
Weight: 9300 kg (9 tons 343 lb)
Barrel length: 6.02 m (19 ft 9 in)
Elevation: -5°/+70°
HE projectile weight: 43.5 kg (95 lb 14 oz)
Range: 24,000 m (15 miles) with standard projectile; 31,500 m (19 miles) with base-bleed projectile
Rate of fire: 6 rounds per minute; 3-round burst in 13 seconds

Assessment
Firepower ★★★★
Range ★★★★
Age ★★★
Worldwide users ★★★

The FH-70 is the highly successful product of a trinational programme, and entered service in the late 1970s. It can fire once every 10 seconds for long periods, which is a better rate of fire than its contemporaries.

155-mm M198

For many years the US Army's 6-inch howitzer was the 1930s vintage M114. By late 1960s standards, it was limited in range and traverse. Research into a successor began in 1968, and in 1978 production of the M198 155-mm howitzer began. The M198 has a split trail carriage with two-position suspension. When firing, a platform is lowered and the wheels are raised clear of the ground. The cradle elevates and traverses, while the top carriage holds the assembly cradle and the hydropneumatic variable-length recoil system. The cannon has a double baffle muzzle brake and a screw-type breech mechanism. The M198 can fire all NATO standard 155-mm rounds, and there are at least 25 different projectiles in the inventory, ranging from smoke and illumination rounds through high explosive and cargo rounds to chemical and nuclear rounds.

Specification
Crew: 11
Calibre: 155 mm
Weight: 7163 kg (7 tons 112 lb)
Barrel length: 6.1 m (20 ft)
Elevation: -5°/+70°
HE projectile weight: 42.9 kg (94 lb 9 oz)
Range: 22,000 m (14 miles) with standard projectile; 30,000 m (19 miles) with rocket-assisted projectile
Rate of fire: 4 rounds per minute

Assessment
Firepower ★★★★
Range ★★★★
Age ★★★
Worldwide users ★★★★

The M198 and its wide range of ammunition entered service with the US Army at the end of the 1970s, when it replaced the M114 howitzer which had been in use all round the world for more than four decades.

155-mm G5

When South African troops intervened at the start of the Angolan civil war in 1975, they found themselves facing powerful Soviet-supplied artillery that far outranged the World War II vintage equipment used by the SADF. However, work had already begun on a new weapon, and with the help of maverick Canadian artillery genius Dr Gerald Bull the South Africans were able to develop and manufacture one of the finest artillery pieces in the world. The G5 155-mm howitzer, which entered service in 1983, features a 45-calibre barrel and a large firing chamber which reduces chamber pressure even at the highest propellant charges. The G5 has a reasonable rate of fire, but its main strength is its extraordinarily long range. G5s used by the Iraqis were a major potential headache for the coalition in the Gulf War, but in the event most were knocked out, thanks to massive allied air superiority.

Specification
Crew: 8
Calibre: 155 mm
Weight: 13,750 kg (13 tons 1187 lb)
Barrel length: 6.97 m (22 ft 10 in)
Elevation: -3°/+75°
HE projectile weight: 45.5 kg (100 lb 5 oz)
Range: 30,000 m (19 miles) with standard projectile; 39,000 m (24 miles) with based-bleed projectile
Rate of fire: 3 rounds per minute

Assessment
Firepower ★★★★
Range ★★★★★
Age ★★★
Worldwide users ★★

The South African-built G5 howitzer is probably the best performing towed artillery piece in service today, being accurate and very long ranged. It is large and heavy, however, and not easily air-portable.

155-mm FH-77A

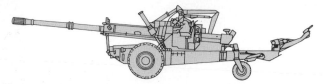

Specification
Crew: 6
Calibre: 155 mm
Weight: 11,500 kg (11 tons 717 lb)
Barrel length: 5.89 m (19 ft 4 in)
Elevation: -3°/+50°
HE projectile weight: 42.6 kg (93 lb 15 oz)
Range: 22,000 m (14 miles)
Rate of fire: 6 rounds every other minute sustained fire; 3-round burst in 8 seconds

Assessment
Firepower   ★★★★
Range   ★★★
Age   ★★★
Worldwide users   ★★

The FH-77 was the subject of the largest export contract in Swedish history, when the Indian government placed an order for as many as 1,500 howitzers. The howitzer can fire a three-round burst in eight seconds.

The first orders for a new towed 155-mm howitzer were placed with Bofors by the Swedish army in 1975. Known as the FH-77A, the howitzer has a 38-calibre barrel fitted with a pepperpot muzzle brake and a vertical sliding breech mechanism. The split-trail carriage has an auxiliary power unit mounted on the front. Elevation and traverse are hydraulic, with manual operation for emergency use. The loading tray holds clips of three rounds, allowing a three-round burst to be fired in under eight seconds. The M/77 shell is an HE projectile with a separate cartridge case. The FH-77B is an export model, with a slightly longer barrel, increased elevation and a mechanised loading system using conventional bagged charges. It has been sold in large numbers to Nigeria and to India.

130-mm M-46

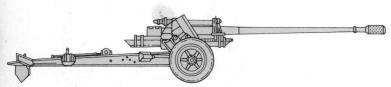

Specification
Crew: 9
Calibre: 130 mm
Weight: 8450 kg (8 tons 717 lb)
Barrel length: 7.6 m (24 ft 11 in)
Elevation: -2.5°/+45°
HE projectile weight: 33.4 kg (73 lb 10 oz)
Range: 27,150 m (17 miles) with standard projectile
Rate of fire: 6 rounds per minute

Assessment
Firepower   ★★★
Range   ★★★★
Age   ★★★★★
Worldwide users ★★★★★

The M-46 130-mm gun outranged Western contemporaries by a considerable margin when introduced in the 1950s. This example was used by Iraqi troops in the Gulf War.

The M-46 field gun is a classic weapon. Developed in the early 1950s, possibly from a naval gun, the M-46 has a very long 58-calibre barrel which gives it exceptional range. It has been used in combat all around the world from Angola to Vietnam. The M-46 is primarily a highly effective counter-battery weapon, and in spite of its age it remains a serious threat to any opposing artillery. The M-46's long barrel has a distinctive pepperpot muzzle brake and a horizontal sliding-wedge breech mechanism. The gun fires separate-loading ammunition, with a variety of projectiles including HE fragmentation, HE rocket assisted, smoke, illumination and an armour-piercing round which will penetrate 230 mm of armour at 1000 m. The M-46 has been used by at least 30 armies.

155-mm CITEFA Model 77

Specification
Crew: 10
Calibre: 155 mm
Weight: 8000 kg (7 tons 1949 lb)
Barrel length: 5.115 m (16 ft 9 in)
Elevation: -0°/+67°
HE projectile weight: 43 kg (94 lb 12 oz)
Range: 22,000 m (14 miles) with standard projectile; 25,300 (16 miles) rocket-assisted projectile
Rate of fire: 1 round per minute sustained fire; 4 rounds per minute for short periods

Assessment
Firepower   ★★★
Range   ★★★
Age   ★★★

The Model 77 is a hybrid artillery piece, utilising an Argentine-designed split-trail towed carriage to which has been married the barrel of a French self-propelled gun of average performance.

Several years ago, Argentina purchased a number of French Mk F3 self-propelled howitzers. In the 1970s, CITEFA developed a new carriage onto which the 33-calibre tube of the F3 could be mounted, and the Argentine army ordered the weapon into production to replace its old M114 howitzers. The F3 barrel is shorter than the 39- or 45-calibre tubes currently standard in NATO, and the Argentine gun has less range than weapons like the FH-70 or the M198. The later Model 81 uses a barrel of Argentine rather than French manufacture, but otherwise differs only in minor details. A battery of Model 77s was deployed to the Falklands in 1982, but because of their weight the guns were restricted to the solid ground around Port Stanley, from where they shelled British forces encircling the town.

155-mm Soltam M-71

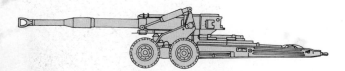

Specification
Crew: 8
Calibre: 155 mm
Weight: 9200 kg (9 tons 123 lb)
Barrel length: 6.67 m (21 ft 11 in)
Elevation: -3°/+52°
HE projectile weight: 43.7 kg (96 lb 5 oz)
Range: 23,500 m (14 miles 1000 yd) with standard projectile; 31,000 m (19 miles) with base-bleed projectile
Rate of fire: 4 rounds per minute; 2 rounds per minute sustained fire

Assessment
Firepower   ★★★★
Range   ★★★★
Age   ★★★
Worldwide users ★★★

The Soltam series of 155-mm howitzers are all very similar, except for the lengths of their barrels. A gun's performance depends on many things, but in general the longer the barrel the longer the range.

Soltam is Israel's only manufacturer of towed artillery. The 155-mm M-68 Gun-Howitzer was developed in the 1960s. Its 33-calibre ordnance was fitted to surplus Israeli Sherman tanks to create a cheap but effective self-propelled gun. The M-71 howitzer uses the same carriage, breech and recoil system as the M-68 but with a lengthened 39-calibre barrel. The Model 839P is the same gun with an auxiliary power system, while the Model 845P has been fitted with an even longer 45-calibre barrel. All of the variants can fire standard NATO 155-mm shells as well as the company's own higher-velocity projectiles. The 155-mm guns manufactured by Soltam have been sold to the [...]li army and have also been exported to at least six other armies, including [...]ore and Thailand.

TOWED ARTILLERY No.2

Even though many modern armies employ self-propelled guns, towed artillery is considerably cheaper and easier to transport by sea or air. Modern guns can come into and out of action with considerable speed, although they are obviously more vulnerable to radar-directed counter-battery fire than self-propelled artillery.

122-mm D-30

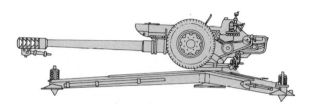

Specification
Crew: 7
Calibre: 122 mm
Weight: 3150 kg (3 tons 224 lb)
Barrel length: 4.88 m (16 ft)
Elevation: -7°/+70°
HE projectile weight: 21.76 kg (47 lb 15 oz)
Range: 15,400 m (9 miles 1000 yd)
Rate of fire: 7–8 rounds per minute

Assessment
Firepower ★★★
Range ★★★★
Age ★★★★
Worldwide users ★★★★

Tough, reliable and hard-hitting, the 122-mm D-30 howitzer was extensively used by the Soviet army, and has been exported to more than 35 nations around the world.

Introduced in 1967, the D-30 was the standard divisional and regimental weapon of the Soviet army. In the last 10 years of its existence the Soviet army made rapid progress towards equipping all mechanised forces with self-propelled artillery. Nevertheless, enormous numbers of D-30 howitzers remain in service with the successor states of the former USSR. Many hundreds of these weapons have been exported. Using separate fixed-charge ammunition, the D-30 is a typical product of the Soviet military machine – a robust, soldier-proof weapon that is reliable under field conditions. Most Arab forces in the Middle East rely on D-30s.

152-mm D-1

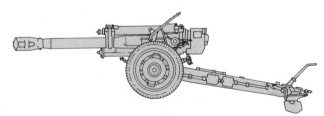

Specification
Crew: 7
Calibre: 152 mm
Weight: 3600 kg (3 tons 1216 lb)
Barrel length: 4.21 m (13 ft 10 in)
Elevation: -3°/+63°
HE projectile weight: 40 kg (88 lb 3 oz)
Range: 12,400 m (8 miles)
Rate of fire: 4 rounds per minute

Assessment
Firepower ★★★★
Range ★★★
Age ★★★★★
Worldwide users ★★★★

First appearing at the height of World War II, the D-1 is a hybrid of two earlier guns. It has a relatively short range but is very hard-hitting.

The D-1 was introduced in 1943, and was used by the Red Army in its great counter-offensives across Poland and into Germany that ended the war in Europe. Until the 1980s each Soviet motorised division had one battalion of D-1s, after that they were progressively replaced by 152-mm self-propelled guns. The D-1s remained in use with lower readiness formations until the end of the USSR. They were widely exported and were used by Arab armies in the 1967 and 1973 Arab-Israeli wars, as well as by the North Vietnamese during their invasion of South Vietnam in 1974-75.

152-mm M1937

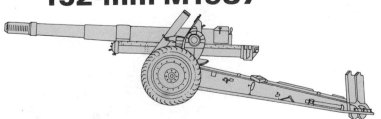

Specification
Crew: 9
Calibre: 152 mm
Weight: 7270 kg (7 tons 347 lb)
Barrel length: 4.93 m (16 ft 2 in)
Elevation: -2°/+65°
HE projectile weight: 43.5 kg (95 lb 14 oz)
Range: 17,265 m (9 miles)
Rate of fire: 4 rounds per minute

Assessment
Firepower ★★★★
Range ★★★★★
Age ★★★★★
Worldwide users ★★★

M1937 guns rumble along the banks of the River Oder at the end of World War II. Conventional in design, the gun is still in service with a number of armies.

The standard weapon of Red Army medium artillery regiments during World War II, the M1937 was replaced after the war by the 152-mm D-20 gun/howitzer. As it was withdrawn from first-line units, the M1937 was issued to lower readiness formations and exported to Soviet allies. It was used in Korea, Vietnam and the Middle East. The M1937 is an unremarkable design, featuring a screw-type breech, hydraulic buffers and it fires cased variable-charge, separate-loading shells. In addition to conventional ammunition, the Soviets developed a 0.2-kiloton tactical nuclear round for all their 152-mm guns.

105-mm OTO-Melara pack howitzer

Specification
Crew: 7
Calibre: 105 mm
Weight: 1290 kg (1 ton 1560 lb)
Barrel length: 1.48 m (4 ft 10 in)
Elevation: -5°/+25°
HE projectile weight: 21.06 kg (46 lb 7 oz)
Range: 10,575 m (6 miles 1000 yd)
Rate of fire: 4 rounds per minute

Assessment
Firepower   ★★
Range   ★★
Age   ★★★★
Worldwide users   ★★★★★

Seen here being pulled by hand off a Royal Marine raft in northern Norway, the Italian OTO-Melara pack howitzer is notable for its small size and ease of handling.

The OTO-Melara pack howitzer was developed during the 1950s and exported to over 25 different countries. It can be dismantled into 11 sub-assemblies for transport across rough terrain, and it can be lifted by light utility helicopters such as the Bell UH-1. It was used by the British Army until its replacement in 1975 by the 105-mm Light Gun. The Argentine army's 3rd artillery battalion of three batteries was deployed to the Falkland Islands as part of the Argentine invasion force. The Argentine guns were used in all the major land actions and were captured by the British forces in June 1982.

105-mm Light Gun

Specification
Crew: 6
Calibre: 105 mm
Weight: 1860 kg (1 ton 1860 lb)
Barrel length: 3.21 m (10 ft 6 in)
Elevation: -5.5°/+70°
HE projectile weight: 16.1 kg (35 lb 8 oz)
Range: 17,200 m (10 miles 1200 yd)
Rate of fire: 3 rounds per minute

Assessment
Firepower   ★★★
Range   ★★★★★
Age   ★★★
Worldwide users   ★★★

The 105-mm Light Gun was developed for the British Army as a replacement for the 105-mm pack howitzer. Vastly more capable, it has been an export success.

The British Army demanded a replacement for its 105-mm OTO-Melara pack howitzers in 1965. It required a weapon with longer range, that could be towed across rough terrain at high speed. Ten years later it received the 105-mm Light Gun, which proved very successful, and has since been adopted by the US Army as the M-119 and by the Australian army. The Light Gun can be carried by a Puma helicopter or split into two loads, each liftable by a single Wessex. Royal Artillery batteries tow their Light Guns with 1-tonne Land Rovers, while US batteries use the AM HMMWV ('Humvee').

25-Pounder

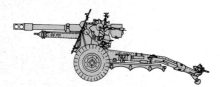

Specification
Crew: 6
Calibre: 87.6 mm
Weight: 1800 kg (1 ton 1730 lb)
Barrel length: 2.35 m (10 ft 6 in)
Elevation: -5°/+40°
HE projectile weight: 11.34 kg (25 lb)
Range: 12,250 m (7 miles 1000 yd)
Rate of fire: 5 rounds per minute

Assessment
Firepower   ★
Range   ★★
Age   ★★★★★
Worldwide users   ★★★★

The British 25-pounder is one of the classic artillery designs. It rose to prominence in the Desert Campaigns of World War II, and although obsolete, it still provides a service in less advanced armies.

The British 25-pounder was one of the classic field artillery pieces of World War II. Entering service at the start of the war, the 25-pounder served in all theatres, from the desert to the jungle. It made its mark during the famous opening barrage at El Alamein in 1942. After the war, the gun could be found wherever the British Army served. Withdrawn from British inventories in the 1970s, except for training or saluting purposes, the 25-pounder is still operational with a dozen armies in the Commonwealth and the Middle East. South African 25-pounders were used operationally in Angola in 1976, where their light weight and ease of use stood them in good stead in spite of being severely out-ranged by opposing guns.

105-mm M101

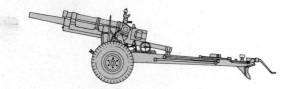

Specification
Crew: 8
Calibre: 105 mm
Weight: 2258 kg (1 ton 497 lb)
Barrel length: 2.57 m (10 ft 6 in)
Elevation: -5°/+66°
HE projectile weight: 21.06 kg (46 lb 7 oz)
Range: 11,270 m (7 miles)
Rate of fire: 3 rounds per minute (sustained)

Assessment
Firepower   ★★
Range   ★★
Age   ★★★★
Worldwide users   ★★★★★

Originally requested after World War I, the M101 howitzer entered service at the beginning of World War II and was used by US forces in Korea and Vietnam. Although far from effective by modern standards, it is one of the most widely used artillery pieces in the world.

Good artillery pieces are among the longest-lived of all military equipment. The M101 began life in 1919, although serious development did not start until the 1930s, and the first equipment, then designated M2, was not put into production until 1940. However, with war looming the howitzer was manufactured in huge numbers, and was used in all theatres of operation. It remained the US Army's standard 105-mm artillery piece in Korea and Vietnam, and did not cease production until 1983. M101s have been widely exported and are still in service with more than 60 armies. M101s fire a wide variety of ammunition, including chemical, high-explosive, anti-personnel, anti-tank, illuminating and smoke rounds. A rocket-assisted projectile has also been developed to improve the howitzer's short range.

SELF-PROPELLED ARTILLERY

Self-propelled artillery is essential on the modern battlefield. Because artillery batteries can be detected almost as soon as they open fire, they need to fire concentrated bursts of fire and then move to avoid retaliation. US gunners christened this tactic 'Shoot and Scoot'. The fate of Iraqi artillery batteries in the Gulf War demonstrated what can happen to artillery that remains in fixed positions.

2S3 152-mm gun

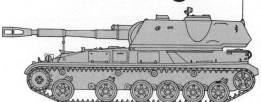

Specification
Crew: 6
Combat weight: 23 tonnes (22 tons 368 lb)
Road speed: 55 km/h (34 mph)
Power-to-weight ratio: unknown
Length: 7.1 m (23 ft 3 in)
Height: 2.7 m (8 ft 10 in)
Armament: 1×152-mm gun; 1×7.62-mm machine-gun

Assessment
Firepower ★★★★
Range ★★★
Age ★★
Worldwide users ★★

The 2S3 is the mainstay of the Russian army's artillery regiments, with each division having 18 of them. It is also nuclear-capable.

The Russian army continued to rely on towed artillery until well into the 1970s. Since then they have adopted a comprehensive series of self-propelled guns, plus armoured forward observer and command vehicles. The 2S3 'Akatsiya' (Acacia) is the broad equivalent of NATO's M109 155-mm guns. Each Russian rifle or tank division has 18 of them. The gun is credited with the comparatively short maximum range of 18 kilometres, and fires the full range of conventional ammunition, chemical or anti-tank rounds. A two-kiloton tactical nuclear round is also issued, but is protected by KGB soldiers.

GCT 155-mm gun

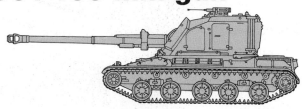

Specification
Crew: 4
Combat weight: 42 tonnes (41 tons 726 lb)
Road speed: 60 km/h (37 mph)
Power-to-weight ratio: 17 hp/tonne
Length: 6.7 m (22 ft)
Height: 3.25 m (10 ft 8 in)
Armament: 1×155-mm gun; 1×7.62-mm machine-gun

Assessment
Firepower ★★★★
Range ★★★★
Age ★★
Worldwide users ★★

The French GCT was used by Iraq in the Gulf War. Its automatic loader has a useful rapid fire capability. The GCT is based on a modified AMX-30 tank chassis.

GIAT Industries completed 500 of these self-propelled guns. They sold them to both Saudi Arabia and Iraq before the Gulf War – in both cases as part of a complete system that included the Thomson-CSF ATILA fire-control system and ammunition. Based on a lightened AMX-30 chassis, the GCT has an automatic loader that allows the crew to be reduced to four and the gun to come into action in less than two minutes. In tests it has fired over 100 rounds per hour, and a burst-fire facility allows a rapid salvo of six rounds in 45 seconds. This is particularly useful in a mobile battle when the gun must move off quickly to avoid counter-battery fire.

M109 155-mm gun

Specification
(M109A2)
Crew: 6
Combat weight: 25 tonnes (24 tons 1366 lb)
Road speed: 56 km/h (35 mph)
Power-to-weight ratio: 16 hp/tonne
Length: 6.1 m (20 ft)
Height: 2.8 m (9 ft 2 in)
Armament: 1×155-mm gun; 1×7.62-mm or 12.7-mm machine-gun

Assessment
Firepower ★★★★
Range ★★★
Age ★★★★★
Worldwide users ★★★★★

Modernised several times since its introduction, the M109 is used by most NATO armies and many others. This US Army M109 is on exercise in Germany.

The first M109s rolled off the production line in 1962, and the US Army fields 2500 of these guns. The guns have undergone several modernisation programmes to maintain effectiveness, but updated fire-control systems and improved ammunition keep it in the front line. It is one of the most widely-used self-propelled guns in the world. The latest version, the M109AC, has machinery to assist the loader, better armour protection and a longer range. M109s in the Gulf were outranged by the Russian and South African guns used by Iraq, but the enemy forces had no fire control or air reconnaissance.

M110 203-mm gun

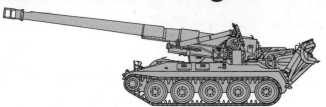

The heaviest self-propelled gun outside Russia, the M110 is operated by a 13-man crew, five riding on the vehicle and the rest in an M548 tracked cargo carrier, which carries the ammunition. The gunners are completely exposed to the elements and enemy fire. The vehicle is not amphibious. The M110 was used by the Royal Artillery in the Gulf War, but it is being phased out in favour of the MLRS. The M110's rate of fire is about one round every two minutes; the ammunition is separate, and all the different types of round weigh over 90 kilograms. Nuclear and chemical shells are available.

Specification
(M110A2)
Crew: 5 (on vehicle)
Combat weight: 28 tonnes (27 tons 1254 lb)
Road speed: 54 km/h (33 mph)
Power-to-weight ratio: 14 hp/tonne
Length: 5.7 m (18 ft 8 in)
Height: 2.9 m (9 ft 6 in)
Armament: 1×203-mm gun

Assessment
Firepower ★★★★★
Range ★★★★
Age ★★★★
Worldwide users ★★★

The 203-mm M110 is the heaviest gun used by NATO forces, but is gradually being phased out in favour of the 227-mm Multiple Launch Rocket System.

G-6 155-mm gun

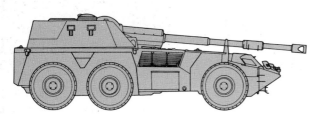

Now in full-scale production for the SADF and the United Arab Emirates, the G-6 is one of South Africa's newest and most effective weapons. Equipped with satellite navigation equipment, a handful of pre-production G-6s were used in combat against Angolan forces in 1987. The longest-ranged gun in service, the G-6 inflicted heavy casualties on FAPLA troops, frequently catching them by surprise with air-burst salvos. In common with modern South African vehicles, the G-6 employs a wheeled chassis which is more suited to travelling long distances in the bush.

Specification
Crew: 6
Combat weight: 36.5 tonnes (35 tons 2060 lb)
Road speed: 90 km/h (56 mph)
Power-to-weight ratio: 14 hp/tonne
Length: 10.4 m (34 ft 2 in)
Height: 3.1 m (10 ft)
Armament: 1×155-mm howitzer; 1×12.7-mm machine-gun; 3 weapon ports for crew personal weapons

Assessment
Firepower ★★★★
Range ★★★★★
Age ★★
Worldwide users ★

The South African G-6 is an outstanding gun that proved highly effective during operations in Angola.

M107 175-mm gun

From the 1960s most NATO armies used three types of SP gun: 155-, 175- and 203-mm. The M107 175-mm gun was used by the US Army in Vietnam, and is still in service with Israel, Greece and Turkey. Some were sold to Iran before the revolution and may still be in service. Most other users have converted their M107s to M110 standard, and the 175-mm gun has been abandoned as being neither one thing nor the other. The new 155-mm guns have a substantially increased range and more lethal ammunition.

Specification
Crew: 5 (on vehicle)
Combat weight: 28 tonnes (27 tons 1254 lb)
Road speed: 56 km/h (35 mph)
Power-to-weight ratio: 14.3 hp/tonne
Length: 5.7 m (18 ft 8 in)
Height: 3.6 m (11 ft 10 in)
Armament: 1×175-mm gun

Assessment
Firepower ★★★★★
Range ★★★★★
Age ★★★★
Worldwide users ★★★

The M107 was used during the Vietnam War, stationed in fire bases to provide support for US troops fighting deep in the jungle.

Abbot 105-mm gun

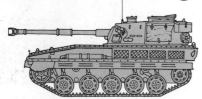

The British Army's Abbot gun has been in urgent need of replacement for many years, and all of them are now in store. It was supposed to have been replaced years ago by the SP70: an Anglo-German co-operative venture that came to nothing. The Abbot's shell is too light by modern standards: it is the same as that fired by the 105-mm light gun. It can maintain a very rapid rate of fire for a short period of time – up to 12 rounds per minute. Six HESH anti-tank rounds are carried in case the enemy front line turns out to be rather closer than anticipated.

Specification
Crew: 4
Combat weight: 16.5 tonnes (16 tons 537 lb)
Road speed: 47 km/h (29 mph)
Power-to-weight ratio: 14.5 hp/tonne
Length: 5.7 m (18 ft 8 in)
Height: 2.5 m (8 ft 3 in)
Armament: 1×105-mm gun; 1×7.62-mm machine-gun

Assessment
Firepower ★★
Range ★★★
Age ★★★★
Worldwide users ★★

The Abbot is an obsolete gun used by the British Army. All of them are now in store and it is being phased out as NATO standardises on 155-mm calibre weapons.

SELF-PROPELLED ARTILLERY

There is a considerable variety of self-propelled artillery. Types of self-propelled artillery pieces range from small guns mounted on converted personnel carriers to massive purpose-built systems. The largest military vehicles currently in service mount huge guns or howitzers and are capable of firing over immensely long ranges.

2S1 122-mm gun

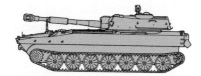

The 2S1 is the smallest of the family of self-propelled guns developed and fielded by the Soviets in the 1970s and 1980s. Roughly comparable in size with Britain's Abbot, but far more capable, the 2S1 carries a 122-mm gun with a maximum range of over 15 kilometres when using conventional ammunition. The gun was usually assigned to Soviet and Warsaw Pact tank divisions. Operating much closer to the front line than their NATO equivalents, and available in large numbers, the 2S1 was a source of valuable firepower to Soviet commanders. Its relatively light weight also means that it is likely to form part of the equipment of the more mobile forces currently being evolved in Russia and the Commonwealth of Independent States.

Specification
Crew: 4
Combat weight: 16 tonnes (15 tons 1680 lb)
Road speed: 60 km/h (37 mph)
Power-to-weight ratio: 15 hp/tonne
Length: 7.3 m (23 ft 11in)
Height: 2.4 m (7 ft 11 in)
Armament: 1×122-mm gun

Assessment
Firepower ★★★
Range ★★
Age ★★★
Worldwide users ★★★★

Originally known in the West as the M1974 Self-propelled Howitzer after the year in which it was first seen, the 2S1 was also known somewhat incongruously to the former Soviet army as the Gvozdika, or Carnation.

2S7 203-mm gun

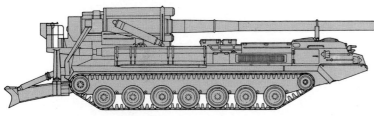

The is the heaviest Russian SP gun, in service for about 10 years and is capable of firing nuclear munitions. Similar in concept to the American M110, the exact capabilities of this gun remain a closely-guarded secret. Its range has been quoted as 30 kilometres, but this is unconfirmed. Nevertheless, the fact that a potential enemy was well provided with such weaponry was a pressing reason for the British Army's replacement of Abbot and its introduction of systems like MLRS and the new AS90 self-propelled howitzer.

Specification
Crew: unknown
Combat weight: 40 tonnes (39 tons 828 lb) (estimated)
Road speed: unknown
Power-to-weight ratio: unknown
Length: 12.8 m (42 ft)
Height: 3.5 m (11 ft 6 in)
Armament: 1×203-mm gun

Assessment
Firepower ★★★★★
Range ★★★★★
Age ★★
Worldwide users ★

The massive 2S7 203-mm self-propelled gun is one of the largest armoured vehicles currently in service anywhere in the world. A sustained rate of fire of one round per minute has been quoted.

2S4 240-mm mortar

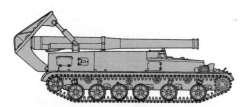

Based on the chassis of the GMZ tracked minelaying vehicle, the 2S4 provided the Russians with overwhelming firepower but a range of only about 13 kilometres. Its breech-loading mortar fires a 130-kilogram HE round which will destroy most bunkers and dug-outs with a single round: opposing guns must hope to locate this beast and destroy it using their superior range. The Russians always enjoyed big mortars; in the late 1950s they deployed several that were nuclear-capable. The 2S4 may well fire nuclear bombs as well.

Specification
Crew: unknown
Combat weight: 30 tonnes (29 tons 1187 lb) (estimated)
Road speed: unknown
Power-to-weight ratio: unknown
Length: 7.5 m (24 ft 7 in)
Height: 2.7 m (8 ft 10 in)
Armament: 1×240-mm mortar

Assessment
Firepower ★★★★★
Range ★
Age ★
Worldwide users ★

The Red Army was always a great believer in mortars, and its successors have inherited one of the largest and most powerful weapons of its type in the shape of the 2S4 self-propelled 240-mm mortar.

DANA 152-mm SP howitzer

Artillery pieces are usually tracked for maximum cross-country mobility, but this means that they are very much slower on the road. The Czechs went a different route with the *vzor* 77 152-mm DANA, which is a wheeled vehicle and is based on the Tatra 815 8x8 truck. Wheeled vehicles are cheaper to build and keep running longer than tracked ones, and they can move far better on roads. Also, the Tatra 815 has one of the best cross-country performances of any wheeled vehicle. The armament is based on that of the Russian 2S3 152-mm howitzer, fitted with an automatic loading system.

Specification
Crew: 3+2
Combat weight: 23 tonnes (22 tons 1434 lb)
Road speed: 80 km/h (50 mph)
Power-to-weight ratio: 15 hp/tonne
Length: 10.4 m (34 ft 2 in) (with gun forward)
Height: 3.5 m (11 ft 6 in)
Armament: 1×152-mm howitzer and 1×12.7-mm AA machine-gun

Assessment
Firepower ★★★
Range ★★★
Age ★★
Worldwide users ★

The Czech DANA is an interesting vehicle with wheels instead of tracks. Operating in a country with a good road system, it trades reduced battlefield mobility for greatly enhanced strategic mobility.

F3 155-mm

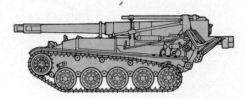

The F3 was developed in the 1950s and has been exported to Latin America and the Middle East. It still serves with the French army, although it is being replaced with the GCT 155-mm gun on an AMX-30 chassis. The F3 uses an AMX-13 light tank chassis with the rear idler removed but, being nearly 2½ tonnes heavier, it is not as agile as the tank. The ordnance which is mounted onto the F3 has been adapted from the M50 155-mm towed howitzer. This was the first piece of artillery developed in France after the end of World War II. The standard HE projectile weighs 43.75 kilograms and has a range of 20 kilometres.

Specification
Crew: 2 (on the weapon)
Combat weight: 17.4 tonnes (17 tons 280 lb)
Road speed: 64 km/h (40 mph)
Power-to-weight ratio: 16 hp/tonne
Length: 6.2 m (20 ft 4 in)
Height: 2.08 m (6 ft 10 in)
Armament: 1×155-mm howitzer

Assessment
Firepower ★★★
Range ★★★
Age ★★★★★
Worldwide users ★★★

Although designed in the 1950s and now outclassed by later weapons, the F3 155-mm gun is still an effective piece of artillery. It has been used by at least a dozen armies.

OTO-Melara Palmaria

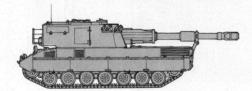

Developed as a private venture for export, OTO-Melara sold 210 of these excellent 155-mm guns to Libya in the early 1980s. The chassis is based on that of the OF-40 MBT, which in turn is derived from that of the German Leopard 1 Main Battle Tank. The 41-calibre ordnance was developed specifically for the Palmaria, and has had a range of ammunition designed to match. Firing conventional 43.5-kilogram 155-mm shells, it has a range of up to 27.5 kilometres, but rocket-assisted rounds will reach 30 kilometres. Automatic loading enables it to fire four rounds per minute, but sustained rate of fire is only one round a minute. It normally carries 30 rounds of ammunition.

Specification
Crew: 5
Combat weight: 46 tonnes (45 tons 650 lb)
Road speed: 60 km/h (37 mph)
Power-to-weight ratio: 16.3 hp/tonne
Length: 7.2 m (23 ft 8 in)
Height: 2.8 m (9 ft 2 in)
Armament: 1×155-mm howitzer

Assessment
Firepower ★★★★
Range ★★★★
Age ★★
Worldwide users ★★

The Palmaria is a well-designed weapon which has not achieved a great deal of export success other than a large order from Libya. Its maximum range with rocket-assisted projectiles is 30 km.

Type 54-1 122-mm SP howitzer

The Chinese army fields two types of SP gun: a 152-mm system similar to the Soviet 2S3, and this 122-mm weapon mounted on the chassis of the YW 531 APC. The current service version has a slightly modified chassis, identifiable by the addition of a fifth road wheel. The gun fitted to the system is a Type 54-1 howitzer, which is a Chinese copy of the pre-war Soviet M-30 122-mm howitzer. It was a good gun in its time, but it is now long past its prime. The HE round weighs 21.76 kilograms and has a maximum range of just under 12 kilometres, so it is outranged by both NATO and Soviet equivalents. A new 122-mm system appeared recently on a lengthened chassis with a sixth road wheel.

Specification
Crew: 7
Combat weight: 15.3 tonnes (15 tons 134 lb)
Road speed: 56 km/h (35 mph)
Power-to-weight ratio: 17 hp/tonne
Length: 5.6 m (18 ft 5 in)
Height: 2.6 m (8 ft 6 in)
Armament: 1×122-mm howitzer

Assessment
Firepower ★★★
Range ★★
Age ★★
Worldwide users ★

It is not surprising that the Type 54 does not measure up to NATO- or modern Soviet-designed equipment, since the tube used is a copy of the Soviet M-30 towed artillery piece, which was originally designed in the 1930s.

COMBAT SUPPORT VEHICLES No. 1

Modern armies require vast quantities of fuel, ammunition and countless other supplies to keep fighting. Specialist support vehicles are used to bring the supplies to the front line and they must have some cross-country capability to deliver the goods on the modern battlefield.

ZIL 130 series

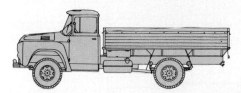

The Soviet army used to operate vast fleets of transport vehicles, although it never freed itself from its reliance on railways to bring forward its supplies. The Soviet forces operated over vast distances and without the network of good roads that is taken for granted in Western Europe. The ZIL series of 4×4 and 6×6 trucks entered production in 1964 and remain in widespread service throughout the former states of the USSR and many ex-Soviet allies. Churned out in their thousands by the Likhachev factory in Moscow, they were basic 1950s-era trucks and compare poorly with Western contemporaries. Poor Soviet engine technology combined with slipshod production quality led to transmission failures and unreliable engines.

Specification
Weight: 4.2 tonnes (4 tons 291 lb)
Length: 6.67 m (21 ft 11 in)
Maximum load: 5.5 tonnes (5 tons 918 lb)
Maximum towed load: 4.5 tonnes (4 tons 960 lb)
Maximum road speed: 90 km/h (56 mph)
Range: 475 km (295 miles)
Fuel: petrol

Assessment
Load ★★★
Range ★★★★
Age ★★★★★
Worldwide users ★★★

The ZIL series of trucks dates back to the 1950s and they have been widely exported to Soviet allies in Africa and Asia. They are still used throughout the former states of the USSR.

Ural-375 6x6 truck

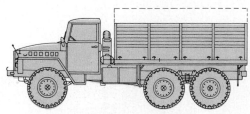

Entering production in 1961 at the Ural factory, the Ural-375 proved to have such a good cross-country performance that it replaced most of the artillery tractors then used to tow Soviet guns. Also very widely exported, the Ural-375 was used for many special purposes, including NBC decontamination (with an old jet engine on the back) and as a multiple rocket launcher (BM-21 122-mm system). Also a common Soviet engineer vehicle and used as a fuel tanker, there was even a specialist 'tropical' version, the Ural-375Y. At least two variants were developed for operations in the arctic tundra of northern Russia.

Specification
Weight: 8.4 tonnes (8 tons 598 lb)
Length: 7.35 m (24 ft 1 in)
Maximum load: 5 tonnes (4 tons 2060 lb)
Maximum towed load: 10 tonnes (9 tons 1881 lb)
Maximum road speed: 75 km/h (46 mph)
Range: 600 km (372 miles)
Fuel: petrol

Assessment
Load ★★★
Range ★★★★★
Age ★★★★★
Worldwide users ★★★★

The Ural-375 was used in a multitude of roles by the Soviet army since its cross-country performance was exceptional. Most BM-21 multiple rocket launchers were mounted on Ural trucks.

KAMAZ 5320 6x4 truck

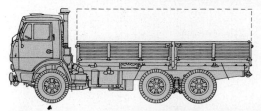

During the 1970s the Soviets acquired a great deal of Western technology, and the Kama river truck factory was one fruit of 'détente' and/or industrial espionage. Located some 900 kilometres due east of Moscow at Naberezhnye Chelny, the Kama plant produces a comprehensive range of 6×4 and 6×6 trucks, all powered by diesel engines. Although the bulk of the factory's annual production of 150,000 plus vehicles went to the civilian sector, all were liable for military requisition and KAMAZ trucks were prominent in the 1979 invasion of Afghanistan and the 10-year guerrilla war that ensued there.

Specification
Weight: 6.8 tonnes (6 tons 1552 lb)
Length: 7.4 m (24 ft 3 in)
Maximum load: 8 tonnes (7 tons 1949 lb)
Maximum towed load: 11.5 tonnes (11 tons 717 lb)
Maximum road speed: 75 km/h (46 mph)
Range: 650 km (405 miles)
Fuel: diesel

Assessment
Load ★★★★
Range ★★★★★
Age ★★★
Worldwide users ★★★

The KAMAZ trucks are primarily built for the civilian market, but the Soviet army used them throughout the war in Afghanistan.

Alvis Stalwart

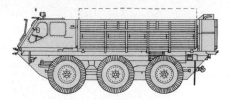

Built as a private venture by Alvis in 1959, the Stalwart caught the interest of the British Army and it was in production as the FV 622 from 1966. Some 1,400 Stalwarts were built until manufacture ceased in 1971, and some remain in service with the British Army; the Austrian and Swedish forces also bought Stalwarts. The Stalwart has a superb cross-country performance and is also fully amphibious, propelled in the water by two marine jets. Able to carry five tonnes of cargo or up to 24 personnel, it has proved very successful. The Royal Artillery uses a version called the FV 623, which has a hydraulic crane attached to load and unload ammunition pallets.

Specification
Weight: 8.9 tonnes (8 tons 1700 lb)
Length: 6.35 m (21 ft 11 in)
Maximum load: 5 tonnes (4 tons 2060 lb)
Maximum towed load: 10 tonnes (9 tons 1881 lb)
Maximum road speed: 63 km/h (39 mph)
Range: 515 km (320 miles)
Fuel: petrol

Assessment
Load ★★★
Range ★★★★
Age ★★★★
Worldwide users ★

The diminutive Alvis Stalwart is a fully amphibious combat support vehicle with excellent cross-country performance and is used by the British Army.

M35/44 6x6 truck

Designed just after World War II, the US Army's M35 2½-ton truck first saw combat during the Korean War, and it has remained in service ever since. Originally built by Reo, production was taken over by the Kaiser Jeep Corporation, which was acquired by American Motors in 1970. Powered by a diesel engine and with a four-speed automatic gear-box, the M35 has proved reliable and relatively easy to maintain. The US Army alone was operating over 60,000 of them during the 1980s and the type has been exported to most US allies in Asia plus several Latin American forces. The basic model has been the basis for a host of variants, including engineer vehicles, fuel tankers and recovery vehicles.

Specification
Weight: 5.9 tonnes (5 tons 1805 lb)
Length: 6.7 m (22 ft)
Maximum load: 4.5 tonnes (4 tons 960 lb)
Maximum towed load: 4.5 tonnes (4 tons 960 lb)
Maximum road speed: 90 km/h (56 mph)
Range: 480 km (300 miles)
Fuel: diesel

Assessment
Load ★★★★
Range ★★★★
Age ★★★★★
Worldwide users ★★★★★

Used in very large numbers by the US Army and many allied nations, the M35 series of diesel-engined trucks has been in service since the 1950s.

MAN 8x8 10-tonne truck

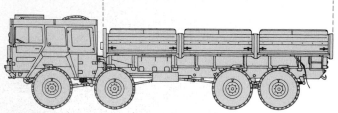

The German truck manufacturer MAN began producing vehicles for the West German army in the 1970s. It has, since delivered a range of 4x4, 6x6 and 8x8 vehicles for many different purposes. The largest of the range is the 10-tonne 8x8, which the German forces use for cargo carrying, launching RPVs and as a radar platform. It has also been tested with Roland SAM launchers. The German forces bought nearly 2,000 10-tonne trucks and the US Army ordered 465 to carry the ground-launched cruise missile and the Pershing II. The MAN 10-tonne truck was also trialled for the 'Heavy Expanded Mobility Tactical Truck' (HEMTT) but the order eventually went to Oshkosh (see below).

Specification
Weight: 15 tonnes (14 tons 1702 lb)
Length: 10.12m (33 ft 3in)
Maximum load: 10 tonnes (9 tons 1881 lb)
Maximum road speed: 90 km/h (56 mph)
Range: 600 km (372 miles)
Fuel: diesel

Assessment
Load ★★★★★
Range ★★★★★
Age ★★
Worldwide users ★★

MAN 10-tonne trucks race across a test track during cross-country performance trials. Widely used by the German army, the MAN trucks are also operated by the US Army.

Oshkosh 8x8 HEMTT

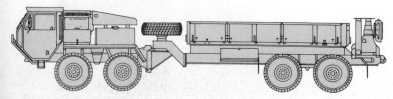

The HEMTT (Heavy Expanded Mobility Tactical Truck) contract was won by Oshkosh in 1981. This 10-tonne truck utilises many commercial automotive components and has a standard Oshkosh cab with an eight-cylinder diesel engine and civilian four-speed automatic gear-box. With sun visors, variable speed windscreen wipers, windscreen washers and comfortable seats, the HEMTT is a far cry from the ageing 1950s designs still in widespread use with the Soviet forces until their demise in 1991. The HEMTT is produced in several versions, including tankers, wreckers and tractors as well as cargo carriers.

Specification
Weight: 16.76 tonnes (16 tons 1108 lb)
Length: 10.17m (33 ft 4in)
Maximum load: 9.79 tonnes (9 tons 1422 lb)
Maximum road speed: 88 km/h (55 mph)
Range: 483 km (300 miles)
Fuel: diesel

Assessment
Load ★★★★★
Range ★★★
Age ★
Worldwide users ★

The Oshkosh HEMTT is the heaviest combat support vehicle expected to move across country. The US Army operates several specialist versions.

MULTIPLE ROCKET LAUNCHERS No. 1

With its ability to destroy enemy area targets by firing massive quantities of high explosive over huge distances in a very short time, the multiple rocket launcher has become an incredibly powerful and destructive weapon.

MLRS

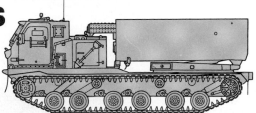

Specification
Crew: 3
Combat weight: 26 tonnes (25 tons 1320 lb)
No. of rockets: 12
Rocket calibre: 227 mm
Warhead weight: variable
Range: 30–40 km (18–25 miles) depending on rocket type

Assessment
Firepower ★★★★★
Accuracy ★★★★
Age ★★
Worldwide users ★★★

The Multiple Launch Rocket System is the most sophisticated weapon of its type in the world today. Sophistication is bought at some cost, but as the war in the Gulf showed, it is also lethally effective.

The US Army displayed little enthusiasm for multiple-launch rocket systems in the years following World War II, but things changed in the 1960s. Development of the Vought Multiple Launch Rocket System (MLRS) was initiated by the US Army in 1976 as a reaction to the vast Soviet force of rocket systems. The MLRS entered service with the US Army in the 1980s, with further examples, manufactured by an international consortium, being purchased by Britain, France, Germany, Italy, the Netherlands and Turkey. Vastly more expensive than primitive Soviet systems, the MLRS fires rockets containing hundreds of anti-personnel and anti-armour sub-munitions with deadly accuracy over ranges of 30 kilometres or more. MLRS systems were used to devastating effect by American and British artillery units during the Gulf War, being used to particular effect against Iraqi artillery positions.

LARS

Specification
Crew: 3
Combat weight: 7 tonnes (6 tons 1949 lb)
No. of rockets: 36
Rocket calibre: 110 mm
Warhead weight: unknown
Range: 14 km (9 miles)

Assessment
Firepower ★★★
Accuracy ★★★
Age ★★★★
Worldwide users ★

The West German LARS was one of the earliest of NATO's modern multiple rocket systems, but the small size of the rocket it fires makes it much less effective than the American-designed MLRS.

West Germany was the first NATO nation to follow the Soviet lead in the deployment of rocket artillery, developing and deploying a multiple rocket system in the 1960s. The relatively simple 6×6 truck-mounted Light Artillery Rocket System or LARS entered service in 1969. Known to the Bundeswehr as the *Artillerie Raketenwerfer 110 SF*, it is issued on a scale of one battery of eight launchers to each army division. Standard warload comprises an HE fragmentation warhead, but a wide variety of rocket types has been tested or is in service, including a parachute-retarded anti-tank mine dispenser. LARS II is the same system mounted on a modern MAN 6×6 seven-ton truck chassis, and features better fire-control systems. LARS seemed advanced when first introduced, but improvements in armour and artillery systems mean that it is now outclassed, which is why the German army has acquired large numbers of the American-designed MLRS.

Valkiri

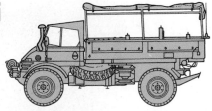

Specification
Crew: 2
Combat weight: 6.4 tonnes (6 tons 670 lb)
No. of rockets: 24
Rocket calibre: 127 mm
Warhead weight: unknown
Range: 22 km (14 miles)

Assessment
Firepower ★★★
Accuracy ★★★
Age ★
Worldwide users ★

South African troops could testify to the effectiveness of multiple rocket fire, being on the receiving end of fire from Soviet-supplied weapons in Angola in the 1970s. The Valkiri was designed to counter such systems.

South African troops operating in Angola in the late 1970s received a painful education into the simplicity and effectiveness of Soviet-supplied arms. Encounters with the BM-21 multiple rocket launcher convinced the South African Defence Force of the value of a simple weapon system which was nevertheless able to deluge an enemy position with high explosive. Inspired by the BM-21, the Valkiri was put into service in the mid-1980s. Mounted on a 4×4 SAMIL truck chassis, Valkiri is a highly-mobile, 24-round, 127-mm rocket system fitted with pre-fragmented, high-explosive warheads ideal for bush warfare. Detonating eight metres above the ground, the warhead covers an area of 1000 square metres with some 8,000 pieces of lethal shrapnel.

BM-21

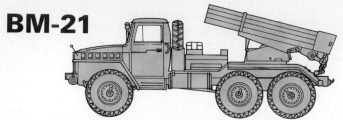

Specification
Crew: 6
Combat weight: 11.5 tonnes (11 tons 717 lb)
No. of rockets: 40
Rocket calibre: 122 mm
Warhead weight: 19.4 kg (42 lb 12 oz)
Range: 20 km (12 miles)

Assessment
Firepower ★★★★
Accuracy ★★
Age ★★★★★
Worldwide users ★★★★★

Entering service in 1964, the BM-21 is a cheap, sturdy, reliable and highly effective weapon system. Far cruder than Western rocket systems, the BM-21 is valued by the Russians for its ability to dump more high explosive onto an area target with a single salvo than an equivalent force of artillery would in 30 minutes. Two types of fin-stabilised rocket are used, the 'long' version with a range of 20 kilometres, and the 'short' version which can reach up to 11 kilometres. BM-21 rockets can be fitted with a variety of warheads, including smoke, high-explosive and fragmentation.

The BM-21 is the world's most widely used multiple rocket system. Simple, even crude, it is nevertheless sturdy and easy to use, and is capable of laying down an awesome amount of fire on a target in a very short time.

BM-27

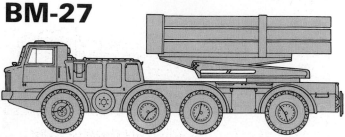

Specification
(estimated)
Crew: 6
Combat weight: 23 tonnes (22 tons 1435 lb)
No. of rockets: 16
Rocket calibre: 220 mm
Warhead weight: unknown
Range: 40 km (25 miles) (approx)

Assessment
Firepower ★★★★★
Accuracy ★★★
Age ★★
Worldwide users ★

The BM-27 was introduced into the Soviet army as a BM-21 replacement in 1977. Known as the *Uragzy* or *Hurricane*, the BM-27 equips artillery brigades and regiments in Combined Arms and Tank Armies. Firing a 220-mm rocket between five and 40 kilometres, the BM-27 is comparable with the American MLRS. The ZIL 135 8×8 chassis has excellent cross-country manoeuvrability, although it cannot compare with a tracked vehicle. Like the MLRS, the BM-27's rockets dispense sub-munitions. These can be incendiary bomblets, fragmentation bomblets, or mines. Once the 16 rockets are fired the launcher can be reloaded from ZIL 8×8 support vehicles in less than 20 minutes. In spite of having been in service for nearly 15 years, few details of the BM-27 have been released to the unclassified world, and the only images available are US Department of Defense artists' impressions.

The BM-27 is a later Soviet system, roughly equivalent to, but probably not as sophisticated as, the MLRS currently in American and NATO service. Like the MLRS, BM-27 rockets are sub-munition dispensers.

RM-70

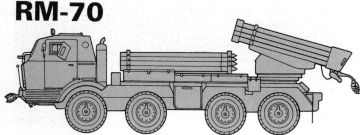

Specification
Crew: 6
Combat weight: 33.7 tonnes (33 tons 376 lb)
No. of rockets: 40
Rocket calibre: 122 mm
Warhead weight: 19.4 kg (42 lb 12 oz)
Range: 20 km (12 miles)

Assessment
Firepower ★★★★
Accuracy ★★
Age ★★★
Worldwide users ★★

Armies which were formerly part of the Warsaw Pact were dominated by the Soviet army, so it is not surprising that they used Soviet weapons and tactics. An exception was Czechoslovakia, whose long-established arms industry continued to produce and export indigenous designs or improved variants of Soviet designs. The RM-70 rocket system, first seen in public in the early 1970s, is basically the Soviet BM-21 122-mm rocket launcher. It is mounted on an armoured version of the excellent Tatra 813 8×8 truck, which has very good cross-country mobility. Forty rockets are carried in the launcher tubes, along with 40 spares which allow for extremely fast reloading. Some vehicles carry a bulldozer blade in front of the cab, which is used to help prepare firing positions. In Czech service, each mechanised or armoured division includes an 18-strong RM-70 battalion.

The RM-70 is basically a copy of the Soviet BM-21, mounted on an 8×8 cross-country truck chassis which also carries a full set of reload rockets, effectively doubling the system's rate of fire.

Type 70

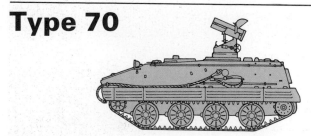

Specification
Crew: 6
Combat weight: 13.4 tonnes (13 tons 426 lb)
No. of rockets: 19
Rocket calibre: 130 mm
Warhead weight: 14.7 kg (32 lb 6 oz)
Range: 10 km (6 miles)

Assessment
Firepower ★★★
Accuracy ★★
Age ★★
Worldwide users ★

The Chinese People's army was heavily influenced by the Soviets in the years following World War II, and even after relations between the two communist giants soured, the Chinese continued to produce Soviet-influenced weapons. China's fast-growing arms industry has produced a number of multiple rocket designs. The 130-mm rocket is used in several launchers, including the 30-round Type 82 and 19-round Type 63 truck-mounted systems, and the 19-round Type 70 which is mounted on a YM531 tracked armoured personnel carrier. Type 70s operate in six-vehicle batteries attached to Chinese armoured divisions, and were used by both sides during China's 1979 border war with Vietnam.

Chinese rocket launchers are obviously influenced by Soviet designs, but they are usually available in a number of forms. The 130-mm rocket used in the Type 70 is also available in towed and truck-mounted forms.

MULTIPLE ROCKET LAUNCHERS No.2

Multiple rocket launchers range in size from heavy rockets, fired from trucks or even tank chassis, to small launchers that can be towed by a jeep or even manhandled.

BM-24

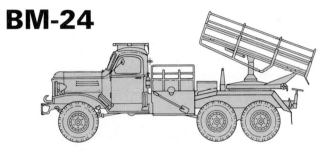

Specification
Crew: 6
Combat weight: 9.2 tonnes (9 tons 123 lb)
No. of rockets: 12
Rocket calibre: 240 mm
Warhead weight: 46.9 kg (103 lb 6 oz)
Range: 11 km (8 miles)

Assessment
Firepower   ★★★★★
Accuracy   ★★
Age   ★★★★★
Worldwide users ★★★

The elderly BM-24 multiple rocket launcher was widely used by Arab forces in the 1967 Arab-Israeli war. This is one of the many that were captured and used against their former owners by the Israelis.

Introduced during the 1950s, the BM-24 240-mm multiple rocket launcher was used by the Soviet army well into the 1970s. It was slowly replaced by the 122-mm calibre BM-21 and was used to equip reserve formations only. Although the BM-24's rockets have warheads twice the size of the BM-21's 122-mm rockets, the system has only 12 tubes as opposed to 40, so it actually delivers less explosive in a single salvo. The BM-24 has been fired in anger in the Middle East; it was the standard Arab multiple rocket launcher during the 1967 war, and the Israelis captured so many that they used whole battalions of BM-24s in the 1973 war. These appeared again in the 1982 invasion of Lebanon, during which the Israeli BM-24s fired a new Israeli-made rocket.

SBAT-70

Specification
Crew: 4
Combat weight: 1 tonne (2195 lb)
No. of rockets: 36
Rocket calibre: 70 mm
Warhead weight: 4 kg (8 lb 13 oz)
Range: 7.5 km (5 miles)

Assessment
Firepower   ★★
Accuracy   ★★★
Age   ★★
Worldwide users ★★

The SBAT-70 is a diminutive trailer-mounted launcher built to fire aircraft rockets fitted with a variety of warheads.

The Brazilian company Avibras manufactures a wide range of multiple rocket launchers, some of which are in service with the Brazilian forces but most are for export. The SBAT-70 system is a land-launched version of the standard Avibras 70-mm aircraft rocket. The LM 70/36 towed launcher has 36 tubes, and weighs only 700 kilograms unloaded and 1000 kilograms when loaded. A 50-metre cable is attached to it for firing the system. A variety of warheads are offered, including HE, HE fragmentation, HEAT (high-explosive anti-tank), practice and white phosphorus.

ASTROS II

Specification
(SS-30)
Crew: 3
Combat weight: 10 tonnes (9 tons 1881 lb)
No. of rockets: 32
Rocket calibre: 127 mm
Warhead weight: 18 kg (39 lb 11 oz)
Range: 30 km (19 miles)

Assessment
Firepower   ★★★★
Accuracy   ★★★
Age   ★★
Worldwide users ★★

The Brazilian ASTROS system uses a common group of launcher, command and fire-control vehicles to deliver three different sizes of unguided rocket.

In service with the Brazilian army and exported in large numbers to Iraq during the Iran-Iraq War, the ASTROS II is a conventional truck-based multiple rocket launcher. The truck is built by Tectran, an Avibras subsidiary, and is a 10-tonne, 6×6 cross-country vehicle with armoured shutters to protect the crew cabin. Three different sizes of rocket launcher are available: the SS-30 (32×127-mm rockets); the SS-40 (16×180-mm rockets) and the SS-60 (4×300-mm rockets) The rockets weigh 68 kilograms, 152 kilograms and 595 kilograms respectively The ASTROS system includes ammunition resupply vehicles, a truck-mounted fire-control radar system and command and control vehicles.

SAKR 122-mm MRL

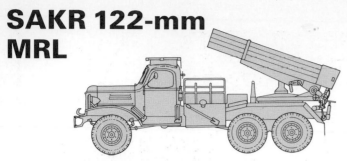

Specification
(30-round SAKR on ZIL-131)
Crew: 3
Combat weight: 11.2 tonnes (11 tons)
No. of rockets: 30
Rocket calibre: 122 mm
Warhead weight: 17.5 kg (38 lb 9 oz)
Range: 32 km (20 miles)

Assessment
Firepower   ★ ★ ★ ★
Accuracy   ★ ★ ★
Age   ★ ★ ★
Worldwide users   ★ ★

An Egyptian SAKR 122-mm multiple rocket launcher in the hands of one of Beirut's innumerable warring militias during the early 1980s.

After breaking with the USSR in the 1970s, Egypt turned to the West for new weapons and also began to develop more of its own military equipment. In 1981, the Egyptian SAKR concern test-fired a development of the Soviet 122-mm rocket fired by the BM-21, which was in service with the Egyptian army. By employing a lighter motor and more efficient rocket propellant, the Egyptians have achieved a major increase in range. Their 122-mm rocket is available in several versions: 30- or 40-round launchers on a Soviet ZIL truck or Japanese Isuzu 6x6, plus a 21-round launcher on a four-tonne Romanian Bucegi 4x4. Several warheads are available, including one with a programmable fuse for delivering sub-munitions.

D-3000

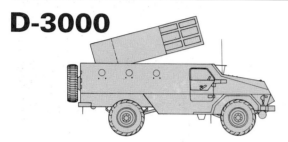

Specification
Crew: 2
Combat weight: unknown
No. of rockets: 12
Rocket calibre: 80 mm
Warhead weight: unknown
Range: 2.5 km (1 mile)

Assessment
Firepower   ★
Accuracy   ★ ★ ★
Age   ★ ★
Worldwide users   ★

D-3000 smoke-laying rocket launchers of the Egyptian army are mounted on Walids – APCs based on the chassis of the Magirus-Deutz 6×4 truck.

The Egyptian army has developed a specialised rocket system for creating massive smokescreens in a very short time. This makes a good deal of sense for an army that is likely to fight in terrain which is notoriously open and lacking in cover, as only armies with the most advanced optics can 'see' through chemical smokescreens. The D-3000 is an 80-mm rocket normally fitted in 12-tube launchers to the Walid 4x4 APC. There is also a larger D-6000 122-mm version, which has been seen mounted in quadruple boxes on either side of a T-62 tank turret. One 12-rocket salvo from a Walid can create a smokescreen up to 1000 metres long that will last for about 15 minutes in normal weather conditions.

RADIRS

Specification
(six-pod launcher)
Crew: 4
Combat weight: depends on vehicle
No. of rockets: 114
Rocket calibre: 70 mm
Warhead weight: 4.5 kg (9 lb 15 oz) (HE)
Range: 15 km (9 miles)

Assessment
Firepower   ★ ★ ★
Accuracy   ★ ★ ★
Age   ★ ★
Worldwide users   ★

The US Army RADIRS system follows the same idea as the SBAT-70 – a low-cost launcher for existing aircraft missiles. It fires pods of HYDRA 70-mm rockets.

BEI Defense Systems developed RADIRS (RApid Deployment Integrated Rocket System) in conjunction with the US Army. Like the Avibras SBAT-70, this employs an aircraft rocket, the 70-mm HYDRA. It is available in a variety of configurations, including towed trailer launchers, vehicle-mounted systems or even a man-packed version. The basic unit is a 19-tube replaceable launcher pod, and up to six can be mounted together on a 2½-tonne truck or three on a Hum-Vee. A single 19-tube launcher can be fired in 0.5 second in 'quick' mode or 1.5 seconds in 'slow' mode. A multitude of different warheads are offered, including HE, HEAT, illumination, flechette and smoke.

Type 63

Specification
Crew: 4
Combat weight: 0.6 tonne (1322 lb)
No. of rockets: 12
Rocket calibre: 107 mm
Warhead weight: 8.33 kg (18 lb 6 oz)
Range: 7.9 km (4 miles 1602 yd)

Assessment
Firepower   ★ ★ ★
Accuracy   ★ ★
Age   ★ ★ ★
Worldwide users   ★ ★ ★ ★

Lebanese militiamen clean the barrels of a Chinese Type 63 rocket launcher. In this case they have fixed the trailer to the back of a truck.

Fired from a light trailer, the Chinese Type 63 12-round multiple rocket launcher is in widespread service with the PLA (People's Liberation Army), as the Chinese army still calls itself. China also supplied large numbers of Type 63s to favoured Afghan guerrilla groups during the Soviet occupation, and it remains in use during the continuing civil war there. The launcher/trailer can be broken down into mule loads for transport across the mountain passes, and the whole system is ideally suited to guerrilla warfare, providing the guerrillas have enough men and animals to carry the 18-kilogram rockets. The Type 63 has been exported to Vietnam and Iraq, where it has seen action, and several Palestinian groups use it as well. The Chinese forces also operate the Type 63 from the back of a 4x4 truck.

ANTI-AIRCRAFT GUNS

Most major armies supplement their anti-aircraft missile systems with mobile anti-aircraft guns. Radar-directed multi-barrel cannon are highly effective against low-flying aircraft and helicopters.

M-163 Vulcan

Specification
Crew: 4
Combat weight: 12 tonnes (11 tons 1814 lb)
Road speed: 67 km/h (41 mph)
Length: 4.86 m (16 ft)
Height: 2.7 m (8 ft 10 in)
Armament: 1×six-barrelled 20-mm cannon

Assessment
Firepower	★★★★
Accuracy	★★
Age	★★★★★
Worldwide users	★★

The ageing Vulcan system needs to be replaced, but will remain in service for some years to come. They are very versatile: the Israelis have used their Vulcans against tower-blocks in the Lebanon.

The M-163 is a six-barrelled 20-mm cannon fitted to the chassis of the M113 armoured personnel carrier. Used in combination with the Chaparral surface-to-air missiles in US anti-aircraft battalions, it provides close-range defence from air attack. The M-163 has been in service since the 1960s and it is showing its age. It lacks the range and firepower of the Soviet ZSU-23-4, and comparative tests have shown it to be less accurate. A replacement, called Sergeant York, was one of the most embarrassing failures of the 1980s, so the M-163 is having to soldier on in the absence of anything better.

ZSU-23-4

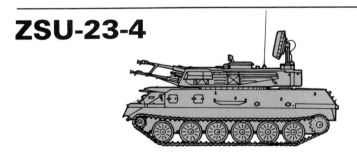

Specification
Crew: 4
Combat weight: 20.5 tonnes (20 tons 394 lb)
Road speed: 44 km/h (27 mph)
Length: 6.54 m (21 ft 6 in)
Height: 3.8 m (12 ft 6 in) (with radar)
Armament: 4×23-mm cannon

Assessment
Firepower	★★★★★
Accuracy	★★★
Age	★★★★
Worldwide users	★★★★

The ZSU-23-4 has proved very successful. Although it is now being replaced in the Russian army by a 30-mm weapon system, it will still be used in Arab armies for many years.

Now being replaced in Russian service by a twin 30-mm system, the ZSU-23-4 has a good combat record. Egyptian ZSUs destroyed 30 Israeli aircraft in the first three days of the 1973 Yom Kippur war. US Army tests of captured ZSUs showed that the system performs very well against helicopters. On the other hand, its vacuum technology and serious cooling problems reduce its potential value, and American electronic counter-measures can jam its radar. In the Russian army they operate in pairs near the headquarters' vehicles of tank and mechanised infantry regiments. They have been widely exported.

Gepard

Specification
Crew: 3
Combat weight: 47 tonnes (46 tons 578 lb)
Road speed: 65 km/h (40 mph)
Length: 6.85 m (22 ft 6 in)
Height: 4.03 m (13 ft 3 in) (radar up)
Armament: 2×25-mm cannon

Assessment
Firepower	★★★★
Accuracy	★★★★
Age	★★★★
Worldwide users	★★

The German Gepard is a highly accurate anti-aircraft system that has recently been improved to keep up with the new generation of fighter bombers and helicopters.

This towering vehicle is the German army's main air defence system. The West German army bought over 400 Gepards between 1976 and 1980, and has recently upgraded them to maintain their effectiveness in the 1990s. Armed with a pair of Oerlikon 35-mm cannon with an effective range of over 3000 metres, the Gepard's radar can detect targets at up to 15 kilometres, and continue to track one target while searching for others. The vehicle has an NBC protection system and carries smoke dischargers. Gepards were exported to Switzerland and the Netherlands.

M-42

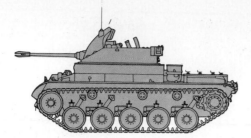

Specification
Crew: 6
Combat weight: 22.4 tonnes (22 tons 103 lb)
Road speed: 72 km/h (45 mph)
Length: 5.8 m (19 ft)
Height: 2.8 m (9 ft 2 in)
Armament: 2×40-mm cannon

Assessment
Firepower	★★
Accuracy	★
Age	★★★★★
Worldwide users	★★

The M-42 Duster is typical of the 1950s self-propelled AA guns, which are no longer adequate against modern ground attack aircraft. This M-42 is in action in Vietnam.

This obsolete system, produced in the 1950s, was taken to Vietnam and used in a ground role. In defence of fire bases or convoys, the M-42's firepower was valuable, although the vehicle offered little protection for the gun crew. It was replaced in the Regular Army by the M-163, but was retained by the National Guard for many years. It was exported to various countries including Austria, Greece, Japan, Jordan, Taiwan and Turkey. The two 40-mm cannon are capable of about 120 rounds per minute per barrel, but the M-42 relies on visually tracking the target; it is therefore useless at night or in poor weather.

V-300

Specification
(V-150 version)
Crew: 4
Combat weight: 10.2 tonnes (10 tons)
Road speed: 88 km/h (55 mph)
Length: 5.68 m (18 ft 7 in)
Height: 2.54 m (8 ft 4 in)
Armament: 1×six-barrelled 20-mm cannon

Assessment
Firepower	★★★★
Accuracy	★★
Age	★
Worldwide users	★

A V-150 with stabilisers deployed to steady the vehicle as the 20-mm cannon blasts a target drone with up to 3,000 rounds per minute.

Several models of the Cadillac Gage Commando armoured personnel carrier are available as air defence vehicles armed with the same weapons system as the M-163. Saudi Arabia bought a number of V-150 Commandos fitted with the 20-mm Vulcan cannon; three hydraulic jacks are deployed to stabilise the vehicle when firing. Cadillac Gage also offer the six-wheeled V-300 as a potential anti-aircraft vehicle. Compared with tracked equivalents, the V-150 or V-300 are far cheaper to build and operate. Cross-country performance is reduced but road speed is substantially better.

Wildcat

Specification
(Prototype 1)
Crew: 3
Combat weight: 18.5 tonnes (18 tons 466 lb)
Road speed: 80 km/h (50 mph)
Length: 6.88 m (22 ft 7 in)
Height: 2.74 m (9 ft) (radar lowered)
Armament: 2×30-mm cannon

Assessment
Firepower	★★★
Accuracy	★★★★
Age	★
Worldwide users	–

Wildcat was one of a series of West German combat vehicles developed for export during the 1970s. Various different weapons fits are available.

Wildcat is a private venture by the German company Krauss Maffei. It is offered in six different versions so that customers have a wide choice of capability. These range from basic day-only fire control to a much more expensive all-weather day/night system. The radar incorporates an automatic IFF system, friendly aircraft are clearly distinguished on the operator's screen. The onboard computer evaluates all target data and controls the duration of the 30-mm cannon bursts.

ZSU-57-2

Specification
Crew: 6
Combat weight: 28 tonnes (27 tons 1254 lb)
Road speed: 50 km/h (31 mph)
Length: 6.22 m (20 ft 5 in)
Height: 2.76 m (9 ft 1 in)
Armament: 2×57-mm cannon

Assessment
Firepower	★★★
Accuracy	★
Age	★★★★★
Worldwide users	★★★

ZSU-57-2s parade through Moscow, their unguided cannon steeply elevated. This system is obsolete, but remains in service with several armies, including Yugoslavia.

The ZSU-57-2 was the Soviet army's first post-war self-propelled anti-aircraft gun. Introduced in the early 1950s, it remains in service with a number of armies, including the Yugoslavian forces which deployed their ZSUs from June 1991 against the breakaway republics of Slovenia and Croatia. The ZSU-57-2 is obsolete: its own S-60 57-mm guns are not radar-guided and rely on manual aiming. It cannot hit anything at night or in bad weather. It has no NBC system, and its large, open-topped fighting compartment is vulnerable to artillery fire or air attack. It was used in Vietnam and in the Middle East, but not with any great success.

SELF-PROPELLED No. 2 ANTI-AIRCRAFT GUNS

Self-propelled anti-aircraft guns vary in calibre from 12.7-mm machine-guns to 76-mm guns. Each weapon system must strike a balance between its firepower and its mobility.

Type 63 37-mm gun

Specification
Crew: 6
Combat weight: 31.5 tonnes (31 tons)
Road speed: 55 km/h (34 mph)
Length: 6.4 m (21 ft)
Height: 2.9 m (9 ft 6 in)
Armament: 2×37-mm guns

Assessment
Firepower   ★★
Accuracy   ★
Age   ★★★★★
Worldwide users   ★★

The Chinese Type 63 is a World War II-style self-propelled anti-aircraft gun. Manually-sighted cannon are mounted on a T-34 tank chassis in a lightly-armoured gun position.

Communist China received vast quantities of military aid from the USSR during the 1950s. Chinese factories soon manufactured direct copies of Soviet equipment from small arms to tanks. Most were identical to the Soviet originals, but there were some unique Chinese variants, including a T-34 tank converted to a mobile anti-aircraft system. The turret was replaced by a large, open gun mounting with twin 37-mm guns. Their cyclic rate was 160-180 rounds per minute and elevation and traverse were manually controlled. With no radar it was limited to daylight/clear-weather engagements. Some Type 63s were supplied to North Vietnam and used along the Ho Chi Minh trail. One example was captured by the ARVN and shipped back to the USA, where it is now at the Aberdeen Proving Ground.

Panhard M3 VDA

Specification
Crew: 3
Combat weight: 6.9 tonnes (6 tons 1747 lb)
Road speed: 90 km/h (56 mph)
Length: 4.45 m (14 ft 7 in)
Height: 2.4 m (7 ft 11 in)
Armament: 2×20-mm cannon

Assessment
Firepower   ★★★
Accuracy   ★★★★
Age   ★★★
Worldwide users   ★★

The Panhard VDA is based on the M3 armoured personnel carrier. To provide the most stable gun platform the chassis can be raised off the ground on jacks.

The Panhard M3 4×4 armoured car has been widely exported since 1970. Over 30 armies use one or more versions of this versatile French vehicle. The M3 VDA (Véhicule de Défense Anti-aérienne) was introduced in 1975 and is in service with several West African armies and in the Middle East. Fitted with a Hispano-Suiza turret with twin 20-mm cannon, it has radar fire control and optical sights. This same turret is compatible with the Renault VAB, Panhard ERC, ENGESA EE-11 and many other armoured personnel carriers. The VDA is equipped with four hydraulic jacks that stabilise the vehicle when firing.

AMX-13 DCA

Specification
Crew: 3
Combat weight: 16.7 tonnes (16 tons 529 lb)
Road speed: 60 km/h (37 mph)
Length: 5.4 m (17 ft 9 in)
Height: 3.8 m (12 ft 6 in)
Armament: 2×30-mm cannon

Assessment
Firepower   ★★★★
Accuracy   ★★★★
Age   ★★★
Worldwide users   ★★

The AMX-13 light tank forms the basis for several AA systems. The DCA has twin 30-mm cannon and radar guidance; this is the cheaper 20-mm gun system.

In 1969 the French army received the first of 60 self-propelled anti-aircraft guns based on the chassis of the AMX-13 light tank. The AMX-13 DCA (Défense Contre Avions) has a steel turret fitted with twin 30-mm cannon. On the back of the turret is the Oeil Noir 1 (Black Eye 1) radar scanner that retracts into the turret bustle when not required. The gunner can select single shot, 15-round bursts or fully automatic. Each gun has 300 rounds and the empty cartridge cases are ejected from the turret together with the links. The DCA turret was also fitted to the hulls of AMX-30 tanks, and the resulting AMX-30SA was bought by the Saudi Arabian army in 1975.

Escorter 35

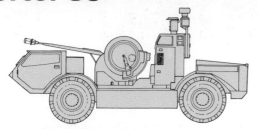

Specification
Crew: 3
Combat weight: 23.6
tonnes (23 tons 508 lb)
Road speed: 120 km/h
(74 mph)
Length: 8.7 m (28 ft 7 in)
Height: 3.9 m (12 ft 10 in)
Armament: 2×35-mm
guns

Assessment
Firepower   ★★★★
Accuracy   ★★★★
Age   ★
Worldwide users   –

Oerlikon designed the Escorter twin 35-mm gun system for export. It is available on either a tracked or wheeled chassis, with long-range search radar as another option.

The Swiss-based company Oerlikon-Bührle is one of the world's main suppliers of towed anti-aircraft guns. The Escorter 35 is a self-propelled version of the company's highly successful 35-mm anti-aircraft gun system. Designed and built as a private venture rather than for a specific army, the Escorter uses either a wheeled chassis or a tracked one, based on the US M113 APC. A day/night fire-control radar plus laser rangefinder are fitted, with the optional addition of a long-range search radar. The twin 35-mm KDF guns each have 430 rounds of ammunition. Their effective range is 3500 metres and an armour-piercing round is available to engage ground targets.

M35/59

Specification
Crew: 6
Combat weight: 9.8
tonnes (9 tons 1445 lb)
Road speed: 60 km/h
(37 mph)
Length: 6.9 m (22 ft 8 in)
Height: 2.5 m (8 ft 3 in)
Armament: 2×30-mm
guns

Assessment
Firepower   ★★★
Accuracy   ★
Age   ★★★★★
Worldwide users   ★★

The Czech M35/59 twin 30-mm anti-aircraft system is another World War II-type weapon. The mounting can be taken off and fired from the ground, and there is no integral radar.

Unlike most Warsaw Pact armies in the 1960s, the Czech forces did not order the Russian ZSU-57-2. Instead, they ordered an anti-aircraft gun based on the chassis of the Praga 6x6 truck. The chassis is protected by a maximum of 10 mm of armour and carries a modified version of the Czech army's M53 towed twin 30-mm anti-aircraft guns. The M35/59 has no fire-control system and no night-vision equipment, so it is limited to clear-weather/daylight operations. The guns have a cyclic rate of 500 rounds per minute but are fed by 50-round top-loading magazines. Maximum range is 3000 metres.

Otomatic

Specification
Crew: 4
Combat weight: 45.2
tonnes (44 tons 1089 lb)
Road speed: 60 km/h
(37 mph)
Length: 7.2 m (23 ft 8 in)
(hull only)
Height: 3.1 m (10 ft)
Armament: 1×76-mm gun

Assessment
Firepower   ★★★★★
Accuracy   ★★★★
Age   ★
Worldwide users   –

The Otomatic 76-mm anti-aircraft gun offers greater range and much greater destructive power than the light cannon universally used by the world's armies.

A private venture by OTO-Melara, the Otomatic uses a modified OF-40 tank chassis to mount a 76-mm gun. The gun is a modified version of the 76-mm compact gun shipped aboard the warships of many nations. This offers several advantages over the conventional 23-mm and 35-mm calibre cannon carried by most self-propelled anti-aircraft guns. It can shoot down helicopters before they come close enough to launch anti-tank missiles, and even the best armoured gunships cannot survive a hit from so large a shell. Directed by a tracking and a search radar, the Otomatic's gun is loaded and fed hydraulically. Targets are normally engaged with bursts of six rounds. The turret holds 70 rounds and another 30 are kept in the hull.

M16 Motor Gun Carriage

Specification
Crew: 6
Combat weight: 8.9
tonnes (8 tons 1700 lb)
Road speed: 60 km/h
(37 mph)
Length: 5.9 m (19 ft 5 in)
Height: 3 m (9 ft 11 in)
Armament: 4×Browning
M2 .50-cal machine-guns

Assessment
Firepower   ★★
Accuracy   ★
Age   ★★★★★
Worldwide users   ★★★

A World War II American M3 half-track in service with the Israeli army in 1973 and fitted with twin 20-mm cannon. Many armies used the quadruple .50-cal machine-gun armament after World War II.

During World War II the US Army used the M3 half-track for an incredible variety of tasks. The M16 was a self-propelled anti-aircraft gun: a basic M3 but with the troop/cargo compartment occupied by a Maxson mount with four .50-cal machine-guns. The Maxson mount was also fitted to a variety of towed carriages and was the US Army's standard anti-aircraft gun. Against the relatively slow-moving aircraft of World War II it was an effective weapon, but in the jet age its limitations became clear. The Israeli Defence Force continued to use M3 half-tracks for many years and it adopted a new anti-aircraft version fitted with its TCM-20 twin 20-mm gun system.

INFANTRY FIGHTING VEHICLES

Modern infantrymen ride to war inside armoured fighting vehicles equipped with cannon and even anti-tank missiles. But although they look like tanks, IFVs are very different. They cannot survive a hit from a large missile or tank gun: their mission is to carry a section of infantrymen that dismounts to fight.

BMP-1

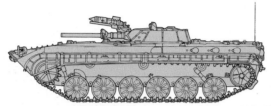

BMP stands for *Boyevaya Mashina Pekhota*, or infantry fighting vehicle. Prior to its appearance in 1967, APCs were just 'battle taxis' for carrying troops to the action. The BMP not only has firing ports from which troops can fight from behind armour, but also a 73-mm cannon and wire-guided anti-armour missiles, which are used to support the foot soldiers in battle. Derived from the chassis of the PT-76 light tank, the BMP shares the low profile common to Russian armoured vehicles, which is a major asset in combat but means that the eight-man troop compartment is horribly cramped and uncomfortable.

Specification
Crew: 3+8
Combat weight: 13.5 tonnes (13 tons 650 lb)
Maximum road speed: 80 km/h (50 mph)
Power-to-weight ratio: 22 hp/tonne
Length: 6.74 m (22 ft 1 in)
Height: 2.15 m (7 ft 1 in)
Armament: 1×73-mm smoothbore gun; 1×7.62-mm machine-gun; 1 launcher rail for 'Sagger' anti-tank missile

Assessment
Firepower ★★
Protection ★★★
Age ★★★★
Worldwide users ★★★★

The Russian BMP was the first true infantry fighting vehicle. At a time when NATO APCs only carried machine-guns, the BMP had a cannon and anti-tank missiles.

BMP-2

The original BMP was used extensively in the Middle East wars of the 1970s and 1980s, but although its design had broken new ground it was soon to be outclassed by Western infantry combat vehicles. The BMP-2, first seen on the 1982 Red Square parade, is a much more dangerous opponent for vehicles like the Bradley and the Warrior. The BMP-2 is fully amphibious and is equipped with an NBC system. It has an effective 30-mm cannon, and the AT-5 'Spandrel' anti-tank guided missile in place of the older-technology AT-3 'Sagger' that arms the earlier BMP-1. Its major handicap remains the small troop compartment: a cross-country run enclosed in any APC will make most people feel sick, but it is even worse in the cramped confines of a BMP.

Specification
Crew: 3+7
Combat weight: 14.6 tonnes (14 tons 828 lb)
Maximum road speed: 65 km/h (40 mph)
Power-to-weight ratio: undisclosed
Length: 6.71 m (22 ft)
Height: 2 m (6 ft 7 in)
Armament: 1×30-mm cannon; 1×7.62-mm machine-gun; 1 launcher for AT-5 'Spandrel' missile

Assessment
Firepower ★★★★
Protection ★★★
Age ★
Worldwide users ★★★

The BMP-2 saw service in Afghanistan where the high elevation of its 30-mm cannon proved useful against guerrillas firing down from the heights. It carries a more effective missile than the BMP-1.

M2 Bradley

The US Army had to wait until 1982 for the M2 Bradley Infantry Fighting Vehicle to enter service. It has replaced the M113 in mechanised units, although not one-for-one since the Bradley is much more expensive than the older design. The M2 has been dogged by questions of safety and reliability, but is nevertheless vastly more capable than the M113, being armed with a potent 25-mm cannon and a pair of long-range TOW anti-tank missiles. The M2's armour consists of two sheets of steel and a thicker aluminium plate, the spaces between each layer providing protection against shaped-charge warheads. The improved M2A1 has additional steel armour on the front and sides, though this has caused weight problems.

Specification
Crew: 3+7
Combat weight: 22.5 tonnes (22 tons 324 lb)
Maximum road speed: 66 km/h (41 mph)
Power-to-weight ratio: 20 hp/tonne
Length: 6.45 m (21 ft 2 in)
Height: 2.97 m (9 ft 9 in)
Armament: 1×25-mm cannon; 1×7.62-mm machine-gun; 2×TOW; 5.56-mm port guns

Assessment
Firepower ★★★★★
Protection ★★★
Age ★
Worldwide users ★

The Bradley proved very effective in the Gulf War: its 25-mm cannon blasted Iraqi bunkers and the thermal sights gave good accuracy during night fighting. Only three out of 2,200 were disabled.

M113

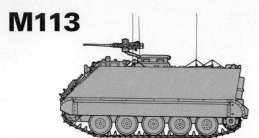

The M113 APC has been produced in greater numbers than any other armoured vehicle. It is in service with more than 50 armies. Typical of APCs developed in the 1950s, the M113 is little more than a bullet-proof armoured box. That simplicity is one of the reasons for its tremendous export success. The M113 is easy to convert to other purposes, and it has been the basis for a bewildering variety of vehicles, ranging from specialist weapons carriers through supply vehicles to command posts. The standard M113 has good battlefield mobility and can be given adequate armament, but it lacks the protection and fighting capability of later generations of infantry vehicles.

Specification
(M113A1)
Crew: 2+11
Combat weight: 11 tonnes (10 tons 1860 lb)
Maximum road speed: 67 km/h (42 mph)
Power-to-weight ratio: 19 hp/tonne
Length: 4.86 m (16 ft)
Height: 2.5 m (8 ft 3 in)
Armament: 1×Browning .50-cal machine-gun

Assessment
Firepower   *
Protection   **
Age   *****
Worldwide users   *****

A US Army M113 ACAV flies a Confederate flag during the Vietnam war when this basic armoured personnel carrier was modified to carry three shielded machine-guns.

Marder

In the 1950s, the Germans designed a family of tracked military vehicles, but the Marder IFV was one of the few to get beyond the drawing board. Very large for its time when introduced in 1968, it was the first Western infantry fighting vehicle. Even today, more than two decades later, it has excellent armour protection and the cross-country capability to enable it to operate with the highly mobile Leopard tanks of the German army. Most Marders were upgraded in the 1980s, with the addition of improved night vision equipment and other minor modifications including a mounting for MILAN anti-armour missiles. The 20-mm cannon is to be replaced by a new 25-mm weapon if funds and the political situation permit.

Specification
Crew: 4+6
Combat weight: 29 tonnes (28 tons 1215 lb)
Maximum road speed: 75 km/h (46 mph)
Power-to-weight ratio: 20.5 hp/tonne
Length: 6.79 m (22 ft 4 in)
Height: 2.98 m (9 ft 9 in)
Armament: 1×20-mm cannon; 1×co-axial 7.62-mm machine-gun; 1×remote-controlled 7.62-mm MG

Assessment
Firepower   ***
Protection   ***
Age   ***
Worldwide users   *

Equipped with cannon and machine-guns, the German army's Marder was the first NATO infantry fighting vehicle. It is twice the weight of equivalent Russian vehicles.

Warrior

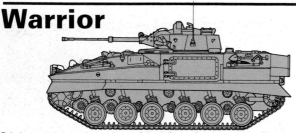

Britain came late to the concept of the infantry fighting vehicle. Entering service in the late 1980s, the Warrior is twice the weight of earlier APCs and carries fewer troops. Nevertheless, it has much better protection and is extremely fast across country. Main armament is the well tried RARDEN 30-mm cannon. This has a low rate of fire, but it is reliable and extremely accurate. Unlike the BMP and the Bradley the troop compartment of the Warrior has no firing ports, but the British Army looks on this as no real handicap. Travelling in a fast-moving tracked vehicle is rather like being bounced around inside a food processor, and it is unlikely that anybody could hit anything smaller than a barn in any case.

Specification
Crew: 3+7
Combat weight: 24.5 tonnes (24 tons 253 lb)
Maximum road speed: 75 km/h (46 mph)
Power-to-weight ratio: 22.5 hp/tonne
Length: 6.34 m (20 ft 10in)
Height: 2.73 m (9 ft)
Armament: 1×30-mm cannon; 1×72-mm Chain Gun

Assessment
Firepower   *****
Protection   ***
Age   *
Worldwide users   *

The British Army re-equipped with Warrior just in time for the Gulf war. Its 30-mm cannon is a proven 'bunker-buster' and its cross-country speed is phenomenal.

AMX-10P

The AMX-10P entered service with the French army in 1973, and with typical energy the French have sold it widely in the Middle East, the Saudis alone buying more than 300 examples. Much smaller than AFVs like the Marder, Bradley and Warrior, the AMX-10P is nevertheless a true infantry combat vehicle. It is armed with a 20-mm dual-feed cannon, whose gunner can select high-explosive or armour-piercing ammunition at the flick of a switch. Apart from the roof hatches and two firing ports in the rear ramp, there is no provision for infantrymen to fire their weapons from within the vehicle. Variants of the AMX-10P include command, amphibious assault, ambulance, repair, anti-armour, mortar, radar, and fire-support vehicles.

Specification
Crew: 3+8
Combat weight: 14.5 tonnes (14 tons 607 lb)
Maximum road speed: 65 km/h (40 mph)
Power-to-weight ratio: 20 hp/tonne
Length: 5.78 m (9 ft 2 in)
Height: 2.57 m (8 ft 5 in)
Armament: 1×20-mm cannon; 1×7.62-mm machine-gun

Assessment
Firepower   **
Protection   ***
Age   ***
Worldwide users   ***

The AMX-10P is the French army's standard tracked infantry fighting vehicle and saw service in the Gulf war with the Saudis. It lacks the cross-country performance of Warrior or the American Bradley.

WHEELED APCs No. 1

Wheeled armoured personnel carriers are used by most armies to supplement their tracked APCs. Wheeled vehicles are much cheaper to manufacture and operate, and their cross-country performance can compare very favourably.

Saxon

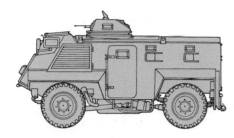

The Saxon is the British Army's latest wheeled APC. It is a lightly armoured, no frills APC/internal security vehicle. The defence budget would not allow all regular, let alone TA battalions, to obtain Warrior IFVs so the Army ordered Saxon instead. Reinforcement battalions for BAOR were to have been re-equipped with it as the old FV432 APC was phased out. This is all open to change with the probability of heavy defence cuts in the next few years. Saxon is replacing the elderly Humber Pigs still serving in Northern Ireland.

Specification
Crew: 2+10
Combat weight: 10.67 tonnes (10 tons 1120 lb)
Maximum road speed: 96 km/h (61 mph)
Power-to-weight ratio: 13.68 hp/tonne
Length: 5.1 m (16 ft 9 in)
Height: 2.6 m (8 ft 6 in)
Armament: various

Assessment
Firepower ★★
Protection ★★★
Age ★★
Worldwide users ★★★

The British Army uses wheeled armoured personnel carriers for rear-of-the-battle-area and line-of-communication duties. The current service vehicle is the GKN Saxon, which is adequate for the task.

VAB

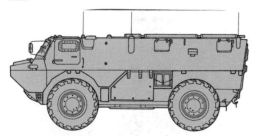

The versatile VAB combat vehicle saw action in the Gulf War with French and Arab forces. A highly successful armoured personnel carrier, it can carry HOT anti-tank guided missiles and operate as a tank destroyer. Four missiles are carried, ready to fire. It can also serve as an ambulance, command post or internal security vehicle. French troops in the Gulf used it to carry MILAN anti-tank guided missile teams and tow Brandt 120-mm mortars. Oman uses 20 VABs fitted with twin 20-mm anti-aircraft guns, and the French army's anti-aircraft VAB will have MATRA SATCP surface-to-air missiles.

Specification
(6×6 version)
Crew: 2+10
Combat weight: 14.2 tonnes (13 tons 2173 lb)
Maximum road speed: 92 km/h (57 mph)
Power-to-weight ratio: 16.5 hp/tonne
Length: 5.98 m (19 ft 7 in)
Height: 2.06 m (6 ft 9 in)
Armament: various

Assessment
Firepower ★★★
Protection ★★★
Age ★★
Worldwide users ★★

The VAB (Véhicule d'Avant Blindé) is one of the most successful of modern wheeled APCs. The French army uses the four-wheeled variant, but six-wheelers have also been sold to a number of other armies.

SIBMAS

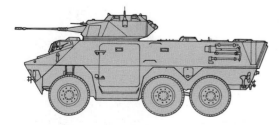

The SIBMAS is a useful APC or weapons carrier produced as a private venture by a Belgian company. Malaysia purchased 162 Armoured Fire Support Vehicles (AFSVs) and 24 Armoured Recovery Vehicle versions for a reported £   million. The AFSVs are armed with a Cockerill 90-mm gun capable of knocking out lightly armoured tanks like the AMX-30 or T-54/55. SIBMAS is only armoured against 7.62-mm armour-piercing bullets, so a cannon or heavy machine-gun could destroy it. SIBMAS is also offered as an APC, anti-aircraft platform or mortar carrier. Its own turret can mount machine-guns, a 60-mm mortar and/or 20-mm cannon.

Specification
Crew: 3+11
Combat weight: 14.5 to 16.5 tonnes (14 tons 607 lb to 16 tons 537 lb), depending on role
Maximum road speed: 100 km/h (62 mph)
Power-to-weight ratio: 19.4 hp/tonne
Length: 7.32 m (24 ft)
Height: 2.24 m (7 ft 4 in)
Armament: various

Assessment
Firepower ★★★
Protection ★★★
Age ★★
Worldwide users ★

The relative simplicity of wheeled vehicles means that they can be produced as private ventures. The Belgian SIBMAS was a good enough machine, but did not sell well in a crowded market, and production has ceased.

Vickers Valkyr

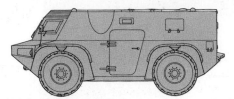

The Vickers Valkyr is another privately-funded, multi-purpose armoured personnel carrier. Designed by Vickers Defence Systems, it follows a similar pattern to the VAB or SIBMAS, with the hull proof against armour-piercing rifle calibre bullets but penetrable by cannon. The armoured glass windscreen and vision blocks are proof against shell splinters. Armament fits include 7.62- and 12.7-mm machine-guns; 20-mm cannon plus 60-mm breech-loading mortar; 90-mm gun or twin 20-mm anti-aircraft guns. It was operated by Kuwaiti forces but is no longer in service.

Specification
Crew: 2+10
Combat weight: 11 tonnes (10 tons 1860 lb)
Maximum road speed: 100 km/h (62 mph)
Power-to-weight ratio: 16.36 hp/tonne
Length: 5.6 m (18 ft 5 in)
Height: 2.05 m (6 ft 9 in)
Armament: various

Assessment
Firepower ★★★
Protection ★★★
Age ★
Worldwide users ★

The Vickers Valkyr was originally designed in Ireland and built under licence in Belgium before being updated by Vickers. Like most modern APCs, it can be fitted with a variety of weapons.

Saracen

Replaced by the FV432 as the British Army's APC during the early 1960s, the Saracen was widely exported to Commonwealth countries and many are still in service. Comparison with modern vehicles like the VAB shows how far APC design has advanced: Saracen has no NBC protection, is not amphibious and its one-man turret mounts a single machine-gun. Because of the large number still in service, some companies are offering modernisation schemes. Some users, e.g. Sri Lanka, have modified their vehicles extensively as a result of combat experience.

Specification
Crew: 2+10
Combat weight: 10.1 tonnes (9 tons 2105 lb)
Maximum road speed: 72 km/h (45 mph)
Power-to-weight ratio: 15.73 hp/tonne
Length: 5.23 m (17 ft 2 in)
Height: 2 m (6 ft 7 in)
Armament: 1×7.62-mm machine-gun

Assessment
Firepower ★
Protection ★★★
Age ★★★★★
Worldwide users ★★★★

The Saracen is from the post-war generation of armoured vehicles. Sturdy and reliable, it has seen service all over the world with the British and a number of Commonwealth armed forces.

Panhard VCR

The Panhard VCR (Véhicule de Combat à Roues) has been sold to several countries including Iraq and the United Arab Emirates. A conventional 6×6 APC, it has a 'V'-shaped hull to minimise damage from land-mines. Following Panhard's traditional design, the middle pair of wheels can be raised off the ground for speedier road travel. Only the front pair of wheels can be steered and the low-pressure tyres enable it to travel 100 km after they have been punctured, provided the speed does not exceed 30 km/h. Armament fits are as diverse as those of most modern APCs and include twin ready-to-launch MILAN missiles.

Specification
Crew: 3+9
Combat weight: 7.9 tonnes (7 tons 1725 lb)
Maximum road speed: 100 km/h (62 mph)
Power-to-weight ratio: 19.6 hp/tonne
Length: 4.87 m (16 ft)
Height: 2.13 m (7 ft)
Armament: various

Assessment
Firepower ★★★
Protection ★★★
Age ★★
Worldwide users ★★★

Developed by Panhard in the 1970s as a private venture, the VCR is available in both four-wheel and six-wheel versions. It saw service on both sides during the Gulf War.

Fahd

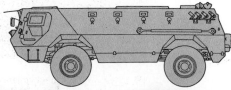

Developed by Thyssen Henschel of Germany, the Fahd is manufactured in Egypt and used by the Egyptian, Kuwaiti and Omani forces. It consists of a Daimler-Benz truck chassis fitted with an armoured body. The use of as many commercially-available components as possible helps reduce costs. Proof against 7.62-mm armoured piercing ammunition, the VAB can carry a wide variety of weapons fits including machine-guns and 20-mm cannon. A central tyre pressure regulation system allows the driver to vary the tyre pressure to suit the terrain; low-pressure/run-flat tyres are used. The crew sit back-to-back facing weapon ports through which they can shoot.

Specification
Crew: 2+10
Combat weight: 11.25 tonnes (11 tons 157 lb)
Maximum road speed: 84 km/h (52 mph)
Power-to-weight ratio: 14.9 hp/tonne
Length: 6 m (19 ft 9 in)
Height: 2.69 m (8 ft 10 in)
Armament: 1×7.62-mm machine-gun or a turret mounting 20-mm cannon. ATGW or MRL

Assessment
Firepower ★★★
Protection ★★
Age ★★
Worldwide users ★★

APCs are easy to build. They are often the first weapons produced by emerging arms industries. The Fahd is typical, with design and components coming from Germany but being built in Egypt.

Nowhere has the spread of armament manufacturing become more apparent than in the production of wheeled armoured vehicles. With manufacture ranging from the Superpowers to the Third World, buyers are faced with a bewildering choice.

Ratel 20 IFV

Specification
Crew: 3+8
Combat weight: 18.5 tonnes (18 tons 466 lb)
Maximum road speed: 105 km/h (65 mph)
Power-to-weight ratio: 15.24 hp/tonne
Length: 7.212 m (23 ft 8 in)
Height: 2.915 m (9 ft 7 in)
Armament: cannon or gun; machine-guns; mortar; port rifles

Assessment
Firepower	★★★
Protection	★★★
Age	★★★
Worldwide users	★

South Africa's arms industry developed to the extent that it did as a result of the United Nations arms embargo. Thrown back onto their own resources, the South Africans developed a series of weapons as good as anything in the world, and well-suited to the long distance operations in bush terrain typical of their country and its borders. The Ratel series of wheeled Infantry Fighting Vehicles are extremely tough, and have excellent cross-country mobility allied to very good range. As with most South African armoured vehicles, it has a 'V'-shaped inner hull for mine protection. The base model Ratel is the Ratel 20, armed with a 20-mm cannon in a two-man turret. Other weapon fits include 60-mm mortar and 90-mm fire-support variants. Ratels have seen extensive service in South Africa's long border war in Namibia and Angola.

South Africa's Ratels saw extensive use in the long-running bush war on the Angola/Namibia border. From the earliest operations in 1978 the Ratels proved reliable and effective.

MOWAG Piranha

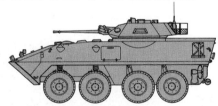

Specification
Crew: 3+6
Combat weight: 12.88 tonnes (12 tons 1523 lb)
Maximum road speed: 100 km/h (62 mph)
Power-to-weight ratio: 23.4 hp/tonne
Length: 6.393 m (21 ft)
Height: 2.69 m (8 ft 10 in)
Armament: cannon; machine-gun; TOW missiles

Assessment
Firepower	★★★
Protection	★★
Age	★★★★
Worldwide users	★★

The Piranha was developed from the late 1960s onwards by the Swiss company MOWAG. It was a private venture, produced without government support. It has since been adopted by a number of nations, the most important of which are Canada and the USA. The Piranha is available in four-, six- and eight-wheeled versions, and is designed to accept a range of armaments. All members of the Piranha family are fully amphibious, having two propellers at the rear of the hull. Canada uses the Piranha in its 6×6 form as the 76-mm Cougar fire-support vehicle, the Grizzly APC, and the Husky armoured recovery vehicle. The 8×8 version is in use with the US Marine Corps as its Light Armored Vehicle, the base model of which is armed with a 25-mm Chain Gun.

The US Marine Corps are among the largest users of Piranha-derived vehicles, operating some 800 Light Armored Vehicles. These were manufactured by General Motors Canada under licence.

ENGESA EE-11 Urutu

Specification
Crew: up to 13
Combat weight: 14 tonnes (13 tons 1747 lb)
Maximum road speed: 105 km/h (65 mph)
Power-to-weight ratio: 18.6 hp/tonne
Length: 6.1 m (20 ft)
Height: 2.72 m (8 ft 11 in)
Armament: gun or cannon; machine-guns

Assessment
Firepower	★★★
Protection	★★
Age	★★★★
Worldwide users	★★★★

In the early 1970s, the Brazilian company ENGESA, which had for some years been successfully converting 4×2 and 6×4 trucks into 4×4 and 6×6 configurations, turned its attention to the development of a range of armoured vehicles. The EE-11 Urutu Armoured Personnel Carrier entered production in 1974. The EE-11 has done much to make Brazil a major arms exporting nation. It has been sold widely: by 1984 more than 3,000 EE-11s had been produced, mostly for export to the Middle East. It is simple, with few technical frills, but in consequence it is easy for poorly-trained Third World troops to maintain. A whole range of variants has been produced or proposed by ENGESA, including ambulance, cargo, command, recovery, anti-tank, anti-aircraft and internal security models. The Urutu is fully amphibious with minimal preparation.

Wheeled APCs are simple to manufacture, and are often the first products of a developing country's armaments industry. The Brazilian ENGESA EE-11 is just such a vehicle, untypical only in that it has had considerable export success.

BMR-600

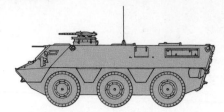

In the early 1970s, the Spanish army issued a requirement for a 6×6 infantry fighting vehicle. The BMR (*Blindado Medio de Ruedas*, or medium-wheeled armoured vehicle) underwent a protracted development process, but is now in production in amphibious and non-amphibious forms. It is relatively lightly armed, and usually has a one-man turret fitted with a remote-firing 12.7-mm gun, or no turret at all. The VEC cavalry scout vehicle is the same basic chassis with a new hull equipped with a two-man power-operated turret mounting a 20- or 25-mm cannon. Some development models have been tested however, including an example with a 90-mm gun and others with varying missile fits.

Specification
Crew: 2+11
Combat weight: 13.75 tonnes (13 tons 1187 lb)
Maximum road speed: 100 km/h (62 mph)
Power-to-weight ratio: 23 hp/tonne
Length: 6.15 m (20 ft 2 in)
Height: 2 m (6 ft 7 in)
Armament: machine-gun; mortar

Assessment
Firepower ★★
Protection ★★
Age ★★★★
Worldwide users ★★

Spain's **Blindado Medio de Ruedas** *is typical of modern wheeled APCs, being designed to accept a variety of armament, ranging from simple pintle-mounted machine-guns to sophisticated two-man turrets mounting 90-mm guns.*

BTR-60P

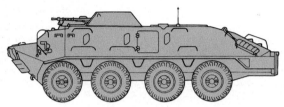

The BTR-60P has been in large-scale use with the Russian army since the 1960s, and can be found in service in most of the armies of the former Warsaw Pact countries as well as Russian allies around the world. There are open-topped and roofed versions. Some models are seen with a small turret containing a 14.7-mm heavy machine-gun, while others are turretless. It is a simple and basic vehicle, with light protection and reasonable mobility. It has been succeeded in production by the marginally improved BTR-70 and the far more capable BTR-80 series.

Specification
Crew: 2+ up to 16
Combat weight: 9.98 tonnes (9 tons 1837 lb)
Maximum road speed: 80 km/h (50 mph)
Power-to-weight ratio: 18 hp/tonne
Length: 7.56 m (24 ft 10 in)
Height: 2.055 m (6 ft 9 in)
Armament: machine-gun

Assessment
Firepower ★
Protection ★
Age ★★★★★
Worldwide users ★★★★★

The BTR-60 is used all over the world. Although of suspect reliability, it is tough, amphibious and has good cross-country mobility. The BTR-60 is equipped with a central tyre pressure regulation system.

BTR-152

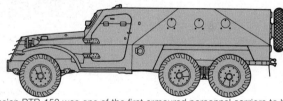

The Russian BTR-152 was one of the first armoured personnel carriers to be introduced after the end of World War II. It is still in service with reserve formations throughout the former Warsaw Pact countries and is widely used in North Africa and the Middle East. The chassis is based on that of the ZIL 6×6 truck. Indeed, the BTR-152 is little more than a bullet-proof lorry. It has no amphibious capability, which the Russian army regarded as a serious disadvantage, and which was to lead to the introduction of the tracked BTR-50 and the wheeled BTR-60 armoured personnel carriers.

Specification
Crew: 2+17
Combat weight: 9 tonnes (8 tons 1926 lb)
Maximum road speed: 75 km/h (46 mph)
Power-to-weight ratio: 12 hp/tonne
Length: 6.83 m (22 ft 5 in)
Height: 2 m (6 ft 7 in)
Armament: 1×7.62-mm machine-gun

Assessment
Firepower ★
Protection ★
Age ★★★★★
Worldwide users ★★★★

Developed in the late 1940s, the BTR-152 was one of the first modern armoured personnel carriers. Although it is little more than a bullet-proof truck, the BTR-152 is still to be seen all over Africa and Asia.

Transportpanzer

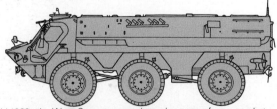

In the mid-1960s the West German army planned a range of new combat vehicles including 4×4, 6×6 and 8×8 trucks, an 8×8 reconnaissance vehicle, and 4×4 and 6×6 personnel carriers. Only the Luchs 8×8 scout vehicle and the Transportpanzer 6×6 APC ever saw the light of day. The Transportpanzer is amphibious and carries a full NBC protection system. In German service, it serves as a supply carrier, ambulance, command and control vehicle, communications vehicle, and combat engineer vehicle. It is also the German Bundeswehr's standard NBC reconnaissance vehicle, in which form it has been sold to the US Army. Some NBC recon vehicles were shipped to the Gulf when the threat of Iraqi chemical attack was at its height.

Specification
Crew: 2+10
Combat weight: 17 tonnes (16 tons 1635 lb)
Maximum road speed: 105 km/h (65 mph)
Power-to-weight ratio: 18.8 hp/tonne
Length: 6.76 m (22 ft 2 in)
Height: 2.3 m (7 ft 7 in)
Armament: 1×7.62-mm machine-gun or 1×20-mm cannon

Assessment
Firepower ★★★
Protection ★★★
Age ★★★
Worldwide users ★

The Transportpanzer is one of the few products of an ambitious German programme of armoured vehicle manufacture. It is a well-made vehicle which has been adapted for a wide variety of roles, from carrying cargo to NBC reconnaissance.

See also: **WEAPON DATA FILE**/APCs No. 1

Wheeled armoured personnel carriers vary from very lightly protected vehicles, weighing 7 tons or less, to 15-ton armoured vehicles capable of withstanding hits from cannon fire.

Cadillac Gage V-150 Commando

Cadillac Gage began work on a low-cost four-wheeled armoured vehicle which would be able to undertake a wide variety of roles. These included convoy escort, reconnaissance, air base security and the basic armoured personnel carrier mission. The V-100 Commando saw extensive service in Vietnam. The V-150 is an improved V-100 which entered production in 1971, and the V-200 is an enlarged variant only in service with Singapore. The current production model is the V-150S, which is heavier and more powerful than the original, and incorporates several automotive improvements. With a wide range of weapon fits, different turret options and the choice of petrol or diesel engines, the Commando has proved popular with Third World armies, and more than 3,500 examples are in service around the world.

Specification
(V-150S with 20-mm cannon)
Crew: 3+2
Combat weight: 10.88 tonnes (10 tons 1411 lb)
Maximum road speed: 88 km/h (55 mph)
Power-to-weight ratio: 20.42 hp/tonne
Length: 5.68 m (18 ft 8 in)
Height: 2.54 m (8 ft 4 in)
Armament: 1×20-mm cannon; 2×7.62-mm machine-guns

Assessment
Firepower ★★★
Protection ★★★
Age ★★★★★
Worldwide users ★★★★★

The Cadillac Gage Commando has achieved a considerable degree of success around the world since its development as a private venture in the 1960s. Available in a wide variety of weapon fits, it has many roles from policing to combat.

Cadillac Gage V-300

Building on the commercial success of the V-100 Commando series, Cadillac Gage developed the V-300 as a private venture in the 1970s. The six-wheeled V-300 is a much larger and more capable vehicle than the Commando. It is amphibious without preparation, and the wide range of optional equipment that can be fitted includes air-conditioning, night vision devices and an NBC system. Armament fits can include 12.7-mm, 20-mm, 25-mm, 76-mm and 90-mm turrets, an 81-mm mortar, and an anti-tank model firing TOW missiles is also available. The V-300 has not matched the success of the smaller Commando. It was unsuccessful in the US Army/US Marine Light Armored Vehicle competition, and except for a small order from Panama has only been sold to Kuwait, many of whose vehicles will have been destroyed in the Gulf War.

Specification
Crew: 3+9
Combat weight: 14.3 tonnes (14 tons 157 lb)
Maximum road speed: 92 km/h (57 mph)
Power-to-weight ratio: 18.6 hp/tonne
Length: 6.4 m (21 ft)
Height: 2.59 m (8 ft 6 in)
Armament: various

Assessment
Firepower ★★★★
Protection ★★★★
Age ★
Worldwide users ★

The V-300 is much larger than its four-wheeled progenitor, and it is much less suited to internal security work. Although it is a much more capable vehicle, it has entered a market where there is a large number of competitors.

Arrowpointe Dragoon

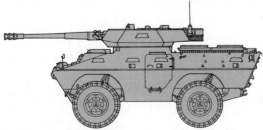

A bold entry into an already crowded market for multi-purpose wheeled vehicles, the Dragoon was designed in response to a US Air Force request for a convoy and base protection vehicle suitable for transport in the C-130 Hercules. The Dragoon was designed from the outset to be tough and easy to maintain. Three-quarters of the vehicle's components are common with the M113 armoured personnel carrier and the M809 five-ton truck. The use of such components means that spares are readily available and mechanics are familiar with their use. The US Army used Dragoons to test a variety of high-tech electronic warfare and surveillance equipment, while the US Navy has a small number in service to patrol nuclear weapons storage facilities. The only major export success to date is a large order from Venezuela.

Specification
Crew: 3+6
Combat weight: 12.7 tonnes (12 tons 1120 lb)
Maximum road speed: 116 km/h (72 mph)
Power-to-weight ratio: 23.62 hp/tonne
Length: 5.58 m (18 ft 4 in)
Height: 2.6 m (8 ft 6 in)
Armament: 1×20-mm cannon; 1×7.62-mm machine-gun

Assessment
Firepower ★★★★
Protection ★★★★
Age ★
Worldwide users ★

The Dragoon is similar to the Cadillac Gage V-150 Commando, and is built with ease of maintenance in mind. The example depicted was operated by the US Army at Fort Lewis in Washington, where it served as an electronic warfare test bed.

Chaimite V-200

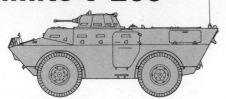

Specification
Crew: 11
Combat weight: 7.3
tonnes (7 tons 403 lb)
Maximum road speed:
99 km/h (61 mph)
Power-to-weight
ratio: 28.76 hp/tonne
Length: 5.6 m (18 ft 5 in)
Height: 2.36 m (7 ft 9 in)
Armament: various

Assessment
Firepower   ★★★
Protection   ★★★
Age   ★★★★★
Worldwide users   ★★

Manufactured by BRAVIA SARL of Portugal, the Chaimite entered service with the Portuguese army in the late 1960s. It looks similar to the Cadillac Gage V-100 Commando, and like the Commando it also has a range of weapons options. The base model is the V-200 and has a one-man turret with two machine-guns. The V-300 can mount 20-mm cannon, and the V-400 has been tested with a variety of 90-mm guns. Other versions include command and communications, mortar, anti-tank, ambulance, crash rescue and riot control. Over 550 have been built and are in service in several countries.

The Chaimite V-200 is almost identical to the Commando, but this has not stopped the Portuguese vehicle from achieving quite a number of export sales. Like the Commando it can mount a variety of weapons.

Simba

Specification
(APC version)
Crew: 2+8
Combat weight: 9.9
tonnes (9 tons 1658 lb)
Maximum road speed:
100 km/h (62 mph)
Power-to-weight
ratio: 21.4 hp/tonne
Length: 5.35 m (17 ft 7 in)
Height: 2.1 m (6 ft 11 in)
to hull top
Armament: 1×7.62-mm
machine-gun on pintle
mount or turret with 1 or
2×7.62-mm machine-guns
or 1×.50-cal Browning
machine-gun

Assessment
Firepower   ★★★★
Protection   ★★★
Age   ★
Worldwide users   ★

The Simba family of 4x4 light combat vehicles has been developed as a private venture by the British company GKN. Aimed at the export market, the Simba is a low-cost multi-purpose wheeled vehicle designed to take a range of armament including guns of up to 90 mm. Its armour is proof against 7.62-mm ball rounds and shell splinters, and the monocoque construction of the hull offers better protection against mines than similar vehicles. The basic APC can carry 10 troops in addition to the commander and driver, but fighting vehicles are limited to a crew of three, the troop-carrying space being lost to make room for two-man 20-mm or 90-mm turrets. As with most modern general-purpose armoured vehicles, Simba can be used in a variety of roles, from mortar carrier to missile-armed tank destroyer.

The GKN Simba is typical of modern private venture wheeled armoured personnel carriers, being relatively simple to operate but which can be upgraded by fitting a variety of weapons and equipment.

PSZH-IV

Specification
Crew: 3+6
Combat weight: 7.5
tonnes (7 tons 851 lb)
Maximum road speed:
80 km/h (50 mph)
Power-to-weight
ratio: 13.3 hp/tonne
Length: 5.7 m (18 ft 8 in)
Height: 2.3 m (7 ft 7 in)
Armament: 14.5-mm
machine-gun; 1×PKT
7.62-mm machine-gun

Assessment
Firepower   ★★
Protection   ★★
Age   ★★★★★
Worldwide users   ★★★★

The Hungarian PSZH-IV was developed in the late 1960s. PSZH stands for *Pancélos Szállitó Harcjármú*, or armoured personnel carrier. Originally thought to have been a scout car, because of its small size, it is amphibious, has an NBC system fitted as standard and also a central tyre pressure regulation system. Armament is a single 14.5-mm KPVT machine-gun in a one-man turret, although there are firing ports in the troop compartment. Variants include command vehicles, ambulances and radiological-chemical recce vehicles. It is in service with Bulgaria, Czech Republic, Hungary and Slovakia.

The PSZH-IV is of the same general configuration as the American Commando, but its thinner armour and lower powered engine mean it is a less capable combat vehicle. It is nevertheless in service with several former Warsaw Pact armies.

SISU XA-180

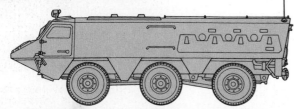

Specification
Crew: 2+10
Combat weight: 15
tonnes (14 tons 1702 lb)
Maximum road speed:
100 km/h (62 mph)
Power-to-weight
ratio: 16 hp/tonne
Length: 7.35 m (24 ft 1 in)
Height: 2.3 m (7 ft 7 in)
Armament: 1×7.62-mm
machine-gun

Assessment
Firepower   ★
Protection   ★★★
Age   ★
Worldwide users   ★

In the early 1980s the Finnish army had a requirement for at least 300 APCs. They found the Russian BTR-60 APC unsatisfactory and ordered the local XA-180 six-wheeled APC from the SISU concern. Development and maintenance costs have been limited by using automotive components from the SISU SA-150 VK 6500-kilogram 4x4 truck. The XA-180 is fully amphibious, powered in the water by two propellers at the hull's rear. It can be fitted with an NBC system. Variants under development include a mortar carrier, an anti-tank weapons carrier, anti-aircraft vehicle, ambulance and command post.

The Finnish SISU XA-180 is nearer the size of the V-300 Commando, and like other modern wheeled APCs it is being tested in a variety of configurations, although its primary function remains to carry troops.

Wheeled APCs are used for a wide range of functions, ranging from anti-tank combat and reconnaissance to keeping public order. Some vehicles are designed for a single purpose, while others cross the divide and are used for a variety of tasks.

MOWAG Roland

The firm of MOWAG Motorwagenfabrik is a well-established manufacturer of military and armoured vehicles, both for the Swiss army and for export. Among its most successful recent exports was the Roland four-wheeled armoured personnel carrier. A specialist internal security vehicle that is much smaller than Saxon and its military equivalents, the Swiss Roland APC is widely used in South America. Like the military vehicles, it is proof against 7.62-mm rifle rounds. Bulletproof wheels are available but maximum speed is reduced to 80 km/h.

Specification
Crew: 3+3
Combat weight: 4.7 tonnes (4 tons 1411 lb)
Maximum road speed: 100 km/h (62 mph)
Power-to-weight ratio: 42.9 hp/tonne
Length: 4.44 m (14 ft 7 in)
Height: 1.62 m (5 ft 4 in) (to hull top)
Armament: 1×7.62-mm machine-gun

Assessment
Firepower   *
Protection   **
Age   ***
Worldwide users *****

Designed by the Swiss firm of MOWAG, the Roland is a small armoured vehicle. Proof against rifle bullets, it would be of marginal use in serious combat, but it is more than sufficient to meet most internal security demands.

Thyssen Henschel Condor

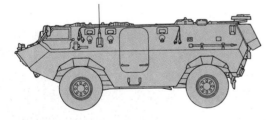

In service with Malaysia, Turkey, Uruguay and various other armies, the Condor is a fully amphibious 4×4 APC capable of carrying many different weapon fits. It has a propeller under the hull rear and optical kit includes NBC system, air-conditioning and night vision equipment. The Condor can manage 50 km/h over 30 km with all tyres punctured. Developed in succession to the earlier UR-416 APC, the Condor is considerably faster than its predecessor even when carrying heavier loads, while its well-sloped sides give much better ballistic protection.

Specification
Crew: 3+9
Combat weight: 12.4 tonnes (12 tons 448 lb)
Maximum road speed: 100 km/h (62 mph)
Power-to-weight ratio: 13.54 hp/tonne
Length: 6.47 m (21 ft 3 in)
Height: 2.47 m (8 ft 2 in)
Armament: 1×7.62-mm machine-gun or turret with twin MGs; .50-cal or 20-mm cannon or ATGWs, e.g. HOT

Assessment
Firepower   ***
Protection   **
Age   ***
Worldwide users ****

A step further up the combat scale, the Thyssen Henschel Condor is a capable APC that is able to carry a variety of armaments while protecting its crew from rifle fire, shell splinters and small mines. The Condor can be used in a variety of roles, including anti-tank, command, ambulance, engineer, cargo and reconnaissance.

TM 170

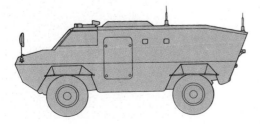

Used by the German Border Guard, the TM 170 is manufactured by Thyssen Henschel and, like the Fahd, is based on a Daimler Benz truck chassis. There are four firing ports in each side, allowing the crew to fire small arms from the troop compartment. TM 170 is fully amphibious and can be fitted with an NBC system. The all-welded hull of the TM 170 provides its crew and passengers with protection against small arms fire and artillery splinters.

Specification
Crew: 2+10
Combat weight: 11.2 tonnes (11 tons)
Maximum road speed: 100 km/h (62 mph)
Power-to-weight ratio: 15 hp/tonne
Length: 6.12 m (20 ft 1 in)
Height: 2.32 m (7 ft 7 in)
Armament: 1×7.62-mm machine-gun or turret mounting twin machine-guns or 20-mm cannon plus HOT or TOW ATGW

Assessment
Firepower   ***
Protection   **
Age   ***
Worldwide users **

Larger and more capable than the Roland, the TM 170 is a dual-purpose vehicle. It has some combat capability, but it is also applicable to police and internal security use. The major TM 170 user is the Federal German Border Guard, the Bundesgrenzschutze.

Humber 'Pig'

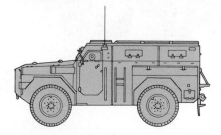

Specification
Crew: 2+8
Combat weight: 5.79 tonnes (5 tons 1568 lb)
Maximum road speed: 60 km/h (37 mph)
Power-to-weight ratio: 20.72 hp/tonne
Length: 4.9 m (16 ft 1 in)
Height: 2.12 m (7 ft)
Armament: none

Assessment
Firepower	–
Protection	*
Age	*****
Worldwide users	*

The Humber APC was one of the earliest vehicles of its type. It was to be retired in the 1960s but was used for many years in Northern Ireland.

The Pig is not a purpose-built IS (Internal Security) vehicle but an obsolete armoured personnel carrier that happened to be available when the British Army found itself deployed to Northern Ireland. Pigs used in service 'over the water' sprouted barricade-removing kit on the hull front, EOD equipment, protected observation positions in the roof and tear-gas launchers. Today, however, all Pigs are now in store.

Shorland SB 501

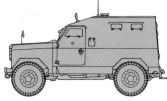

Specification
Crew: 2+6
Combat weight: 3.6 tonnes (3 tons 1216 lb)
Maximum road speed: 105 km/h (65 mph)
Power-to-weight ratio: 31.2 hp/tonne
Length: 4.26 m (14 ft)
Height: 2.03 m (6 ft 8 in)
Armament: optional grenade launchers and/or 7.62-mm machine-gun

Assessment
Firepower	*
Protection	*
Age	***
Worldwide users	****

Another vehicle developed as a result of Northern Ireland's troubles, the Shorland is built on the long wheelbase Land Rover chassis.

Built by Short Brothers in Northern Ireland, this is based on the 110-in Land Rover military chassis. Sharing 85 per cent of the components of the Land Rover, it is simple and easy to operate, purpose-built for internal security and used in at least 17 countries. Its armour will stop 7.62-mm×51 rounds from over 23 metres, and the vehicle is shaped so that blazing petrol cannot enter and grenades will roll off the roof.

Hotspur Hussar

Specification
Crew: 1+13
Combat weight: 4.7 tonnes (4 tons 1411 lb)
Maximum road speed: 95 km/h (59 mph)
Power-to-weight ratio: 24 hp/tonne
Length: 5.74 m (18 ft 10 in)
Height: 2.1 m (6 ft 11 in)
Armament: optional 1×7.62-mm machine-gun

Assessment
Firepower	*
Protection	*
Age	*
Worldwide users	**

A larger vehicle than the Shorland, the Hotspur Hussar is a capable internal security vehicle. It too was inspired by the troubles in Ulster, and like the Shorland it is also based on a Land Rover chassis.

Based on the chassis of the Land Rover 110 but with an extra powered axle, the Hussar is armoured against 7.62-mm×51 from over 25 metres and against SMG or pistol ammunition from any range. The windscreen is made from armoured glass and can be additionally protected with polycarbonate shields.

Commando Ranger

Specification
Crew: 2+6
Combat weight: 4.5 tonnes (4 tons 963 lb)
Maximum road speed: 112 km/h (69 mph)
Power-to-weight ratio: 40 hp/tonne
Length: 4.69 m (15 ft 5 in)
Height: 1.9 m (6 ft 3 in)
Armament: optional turret or roof-mounted 7.62-mm or .50-cal machine-gun

Assessment
Firepower	*
Protection	**
Age	**
Worldwide users	**

The Commando Ranger is based on commercial light truck components. With its limited range of functions, it is cheaper to acquire and operate than specially-designed armoured fighting vehicles.

This was built to a US Air Force requirement for an airbase security vehicle and it is now used by the USAF and the US Navy. Based on a Chrysler truck chassis, the hull is protected by Cadloy armour, which is proof against small arms fire, and the combat tyres are foam-filled run-flats good for another 80 kilometres after being shot out. The Ranger is intended less for riot control and more for dealing with an armed threat to a base facility.

Using tracked vehicles to carry supplies was tried successfully as far back as World War I. Since 1945, the armoured personnel carrier has become a vitally important element in modern mechanised warfare.

BMD

Each of the seven Russian airborne divisions can field 330 of these armoured personnel carriers, which give the Russian paratroopers a substantial advantage over their Western counterparts. Nearly six tons lighter than the BMP from which it is developed, the BMD can be dropped by parachute and is fully amphibious. It has obvious limitations as an APC, principally its lack of room, but in the right place at the right time it could make all the difference.

Specification
Crew: 2+6
Combat weight: 8.9 tonnes (8 tons 1700 lb)
Maximum road speed: 80 km/h (50 mph)
Power-to-weight ratio: 35 hp/tonne
Length: 5.4 m (17 ft 9 in)
Height: 1.85 m (6 ft 1 in)
Armament: 1×73-mm smoothbore gun; 1 launcher rail for 'Sagger' or 'Spigot' anti-tank missiles; 1×7.62-mm machine-gun

Assessment
Firepower   ★★★★★
Protection   ★★
Age   ★★★
Worldwide users   ★

The BMD looks like a reduced size version of the BMP infantry fighting vehicle, and it carries similar armament. It is very small, however, and an infantry section would find it a tight squeeze.

MT-LB

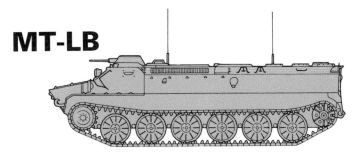

Primarily used to tow artillery, the Russian MT-LB also serves as an APC, mine layer and signals vehicle. It is slightly faster than the FV 432 and more mobile over snow or boggy ground. It is amphibious without preparation, but has a shorter range than the FV 432. Its small turret houses a 7.62-mm machine-gun, and its troop compartment is roomier, able to accommodate 11 troops and their equipment.

Specification
Crew: 2+11
Combat weight: 11.9 tonnes (11 tons 1590 lb)
Maximum road speed: 61.5 km/h (38 mph)
Power-to-weight ratio: 20 hp/tonne
Length: 6.45 m (21 ft 2 in)
Height: 1.86 m (6 ft 1 in)
Armament: 1×7.62-mm machine-gun

Assessment
Firepower   ★★
Protection   ★
Age   ★★★★
Worldwide users   ★★★★

The MT-LB's wide tracks and low ground pressure make it a highly suitable vehicle for carrying personnel across boggy and arctic terrain.

NVH-1

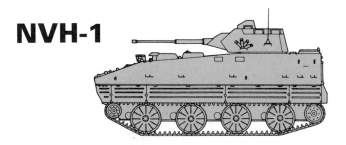

This is an interesting co-operative venture by Vickers and Norinco, the Chinese state arms manufacturing business. The APC is a much improved version of the Type 531 APC, powered by a licence-built German diesel engine and carrying a Vickers two-man turret. This can carry either 30-mm RARDEN or 25-mm Oerlikon-Bührle cannon plus a co-axial 7.62-mm McDonnell Douglas Chain Gun. It is fully amphibious without preparation.

Specification
Crew: 2+9
Combat weight: 16 tonnes (15 tons 1680 lb)
Maximum road speed: 65 km/h (40 mph)
Power-to-weight ratio: 20 hp/tonne
Length: 6.1 m (20 ft)
Height: 2.77 m (9 ft 1 in)
Armament: 25- or 30-mm cannon plus 7.62-mm Chain Gun

Assessment
Firepower   ★★★★
Protection   ★★★
Age   ★
Worldwide users   –

China has been struggling to modernise its archaic armed forces for many years. The NVH-1 is a combination of Soviet-influenced vehicle technology and Western armament in a British turret.

AMX-13 VCI

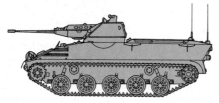

Specification
Crew: 3+10
Combat weight: 15 tonnes (14 tons 1702 lb)
Maximum road speed: 60 km/h (37 mph)
Power-to-weight ratio: 16.6 hp/tonne
Length: 5.7 m (18 ft 8 in)
Height: 2.41 m (7 ft 11 in)
Armament: 1×20-mm cannon; 12.7-mm or 7.62-mm machine-gun

Assessment
Firepower   ★★★
Protection   ★★★
Age   ★★★★★
Worldwide users   ★★★★

The AMX-13 series of light armoured vehicles was one of France's most successful designs of the 1950s and 1960s. The VCI, or Véhicule de Combat Infantérie, is the APC variant.

The AMX-13 VCI is the last APC version of this series of armoured vehicles based on the chassis of the AMX-13 light tank. Although the AMX-13 was a nimble light tank when introduced in the 1950s, it lacks the cross-country speed and acceleration of the later British Scorpion family. On the other hand, the larger hull can accommodate bigger loads like a 155-mm howitzer or 120-mm mortar.

Saurer 4K 4FA

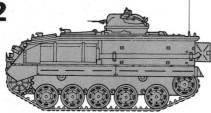

Specification
Crew: 2+8
Combat weight: 14.8 tonnes (14 tons 1277 lb)
Maximum road speed: 64 km/h (40 mph)
Power-to-weight ratio: 21.6 hp/tonne
Length: 5.87 m (19 ft 3 in)
Height: 1.6 m (5 ft 3 in)
Armament: 1×12.7-mm machine-gun

Assessment
Firepower   ★★
Protection   ★★★
Age   ★★★
Worldwide users   ★

Designed in the late 1950s by Steyr-Daimler-Puch, the 4K 4FA is a fairly competent vehicle. In service with the Austrian army, it can withstand 20-mm cannon fire.

Comparing the Saurer with a lightweight tracked APC like the British Spartan series graphically shows the trade-off between mobility/protection and cost. Spartan and weapons carrier versions using the same chassis are smaller and faster than similar derivatives of the Saurer, but the Austrian vehicle is built to withstand hits from a 20-mm cannon which would chew up the lighter British AFVs. Like the Stormer, the basic Saurer APC accommodates a full section.

FV 432

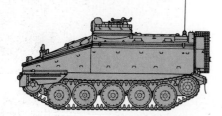

Specification
Crew: 2+10
Combat weight: 15 tonnes (14 tons 1702 lb)
Maximum road speed: 52 km/h (32 mph)
Power-to-weight ratio: 15.7 hp/tonne
Length: 5.25 m (17 ft 3 in)
Height: 1.87 m (6 ft 2 in)
Armament: 1×7.62-mm machine-gun

Assessment
Firepower   ★
Protection   ★★★
Age   ★★★★★
Worldwide users   ★

Britain's FV 432 is a contemporary of the American M113. With similar capacity, it is a less mobile vehicle, but it has nevertheless been in front-line service with the British Army for nearly 30 years.

The FV 432 has served the British Army well, and will remain in service for some time as the MCV-80 slowly percolates into the mechanised battalions. Most have now had their tiresome amphibious kits removed, but the NBC overpressure and filtering system remain a serious weakness. Various specialist vehicles are likely to outlast the conventional APC, although the cost of converting an FV 432 to, say, the ambulance role is almost as high as buying a new vehicle from the CVR(T) series produced by Alvis.

FV 103 Spartan APC

Specification
Crew: 3+4
Combat weight: 8.17 tonnes (7 tons 889 lb)
Maximum road speed: 80+ km/h (50+ mph)
Power-to-weight ratio: 23.25 hp/tonne
Length: 5.1 m (16 ft 9 in)
Height: 2.28 m (7 ft 6 in)
Armament: 1×7.62-mm machine-gun

Assessment
Firepower   ★
Protection   ★★
Age   ★
Worldwide users   ★★★

Smaller and more mobile than the FV 432, the Alvis Spartan is a member of the Scorpion family of tracked combat vehicles. It is used by the British Army in specialist roles, such as carrying Javelin SAM or MILAN ATGW missile teams.

Spartan has now been in service for 10 years performing a number of roles, carrying Blowpipe and Javelin SAM teams, supplies of Swingfire anti-tank missiles for the Striker anti-tank vehicle and as an APC for the RAF regiment. Its small troop compartment has room for only four men, so it cannot really be compared with APCs designed to carry a full section into combat. Compact and with unrivalled cross-country mobility, it is ideal for smaller units.

TRACKED APCs No.2

Tracked APCs come in a variety of shapes and sizes. Originally they were generally simple armoured boxes with tracks, but in recent years many have acquired powerful weaponry and are now effective fighting vehicles.

FMC AIFV

FMC developed their AIFV from the proven M113 armoured personnel carrier to a US Army requirement for a vehicle with firing ports and a fully enclosed main armament. The US Army eventually bought the Bradley, but the AIFV has been exported to Belgium, the Netherlands and the Philippines. Its laminate armour provides a high degree of protection for a vehicle of its size, and its armament and cross-country performance are quite adequate. It is certainly more cost-effective than the Bradley.

Specification
Crew: 3+7
Combat weight: 13.6 tonnes (13 tons 874 lb)
Maximum road speed: 61 km/h (37 mph)
Power-to-weight ratio: 19 hp/tonne
Length: 5.25 m (17 ft 3 in)
Height: 2.6 m (8 ft 6 in)
Armament: 1×Oerlikon 25-mm cannon; 1×7.62-mm machine-gun

Assessment
Firepower ★★
Protection ★★
Age ★★
Worldwide users ★★

The FMC Armoured Infantry Fighting Vehicle is a heavily-armed infantry combat vehicle. Developed from the ubiquitous and well-proven M113 armoured personnel carrier, it is much cheaper than IFVs like the Bradley and the Warrior.

AAV7

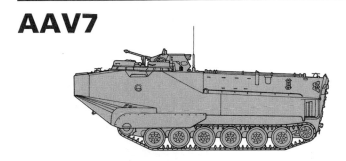

Just as the United States is the only nation to field as large and powerful an amphibious assault force as the US Marines, so no other country has developed an amphibious assault vehicle like the Marine Corps' AAV7. Entering service just after the end of the Vietnam War, the AAV7 (then known as the LVTP7) is the latest in a long series of American amphibious tracked vehicles dating back to World War II. Larger than most APCs, it has excellent performance in the water, and is armoured to protect its crew from small-arms fire and shell splinters.

Specification
Crew: 3+25
Combat weight: 22.8 tonnes (22 tons 985 lb)
Maximum road speed: 64 km/h (40 mph)
Power-to-weight ratio: 17.5 hp/tonne
Length: 7.8 m (25 ft 6 in)
Height: 3.2 m (10 ft 6 in)
Armament: 1×.50-cal machine-gun

Assessment
Firepower ★
Protection ★
Age ★★★
Worldwide users ★★★

Too large to be a practical armoured personnel carrier, although it is often used as such, the AAV7 comes into its own in amphibious operations, when its excellent waterborne capability enables it to outperform other fighting vehicles.

BTR-50

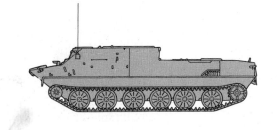

First seen in public 30 years ago, the BTR-50 was the standard APC carrying the infantry battalions in Russian tank divisions. Now largely replaced by BMP, it soldiers on with former Warsaw Pact armies and one-time Russian client states. While swimming, the engine can only be run at full power for about eight minutes due to cooling problems; it is uncontrollable in a current faster than 8 km/h and has trouble getting out of the water. It has only slightly more amphibious ability than the standard M113.

Specification
Crew: 2+20
Combat weight: 14 tonnes (13 tons 1747 lb)
Maximum road speed: 44 km/h (27 mph)
Power-to-weight ratio: 16.9 hp/tonne
Length: 7 m (23 ft)
Height: 2 m (6 ft 7 in)
Armament: 1×7.62-mm machine-gun

Assessment
Firepower ★
Protection ★
Age ★★★★★
Worldwide users ★★★★

The BTR-50 was one of the first tracked vehicles designed specifically as an armoured personnel carrier to be fielded by any army. Still in service around the world, it is now showing its age.

YW 531

Specification
Crew: 4+10
Combat weight: 12.6 tonnes (12 tons 896 lb)
Maximum road speed: 65 km/h (40 mph)
Power-to-weight ratio: 25 hp/tonne
Length: 5.4 m (17 ft 9 in)
Height: 2.5 m (8 ft 3 in)
Armament: 1×12.7-mm machine-gun

Assessment
Firepower   *
Protection   **
Age   ***
Worldwide users   ****

As with many armoured personnel carriers, the Chinese *YW 531* has been used as a weapons carrier as well as being a personnel carrier. This version is fitted with a *Type 63* multiple rocket launcher.

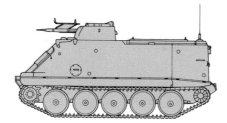

Developed in the late 1960s, this Chinese APC has seen action in Vietnam, Uganda (the Tanzanians use them) and in Angola by Zaïrean forces in 1976. It is a straightforward 1960s' design: an armoured box with a 12.7-mm machine-gun on top. Ambulance, command post and 120-mm mortar-carrying versions are also produced.

Pansarbandvagn 302

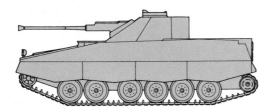

Specification
Crew: 2+10
Combat weight: 13.5 tonnes (13 tons 650 lb)
Maximum road speed: 66 km/h (41 mph)
Power-to-weight ratio: 21 hp/tonne
Length: 5.35 m (17 ft 7 in)
Height: 2.5 m (8 ft 3 in) (to turret top)
Armament: 1×20-mm cannon

Assessment
Firepower   ***
Protection   ***
Age   ***
Worldwide users   *

Sweden's *Pansarbandvagn 302* is an armoured box, similar in concept to the American *M113* or the British *FV 432*. However, it has better protection and was one of the first such APCs to be armed with a cannon.

The Swedish army was one of the first to fit a cannon to its standard APC: the Pbv 302 entered service in 1966. Fully amphibious, it has a small turret on the left-hand side fitted with a 20-mm Hispano Suiza cannon which fires HE and AP ammunition. The front of the vehicle is proof against 20-mm cannon fire and the double-skinned hull gives added buoyancy and protection against HEAT rounds.

Stridsfordon 90

Specification
Crew: 3+8
Combat weight: 20 tonnes (19 tons 1523 lb)
Maximum road speed: 70 km/h (43 mph)
Power-to-weight ratio: 25 hp/tonne
Length: 6.4 m (21 ft)
Height: 2.5 m (8 ft 3 in)
Armament: 1×25-mm cannon; 1×7.62-mm machine-gun

Assessment
Firepower   ****
Protection   ***
Age   *
Worldwide users   –

The hull of an *Ikv-91* tank-destroyer has been used as a test-rig during the development of the 40-mm turret used in the infantry combat version of the *Stridsfordon 90*.

The Swedish army tested the Alvis Scorpion and Stormer in 1984 and found their cross-country performance excellent even in deep snow. However, the Swedes decided to develop their own light armoured vehicle armed with cannon and possibly the Bofors BILL anti-tank guided missile. The profile is deliberately low and armour protection an improvement over the old Pbv 302. Fire support models have been trialled with 40- and 57-mm Bofors guns.

Stormer

Specification
Crew: 3+8
Combat weight: 12.7 tonnes (12 tons 1120 lb)
Maximum road speed: 80 km/h (50 mph)
Power-to-weight ratio: 19.6 hp/tonne
Length: 5.69 m (18 ft 8 in)
Height: 2.27 m (7 ft 5 in)
Armament: 1 or 2×7.62-mm machine-guns or 20-mm cannon

Assessment
Firepower   ***
Protection   ***
Age   **
Worldwide users   *

Although using many components of the lightweight Scorpion family, the *Stormer* is a larger, heavier vehicle which can carry a full eight-man infantry section into battle.

A lengthened, much heavier, diesel-powered development of the Scorpion chassis, the Stormer is produced by Alvis for export. The larger troop compartment has room for an eight-man section and it can be fitted with several different turrets mounting one or two 7.62-mm machine-guns or 20-mm cannon. With a front flotation screen, Stormer is fully amphibious, and optional equipment includes an NBC system and air-conditioning.

LIGHT VEHICLES No.1

Light utility vehicles have become essential items in the inventory of the modern army, having proved their worth in World War II. They are used for an astonishing array of tasks, both in combat and in rear echelon roles, and without them it would be difficult to carry out the most routine of duties.

Series III ¾-ton Land Rover

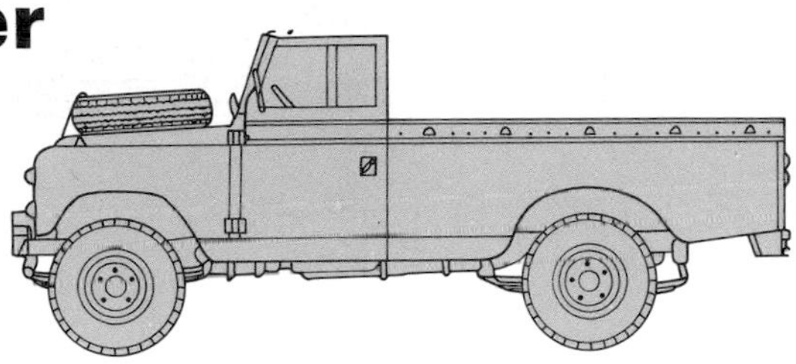

Of all the vehicles in the lightweight military class, Land Rover is the only one in service worldwide, irrespective of the political affiliations of the user nation. Due to its relatively low cost and mechanical simplicity, even Third World countries find it ideal for their needs. To high-tech nations, however, the design is now regarded as outdated, having been largely unchanged for over a quarter of a century.

Specification
Seating: 1+10
Cross-country load: 850 kg (1874 lb)
Range: 600 km (372 miles)
Gradient: 100 per cent
Engine: four-cylinder petrol
Power: 69 hp at 4000 rpm
Gears: four forward and one reverse gears
Transfer box: two-speed
Body material: aluminium alloy

Assessment
Carrying ability *****
Pulling power ***
Cargo space *****
Body variants *****

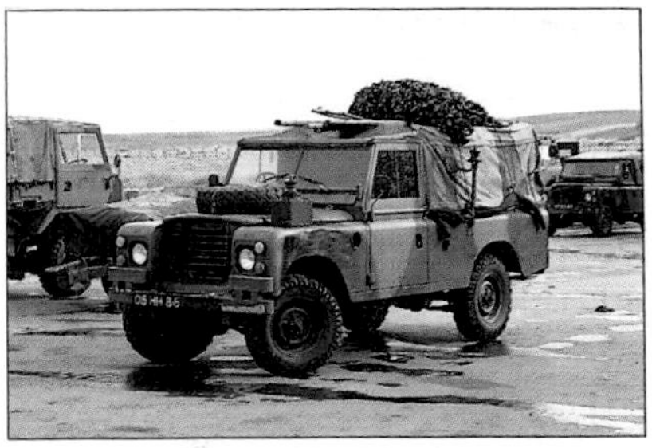

The Series III Land Rover of the 1970s is similar to earlier Land Rovers, with a number of cosmetic changes. These include moving the headlamps from the grille to the front wings for safety reasons.

Land Rover 110

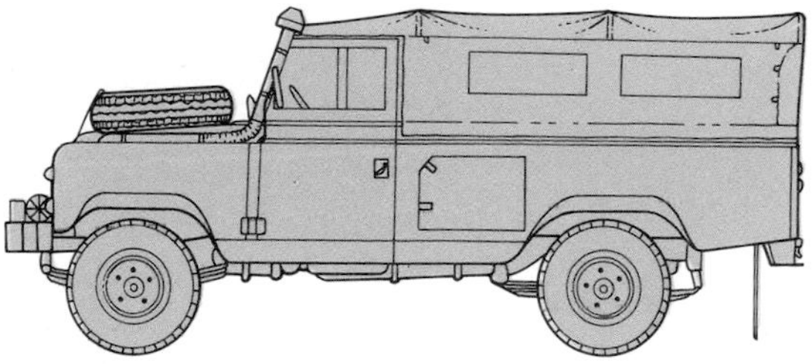

After nine years in service, the One-Ten has successfully inherited the throne vacated by the leaf-springed Land Rovers of the 1960s and 1970s. Combining new technology with a proven design, it provides good load-carrying ability.

Specification
Seating: 1+10
Cross-country load: 1100 kg (1 ton 179 lb)
Range: 565 km (351 miles)
Gradient: 100 per cent
Engine: four-cylinder petrol
Power: 83 hp at 4000 rpm
Gears: four forward and one reverse gears
Transfer box: two-speed
Body material: aluminium alloy

Assessment
Carrying ability *****
Pulling power ****
Cargo space *****
Body variants *****

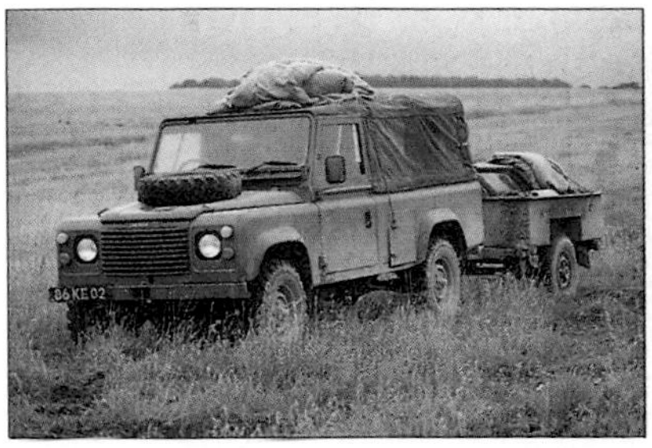

The Land Rover 110 retains all of the type's ruggedness and dependability, combined with excellent new features taken from the sophisticated and successful Range Rover.

M151A2

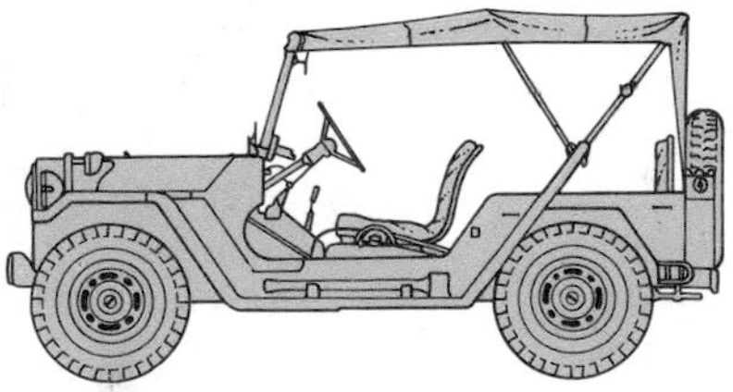

The M151 can reasonably be described as the third generation of the 'jeep' concept, and is an ideal light, quick response vehicle. The biggest drawback of this series is the very limited troop and cargo-carrying capability, which means that a second type of vehicle, normally the M715 series, is required for many of the duties which would usually be carried out by the Land Rover or UAZ 469.

Specification
Seating: 1+3
Cross-country load: 363 kg (800 lb)
Range: 480 km (300 miles)
Gradient: 60 per cent
Engine: four-cylinder petrol
Power: 72 hp at 4000 rpm
Gears: four forward and one reverse gears
Transfer box: single-speed
Body material: steel

Assessment
Carrying ability **
Pulling power ***
Cargo space **
Body variants ****

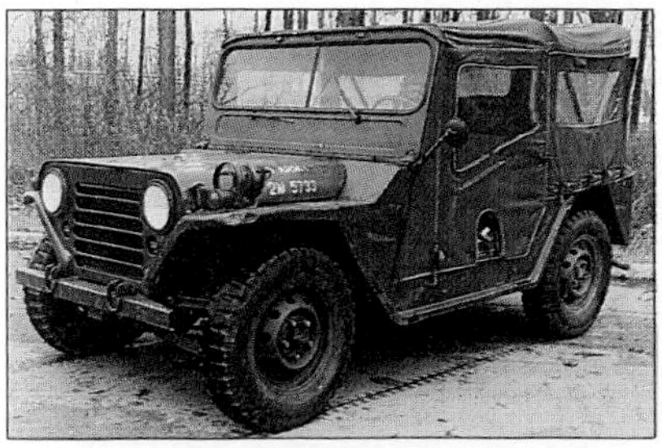

The M151 is descended from the famous Willys Jeep of World War II. A small cargo capacity limits its use, however, and it is being superseded in US military service by the much larger 'Hummer'.

M998 HMMWV

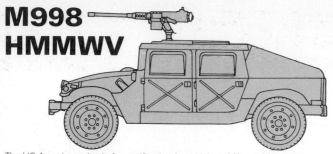

Specification
Seating: 1+3 (+8 when used as a troop carrier)
Cross-country load: 1134 kg (1 ton 1260 lb)
Range: 580 km (1212 miles)
Gradient: 60 per cent
Engine: V-8 air-cooled
Power: 135 hp at 3600 rpm
Gears: automatic with three forward and one reverse
Transfer box: two-speed with permanent four-wheel drive
Body material: steel

Assessment
Carrying ability	★★★★★
Pulling power	★★★★★
Cargo space	★★★★★
Body variants	★★★★★

Large, powerful and with superb cross-country mobility, the M998 HMMWV is vastly superior to the preceding M151 'jeep', but at more than $30,000 it is also vastly more expensive.

The US Army issued a draft specification for a high-mobility multi-purpose wheeled vehicle (HMMWV, otherwise known as the 'Hummer' or 'Hum-Vee') in 1979. Considerably larger than the M151 'jeep' it replaces, the Hummer is also used in place of the M274 Mule, the M561 Gama Goat and the M880 series of commercial pick-up trucks. There are many variants of the 'Hummer', including cargo/troop carriers, TOW carriers, armament carriers, ambulances and shelter carriers. It is also the basis for the Avenger surface-to-air gun/missile system used in the US Army's Forward Area Air Defense System.

UAZ 469B

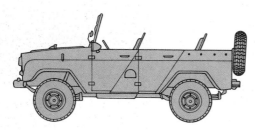

Specification
Seating: 1+6
Cross-country load: 600 kg (1323 lb)
Range: 750 km (466 miles)
Gradient: 62 per cent
Engine: four-cylinder petrol
Power: 75 hp at 4000 rpm
Gears: four forward and one reverse gears
Transfer box: two-speed
Body material: steel

Assessment
Carrying ability	★★★
Pulling power	★★★
Cargo space	★★★★
Body variants	★★

The UAZ 469 is not a sophisticated vehicle, but it is tough. It also has good ground clearance, which is one of the major factors deciding cross-country performance in all but the most extreme of terrain.

Until the 1970s, the standard Soviet vehicle in this class was the GAZ 69, which was a derivative of the World War II Jeep. The production replacement for the GAZ was the UAZ 469B, which bears more than a passing resemblance to the Land Rover and shares many of its design features. Unfortunately the vehicle tends to rust prematurely due to the steel body panels, and although a hard top is available it is very seldom seen, even in adverse climates.

Mercedes-Benz G Wagen

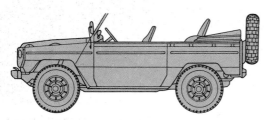

Specification
Seating: 1+5
Cross-country load: 750 kg (1653 lb)
Range: not available
Gradient: 80 per cent
Engine: four-cylinder petrol
Power: 90 hp at 4800 rpm
Gears: four forward and one reverse gears
Transfer box: single-speed
Body material: steel

Assessment
Carrying ability	★★★★
Pulling power	★★★★★
Cargo space	★★★
Body variants	★★★★

The G Wagen is built for Mercedes by Steyr-Daimler-Puch of Austria, who sell it in some markets as the Puch. It is also built for the French army under licence by Peugeot.

This high-quality vehicle, although in service with the German Border Guard and several other nations as well as many European Emergency Services and civilian organisations, is not actually used in large numbers by the German army. Cost tends to be the limiting factor to more widespread sales of what is unquestionably a very good vehicle, and once again the steel body poses drawbacks with vehicle life expectancy.

Fiat 1107AD Campagnola

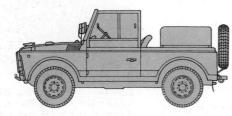

Specification
Seating: 1+6
Cross-country load: 610 kg (1345 lb)
Range: 400 km (248 miles)
Gradient: 100 per cent
Engine: four-cylinder petrol
Power: 80 hp at 4600 rpm
Gears: five forward and one reverse gears
Transfer box: two-speed
Body material: steel

Assessment
Carrying ability	★★★
Pulling power	★★★★
Cargo space	★★★
Body variants	★★

Although it looks very much in the Land Rover mould and has similar capacity and performance to the older short-wheelbase variants, the Fiat 1107 lacks the British vehicle's rust-proof aluminium body.

Apart from Tunisia and Yugoslavia, where the Campagnola has been licence-produced, bulk sales of this respected vehicle have been limited to the Italian armed forces. This product from the Fiat stable has the features and looks of a short-wheelbase Land Rover, and mechanically it possesses similar qualities.

COMBAT ENGINEER VEHICLES No.1

Combat engineer vehicles are an essential part of modern mechanised warfare, being used for tasks as varied as preparing firing positions, breaching obstacles, mine clearing and retrieving broken-down AFVs.

Centurion AVRE

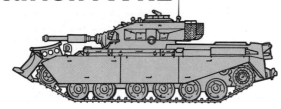

Developed from the classic Centurion medium tank, the Centurion AVRE (Armoured Vehicle Royal Engineers) was the successor to the wartime 'funny' tanks used in the 1944 invasion of Normandy. Deployed with 32 Armoured Engineer Regiment in Germany, the Centurion AVRE is now supplemented by the CET but remains an important vehicle. From 1984 the Royal Artillery handed over the Centurions it used to be employed as forward observation posts, and these have now been added to the AVRE fleet.

Specification
(165 AVRE)
Crew: 5
Combat weight: 51.8 tonnes (50 tons 2195 lb)
Road speed: 34 km/h (21 mph)
Length: 8.68 m (28 ft 6 in)
Height: 3 m (9 ft 11 in)
Armament: 1×165-mm demolition gun; 2×7.62-mm machine-guns

Assessment
Firepower ★★★★
Versatility ★★★★★
Age ★★★★★
Worldwide users ★

The Centurion is one of the classic armoured vehicles, with a career stretching back to the final years of World War II. Engineer variants of the tank are the last to serve with the British Army.

CET

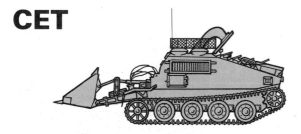

The first CET was accepted by the British Army in 1978 and it has proved itself to be a very useful engineer vehicle indeed. Designed to provide integral engineer support to the now re-designated BAOR battle groups, the CET is used to excavate firing positions, move disabled vehicles, repair and maintain roads, and prepare or remove battlefield obstacles. On top of the hull it has a rocket-propelled, self-emplacing earth anchor.

Specification
Crew: 2
Combat weight: 17.7 tonnes (17 tons 940 lb)
Road speed: 56 km/h (35 mph)
Length: 5.3 m (17 ft 5 in)
Height: 2.83 m (9 ft 4 in)
Armament: 1×7.62-mm machine-gun

Assessment
Firepower ★
Versatility ★★★★
Age ★★★
Worldwide users ★

The Combat Engineer Tractor is far more than the armoured earth-mover that it appears to be. It is a tough and versatile machine, capable of undertaking the majority of tasks required of combat engineer vehicles.

M728

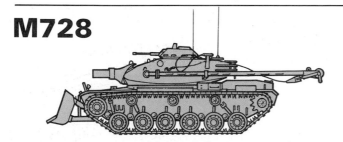

The standard US Army combat engineer vehicle, the M728, is an M60A1 MBT with its 105-mm gun replaced by a 165-mm demolition gun which fires a HESH round. The vehicle is fitted with a dozer blade and carries an 'A' frame over the turret, which can lift up to 15 tonnes. A 7.62-mm machine-gun is mounted co-axially with the main armament, and the commander's cupola carries a .50-cal Browning.

Specification
Crew: 4
Combat weight: 53.2 tonnes (52 tons 358 lb)
Road speed: 48 km/h (30 mph)
Length: 8.92 m (29 ft 3 in)
Height: 3.2 m (10 ft 6 in)
Armament: 1×165-mm demolition gun; 1×7.62-mm machine-gun; 1×.50-cal machine-gun

Assessment
Firepower ★★★★
Versatility ★★★★★
Age ★★★★
Worldwide users ★★★

Like the Centurion, the M728 is based upon a Main Battle Tank, which in this case is the US Army's M60A1 MBT. Like the Centurion, it is equipped with a large, short-range gun which is used for demolition work.

Leopard AEV

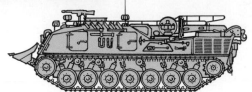

Based on the chassis of the Leopard 1 Main Battle Tank, the AEV can rip up roads, dig holes, prepare or remove battlefield obstacles, excavate tank firing positions and prepare river banks for water crossing. The German army has some 37 Leopard AEVs, and the vehicle is also used by Belgium, Italy and the Netherlands. The crane can lift up to 20 tonnes and the maximum tractive effort of the winch is 70 tonnes.

Specification
Crew: 3
Combat weight: 40.8 tonnes (40 tons 336 lb)
Road speed: 65 km/h (40 mph)
Length: 7.98 m (26 ft 2 in)
Height: 2.69 m (8 ft 10 in)
Armament: 1×7.62-mm machine-gun in bow; 1×7.62-mm AA machine-gun

Assessment
Firepower   *
Versatility   * * * *
Age   * * * *
Worldwide users   * *

The German Leopard 1 tank was probably the most mobile of post-war Main Battle Tanks, and the Leopard armoured engineer vehicle uses the same chassis and powerpack. It is a highly versatile vehicle.

IMR

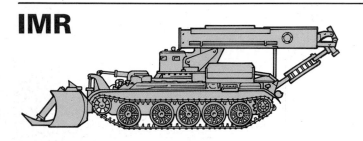

The IMR, based on the chassis of the T-55, was the standard Russian armoured engineer vehicle and is widely used throughout the former Warsaw Pact countries. Unlike the Centurion, EBG and M728, the IMR has no demolition capacity. The tank turret is replaced by a hydraulically-operated crane with 360-degree traverse and two pincer-type grabs for ripping up trees and small obstacles. Its dozer blade can be used straight or in a 'V' configuration, but is unable to angle doze.

Specification
Crew: 2
Combat weight: 34 tonnes (33 tons 1030 lb)
Road speed: 48 km/h (30 mph)
Length: 6.45 m (21 ft 2 in)
Height: 2.48 m (8 ft 2 in)
Armament: none

Assessment
Firepower   –
Versatility   * * *
Age   * * * * *
Worldwide users   * * * *

The IMR has no demolition or mine-clearing capacity, but this is no handicap as Russian doctrine calls for specialised vehicles for each of these tasks.

AMX-13 VCG

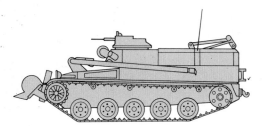

The French army's AMX-13 *Véhicule de Combat de Génie*, or combat engineer vehicle, demonstrates that engineer vehicles do not have to be of Main Battle Tank size to be effective. Based on the AMX-13 personnel carrier, the VCG's main task is the carriage of an engineer field troop into the combat area and to enable that field troop to clear a passage through obstacles, or to launch light bridges, or to carry out demolitions. It is fitted with a dozer blade, shear legs and a winch.

Specification
Crew: 2+7 engineers
Combat weight: 17.6 tonnes (17 tons 717 lb)
Road speed: 60 km/h (37 mph)
Length: 6.05 m (19 ft 10 in)
Height: 2.41 m (7 ft 11 in)
Armament: 1×12.7-mm machine-gun

Assessment
Firepower   *
Versatility   * * * *
Age   * * * * *
Worldwide users   *

The VCG differs slightly from other engineer vehicles. Based on an APC chassis, it is more of a support vehicle for the engineer field troop that it carries than a pure engineer vehicle like the converted MBTs.

AMX-30 EBG

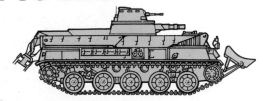

The AMX-30 EBG uses the same chassis as the AMX-30 bridgelayer, but with the engine, suspension and transmission of the more modern AMX-30B2. Fitted with a dozer blade able to dig 120 cubic metres of earth per hour, the EBG also carries a scarifier. When this is swung into position the EBG can slow reverse along a road, ripping it up as it goes along. The EBG has four tubes for launching mines, a demolition charge launcher and a demolition gun firing a 17-kilogram round.

Specification
Crew: 3
Combat weight: 38 tonnes (37 tons 896 lb)
Road speed: 65 km/h (40 mph)
Length: 7.9 m (26 ft)
Height: 2.94 m (9 ft 8 in)
Armament: 1×142-mm demolition gun; 1×7.62-mm machine-gun; 4×mine projectors

Assessment
Firepower   * * * * *
Versatility   * * * * *
Age   * * *
Worldwide users   *

The versatile AMX-30 EBG (Engin Blindé du Genie, or armoured engineer vehicle) is based on the chassis of the AMX-30 tank. As with most Western engineer vehicles, it can be used to perform a variety of combat engineer tasks.

ANTI-TANK GUIDED MISSILES

No. 1

For the last 30 years the supremacy of the tank has been challenged by increasingly accurate guided weapons. Fitted with large warheads able to penetrate over 500 mm of armour plate, they are a key weapon on the modern battlefield.

TOW

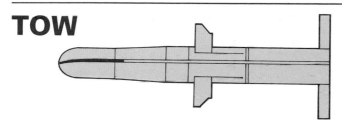

The Hughes TOW entered service in 1970 and has proved to be one of the most successful of anti-tank weapons. Today, it is used by 40 different nations. TOW's large size and heavy weight make it unsuitable as a mobile infantry weapon: it is usually mounted on a light vehicle, APC or helicopter. The basic missile is designated BGM-71A and consists of a shaped-charged warhead with a launch motor and a flight motor. Thermal and xenon beacons identify the missile in flight and help the operator steer it onto the target. The US Army now uses two later versions, TOW2A and TOW2B.

Specification
(TOW 2)
Missile weight: 28 kg (61 lb 12 oz)
Launcher weight: 93 kg (205 lb)
Warhead: 5.9 kg (13 lb)
Minimum range: 65 m (213 ft)
Maximum range: 3750 m (4100 yd)
Armour penetration: 800+ mm (31+ in)

Assessment
Reliability	★★★★
Accuracy	★★★★
Age	★★
Worldwide users	★★★★

IS soldier in unusually elaborate face camouflage drives an M151 utility vehicle fitted with a TOW anti-tank guided missile launcher. TOW is really too heavy for use in the dismounted role.

HOT

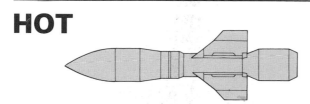

HOT (*Haut subsonique Optiquement, Téléguidé*) has a similar performance to TOW. A second-generation weapon developed jointly by the Franco-German Euromissile consortium, it is in service with some 15 armies, including Iraq and Syria. The Russian AT-5 'Spandrel' is suspected to be based on stolen HOT technology. HOT's long range enables it to engage older types of tank beyond the effective range of their main armament. Fitted to missile-firing tank-destroyers, it proved highly effective, although reloading is obviously much slower than on the gun-armed *Jagdpanzers*.

Specification
Missile weight: 23.5 kg (51 lb 13 oz)
Launcher weight: 8.5 kg (18 lb 12 oz) (launch tube only)
Warhead: 6-kg (13 lb 4 oz) hollow-charge HE
Minimum range: 75 m (245 ft)
Maximum range: 4000 m (4370 yd)
Armour penetration: 1300+ mm (51+ in) (HOT 2)

Assessment
Reliability	★★★★
Accuracy	★★★★★
Age	★★
Worldwide users	★★★

The West German army developed a range of tank destroyers during the 1960s and equipped some with 90-mm guns and others with early ATGMs. The latter now use HOT missiles.

MILAN

The man-portable MILAN is the best of the second-generation wire-guided anti-tank missiles, and is primarily designed to be used by infantry firing from a defensive position. Produced by Euromissile, it is manufactured under licence in Britain. The Russian AT-4 'Spigot' is closely based on the same design. The missile comes in factory-sealed tubes which are fitted to the firing post; on firing, a gas generator inside the tube blows the missile forward and, after it has travelled a safe distance from the firing post, its own motor powers it on its 13-second flight to the target. The latest version is the MILAN 2.

Specification
Missile weight: 11.3 kg (24 lb 15 oz)
Launcher weight: 6.4 kg (14 lb 2 oz)
Warhead: 1.45 kg (3 lb 3 oz) shaped-charge high-explosive
Minimum range: 25 m (82 ft)
Maximum range: 2000 m (2190 yd)
Armour penetration: 1000+ mm (39+ in)

Assessment
Reliability	★★★★
Accuracy	★★★★★
Age	★★
Worldwide users	★★

MILAN is the most successful Western anti-tank guided missile and is in service with many different armies. When fired, the tube flies back off the launcher while the missile flies down range.

Dragon

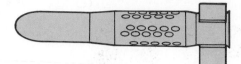

The US Army's equivalent of MILAN, but is much older and less capable. Its maximum range of 1000 metres is now inadequate and its unusual propulsion system offers little advantage. It has 60 side-thrust rocket motors on its outer surface and rolls as it flies. A central rocket provides forward thrust, while the side-thrust rockets fire as they reach the bottom centre to give the missile lift. They are also fired by signals sent down the wire to alter the missile's course. The current service version is the M47 Dragon II, which has better penetration but the same range, and Dragon III is in development.

Specification
Missile weight: 6.2 kg (13 lb 4 oz)
Launcher weight: 7.6 kg (16 lb 12 oz)
Warhead: 2.45 kg (5 lb 6 oz)
Minimum range: 75 m (245 ft)
Maximum range: 1000 m (1100 yd)
Armour penetration: 600 mm (24 in)

Assessment
Reliability ★★★
Accuracy ★★
Age ★★★
Worldwide users ★★★

The M47 Dragon can be fired by one man: the large cap at the back blows off while the tube remains on the firer's shoulder. Dragon has only half the range of MILAN and is due to be replaced.

AT-3 'Sagger'

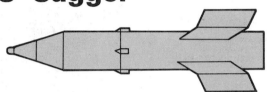

'Sagger' is the NATO reference name for this Russian anti-tank guided missile, which is used as an infantry weapon and mounted on vehicles and helicopters. Thanks to 'Sagger' Egyptian infantry inflicted a surprise defeat on the Israeli armoured corps in the first days of the 1973 Arab-Israeli war. Early 'Saggers' were manually controlled but, during the late 1970s, the Russians introduced a version with semi-automatic guidance. Between its minimum range of 300 metres and about 1 kilometre, it is guided to the target by eye. At longer ranges, the operator uses the x10 magnification optical sight.

Specification
Missile weight: 11.3 kg (24 lb 15 oz)
Launcher weight: not applicable
Warhead: 3 kg (6 lb 10 oz) HEAT
Minimum range: 300 m (328 yd)
Maximum range: 3000 m (3280 yd)
Armour penetration: 410+ mm (16+ in)

Assessment
Reliability ★★
Accuracy ★★
Age ★★★
Worldwide users ★★★★

Seen here mounted above the main armament of a BMP infantry fighting vehicle, 'Sagger' made an enormous impact in 1973 when Egyptian soldiers inflicted a surprise defeat on the Israeli armoured forces.

AT-4 'Spigot'

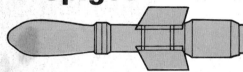

Introduced in the 1980s, the AT-4 'Spigot' is a Russian man-portable system that has also been fitted to vehicles. Its similarity to MILAN may be due to technology stolen from Euromissile. It is a little smaller than MILAN but details about its performance are only just emerging now that East German weapons are in the hands of the unified German army. It is a major advance over the old manual command weapons like 'Sagger', but it is known to have been supplemented from the mid-1980s by an even better missile. The latter has the NATO codename 'Saxhorn' but performance details are not available.

Specification
Missile weight: 10–12 kg (22–26 lb) (estimated)
Launcher weight: 40 kg (88 lb 3 oz) approx. (including missile)
Warhead: HEAT (slightly heavier than MILAN)
Minimum range: unknown
Maximum range: 2000 m (2190 yd) (approx.)
Armour penetration: at least 500 mm (20 in), possibly 850 mm (31 in) or more

Assessment
Reliability ★★★
Accuracy ★★★★
Age ★★
Worldwide users ★★

'Spigot' is the Russian equivalent of MILAN, seen here in service with the late, unlamented East German army. The soldiers are wearing Russian-type padded helmets.

ADATS

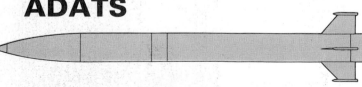

The dual-purpose Air-Defence Anti-Tank System, or ADATS, is a joint development by Oerlikon of Switzerland and Martin Marietta of the USA. Designed to engage fast-moving airborne targets as well as tanks, ADATS is much larger and faster than dedicated anti-tank weapons. It also has a much longer range, although terrain features usually restrict this advantage. The Mach 3 missile has impact and proximity fuses and is laser-guided. The launch system is equipped with surveillance radar, FLIR (Forward-Looking Infra-Red), low-light TV and a laser rangefinder. ADATS is primarily intended as an anti-aircraft weapon, with the anti-tank capability very much a secondary role. It can be mounted on the M113A2 armoured personnel carrier as shown here, or on the MOWAG Shark 8×8 or even the Bradley M3 Cavalry Fighting Vehicle.

Specification
Missile weight: 51 kg (112 lb 7 oz)
Launcher weight: not known
Warhead: dual-purpose 12 kg (26 lb) + HE
Minimum range: 500 m (550 yd)
Maximum range: 6000 m (6570 yd) (ground); 8000 m (8750 yd) (air)
Armour penetration: 900+ mm (35+ in)

Assessment
Reliability ★★★★
Accuracy ★★★★★
Age ★
Worldwide users ★

ADATS blasts off from the octuple launcher on an M113 armoured personnel carrier. This unusual missile is capable of engaging either tanks or aircraft.

ANTI-TANK GUIDED MISSILES

HEAT warheads were developed during World War II, but their ability to penetrate armour has increased considerably since 1945. Modern weapons such as the LAW 80 can penetrate over 600 mm of steel armour plate, making them a serious threat to all armoured vehicles.

Bantam

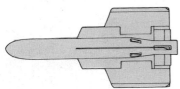

The Bofors Bantam is a man-portable first-generation anti-tank guided missile purchased by the armies of Switzerland and Sweden in the 1960s. The missile is supplied in a container with a 20-metre control cable that is connected to a control unit. Each control unit can take up to three missiles, although by using distribution boxes this total can be increased to 18. The missile is manually guided to the target; bright flares burn in its tail to help the operator see where it is going. One of the smallest and lightest of early ATGMs, the Bantam was well-suited to helicopter operations.

Specification
Missile weight: unknown
Launcher weight: 11.5 kg (25 lb)
Warhead: unknown
Minimum range: 300 m (330 yd)
Maximum range: 2000 m (2190 yd)
Armour penetration: 500 mm (20 in)

Assessment
Reliability   ★★★
Accuracy   ★★
Age   ★★★★
Worldwide users   ★

The Bofors Bantam was one of the first man-portable anti-tank guided missiles to enter service. A single launcher unit could be wired up to 18 missiles, although they had to be fired one at a time.

AT-1 'Snapper'

The AT-1 'Snapper' was the first anti-tank missile to enter service with the Red Army. The designation and reporting name are both NATO terms; the Soviets are believed to have described it as the 3M6 missile. Suspiciously similar to the French SS-10, the AT-1 has the same general layout and is manually guided to the target. Any disturbance to the operator's concentration is likely to cause the AT-1 to miss. It has seen limited action, mainly in the Middle East, where it made an undistinguished contribution to the Arab effort in the 1967 Six-Day War. The AT-1 was replaced by 'Swatter' and 'Sagger' and is probably no longer in service anywhere today.

Specification
Missile weight: 22.25 kg (49 lb)
Launcher weight: not applicable
Warhead: 5.25 kg (11 lb 9 oz)
Minimum range: 400 m (440 yd)
Maximum range: 2700 m (2950 yd)
Armour penetration: 1350 mm (53 in)

Assessment
Reliability   ★★
Accuracy   ★★
Age   ★★★★★
Worldwide users   ★★★

AT-1 'Snapper' missiles on a BRDM armoured car. These manually-guided weapons were able to knock out most tanks, but their accuracy was poor, especially if the target fired back.

LAW 80

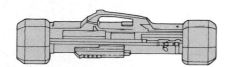

LAW 80 is a one-shot disposable rocket launcher adopted by the British Army during the late 1980s. One metre long and weighing 10 kilograms, it is just possible for riflemen to carry in addition to their standard kit. The dimensions are dictated by the need to carry a large enough warhead to threaten modern tanks. The 1960s American LAW, used by British soldiers in the Falklands to attack enemy bunkers, fires a 66-mm rocket that is ineffective against MBTs. LAW 80 has a 94-mm rocket capable of destroying most likely targets. It has an integral spotting rifle that fires tracer rounds, enabling the operator to correct his aim before letting go with the main round. Straightforward to operate and highly reliable, the LAW 80 is an essential addition to the infantry soldier's armoury.

Specification
Missile weight: unknown
Launcher weight: 10 kg (22 lb 1 oz)
Warhead: unknown
Minimum range: 20 m (65 ft)
Maximum range: 500 m (550 yd)
Armour penetration: 600+ mm (24+ in)

Assessment
Reliability   ★★★★
Accuracy   ★★★★
Age   ★
Worldwide users   ★

LAW 80 is 1.5 metres long when extended for firing. It is the largest size practical for an infantryman to carry and it incorporates a spotting rifle to assist in aiming it.

SPG-9

Specification
Missile weight: 1.3 kg
(2 lb 14 oz)
Launcher weight: 60 kg
(132 lb 4 oz)
Warhead: HEAT or HE
Minimum range: 50 m
(164 ft)
Maximum range:
1960 m (2140 yd)
Armour penetration:
400 mm (16 in)

Assessment
Reliability   ★★★★★
Accuracy   ★★
Age   ★★★
Worldwide users   ★★★★

Lebanese militiamen load a 73-mm round into an SPG-9 recoilless rifle. The pop-out fins that stabilise the missile in flight are clearly visible.

The SPG-9 is a lightweight recoilless anti-tank gun widely used in the former Soviet army and supplied to Warsaw Pact forces, including Bulgaria, East Germany, Hungary and Poland. Operated by a two-man crew, its 73-mm fin-stabilised rounds are rocket-assisted and have a muzzle velocity of over 700 metres per second. Otherwise very similar in performance to the 73-mm gun fitted to BMP and BMD infantry fighting vehicles, the SPG-9 is mounted on a light tripod and is normally carried inside a vehicle. Introduced in 1969 to replace the B-10 and B-11 recoilless rifles, it has seen action in Afghanistan. The anti-tank platoon of each Soviet Motor Rifle battalion was equipped with two SPG-9s.

3.5-in M20 rocket launcher

Specification
Missile weight: 4 kg
(2 lb 14 oz)
Launcher weight: 5.9 kg
(8 lb 13 oz)
Warhead: 0.87 kg
(1 lb 15 oz)
Minimum range: 20 m
(65 ft)
Maximum range: 100 m
(328 ft)
Armour penetration:
250 mm (10 in)

Assessment
Reliability   ★★★★
Accuracy   ★
Age   ★★★★★
Worldwide users   ★★★★

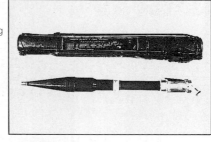

US soldiers in Korea fire a 3.5-in rocket launcher at night. Note the conspicuous launch signature that immediately betrays their position to the enemy.

The US 3.5-in rocket launcher was widely known as the 'super bazooka', as it replaced the 2.36-in Bazooka of World War II fame. Adopted after World War II by many NATO armies, it has been superseded in most major armies but remains in use elsewhere. Versions of the M20 were still being manufactured until recently in Austria and Spain. The launcher itself is little more than an aluminium tube with a firing mechanism – magneto or two AA batteries in more modern versions – that launches fin-stabilised rockets at the modest velocity of 160 metres per second. Very simple to use, the M20 is handicapped by its short range and limited armour penetration. Since its introduction, HEAT warheads have been much improved and its performance is poor by comparison.

RPG-18

Specification
Missile weight: 1.4 kg
(3 lb 1 oz)
Launcher weight: 2.7 kg
(5 lb 15 oz)
Warhead: unknown
Minimum range: 20 m
(65 ft)
Maximum range: 200 m
(656 ft)
Armour penetration:
375 mm (15 in)

Assessment
Reliability   ★★★
Accuracy   ★★
Age   ★
Worldwide users   ★★★

An RPG-18 in carrying position with a missile below it. This is the Russian equivalent of the 66-mm LAW used by many NATO armies since the 1970s.

The RPG-18 is the Russian equivalent of the US M72 LAW and follows the same format. It is a one-shot disposable weapon – an extendable tube with pop-up sights and cartoon instructions painted on the side. It fires a 64-mm calibre shaped charge, compared with the 66-mm warhead of the old US weapon. Effective enough against APCs and light vehicles, it does not have sufficient penetration to knock out the latest generation of Western – or even Russian – tanks. Several Warsaw Pact countries had begun to manufacture the RPG-18 by the time the alliance disintegrated at the end of the 1980s.

106-mm M40 recoilless rifle

Specification
Missile weight: 16.9 kg
(37 lb 4 oz)
Launcher weight:
209 kg (460 lb)
Warhead: 7.9 kg
(17 lb 7 oz)
Minimum range: 20 m
(65 ft)
Maximum range:
1100 m (1200 yd)
Armour penetration:
400 mm (16 in)

Assessment
Reliability   ★★★★★
Accuracy   ★★★
Age   ★★★★★
Worldwide users   ★★★★★

Austrian troops prepare to fire a 106-mm recoilless rifle. The widely-used US M40 is the most successful design of its type and is likely to remain in service for many years to come.

Entering service in the 1950s, the US M40 106-mm recoilless rifle is the most successful weapon of its type. Adopted by over 30 armies and still widely encountered today, the 106-mm recoilless rifle was the first to be fitted with a spotting rifle. By firing a few shots with this, the operator can adjust his aim ready for the main round, greatly improving his chance of hitting the target. The 'wheelbarrow'-like mounting can be manoeuvred on the ground or clamped to a vehicle – typically a jeep. The HEAT round is supplemented by a HEP (High-Explosive Plastic) round, similar to the British HESH ammunition, plus a specialised anti-personnel round widely used in Vietnam. Spain and Austria both manufacture very similar weapons.

ANTI-TANK WEAPONS

Anti-tank weapons come in a range of sizes and capabilities, from the simplest of launchers to sophisticated guided missiles, with high speed, great accuracy, and warheads that are large enough to smash through almost any known tank armour.

MBB Cobra

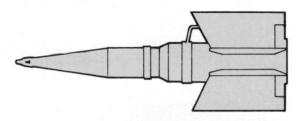

This German missile is typical of the first generation of anti-tank guided weapons which are now obsolete. The missile is placed on the ground, pointing towards the target; up to eight can be connected to the same control box. On firing, the missile is boosted vertically into the air, then its own sustainer cuts in to propel it towards the target. The operator controls it with a joystick on his control box connected to the missile by a wire. It requires considerable concentration to control the rapidly moving missile and steer it onto the target, and if the operator comes under enemy fire he is unlikely to score a hit.

Specification
Missile weight: 10.3 kg (22 lb 11 oz) at launch
Launcher weight: not applicable
Warhead: 7 kg (15 lb 7 oz) shaped-charge HE
Minimum range: 400 m (440 ft)
Maximum range: 2000 m (2190 yd)
Armour penetration: 500 mm (20 in)

Assessment
Reliability ★★
Accuracy ★★
Age ★★★★★
Worldwide users ★★★★

The MBB Cobra is command-guided, meaning that the operator has to 'fly' the missile all the way to the target, using a joystick to send commands to the missile. A first generation missile, the Cobra was exported to at least a dozen countries. More than 170,000 were manufactured.

Bofors BILL

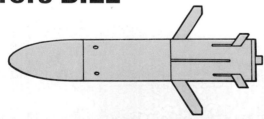

Properly known as the Bofors RBS-56, BILL means 'Bofors, Infantry, Light and Lethal'. BILL is programmed to fly exactly one metre above the sight line and across the top of the tank. A proximity fuse detects the target electronically and automatically fires the warhead when it is within lethal range. The explosive jet shoots down through the thin roof of the tank, with devastating effect on the interior. BILL is in use by the Swedish army and a number were purchased by the US Army for evaluation. BILL has a maximum range of 2000 metres.

Specification
Missile weight: 16 kg (35 lb 4 oz)
Launcher weight: 27 kg (59 lb 8 oz)
Warhead: shaped-charge pointing downwards
Minimum range: 150 m (490 ft)
Maximum range: 2000 m (2190 yd)
Armour penetration: classified

Assessment
Reliability ★★★★
Accuracy ★★★★
Age ★
Worldwide users ★

The BILL is a very effective missile, with its unique top-attack capability, but it requires a four-man team to support it adequately in the field. This is why the US Army has not adopted the weapon, even though it out-performed the Dragon 2 in trials.

Swingfire

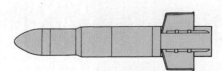

Swingfire is the British equivalent of TOW. It utilises a similar guidance system, allied to an even larger warhead capable of penetrating all current armour types. First entering service in 1969, Swingfire is mounted on the Striker armoured vehicles of the British and Belgian armies. A palletised version is built under licence in Egypt, which can be mounted on any vehicle or trainer of Land Rover size or larger. In separated fire mode the operator's sight can be connected to the launcher by a separation cable up to 100 metres in length.

Specification
Missile weight: 27 kg (59 lb 8 oz)
Launcher box weight: 10 kg (22 lb)
Warhead: 7 kg (15 lb 7 oz) hollow-charge HE
Minimum range: 150 m (490 ft)
Maximum range: 4000 m (4370 yd)
Armour penetration: 800+ mm (31+ in)

Assessment
Reliability ★★★
Accuracy ★★★★
Age ★★★
Worldwide users ★★

Introduced in 1969, Swingfire was a match for any known tank. Although still a powerful missile, it is hampered by being command-guided, requiring a skilled operator to 'fly' the missile using a joystick.

40-mm RPG-7

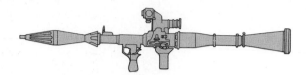

Specification
Launcher weight: 7.9 kg (17 lb 7 oz)
Round weight: 2.25 kg (5 lb)
Muzzle velocity: 120 m (394 ft) per second
Maximum velocity: 300 m (984 ft) per second
Effective range: 300 m (328 yd)
Armour penetration: 330 mm (13 in)

Assessment
Reliability ★★★
Accuracy ★★
Age ★★★★★
Worldwide users ★★★★★

The RPG-7 was evolved from the RPG-2, which was itself inspired by the German Panzerfaust of World War II. Not really effective against the latest MBTs, it remains useful against lighter armour.

Firing a muzzle-loaded 85-mm (in the standard PG-7 version) grenade, the RPG-7 will be seen in trouble spots around the world for many years to come. It has been produced in Russia, China and a number of licensed and unlicensed Third World nations. Both sides in the Iran–Iraq war used RPG-7s. Ironically, RPG-s have been used more often against Communist forces – in Afghanistan, Nicaragua and Angola – than by them.

84-mm M2 Carl Gustav

Specification
Launcher weight: 14.2 kg (31 lb 5 oz)
Round weight: 1.7 kg (3 lb 12 oz)
Muzzle velocity: 310 m (1017 ft) per second
Maximum velocity: 310 m (1017 ft) per second
Effective range: 450 m (492 yd)
Armour penetration: 450 mm (18 in)

Assessment
Reliability ★★★★
Accuracy ★★★
Age ★★★★★
Worldwide users ★★★★

Until recently the standard medium anti-armour weapon of the British Army, the Swedish-built Carl Gustav recoilless gun is one of the world's most widely-used anti-tank weapons.

This Swedish-designed recoilless rifle remains in service worldwide, and was until recently the British Army's standard section medium anti-tank weapon. Unlike the US Army, which uses the M47 Dragon anti-tank guided missile as its medium anti-tank weapon, many armies have continued to keep an unguided anti-tank weapon with the fighting troops. It has a higher potential rate of fire than the RPG-7.

82-mm B-300

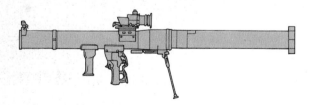

Specification
Launcher weight: 3.5 kg (7 lb 11 oz)
Round weight: 4.5 kg (9 lb 15 oz)
Muzzle velocity: 280 m (918 ft) per second
Maximum velocity: over 280 m (918 ft) per second
Effective range: 400 m (440 yd)
Armour penetration: 400+ mm (16+ in)

Assessment
Reliability ★★★★
Accuracy ★★★
Age ★★
Worldwide users ★★

As with all light anti-tank weapons, the B-300 is small enough and handy enough to be carried and operated by one man. It has an effective range of about 400 metres.

Developed from the RPG-7 and the French LRAC 89, this Israeli system's innovation is that it consists of two parts: a re-usable sight and a gripstock connected to the muzzle, to which the rounds, packed in the disposable tubes that include the breech, are inserted before firing. It fires rocket-powered fin-stabilised rounds. The B-300 has been ordered by the US Marine Corps as an anti-bunker and anti-tank weapon.

120-mm SEP DARD 120

Specification
Launcher weight: 4.5 kg (9 lb 15 oz)
Round weight: 8.9 kg (19 lb 10 oz)
Muzzle velocity: 280 m (918 ft) per second
Maximum velocity: 280 m (918 ft) per second
Effective range: 600 m (655 yd)
Armour penetration: 500+ mm (20+ in)

Assessment
Reliability ★★★★
Accuracy ★★★★
Age ★
Worldwide users ★

The larger the calibre of a shaped-charge warhead, the better is its armour-piercing capability. No heavier than the Carl Gustav, the French DARD 120 has a 50 per cent larger warhead, and much greater tank-killing power.

Developed by the French, the DARD 120 is the 'big game hunter's' choice among modern man-portable unguided anti-armour systems. Its calibre – larger than that of any other of these weapons – is intended to give it a better chance of killing a modern Main Battle Tank from the front. Probably neither a Carl Gustav, an RPG-7, nor an RPG-16 can knock out a modern tank from the front, but the DARD can penetrate the NATO Heavy Triple Target. Like the B-300, it consists of a re-usable sight and gripstock.

SURFACE-TO-AIR MISSILES

Surface-to-air missiles are used by armies to defend themselves against fixed-wing aircraft and helicopters. All major armies, except the British, complement their SAMs with anti-aircraft cannon designed to destroy aircraft that attack at very low level where SAMs are least effective.

Rapier

The Rapier low-level surface-to-air radio command to line-of-sight missile system has been in service for many years, development beginning as a private venture in the early 1960s, with the first production models being delivered to the British Army in the early 1970s. Rapier's performance and ECCM capabilities have been updated to meet new aircraft threats, and the Rapier 2000 will take the British Army into the 21st century. Rapier was initially only available in a towed version, but the self-propelled Tracked Rapier was introduced to give British Army formations their own integral air defence capability.

Specification
Guidance: optical or radar CLOS
Weight: 42.6 kg (93 lb 15 oz)
Length: 2.24 m (7 ft 4 in)
Span: 0.381 m (15 in)
Speed: Mach 2
Operating altitude: very low to +3000 m (9840 ft)
Operating range: 400–7000 m (440 yd–4 miles)

Assessment
Mobility ★★★★
Accuracy ★★★★
Age ★★★
Worldwide users ★★★★★

Fast reaction time and the ability to score direct hits make the British Rapier a formidably effective system.

RBS-70

The RBS-70 laser-beam-riding guided surface-to-air missile was developed by the Swedish armaments company Bofors. It is a very small missile which can be broken down into three sections and which is easily man-portable. It is also produced as a vehicle-mounted system, and has been successfully tested on light 4×4 vehicles such as the Land Rover. The latest version, the RBS-70 ARMAD, is a three-man armoured turret which is equipped with a surveillance radar and all the fire-control systems necessary for a successful engagement.

Specification
Guidance: laser-beam-riding
Weight: 24 kg (53 lb)
Length: 0.42 m (16 in)
Span: 0.106 m (4 in)
Speed: Mach 1
Operating altitude: 3000 m (9840 ft)
Operating range: 5000 m (3 miles)

Assessment
Mobility ★★★★★
Accuracy ★★★
Age ★★★★
Worldwide users ★★★

The Swedish RBS-70 system is a laser-beam-riding missile which is man-portable.

SA-8 'Gecko'

The SA-8 'Gecko' low- to medium-level surface-to-air missile was first deployed with Russian army divisions in the early 1970s. It is a completely self-contained system, mounted on a 6x6 amphibious vehicle, which is equipped with its own tracking and surveillance radars. In operation, however, SA-8 batteries are usually controlled by external height-finding and surveillance radars. Larger than the British Rapier system, the SA-8 was superseded in the 1980s by the improved SA-8B, which is a slightly larger missile with improved speed, range and electronics.

Specification
Guidance: semi-active radar or IR homing
Weight: 170 kg (375 lb)
Length: 3.1 m (10 ft)
Span: 1.64 m (5 ft 5 in)
Speed: Mach 2
Operating altitude: 10–13,000 m (33–42,650 ft)
Operating range: 1600–12,000 m (1–7 miles)

Assessment
Mobility ★★★★
Accuracy ★★★
Age ★★★★
Worldwide users ★★★★★

The SA-8 has been in service with the Russian army for nearly 20 years. The amphibious vehicle it is mounted on is based on a cross-country truck chassis.

SA-9 'Gaskin'

The SA-9 'Gaskin' seems to have been developed at about the same time as the larger SA-8, first being seen in public during the 1970s. Deployed at regimental level with the Russian army, the SA-9 is a short-range weapon that has been exported to more than 25 countries. The 'Gaskin' was at first thought to have been a vehicle-launched version of the man-portable SA-7 'Grail', but it is in fact a larger, faster missile with greater range and altitude performance. The SA-9 has been supplemented by the similar but slightly larger SA-13 'Gopher', which is mounted on a tracked chassis.

Specification
Guidance: IR homing
Weight: c.30 kg (c.66 lb)
Length: 1.8 m (5 ft 11 in)
Span: 0.30 m (12 in) approx.
Speed: Mach 1.5+
Operating altitude: c.4000 m (c.13,100 ft)
Operating range: c.8000 m (c.5 miles)

Assessment
Mobility   ★★★★
Accuracy   ★★★
Age   ★★★★
Worldwide users ★★★★★

The SA-9 has been widely exported to Soviet allies, and is deployed to regimental air defence companies within the Soviet forces.

M48A1 Chaparral

The Chaparral is a surface-to-air heat-seeking missile developed in the 1960s to meet a US Army requirement for a low-level air defence system. Chaparral was evolved from the AIM-9D variant of the well-tried Sidewinder air-to-air missile. It is optically sighted, with the latest variant incorporating a thermal imager to give the formerly clear-weather-only system some night and poor weather capability. The US Army bought some 500 systems, operating them in composite battalions with M163 Vulcan anti-aircraft guns. Chaparral has seen some combat use with the Israelis in 1973 and 1982.

Specification
Guidance: IR homing
Weight: 86.2 kg (190 lb)
Length: 2.9 m (9 ft 6 in)
Span: 0.64 m (25 in)
Speed: Mach 1+
Operating altitude: 50–3000 m (164–9840 ft)
Operating range: 6000 m (4 miles)

Assessment
Mobility   ★★★★
Accuracy   ★★★
Age   ★★★
Worldwide users ★★★

Chaparral fires a heat-seeking missile which automatically homes in on the target. It was first used in action by the Israelis during the 1973 Yom Kippur War.

Crotale

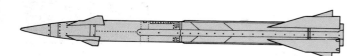

Development of the Crotale missile system began in France in the mid-1960s. Designed for all-weather interception of low-level targets, Crotale can be mounted on trailers, wheeled vehicles, tracked vehicles, and on ships. A typical system will consist of an acquisition and co-ordination unit linked to two or three fire units. A more advanced version mounted on an AMX-30 tracked chassis was sold to Saudi Arabia as the Shahine system. The Crotale missile is larger than the British Rapier, but smaller than the Soviet 'Gecko'. It has been sold to a dozen countries, in addition to being in service with both the French army and the French navy.

Specification
Guidance: radar/IR
Weight: 85 kg (187 lb)
Length: 2.89 m (9 ft 6 in)
Span: 0.54 m (21 in)
Speed: Mach 2.3
Operating altitude: 15–5000 m (50–16,400 ft)
Operating range: 500–10,000 m (550yd–6 miles)

Assessment
Mobility   ★★★
Accuracy   ★★★
Age   ★★★★★
Worldwide users ★★★★

The French Crotale missile has a focused splintering warhead detonated by an infra-red proximity fuse. Several missile units are usually linked to a target acquisition vehicle.

Roland

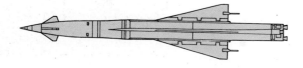

Roland was developed by Euromissile, a joint development by France and Germany. It is a low- to medium-altitude system available in all-weather and clear-weather variants. From the start the Roland system was designed to be incorporated into a variety of launch vehicles. In German service it has been fitted to Marder infantry fighting vehicles and MAN eight-wheel trucks. France mounts Roland on an AMX-30 tank chassis. Since its first delivery in the late 1970s, Roland has been sold to about a dozen countries.

Specification
Guidance: optical radar
Weight: 66.5 kg (146 lb 10 oz)
Length: 2.4 m (7 ft 11 in)
Span: 0.5 m (20 in)
Speed: Mach 1.6+
Operating altitude: 120–3000 m (395–9840 ft)
Operating range: 500–6300 m (550yd–4 miles)

Assessment
Mobility   ★★★★
Accuracy   ★★★★
Age   ★★
Worldwide users ★★★★

The German army's Roland SAMs are mounted on a Marder armoured personnel carrier chassis. French Rolands are carried on a modified AMX-30 tank hull.

SURFACE-TO-AIR MISSILES

Surface-to-air missiles are a post-World War II phenomenon, first becoming operational in the 1950s. They were often huge pieces of high performance machinery, and some have remained in service for more than three decades.

SA-1 'Guild'

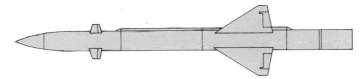

Although not seen until the Revolution Day parade in 1960, the SA-1 entered service in 1954. Development must have started immediately after World War II. It is a large, liquid-propelled missile, with a range initially estimated at about 30 kilometres, though later assessments were to increase that figure to at least 50 kilometres. 'Guild' was radio-command guided by an immensely powerful radar known as 'Yo-Yo', which was reportedly able to track up to 30 targets at once. Hundreds of batteries were deployed in the 1960s, but the numbers gradually declined as more modern weapons entered service.

Specification
Guidance: radio-command or semi-active radar homing
Weight: 3200 kg (3 tons 336 lb)
Length: 12 m (40 ft)
Span: 2.8 m (9 ft 2 in)
Speed: Mach 2+ (estimate)
Operating altitude: maximum more than 15,000 m (49,200 ft)
Operating range: up to 50 km (31 miles)
Warhead: high explosive

Assessment
Mobility	★
Accuracy	★★
Age	★★★★★
Worldwide users	★

SA-1 'Guild' missiles parade through Red Square. It was ceremonial occasions such as the anniversary of the October Revolution which often gave Westerners their first view of such weapons, usually several years after their entry into service.

SA-2 'Guideline'

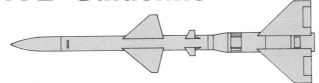

Unlike the SA-1, the SA-2 'Guideline' seems to have been intended from the outset to be a mobile system, although as such it is very bulky. It is liquid-fuelled, but has a solid booster rocket. The SA-2 first entered service in 1956 as a bomber destroyer, being designed to engage fast, high-flying targets. Just how high was not known until 1960, when an SA-2 brought down the CIA U-2 flown by Gary Powers. This single incident more than any other forced the change in tactics which brought modern warplanes down to treetop height. SA-2s brought down five more U-2s over China and Cuba. The missile was used in anger during the Indo-Pakistan War of 1965, in the Six Day War, in Vietnam and during the Yom Kippur War. By the end of that time, attacking aircraft had the SA-2's measure, and it was not particularly successful. It nevertheless remains in service in 20 countries, and a copy is built in China.

Specification
Guidance: radio-command or semi-active radar homing
Weight: 2300 kg (2 tons 590 lb)
Length: 10.8 m (35 ft 5 in)
Span: 1.7 m (5 ft 8 in) (missile) 2.2 m (7 ft 3 in) (booster)
Speed: Mach 3.5
Operating altitude: maximum 28,000 m (92,000 ft)
Operating range: 50 km (31 miles)
Warhead: 130 kg (287 lb) HE with proximity fuse

Assessment
Mobility	★★
Accuracy	★★
Age	★★★★★
Worldwide users	★★★★★

Although the SA-2 'Guideline' was supposed to be a mobile system, the entire launch unit (including radar, launcher, missiles, fuelling units, and the like) weighed in at more than 100 tons, and required a fair-sized convoy to move anywhere.

SA-3 'Goa'

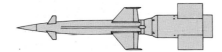

Essentially a medium altitude complement to the 'Guideline', the solid-fuelled SA-3 'Goa' is of the same generation. Considerably smaller than the SA-2, 'Goa' is much more manoeuvrable. Although technically a mobile system, being mounted in pairs on rails towed behind ZIL-157 tractors, 'Goa' is somewhat cumbersome. However, it remains a reasonably effective missile, so ex-army mobile systems have largely been transferred to the air forces of their users, primarily for short-range airfield defence. The SA-3 was first used in combat during the Middle East's 'War of Attrition' in the early 1970s but without much success, since countermeasures developed against the SA-2 also worked against the SA-3. It was nevertheless the most numerous Arab SAM during the 1973 Yom Kippur War. 'Goa' was widely exported to Soviet client states, and it remains in service with about 24 countries.

Specification
Guidance: radio-command
Weight: 636 kg (1380 lb)
Length: 6.7 m (22 ft)
Span: 1.2 m (3 ft 11 in) (missile) 1.5 m (4 ft 11 in) (booster)
Speed: Mach 3.5
Operating altitude: 1500–13,000 m (4900–42,640 ft)
Operating range: 30 km (19 miles)
Warhead: 60 kg (132 lb) HE with proximity fuse

Assessment
Mobility	★★
Accuracy	★★
Age	★★★★★
Worldwide users	★★★★★

Originally mounted in pairs on a mobile launcher, the SA-3 'Goa' is now a fixed missile, usually guarding airbases. It is often seen on triple or even quadruple mounts, as seen on this Finnish example.

SA-4 'Ganef'

Contemporary with the SA-2 and SA-3, the SA-4 'Ganef' was first seen during a Red Square parade in 1964. Known as 'Krug' to its former operators in the Soviet army, the SA-4 is a fully mobile system with two missiles carried on a tracked transporter-erector-launcher. 'Ganef' is very different to the preceding missiles. It is launched by four strap-on solid rocket boosters, which fall away once the main ramjet sustainer motor ignites. Sensors associated with the SA-4 include the 'Long Track' surveillance radar, 'Thin Skin' height-finding radar and 'Pat Hand' fire-control and command-guidance radar. 'Ganef' is radio-command guided for the first part of its flight, with semi-active homing for the terminal stage. SA-4 is an army-level air-defence system, which is in service with some former Warsaw Pact nations and with Libya.

Specification
Guidance: radio-command with terminal semi-active radar homing
Weight: 2400 kg (2 tons 806 lb)
Length: 8.8 m (28 ft 10 in)
Span: 2.3 m (7 ft 7 in) (wing) 2.6 m (8 ft 6 in) (tail)
Speed: Mach 2.5
Operating altitude: 1100–24,000 m (3600–78,700 ft)
Operating range: 70+ km (43+ miles)
Warhead: 135 kg (298 lb) HE with proximity fuse

Assessment
Mobility   ★★★
Accuracy   ★★
Age   ★★★★★
Worldwide users ★★★

The large SA-4 was classed as a medium-range system by the Soviet army. In the Warsaw Pact days the 'Ganef' was an army-level asset, and although it is a hefty piece of equipment it is fully mobile.

Bloodhound

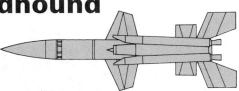

Development of the Bloodhound surface-to-air missile began in the late 1940s, with the first production examples being delivered in 1958. Further development resulted in the much improved Bloodhound Mk 2, which entered service with the Royal Air Force in 1964. It was to remain in service for a quarter of a century, and was exported to Singapore, Switzerland and Sweden. Bloodhound is similar in performance and operation to the contemporary Soviet SA-4, although the British missile is faster and has a longer range. Targets are detected by a surveillance radar system which passes information to a target illumination radar. The missile is launched by four strap-on solid propellant boosters, which take the missile to supersonic speed. Propulsion is then provided by two ramjets which accelerate the missile to Mach 3.5. The missile is guided by homing in on radar reflections off the target.

Specification
Guidance: semi-active radar homing
Weight: 2300 kg (2 tons 590 lb)
Length: 7.75 m (25 ft 5 in)
Span: 2.83 m (9 ft 4 in)
Speed: Mach 3+
Operating altitude: 100–23,000 m (330–75,400 ft)
Operating range: 80+ km (50+ miles)
Warhead: HE with proximity fuse

Assessment
Mobility   ★
Accuracy   ★★★
Age   ★★★★★
Worldwide users ★★

Similar in size and performance to the contemporary Soviet SA-4, the British Bloodhound differed in that it was a non-mobile system. Its main deployment was in the protection of RAF airfields.

Nike Hercules

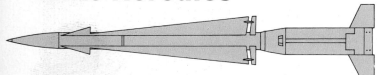

Nike Ajax was the world's first operational guided SAM. A slender, elegant missile, it went into service outside Washington DC in December 1953. It required massive fixed-firing facilities, however, and even before it was deployed it was recognised that it would not be effective for long. Nike Hercules was a far superior missile that could be grafted onto Ajax sites, using Ajax radars and fire-control systems. It began to enter service in 1958 and had phenomenal performance. In trials in 1960, one Nike Hercules proved able to intercept incoming Corporal ballistic missiles, and in a spectacular feat, one Hercules intercepted another some 50 kilometres from the launch site, at an altitude of 30000 metres and with closing speeds in excess of Mach 7. By 1963, 134 batteries were operational. Nike Hercules systems were exported to eight NATO countries, as well as Taiwan, Japan and Korea.

Specification
Guidance: radio-command
Weight: 4850 kg (4 tons 1725 lb)
Length: 12.5 m (41 ft)
Span: 1.88 m (6 ft 2 in)
Speed: Mach 3.7
Operating altitude: maximum 45,000 m (148,000 ft)
Operating range: 140+ km (87+ miles)
Warhead: HE or (US versions only) nuclear

Assessment
Mobility   ★
Accuracy   ★★★★★
Age   ★★★★★
Worldwide users ★★★

Very large and of extremely long range, the Nike Hercules was one of the first missiles to have the accuracy and performance to be able to intercept other missiles.

HAWK

The HAWK missile was developed in the 1950s, the first guided launch taking place in June 1956. The name is an acronym standing for Homing All the Way Killer, and as it implies, the missile utilises semi-active radar homing from the moment of launch. It entered service in 1960, and since that time it has been acquired by another 21 nations around the world. Since its first introduction, HAWK has been continually upgraded. Its first combat use was in 1973 when Israeli missiles were credited with destroying some 20 Egyptian and Syrian aircraft. The MIM-23B Improved HAWK currently in service is the same basic missile as that which first flew over 35 years ago, but its guidance and fire-control systems have changed out of all recognition. Improved HAWK has a new, continuous wave acquisition radar, a high-powered illuminator radar, a passive tracking adjunct system which allows for long-range optical engagements, and a highly computerised battery-control system which enables the system to be used against multiple targets at low level.

Specification
Guidance: semi-active radar homing
Weight: 626 kg (1380 lb)
Length: 5.12 m (16 ft 9 in)
Span: 1.22 m (4 ft)
Speed: Mach 2.5
Operating altitude: 30–16,000 m (98–52,500 ft)
Operating range: 40 km (25 miles)
Warhead: 330 kg (727 lb) HE with radio-proximity and impact fuse

Assessment
Mobility   ★★★
Accuracy   ★★★
Age   ★★★★★
Worldwide users ★★★★★

The HAWK missile remains in front-line service, more than 35 years after its first flight. During that time the HAWK's guidance and fire-control systems have been continually upgraded to enable the weapon to deal with new threats.

SURFACE-TO-AIR MISSILES

Since the 1960s aircraft have carried electronic warfare equipment designed to defeat radar-guided surface-to-air missiles. The electronic advantage has swung back and forth ever since; sometimes the aircraft can jam everything fired at them, on other occasions they have suffered terrible losses.

SA-6 'Gainful'

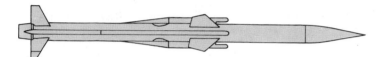

Specification
Guidance: semi-active radar homing
Weight: 550 kg (1212 lb)
Length: 6.2 m (20 ft 4 in)
Span: 1.52 m (4 ft 11 in)
Speed: Mach 2.8
Operating altitude: 100–9000 m (328–29,500 ft)
Operating range: 22–30 km (14–19 miles)
Warhead: c.80 kg (c.176 lb)

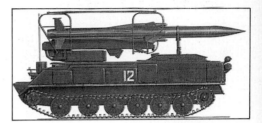

The SA-6 missile came as a disagreeable surprise to the Israeli air force in the opening battles of the 1973 Arab-Israeli war. Supplied in large quantities to Syria and Egypt, it had been regarded as no more effective than other Russian missiles known to the West. But Israeli ECM had no effect on the SA-6 batteries and their fighter-bombers suffered grave losses. The SA-6 has been exported to most Russian client states and allies since the late 1960s, and is still widely encountered today. It is fired from tracked launcher vehicles based on the chassis of the ZSU-23-4 self-propelled anti-aircraft gun.

Assessment
Mobility ★★★★★
Accuracy ★★★
Age ★★★★
Worldwide users ★★★★★

The tracked launcher vehicle carries three SA-6 missiles. The SA-6 was a significant improvement over SA-2 and SA-3, although US forces soon developed countermeasures.

SA-10 'Grumble'

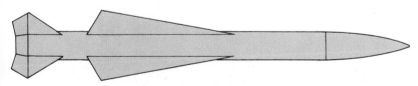

Specification
Guidance: unknown
Weight: c.1500 kg (1 ton 1075 lb)
Length: 7 m (23 ft)
Span: 1 m (3 ft 3 in)
Speed: Mach 6
Operating altitude: unknown
Operating range: unknown
Warhead: HE, probably nuclear-capable

The Russian SA-10, given the name 'Grumble' by NATO, has not been supplied to any of Russia's allies. It is a mobile SAM system designed for defence of strategically important sites. It is fired from fixed positions or 8x8 MAZ-7910 transport/launcher vehicles; in either case the launch takes place with the missile positioned vertically. Deployed since the early 1980s, SA-10 has the ability to attack low-flying targets such as cruise missiles, as well as bombers at very high altitudes.

Assessment
Mobility ★
Accuracy ★★★★
Age ★★
Worldwide users ★

The Russian long-range mobile SAM system known to NATO as the SA-10. It is a very fast missile that can destroy supersonic targets.

SA-12 'Gladiator'

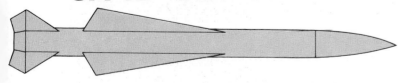

Specification
Guidance: unknown
Weight: 2000 kg (1 ton 2172 lb)
Length: 7.2 m (23 ft 8 in)
Span: 1.5 m (4 ft 11 in)
Speed: Mach 3
Operating altitude: 90–30,000 m (245–98,400 ft)
Operating range: 5.5–90 km (4–56 miles)
Warhead: 150 kg (330 lb) HE

The SA-12 was introduced in the last years of the former USSR. It was designed to replace the huge SA-4 'Ganef' missiles that provided long-range SAM capability to front- and army-level formations. It is essentially the Russian equivalent of the US Patriot system: a long-range missile capable of intercepting ballistic missiles as well as aircraft. It has one warhead designed to intercept supersonic cruise missiles and supersonic aircraft.

Assessment
Mobility ★★★
Accuracy ★★★★
Age ★★
Worldwide users ★

The SA-12 is similar to the SA-10: another long-range SAM system. It was built to replace the SA-4 'Ganef' long-range missile.

Patriot

Specification
Guidance: command and semi-active radar homing
Weight: 1000 kg (2205 lb)
Length: 5.18 m (17 ft)
Span: 0.91 m (2 ft 11 in)
Speed: Mach 3
Operating altitude: up to 24,000 m (78,700 ft)
Operating range: 60 km (37 miles)
Warhead: HE or nuclear

Assessment
Mobility   ★★★
Accuracy   ★★★★★
Age   ★★★
Worldwide users   ★★★

The Patriot missile won instant fame during the Gulf War when it was used to intercept 'Scud' surface-to-surface missiles fired into Saudi Arabia and Israel by the Iraqi army.

The SAM system made famous by the Gulf War, Patriot had a long development history punctuated by technological problems and political vacillation. Design began in 1965 on a missile to replace the US Army's HAWK system but, although test launches took place by 1970, it was another 13 years before Patriot entered service. Supplied in a sealed canister and requiring no maintenance in the field, Patriot missiles are fired from a semi-trailer that has its own generator. The control station is fitted to a long-wheelbase M816 6x6 truck. Several modes of operation are possible, ranging from manual with computer assistance to fully automated with manual override. Surveillance, target detection, tracking and missile guidance are all provided by the AN/MPQ-53 radar set.

Thunderbird

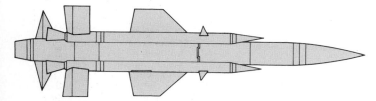

Specification
Guidance: semi-active radar homing
Weight: unknown
Length: 6.35 m (20 ft 10 in)
Span: 1.63 m (5 ft 4 in)
Speed: unknown
Operating altitude: unknown
Operating range: up to 75 km (47 miles)
Warhead: c.80 kg (c.50 lb) HE

Assessment
Mobility   ★
Accuracy   ★★★
Age   ★★★★★
Worldwide users   ★

Thunderbird was similar to the Bloodhound missile operated by the RAF. The British Army's first SAM, it was used by the British Army of the Rhine from 1959 to 1978.

Thunderbird was the British Army's first operational surface-to-air missile. Entering service in 1959, it had four Bristol-Aerojet rocket boosters wrapped around its body to deliver the enormous acceleration necessary. Thunderbird was deployed in batteries of six firing troops, each with three launchers. In 1963 the system was improved to Thunderbird Mk 2 standard, which had higher impulse boost and sustainer motors. Its Ferranti 'Firelight' radar was designed to defeat enemy ECM and enabled Thunderbird to intercept targets at low level. Some of the Thunderbird Mk 1s were sold to Saudi Arabia, but an export order from Libya was cancelled by Colonel Khadaffi after his 1969 coup d'état. Thunderbird was replaced by US HAWK missiles in the British Army in 1976.

Spada

Specification
Guidance: semi-active radar
Weight: 220 kg (485 lb)
Length: 3.7 m (12 ft 2 in)
Span: 625 mm (25 in)
Speed: Mach 2+
Operating altitude: unknown
Operating range: unknown
Warhead: high explosive

Assessment
Mobility   ★
Accuracy   ★★★★★
Age   ★★★
Worldwide users   ★

The business end of the Spada point defence system is the Aspide missile. Spada is designed to defend high-value strategic targets from a concentrated air attack.

The Spada point defence system was developed by Selenia for the Italian armed forces. It is intended to provide close-range defence for strategically important positions. The likely targets are fast jets capable of very low-level attacks and hard manoeuvres, plus air-launched and cruise missiles. The Spada system is designed to shoot them down despite enemy electronic countermeasures. Firing Aspide missiles from static launch sites, Spada has a very short reaction time and each system has 18 quadruple missile launchers – 72 missiles – under its control. It is designed to be computer-linked to the Italian national air defence radar net. The first operational deployment of this highly automated system took place in 1982-83 and 12 Spada systems were ordered during the mid-1980s.

Tigercat

Specification
Guidance: command, TV or radar
Weight: 63 kg (139 lb)
Length: 1.48 m (4 ft 10 in)
Span: 650 mm (26 in)
Speed: unknown
Operating altitude: up to 5500 m (18,000 ft)
Operating range: 5000 m (3 miles)
Warhead: high explosive

Assessment
Mobility   ★★
Accuracy   ★★★
Age   ★★★
Worldwide users   ★★★

Tigercat is a land-based version of the Short Brothers Sea Cat naval SAM. It is able to engage targets at extremely low level and is available with a number of guidance systems.

Tigercat is a land-based version of the Sea Cat surface-to-air missile used by Royal Navy warships to defend themselves against Argentine aircraft during the Falklands war. Ironically, it was deployed to Port Stanley by the Argentine army which had bought Tigercat during the 1970s. Like its nautical variant, Tigercat is designed for immediate reaction. It can be manually-guided by means of a thumb-operated control that steers the missile via a radio-link, the flares at the rear of the missile helping the operator to see where it is going. Alternatively, Tigercat can be fitted with radar or TV guidance. Fire-control radar can also be added, enabling Tigercat to operate at night or in poor visibility. Other export customers have included India, Iran and South Africa.

ASSAULT RIFLES No. 1

The heart of all combat forces is the infantryman, and the infantryman's most important weapon is his rifle. Modern assault rifles give an infantry squad of the 1990s more firepower than a company possessed during World War II.

Armalite AR-15 (M-16) rifle

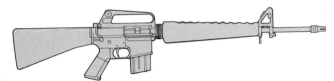

The AR-15 was one of the first of the modern 5.56-mm calibre rifles to enter service. Designed by Eugene Stoner in the late 1950s, the AR-15 made extensive use of pressed steel and plastic in its construction. Although it looked like a toy, it was a serious weapon. Firing high-velocity 5.56-mm ammunition, much smaller than the then standard 7.62-mm NATO round, it allowed soldiers to carry more ammunition into combat. It was designated M16 when issued to the US Air Force, and was to go on to achieve fame as the US Army's standard rifle in Vietnam. After initial reliability problems the M16 proved to be an effective battlefield weapon, and the current M16A2 variant is much improved.

Specification
(M16A2)
Cartridge: 5.56-mm NATO
Weight: 4 kg (8 lb 13 oz)
Length: 1000 mm (39 in)
Cyclic rate of fire: 600 rounds per minute
Magazine: 20- or 30-round box
Effective range: 500 m (550 yd)

Assessment
Reliability ★★★★
Accuracy ★★★
Age ★★★★
Worldwide users ★★★★

The M16 has been in service for 30 years, coming to the fore in Vietnam, and in that time it has almost become a symbol for the American fighting man as well as having a great deal of influence on many other assault rifle designs.

Enfield SA80 Individual Weapon

The British Army was late to adopt a small-calibre battle rifle, in spite of the fact that much of the pioneering work on such weapons had been done in Britain. The 5.56-mm Enfield SA80 Individual Weapon, designated L85 by the British Army, entered service in the mid-1980s, replacing the L1A1 version of the classic FN FAL. The SA80 is a 'bullpup' design with the magazine located behind the trigger. Short and handy, it is well suited to urban combat and mechanised warfare. Equipped with a 4× sight, especially valuable when fighting in poor light, it is one of the most accurate assault rifles in service today. Unfortunately its reliability is not of the same high standard, being prone to break when used in combat conditions.

Specification
Cartridge: 5.56-mm NATO
Weight: 5 kg (11 lb)
Length: 785 mm (31 in)
Cyclic rate of fire: 800 rounds per minute
Magazine: 30-round box
Effective range: 500 m (550 yd)

Assessment
Reliability ★★
Accuracy ★★★★★
Age ★
Worldwide users ★

The Enfield SA 80 Individual Weapon is one of the finest rifles ever produced, as long as it remains on the firing range. Under battlefield conditions, however, it has an alarming tendency to break, to shed parts or even to fall apart.

FA MAS rifle

20th century small arms design has generally lagged well behind the rest of the world, but with the FA MAS assault rifle it made up ground with a vengeance. A 'bullpup' design like the British SA80 and the Austrian AUG, the FA MAS is even shorter than its contemporaries. It fires the NATO standard 5.56-mm round, but has a very high rate of fire and needs a delicate finger on the trigger when firing automatically to avoid wasting ammunition. Despite its unusual appearance, giving rise to its French nickname of 'Le Clarion' (the Bugle), the FA MAS is relatively easy to handle and fire. It has proved to be an effective assault rifle in service, although its trigger pull is not all that could be desired and requires practice to master. As with all bullpups it has a tactical drawback, in that without modification it cannot be fired left-handed.

Specification
Cartridge: 5.56-mm×45
Weight: 4.5 kg (9 lb 15 oz)
Length: 757 mm (30 in)
Cyclic rate of fire: 900–1000 rounds per minute
Magazine: 25-round box
Effective range: 400 m (440 yd)

Assessment
Reliability ★★★
Accuracy ★★★
Age ★
Worldwide users ★

Slung over the back of a French soldier, it is easy to see why the FA MAS rifle has been nicknamed 'the Bugle'. It has all the advantages offered by its 'bullpup' layout, being an effective combat rifle that is easy to handle.

Steyr AUG

Specification
Cartridge: 5.56-mm×45
Weight: 4.1 kg (9 lb)
Length: (overall) 790 mm
(31 in)
Barrel length: 508 mm
(20 in)
Cyclic rate of fire: 650
rounds per minute
Magazine: 30-round box

Assessment
Reliability   ★★★★★
Accuracy   ★★★★
Age   ★★
Worldwide users   ★★

The Steyr Armee Universal Gewehr still has an arresting appearance, 15 years after it entered service. It is one of the most reliable assault rifles made, with few faults.

In spite of its space-age appearance, the Steyr *Armee Universal Gewehr* has been in service for more than 15 years. The first of the modern 'bullpup' rifles, the AUG has won an enviable reputation for toughness and reliability. Its transparent plastic magazine lets the firer know at a glance just how many rounds he has left. It is also highly damage-resistant, unlike the metal magazines of other 5.56-mm rifles. The AUG is the standard rifle of the Austrian army, where it is known as the Sturmgewehr 77, and it is also used by armies and law enforcement agencies around the world, from Australia to the United States.

Beretta AR70

Specification
Cartridge: 5.56-mm×45
(M193 or SS109)
Weight: 4.1 kg (9 lb)
Length: (overall) 955 mm
(37 in)
Barrel length: 450 mm
(18 in)
Cyclic rate of fire: 650
rounds per minute
Magazine: 30-round box

Assessment
Reliability   ★★★
Accuracy   ★★★
Age   ★
Worldwide users   ★

The Beretta AR70 displays the clean lines and good finish typical of weapons manufactured by Beretta. Like most modern rifles, it can be fitted with a variety of accessories.

The AR70 was developed by the Italian firm of Beretta in the 1970s after a careful study of existing small-calibre combat rifles. It is a straightforward 5.56-mm assault rifle with few frills, carefully designed to minimise the amount of dirt that can enter the weapon. Capable of automatic fire, its only problem is that the cocking handle is the only part connecting gas piston to bolt carrier: lose the handle and the weapon is unusable. The Beretta 70/90 is an improved version developed for the Italian army. It is exceptionally easy to strip and maintain, and can take any M16-type magazine.

Heckler & Koch G41

Specification
Cartridge: 5.56-mm×45
Weight: 4.1 kg (9 lb)
Length: (overall) 997 mm
(39 in)
Barrel length: 450 mm
(18 in)
Cyclic rate of fire: 850
rounds per minute
Magazine: 30-round box

Assessment
Reliability   ★★★★
Accuracy   ★★★★
Age   ★
Worldwide users   ★

Heckler & Koch have taken their G3 rifle and used it as a basis for a whole family of weapons. The G41 is a robust weapon capable of taking a variety of NATO standard sights and magazines.

The G3 manufactured by the German firm of Heckler & Koch was one of the classic post-war full-power rifle designs. Used extensively around the world, its operating system formed the basis for a number of smaller designs, including the MP5 and HK53 sub-machine guns in 9-mm and 5.56-mm calibre respectively, and the HK33 and G41 assault rifles, also in 5.56-mm calibre. The G41 has been developed specifically to fire the current NATO standard SS109 round. It can accept M16-type magazines, gives three-round bursts or fully automatic fire, and has a built-in mount for night and telescopic sights.

Fabrique National FNC

Specification
Cartridge: 5.56-mm×45
(M193 or SS109)
Weight: 3.8 kg (8 lb 6 oz)
Length: (overall) 997 mm
(39 in)
Barrel length: 449 mm
(18 in)
Cyclic rate of fire: 600–
700 rounds per minute
Magazine: 30-round box
Effective range: 200 m
(220 yd)

Assessment
Reliability   ★★★
Accuracy   ★★★
Age   ★
Worldwide users   ★

Fabrique National entered the 5.56-mm stakes with the FNC carbine, which adopted features from the world-beating FN FAL.

Fabrique National are well known for their 7.62-mm FN FAL rifle, which has been a world standard weapon since the 1950s and has been used by more than 90 countries. The FNC is Fabrique National's response to the trend towards smaller calibre battlefield weapons. It is a lightweight 5.56-mm rifle originally intended for infantry operating without continuous logistic support, or who are in difficult terrain such as jungles or mountains. The FNC is gas-operated, with a piston and cylinder above the barrel. It has been tested by many countries and has been adopted by at least seven armies, including those of Belgium and Sweden.

Over the last 20 years most armies have adopted rifles that fire relatively light cartridges. Rifles like the AK-74 are easier to shoot than older weapons, and individual soldiers can carry much more ammunition. On the other hand, there is no doubt that 7.62-mm bullets do a great deal more damage.

AK-47

Specification
Cartridge: 7.62-mm×39
Weight: 3.15 kg (7 lb)
Length: 876 mm (34 in)
Cyclic rate of fire: 600 rounds per minute
Magazine: 30-round box

Assessment
Reliability   ★★★★
Accuracy   ★★★
Age   ★★★★★
Worldwide users ★★★★★

The cocking handle on the Kalashnikov series of rifles is unhelpfully positioned on the right, which forces the shooter to reach over the weapon with his left hand.

Firing a lower-powered cartridge than the rifles it replaced, the AK was designed for battlefield ranges of under 300 metres. Combat experience in World War II showed that it was rare for infantrymen to fire at longer ranges. With its capacity for automatic fire and exceptional reliability, the AK-47 was superior to its contemporaries. In 1959 the USSR adopted an improved version, designated AKM. Cheaper and easier to produce, this was replaced by the AK-74, although many reserve units still use the AKM. The AK series is the most widely manufactured military rifle of all time.

AK-74

Specification
Cartridge: 5.45-mm×39.5
Weight: 3.6 kg (7 lb 15 oz)
Length: 930 mm (36 in)
Cyclic rate of fire: 650 rounds per minute
Magazine: 30-round plastic magazine

Assessment
Reliability   ★★★★
Accuracy   ★★★★
Age   ★
Worldwide users ★

The AK-74 has prominent grooves in the stock and foregrip to make it immediately distinguishable from earlier AKs. This is essential because it takes different ammunition.

As Western armies adopted weapons in 5.56-mm calibre, the Russians re-equipped with this new version of the AKM. It is operated like all other Kalashnikov rifles, but fires a 5.45-mm cartridge which produces almost no recoil. It feels much the same as firing a .22 target rifle – but the 5.45-mm bullet travels at high velocity, and is designed to deform when it strikes the target. Its performance is similar to that of a soft-nosed bullet. The AK-74 produces a fearsome muzzle blast. It looks very similar to the AKM but has a different muzzle brake and a groove running along the stock and foregrip.

Galil

Specification
Cartridge: 7.62-mm×51
Weight: 4.9 kg (9 lb 15 oz)
Length: 1050 mm (41 in)
Cyclic rate of fire: 600 rounds per minute
Magazine: 25-round box

Assessment
Reliability   ★★★★
Accuracy   ★★★★
Age   ★★
Worldwide users ★★

A South African soldier uses the locally-made R4 variant of the Israeli Galil. This strongly-built rifle has performed well in the harsh conditions of war in the bush.

With almost every Arab opponent armed with the AK-47, the Israeli Defence Force has unrivalled experience of the Russian weapon's strengths and weaknesses. The Israelis noted the exceptional strength and reliability of the AK as well as its simplicity – it does not take long to teach someone to shoot a Kalashnikov. Israel developed the Galil rifle along very similar lines and improved its accuracy. Available in 5.56-mm or 7.62-mm, and in a choice of barrel lengths, the Galil has proved very successful. South African forces also adopted a version of the Galil under the designation R4.

M14

Specification
Cartridge: 7.62-mm×51
Weight: 5.1 kg
(11 lb 4 oz)
Length: 1120 mm (44 in)
Cyclic rate of fire: 700
rounds per minute
Magazine: 20-round box

Assessment
Reliability   ★★★
Accuracy   ★★★
Age   ★★★★★
Worldwide users   ★

*US soldiers with a mixture of M14s
and M16s are ready to board a
helicopter during the Vietnam War.*

In the 1950s the US Army refused to follow the trend towards smaller bullets
and forced all NATO armies to adopt the 7.62-mm × 51 cartridge as standard.
Ten years after the Soviets deployed their revolutionary Kalashnikov, US troops
received the M14. Although accurate and manufactured to very high standards, it
was a throw-back to World War II, and was clearly obsolete as a combat rifle.
Used in the early days of the Vietnam War, it was rapidly replaced by the
5.56-mm M16, and had one of the shortest service careers of any modern rifle.

FN FAL

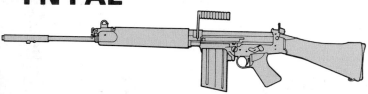

Specification
Cartridge: 7.62-mm×51
Weight: 5 kg (11 lb)
Length: 1143 mm (45 in)
Cyclic rate of fire: 650
rounds per minute
(automatic versions)
Magazine: 20-round box

Assessment
Reliability   ★★★
Accuracy   ★★★
Age   ★★★★★
Worldwide users   ★★★★★

*The FN FAL, known to a generation of
British soldiers as the SLR, remains
one of the most successful service
rifles since World War II.*

The FN was originally designed to fire the 7.92-mm *Kurz* cartridge used by the
World War II German weapons that so influenced the Kalashnikov. However, US
pressure for a more powerful cartridge produced the compromise 7.62-mm × 51
as the NATO standard. FN rebuilt their rifle to fit the new cartridge and promptly
cornered the market. The British Army used it until the late 1980s, and many
remain in service with reserve and support units. British and Australian FNs were
modified to prevent fully automatic fire which is almost impossible to control.

Heckler & Koch G3

Specification
Cartridge: 7.62-mm×51
Weight: 5.1 kg
(11 lb 4 oz)
Length: 1025 mm (40 in)
Cyclic rate of fire: 600
rounds per minute
Magazine: 20-round box

Assessment
Reliability   ★★★
Accuracy   ★★★
Age   ★★★★
Worldwide users   ★★★★

*The Heckler & Koch G3 is in service
all over the world. It employs the
same roller-locking system used by
H&K in the MP5 sub-machine gun.*

This is one of the few rifles firing a full-sized cartridge and working on delayed
blowback using the roller-locking system perfected by Heckler & Koch. Slightly
heavier than the FN FAL and with the cocking lever in a rather awkward position,
the G3's accuracy and overall performance is so similar to that of the Belgian rifle
as to be indistinguishable in average hands. With a few notable exceptions, the
G3 has been adopted everywhere the FN FAL missed. Like the FN, the G3
design has been modified for 5.56-mm weapons, but these have not prospered
like their larger predecessors.

Simonov SKS

Specification
Cartridge: 7.62-mm×39
Weight: 3.85kg (8 lb 8 oz)
(empty)
Length: 1021 mm (40 in)
Cyclic rate of fire:
single shot
Magazine: 10-round box
internal magazine

Assessment
Reliability   ★★★
Accuracy   ★★
Age   ★★★★★
Worldwide users   ★★

*The SKS was to have been the Soviet
service rifle after World War II, but it
was rapidly eclipsed by the AK-47 and
passed on to guerrilla armies and
other Soviet allies.*

The SKS fires the same 7.62-mm × 39 cartridge as the Kalashnikov it was
supposed to serve alongside. Because the AK-47 proved so successful, the
Soviets abandoned the SKS within a few years, retaining them for parade duty
only. The SKS is very light, but this means the recoil from its light round feels
proportionately heavier. Capable of reasonable accuracy to about 400 metres,
the SKS was supplied to most Soviet-equipped armies, and has been widely
used in Africa, the Middle East and South East Asia.

Rifles remain the basic weapon of warfare, arming the infantrymen without whom no battle can be won. Most armies now equip their men with small-calibre weapons, often firing the 5.56-mm NATO round.

M16A2

Specification
Cartridge: 5.56-mm×45
Weight: 3.85 kg
(8 lb 8 oz)
Length: 1000 mm (39 in)
Cyclic rate of fire: 600
rounds per minute
Magazine: 30-round box

Assessment
Reliability	★★★★
Accuracy	★★★★
Age	★
Worldwide users	★★★

Unlike the British army's SA80 rifle, the M16A2 can be fired from the left shoulder – an essential feature on a modern combat weapon. The US Army is now upgrading its M16s to M16A3 standard by fitting an optical sight.

Eugene Stoner's revolutionary AR-15 design first entered widespread service in the 1960s. After initial teething troubles, it became the standard by which other small-calibre, high-velocity assault rifles were judged. After 20 years, however, it was starting to show its age. The M16A2 is essentially the M16 modified to fire the harder-hitting SS109 round that has become standard in NATO. The weapon incorporates a number of improvements, being more solidly built and with a heavier barrel than preceding M16s. US Army versions fire three-round bursts, but not fully automatically. Still as light and handy as the original, the M16A2 is a first-class, modern assault rifle.

SAR 80

Specification
Cartridge: 5.56-mm
(US M193 or M196)
Weight: 3.7 kg
(8 lb 2 oz) (unloaded)
Length: 970 mm (38 in)
(overall)
Cyclic rate of fire: 600–
850 rounds per minute
Magazine: 20- or 30-
round box

Assessment
Reliability	★★★
Accuracy	★★★
Age	★
Worldwide users	★

Singapore's growing armaments industry has produced a series of cheap but effective infantry weapons. The SAR 80 series 5.56-mm rifles have been seen recently in the hands of Croatian militia, who acquired a large consignment in early 1991.

The rapidly developing island state of Singapore has one of the most advanced industrial capabilities in Asia. That industry is making a play for exports in a number of markets, one of which is in the field of small arms. The SAR 80 is produced by Chartered Industries of Singapore, the firearms division of which was founded in 1967 to manufacture the M16 under licence. Designed with the help of the British company Sterling, the SAR 80 is at least as effective as the American rifle, but is cheaper to build using the latest production techniques. The result is a basic, gas-piston assault rifle with an attractive price tag.

CETME Model L

Specification
Cartridge: 5.56-mm
Weight: 3.6 kg
(7 lb 15 oz)
Length: 925 mm (36 in)
Cyclic rate of fire: 700–
800 rounds per minute
Magazine: 30-round box

Assessment
Reliability	★★★
Accuracy	★★★
Age	★
Worldwide users	★

The CETME Model L rifle uses NATO standard magazines and is very similar in performance and construction to the Heckler & Koch G3 derivatives chambered for the 5.56-mm NATO cartridge. It has not been widely exported.

The foundation of the CETME concern was a group of German engineers who moved to Spain after World War II. There they developed the roller locking system adopted by Heckler & Koch. Like many other manufacturers, CETME have adapted their basic 7.62-mm battle rifle design to create an assault rifle firing the smaller NATO 5.56-mm round. As with a number of contemporary designs, the Model L offers three-round bursts as well as single-shot and full-auto fire. Originally offered with 20-round magazines, the Model L will now accept standard M16-pattern magazines, which may be prone to damage, but which are cheap and available all over the world.

Ruger Mini-14

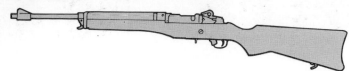

Specification
(Self-loading Mini-14)
Cartridge: 5.56-mm×45
Weight: 2.9 kg (6 lb 6 oz)
(gun empty)
Length: 946 mm (37 in)
Rate of fire: semi-
automatic only
Magazine: 5-, 20- or 30-
round box

Assessment
Reliability   ★★★
Accuracy   ★★★
Age   ★★
Worldwide users ★★★

The Ruger Mini-14 is used in military service, law enforcement and is a very popular plinking/varmint rifle in the USA. In Britain it is used by the Royal Ulster Constabulary.

The Ruger Mini-14 could be described as a scaled-down version of the M14 battle rifle, although a number of changes have been made to allow the weapon to cope with the higher chamber pressures generated in firing high-velocity 5.56-mm rounds. Light and hardy, the Mini-14 is an extremely well-made piece which has found favour with police and security forces around the world. A number of variants have been produced, including the AC-556 selective-fire version, and one model chambered for the standard Russian 7.62-mm x 39 round, as fired by the famous Kalashnikov.

Beretta AR70/90

Specification
Cartridge: 5.56-mm×45
Weight: 3.99 kg
(8 lb 12 oz)
Length: 986 mm (39 in)
Cyclic rate of fire: not
disclosed, but probably
about 650 rounds per
minute
Magazine: 30-round box

Assessment
Reliability   ★★★★
Accuracy   ★★★★
Age   ★
Worldwide users ★

The Beretta AR70/90 was used by Italian paratroops and marines while the rest of the Italian army soldiered on with 7.62-mm BM59s. Now the whole army is adopting AR70/90s.

The Italian firm of Beretta started developing a 5.56-mm assault rifle in the late 1960s. The AR70/223 which emerged was a conventional gas-piston-operated design. It achieved a limited amount of export success, but it also formed the basis of the AR70/90. This is an improved version of the older rifle, incorporating the latest features such as a three-round burst facility, but which also takes in ideas and suggestions from military users of the AR70. As with most modern assault rifles, its magazine housing is compatible with M16-type magazines.

Armalite AR-18

Specification
Cartridge: 5.56-mm
M193
Weight: 3.17 kg
(8 lb 2 oz) (empty)
Length: 940 mm (37 in)
(stock extended); 736 mm
(29 in) (stock folded)
Cyclic rate of fire: 650
rounds per minute
Magazine: 20-, 30- or 40-
round box

Assessment
Reliability   ★★★★
Accuracy   ★★★
Age   ★★★
Worldwide users ★

Designed to be manufactured on primitive machine tools, the AR-18 is nevertheless an accurate and effective weapon. It was built in Britain and Japan but is no longer in production.

The AR-18 was developed in the early 1960s by the Armalite concern. It is not a variant of the AR-15, although it uses some of the ideas from the earlier AR-15/M16 series. Designed as a cheap, alternative weapon for countries that could not afford the latest Western technology, it could not compete with the ubiquitous M16. The AR-18 is nevertheless a light, accurate, easy to handle assault rifle. The rotary bolt and gas piston have been copied to some extent in the British SA80 bullpup assault rifle.

Heckler & Koch HK33

Specification
Cartridge: 5.56-mm
M193
Weight: 3.65 kg (8 lb)
Length: 920 mm (36 in)
Cyclic rate of fire: 600
rounds per minute
Magazine: 25-round box

Assessment
Reliability   ★★★★
Accuracy   ★★★★
Age   ★★★
Worldwide users ★★★★

A short burst is fired from the Heckler & Koch HK33 5.56-mm rifle. Employing the same locking system as the G3, the HK33 is accurate and easily controllable.

The almost bewildering variety of weapons manufactured by Heckler & Koch to use their roller locking system covers everything from sub-machine guns, through rifles and sniper rifles, to medium machine-guns. The HK33 is a top-of-the-line 5.56-mm calibre assault rifle which is scaled down from the full-power G3 rifle. The weapon is well-manufactured, and it shoots and handles well. The HK33 has achieved a considerable degree of export success in Asia, Africa and South America.

The 1950s was a time of transition in small arms design, with weapons that were modified from wartime rifles being joined in service by new designs, which included some that were to serve for 30 years and more.

7.62-mm L1A1 Self-Loading Rifle

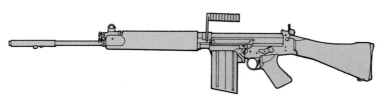

Specification
(SLR)
Cartridge: 7.62-mm×51
Weight: 5 kg (11 lb)
Length: 1143 mm (45 in)
Cyclic rate of fire:
semi-automatic only
Magazine: 20-round box

Assessment
Reliability ★★★
Accuracy ★★★
Age ★★★★★
Worldwide users ★★★★★

The FN FAL is a post-war classic, used by more armies than any other rifle. In its L1A1 SLR form, it was the British Army's standard rifle for three decades from the mid-1950s. During that time it has seen service from the arctic cold of Norway to the desert heat of Oman.

Developed by the Belgian firm of Fabrique Nationale, the Fusil Automatique Legère or FN FAL is possibly the greatest of all post-war military rifles. Developed from the FN Model 49, it is a tough, accurate and supremely reliable design. The British Army is one of about 90 armies to use a version of the FAL. Built under licence as the L1A1 SLR (self-loading rifle), it has been in service for some 30 years, seeing service from Malaya to the Falklands. It has now been replaced by the SA80, largely because the original rifles are getting old and have seen some hard service. Many regiments have found teaching marksmanship with worn-out weapons to be an impossible task.

CETME

Specification
(CETME C3)
Cartridge: 7.62-mm×51
NATO
Weight: 4.5 kg
(9 lb 15 oz) (unloaded)
Length: 1015 mm (40 in)
Cyclic rate of fire: 550–
650 rounds per minute
Magazine: 20-round box

Assessment
Reliability ★★★
Accuracy ★★★
Age ★★★★★
Worldwide users ★

The CETME was developed from German World War II experimental designs. It is also the progenitor of the Heckler & Koch G3 rifle, the only full-power rifle to rival the FN FAL in worldwide popularity. The same basic rifle in 5.56-mm calibre is the standard service rifle of the Spanish army.

CETME was the product of a team of German designers from Mauser who set up shop in Spain in the years following the end of World War II. Originally intended to fire a reduced-power 7.92-mm round, the first production CETME rifle, which appeared in 1958, fired a unique cartridge. It was the same size as the then new 7.62-mm NATO standard round but of lower power. The CETME was the first rifle to use the roller-locking system later taken up by Heckler & Koch. The CETME C3 is the latest model of the rifle, and can fire full-power NATO rounds as well as the unique reduced-power round. A 5.56-mm variant of the CETME is now being manufactured. Known as the Model L, it is replacing the C3 in use with the Spanish army.

Valmet M76

Specification
(M76)
Cartridge: 7.62-mm×39
or 5.56-mm×45
Weight: 4.51 kg
(9 lb 15 oz) (7.62-mm
model with 30-round mag)
Length: 914 mm (36 in)
Cyclic rate of fire: 650
rounds per minute
Magazine: 15-, 20- or 30-
round box

Assessment
Reliability ★★★★
Accuracy ★★★
Age ★★★★
Worldwide users ★

In the 1950s, Valmet of Finland produced an updated version of the Soviet AK-47. Mechanically similar, it has more modern fittings.

Valmet of Finland make an improved Kalashnikov in 5.56- and 7.62-mm calibres, and there is probably very little to choose between these and the Israeli Galils. There is also a heavy-barrel version, the M78, for use as a machine-gun. However, for sniping they offer the M86, a superbly accurate conventional bolt-action single-shot weapon.

Fusil Automatique Modèle 49

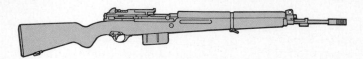

Specification
Cartridge: 7-mm, 7.65-mm, 7.92-mm or .30 cal
Weight: 4.31 kg (9 lb 8 oz)
Length: 1116 mm (44 in)
Cyclic rate of fire: single shot
Magazine: 10-round box

Assessment
Reliability   ★★★
Accuracy   ★★★
Age   ★★★★★
Worldwide users   ★

FN's Modèle 49 was a pre-war design dating from the 1930s. Comparable with the American Garand, it was the basis from which the highly successful FN FAL was to be developed in the early 1950s.

Also known as the 'SAFN', 'ABL' or 'Saive', this gas-operated self-loading rifle was designed before World War II by D. J. Saive in the FN works in Belgium. He fled to England during the war and continued to develop the gun, offering it to the British Army, which rejected it. Back in Belgium after the war it was placed in production and did very well. Built to a high standard, it was expensive to manufacture but proved popular, partly because it was available in many calibres.

MAS 49/56

Specification
Cartridge: 7.5-mm×54
Weight: 4.5 kg (9 lb 15 oz)
Length: 1010 mm (40 in)
Cyclic rate of fire: single shot
Magazine: 10-round box

Assessment
Reliability   ★★★
Accuracy   ★★★
Age   ★★★★★
Worldwide users   ★★

The MAS 49/56 is a tough, handy weapon which is very reliable. It was used by the French army well into the 1980s, until it was replaced by the revolutionary 5.56-mm FAMAS.

The French were the last army to develop a bolt-action service rifle, but wartime experience showed that they needed a self-loader. The tough and very reliable MAS 49 was the result. It served the French army very well in Indo-China and Algeria. The only drawback for non-French forces, is the use of the French 7.5-mm cartridge, but some have been produced in 7.62-mm NATO.

vz 52

Specification
Cartridge: 7.62-mm vz 52
Weight: 4.6 kg (10 lb 15 oz)
Length: 1003 mm (39 in)
Cyclic rate of fire: single shot
Magazine: 10-round box

Assessment
Reliability   ★★★
Accuracy   ★★★
Age   ★★★★★
Worldwide users   −

The vz 52 was not one of the long-established Czech armaments industry's success stories. No more than reasonable, it was produced for about five years in the 1950s.

The vz 52 was a self-loading rifle developed in Czechoslovakia in the brief interlude between German and Soviet occupation. Its operation was largely cribbed from the MKb42(W), a Walther-designed wartime German assault rifle, and the trigger was copied from the M1 Garand. Chambered for the Czech 7.62-mm round, some were modified to fire 7.62-mm × 39 after the Czech forces were incorporated into the Warsaw Pact. The Czech army dropped the vz 52 like a brick as soon as supplies of the vz 58 assault rifle began to arrive.

Beretta BM 59

Specification
Cartridge: 7.62-mm NATO
Weight: 4.6 kg (10 lb 2 oz)
Length: 1095 mm (43 in)
Cyclic rate of fire: 750 rounds per minute
Magazine: 20-round box

Assessment
Reliability   ★★★
Accuracy   ★★★★
Age   ★★★★
Worldwide users   ★★

The Beretta BM 59 was designed to fire the NATO standard 7.62-mm round introduced in the 1950s. Like the M14, it is an updated version of the US Army's pre-war M1 Garand rifle.

Beretta began making Garand rifles for the Italian army soon after World War II, and in 1959 they redesigned it. The result was the BM 59: an M1 modified to take a 20-round magazine and fire full-auto. It was very successful and Beretta went on to make a heavy-barrel model, then modified the gas system to improve accuracy and cut down the rate of fire.

During the 1980s the US Army funded a comprehensive research programme to find a new rifle that offered a 100 per cent improvement over the M16. None of the designs submitted could achieve this. There has been no radical improvement in service rifles since Stoner's work in the 1950s.

R4

The South African Defence Force (SADF) and the Republic's police units have recently been re-equipped with the R4 and R5 5.56-mm rifles in place of the FN FALs and Heckler & Koch G3s of the 1970s. The R4 is a development of the Israeli Galil, in turn a development of the Kalashnikov. The SADF's version of the Galil is a much more robust weapon and has a longer butt to suit the larger-statured South African soldiers. Generally issued with nylon furniture and a plastic 35-round magazine, it includes the popular beer-bottle opener on the integral bipod. A thumb-operated safety above the pistol grip is also used to select single-shot or fully automatic operation. The sights have tritium inserts for night firing, set to 200 metres, below which the R4 has a basically flat trajectory The R5 is a carbine version, similar in concept to the AKSU or Colt Commando.

Specification
Cartridge: 5.56-mm
Weight: 4.3 kg
(9 lb 8 oz) (empty); 4.83 kg
(10 lb 10 oz) (loaded)
Length: 740 mm (29 in)
(butt folded); 1005 mm
(39 in) (butt extended)
Cyclic rate of fire: 650
rounds per minute
Magazine: 35-round box

Assessment
Reliability   ★★★★
Accuracy   ★★★★
Age   ★
Worldwide users   ★★

An equestrian unit of the SADF (South African Defence Force) equipped with R4 assault rifles. The smaller R5 is used by vehicle crew and some paramilitary formations.

SIG SG540

Manufactured under licence by Mannhurin in France, the Swiss SG540 series of rifles has been very widely exported to African nations, particularly those formerly ruled by France. It is also used by the armed forces of Bolivia, Ecuador, Paraguay and Indonesia. There are three types: the SG540 and SG543 are chambered for the M193 5.56-mm cartridge, while the SG542 fires the 7.62-mm×51 NATO round. All are gas-operated weapons with a rotating bolt, and the gas pressure can be adjusted to overcome resistance from dirt or snow in the mechanism. The rifles have a tilted drum rear sight, which is rotated to give range settings in 100-metre increments. The rifles can be fired single shot, fully automatic or in three-round bursts. In the latter case they fire three rounds in 0.25 seconds.

Specification
(SG540 with fixed butt)
Cartridge: 5.56-mm
Weight: 3.26 kg
(7 lb 3 oz) (empty); 3.79 kg
(8 lb 5 oz) (loaded)
Length: 950 mm (37 in)
Barrel length: 460 mm
(18 in)
Cyclic rate of fire: 650–
800 rounds per minute
Magazine: 30-round box

Assessment
Reliability   ★★★
Accuracy   ★★★
Age   ★★★★
Worldwide users   ★★★★

The SG540 is now supplemented by the SG550, which is used by the Swiss army and widely sold to civilians in Switzerland. Swiss law requires all men to own an assault rifle, yet armed crime in the country is negligible.

M1 carbine series

Many modern rifles employ short-stroke piston operation; this was invented by David M. Williams and was first used on this light and handy carbine produced by Winchester in 1941. Supplied to fulfil a US Ordnance Department request for a light rifle not exceeding 2.5 kilograms and capable of fully automatic fire, the M1 became standard issue to the US airborne forces during World War II and very popular throughout the Free World afterwards. Although the .30-cal cartridge is little more than a pistol round, it is accurate at combat ranges and is easily controllable. Popular as an officer's sidearm as well, it was widely used in Asia after World War II – by French, then Vietnamese and US forces in Indo-China and by the British in Malaya. Over six million M1s were made, most were semi-automatic only, but over 500,000 fully automatic M2s were produced in 1944-45. There was also an M3: fitted with a flash hider and designed to carry an infra-red night sight, only 2,100 were made.

Specification
Cartridge: .30 M1
Weight: 2.36 kg
(5 lb 3 oz) (empty); 2.62 kg
(5 lb 12 oz) (loaded with a
30-round box)
Length: 904 mm (35 in)
Barrel length: 458 mm
(18 ln)
Cyclic rate of fire: (M2
and M3 only) 750 rounds
per minute
Magazine: 15- or 30-
round box

Assessment
Reliability   ★★★
Accuracy   ★★★★
Age   ★★★★★
Worldwide users   ★★★

A British paratrooper fires an M1 carbine at Arnhem. Used by US and Allied forces during World War II, the M1 continued to serve in the guerrilla wars in Malaya, Borneo and Vietnam.

AKSU

Specification
Cartridge: 5.45-mm
Weight: 3.4 kg
(7 lb 7 oz) (loaded)
Length: 420 mm (16 in)
(butt folded); 675 mm (26
in) (butt extended)
Cyclic rate of fire: 800
rounds per minute
Magazine: 30-round box

Assessment
Reliability ★★★
Accuracy ★★★★★
Age ★★
Worldwide users ★★★★

The AKSU is a shortened version of the Kalashnikov AK-74 and fits very nicely under a greatcoat. It was widely used in Afghanistan by vehicle crew and airborne forces.

The AKSU is a shortened version of the Kalashnikov AK-74. Like the Colt Commando version of the M16, it retains the same grips, breech mechanism and magazines as the full-size rifle, but has a drastically shortened barrel. It was issued to vehicle crew and the Russian airborne forces that played such a leading role in Afghanistan. Within 200 metres or so its performance is quite adequate, though fully automatic fire is very unselective. The muzzle brake is nothing fancy, but it does work effectively, diverting the propellant gases either side. Its size and compact folding stock make it easy to conceal.

EM-2

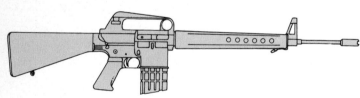

Specification
Cartridge: 7-mm×44
Weight: 3.4 kg
(7 lb 7 oz) (empty); 4.7 kg
(10 lb 6 oz) (loaded)
Length: 889 mm (35 in)
Cyclic rate of fire: 600
rounds per minute
Magazine: 20-round box

Assessment
Reliability ★★★
Accuracy ★★★★
Age ★★★★★
Worldwide users ★

The EM-2 was an innovative assault rifle that the British Army tried to adopt just after World War II until US pressure forced NATO armies to use a 7.62-mm weapon.

Known to the post-war British Army as the 7-mm Rifle, Automatic, No. 9 Mk 1, the EM-2 was a radical assault rifle intended to replace the .303 Lee-Enfield. Firing a new 7-mm×44 cartridge, it had a 'bullpup' layout, i.e. the magazine was behind the pistol grip. Gas-operated and capable of fully automatic fire, it fired from a closed breech and had an optical sight as standard. However, although the British Army planned to adopt it, the EM-2 was dropped when the USA insisted that NATO armies must use a weapon chambered for the 7.62-mm×51 cartridge. The EM-2 could not fire this more powerful round. It should be noted that although the SA80 rifle now in service shares some external features with the EM-2, the latter was lighter, better balanced and internally quite different.

Armalite AR-10

Specification
Cartridge: 7.62-mm×51
Weight: 3.4 kg
(7 lb 7 oz) (empty); 4.8 kg
(10 lb 9 oz) (loaded)
Length: 1029 mm (40 in)
Cyclic rate of fire: 700
rounds per minute
Magazine: 20-round box

Assessment
Reliability ★★★
Accuracy ★★★★
Age ★★★★★
Worldwide users ★

The Armalite AR-10 was a fine 7.62-mm rifle that proved commercially unsuccessful despite its capabilities. It was later scaled down to become the AR-15 5.56-mm rifle, also known as the M16.

The AR-10 was the ancestor of the AR-15, alias the M16, the Western world's finest assault rifle. Introducing the general layout that was to become so familiar in the 1960s, the AR-10 appeared in 1955 but was chambered for the then-standard 7.62-mm×51 NATO cartridge. It was an excellent weapon, better than most of its contemporaries and a pleasure to shoot. Unfortunately, by the time it was ready for production most NATO armies had just ordered either FN FALs or Heckler & Koch G3s. Orders were tiny: the Portuguese took 1,500 AR-10s for their colonial troops fighting in Africa and some went to Sudan. This was not enough to keep the weapon in production and manufacture ceased in 1961.

M1 Garand

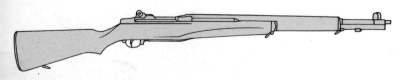

Specification
Cartridge: .30 '06
Weight: 4.37 kg
(9 lb 10 oz) (empty)
Length: 1103 mm (43 in)
Cyclic rate of fire:
semi-automatic only
Magazine: 8-round clip

Assessment
Reliability ★★★★★
Accuracy ★★★★
Age ★★★★★
Worldwide users ★★★

The M1 Garand was the first self-loading rifle to be adopted as a standard service weapon. Robust and accurate, it served the US Army well from World War II to Korea and is still very popular as a sports shooting rifle.

The first self-loading rifle to be adopted as a standard service weapon, the M1 Garand was adopted in 1932 and issued in quantity four years later. Used by the US Army throughout World War II and Korea, some 5.5 million M1s had been made by the time manufacture ceased in the 1950s. Still a popular target-shooting rifle in the USA, and now produced by Springfield Armory, the M1 was supplied to many US allies, including South Vietnam and Italy, where it was made under licence by Beretta. A big, strong rifle, the M1 earned its reputation for reliability under combat conditions from the jungles of the Philippines to the frozen hills of Korea.

SNIPER RIFLES No. 1

The sniper has had an influence upon the conduct of war out of all proportion to the numbers involved in his deadly trade. The long-range and pinpoint accuracy of his weapon allows the sniper to dominate huge areas, bringing the whole delicately balanced military machine grinding to a halt.

SVD Dragunov

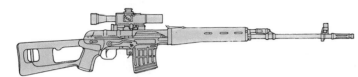

Specification
Cartridge: 7.62x54R
Weight: 4.3 kg (9 lb 8 oz)
Length: 1225 mm (48 in)
Barrel length: 622 mm (25 in)
Magazine: 10-round box

Assessment
Reliability	★★★★
Accuracy	★★★
Age	★★★★★
Worldwide users	★★★★★

Designed in the 1960s, the SVD sniper rifle is a simple, sturdy, self-loading weapon. It is considerably more suited to field use than many more accurate weapons, but is nevertheless accurate to 800 metres in good hands.

The Russian army has always recognised the value of the sniper, but since the Kalashnikov rifles and light machine-guns used in a platoon are not accurate beyond 400 metres, a long-range weapon is essential. The *Snaiperskaya Vintovka Dragunova*, or SVD sniper rifle, is light, well balanced and simple to operate. It uses the basic Kalashnikov action, modified to handle the much more powerful 7.62-mmx54 rimmed cartridge, which though dating back to the last century remains highly accurate. Equipped with a PSO-1x4 scope, the Dragunov can achieve single shot kills at 800 metres.

Walther WA 2000

Specification
Cartridge: .300 Winchester Magnum
Weight: 8.3 kg (18 lb 5 oz)
Length: 905 mm (35 in)
Barrel length: 650 mm (26 in)
Magazine: 6-round box

Assessment
Reliability	★★★
Accuracy	★★★★
Age	★★★
Worldwide users	★

The Walther WA 2000 is one of the most accurate sniping rifles currently available. This accuracy is bought at some cost. Its sophisticated design is more suited to police and security use than the rough and tumble of the field.

The Walther WA 2000 was introduced in 1981 and immediately made an impact with its futuristic design. Sold as the 'Rolls-Royce' of sniper rifles, it comes with an appropriate price tag. It is a gas-operated bullpup design, with a heavy barrel carried in a rigid frame. The barrel is fluted externally, making it resistant to vibration, and it lies in a straight line with the shoulder, which counteracts muzzle rise. It is chambered for the .300 Winchester Magnum round, which Walther decided was the most accurate commercially available. The WA 2000 is hardly a combat rifle, needing fine tuning and careful handling for maximum performance, but for police, internal security and counter-terrorism sniping it is highly effective.

Heckler & Koch PSG 1

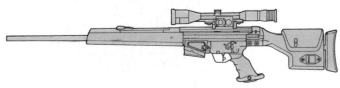

Specification
Cartridge: 7.62x51
Weight: 7.48 kg (16 lb 8 oz) (with 20-round mag)
Length: 1208 mm (47 in)
Barrel length: 650 mm (26 in)
Magazine: 5- or 20-round box

Assessment
Reliability	★★★★★
Accuracy	★★★★
Age	★★★
Worldwide users	★★

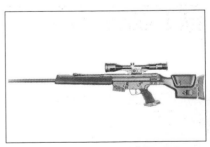

The PSG 1 bears a resemblance to the G3 rifle from which it is descended, but it is really a new weapon. It is extremely accurate at battlefield ranges, producing three-inch groups with 20 rounds at 300 metres.

Heckler & Koch have been ringing the changes on their basic 7.62-mm G3 rifle design for 30 years. The Präzisionsschützengewehr or PSG 1 is derived from the G3, and uses the standard Heckler & Koch roller locking system. It is nevertheless a dedicated sniping weapon, with a heavy barrel, adjustable butt, and trigger. The PSG 1 is semi-automatic, firing single shots from a five- or 20-round magazine. The ×6 telescopic sight has an illuminated reticle with six sight settings, from 100 to 600 metres. It fires standard 7.62-mm ×51 NATO ammunition, but the wise sniper will make sure that all his ammunition is of match grade for maximum accuracy.

Galil sniper

Specification
Cartridge: 7.62×51
Weight: 6.4 kg
(14 lb 2 oz) (empty, without sight)
Length: 1115 mm (44 in)
Barrel length: 508 mm (20 in)
Magazine: 20-round box

Assessment
Reliability   ★★★★★
Accuracy   ★★★★
Age   ★★
Worldwide users   ★★

The Galil sniper rifle resembles the assault rifle from which it was developed. It has been redesigned and manufactured to the finest tolerances. The Galil is fitted with a heavy barrel to which has been added a muzzle brake/compensator. The solid butt, which can be folded forwards for carriage, has an adjustable butt pad and cheek rest, while a Nimrod ×6 sight is standard. The Galil's assault rifle descent suits it to the rigours of combat better than many more modern, super-accurate, but fragile rifles. Using the attached bipod, the Galil can group rounds in a 30-cm circle at 600 metres, which is more than adequate for most sniping purposes.

The Galil sniper has been shaped by the Israeli Defence Force's battlefield experience. As a result, the gun is built more for combat reliability than for exceptional accuracy in perfect conditions.

M21

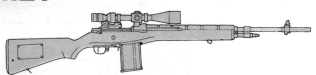

Specification
Cartridge: 7.62×51
Weight: 7.15 kg
(15 lb 10 oz)
Length: 1120 mm (44 in)
Barrel length: 559 mm (22 in)
Magazine: 20-round box

Assessment
Reliability   ★★★★
Accuracy   ★★★
Age   ★★★
Worldwide users   ★★

The M21 is the standard US Army sniping rifle. It is an enhanced version of the 7.62-mm M14 rifle. Originally known as the Rifle, M14, National Match (Accurized), it retains the appearance and basic mechanism of the M14, but only uses selected barrels manufactured to the closest tolerances. The trigger mechanism is assembled by hand and is adjusted to provide a crisp and consistent release. The gas-operation mechanism has also been worked over for smoothness of action. The ×3 sight has the usual cross hairs, but it also has a system of graticules that allows the sniper to judge accurately the distance to a man-sized target.

With a design history reaching back to the original M1 rifle of the 1930s, the M21 is nothing if not reliable. It is also accurate, at least at battlefield sniping distances.

Parker Hale Model 85

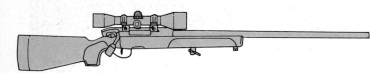

Specification
Cartridge: 7.62×51
Weight: 13.75 kg
(30 lb 5 oz) (including sight)
Length: 1150 mm (45 in)
Barrel length: 700 mm (27 in)
Magazine: 10-round box

Assessment
Reliability   ★★★★
Accuracy   ★★★★
Age   ★
Worldwide users   ★★

The British firm of Parker Hale has been in the business of manufacturing competition and hunting rifles for many years. It was a natural step to produce sniper rifles for military and security use. The Parker Hale 85 has a Mauser-style bolt action allied to a heavy free-floating barrel guaranteed accurate for 5,000 rounds. The trigger is adjustable for weight and pull, and the butt can be altered to suit the firer. The Model 85 can take a variety of telescopes and vision devices, but with a standard ×6 sight it should guarantee first-round hits at 600 metres and 85 per cent hit probability at ranges up to 900 metres.

The Parker Hale Model 85 is an accurate bolt-action rifle with a heavy free-floating barrel, forged from chrome-molybdenum steel. As with most modern sniping rifles, its butt can be adjusted to suit the firer.

Beretta Sniper

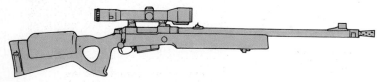

Specification
Cartridge: 7.62×51 NATO
Weight: 7.2 kg
(15 lb 4 oz) (with telescope and bipod)
Length: 1165 mm (45 in)
Barrel length: 586 mm (23 in)
Magazine: 5-round box

Assessment
Reliability   ★★★★
Accuracy   ★★★★
Age   ★
Worldwide users   ★★★★

When the market for high-precision sniper rifles expanded in the 1970s, virtually every major European small arms manufacturer produced designs. The Italian firm of Beretta was no exception. The Beretta Sniper is an orthodox bolt-action design built to the usual high Beretta standard. It is recognisable by its adjustable stock with thumb-hole, bipod, and bell-mouthed flash hider. The bipod mount can also contain a harmonic balancer, a device which damps out barrel vibration to give superbly consistent shooting. The Beretta Sniper can take any NATO standard sight, although the Zeiss Diavari ×1.5-×6 zoom scope is recommended.

Like the Parker Hale, the Beretta Sniper is a heavy-barrelled bolt-action rifle. Beautifully manufactured, it is fitted with NATO standard sight mounts, which means it can be fitted with a wide range of night and telescopic sights.

SNIPER RIFLES No. 2

The makers of sniper rifles try to iron out every inconsistency that can lead to the soldier missing his target. Individual rifles may cost several thousand pounds — but it costs far more than that to train an army sniper to the highest standards.

L42A1

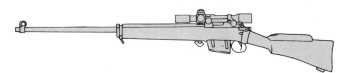

Specification
Cartridge: 7.62-mm NATO
Weight: 4.43 kg (9 lb 12 oz)
Length: 1181 mm (46 in)
Barrel length: 699 mm (27 in)
Magazine: 10-round box

Assessment
Reliability ★★★★★
Accuracy ★★★★
Age ★★★★★
Worldwide users ★★

The L42 sniper rifle is the last version of the famous Lee-Enfield rifle to see active service with the British Army. Note how the sniper has used hessian and scrim net to conceal the tell-tale shape of his rifle.

The British Army invested little time in sniper training during the 1960s, but the Royal Marines maintained an excellent sniper training programme that came to influence the Army when it 'rediscovered' sniping. Until the late 1980s when the L96 was adopted, British snipers used the L42 – a version of the famous Lee-Enfield bolt-action weapon carried by British infantry since 1895. L42s were converted from World War II-era No. 4 Mk 1(T) .303 rifles that were already fitted with a telescopic sight. Open sights were retained as well, and eight different sized foresights were provided for zeroing. Although the stock terminated about halfway along the barrel, both were invariably shrouded in hessian and/or scrim scarf to camouflage the tell-tale shape of the rifle. Used from the Middle East to the Falklands, the L42 gave good service, but it is now outclassed by the latest high-tech rifles entering service.

L96A1

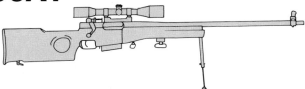

Specification
Cartridge: 7.62×51
Weight: 6.2 kg (13 lb 11 oz)
Length: 1163 mm (45 in)
Barrel length: 655 mm (26 in)
Magazine: 10-round detachable box

Assessment
Reliability ★★★★
Accuracy ★★★★★
Age ★
Worldwide users ★

A Royal Marine sniper searches for his target with binoculars, his L96 sniper rifle ready for action. Developed from a sporting rifle, the L96 is an extremely accurate weapon that is just entering service with the Army and Royal Marines.

The L96A1 is the British Army's current sniper rifle and is issued to Army and Royal Marine snipers. Designed and manufactured by Accuracy International, it fulfils the British forces' requirement for a guaranteed hit at 600 yards. The stainless steel barrel is free floating within the ambidextrous stock. The L96A1 has an integral bipod and it can also be fitted with a retractable spike under the butt. The rifle can be stripped down in about five minutes using three Allen keys and a screwdriver, and the barrel can be changed in a similar time without having to strip the rest of the weapon. The trigger too can be removed and adjusted without dismantling the entire weapon. The makers offer other versions of the rifle, including a suppressed model which has an effective range of 300 metres using subsonic 7.62-mm ammunition. There is also a 'Super Magnum' version which fires .338 Lapua Magnum, .300 Winchester Magnum or 7-mm Remington Magnum. All three calibres offer a significant range advantage over 7.62-mm ammunition.

FR-F2

Specification
Cartridge: 7.62×51
Weight: 5.34 kg (11 lb 12 oz) (wooden stock version with scope); 5.74 kg (12 lb 10 oz) (composite stock model with scope)
Length: 1200 mm (47 in)
Barrel length: 650 mm (26 in)
Magazine: 10-round box

Assessment
Reliability ★★★★
Accuracy ★★★★★
Age ★★
Worldwide users ★

A French sniper armed with the FR-F1 sniper rifle from which the current FR-F2 was developed. The two rifles can be distinguished by the location of the bipod and the thermal sleeve fitted to the FR-F2.

The FR-F2 is the current French sniper rifle. It is a development of the 7.5-mm FR-F1, first issued in 1966 and chambered for the M1936 7.5-mmx54 cartridge: one unique to France. Although some were modified to fire 7.62-mm NATO, it was only used by French forces. The FR-F2 introduced some significant changes. Apart from the inevitable switch to NATO standard 7.62-mm ammunition, it has the bipod just forward of the magazine so the sniper can adjust it without having to move out of firing position. The fore-end is made of metal not wood and is covered in matt-black plastic. The barrel is sheathed in a plastic thermal sleeve, which minimises the weapon's infra-red signature and prevents the heat from the barrel interfering with the shooter's sight picture. Designed to achieve a first-round hit on a man-sized target at 600 metres, the FR-F2 can group all 10 shots within 20 cm at that range. At 200 metres, it groups to within 5 cm.

Barrett sniper rifles

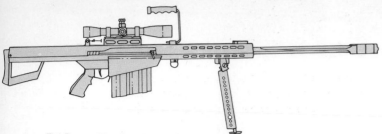

Specification
(Model 82A1)
Cartridge: .50 Browning
(12.7×99)
Weight: 13.4 kg
(29 lb 8 oz)
Length: 1549 mm (61 in)
Barrel length: 737 mm
(29 in)
Magazine: 11-round
detachable box

Assessment
Reliability   ★★★★
Accuracy   ★★★★
Age   ★
Worldwide users   ★★

Detail of the scope and scope mount fitted to the Barrett .50-calibre rifle. The optics have to be able to survive the punishing recoil and muzzle blast of this incredible weapon.

The Barrett .50-calibre sniper rifle was credited with a confirmed kill at 1800 metres during the Gulf War. Since the mid-1980s, several manufacturers have supplied small quantities of .50-calibre rifles to the US Army and the Marine Corps. The Barrett Model 82A1 semi-automatic rifle proved the most popular and, in September 1991, Barrett won an order for 300 of these huge rifles. .50-calibre weapons guarantee to cause massive injury and at far greater range than is possible with conventional rifle ammunition. The penetrative power of the .50-calibre round also enables it to destroy light vehicles, aircraft and helicopters. The Model 82A1 overcomes the formidable recoil of the .50-calibre round by using a muzzle brake that diverts much of the propellant gas sideways.

McMillan sniper rifles

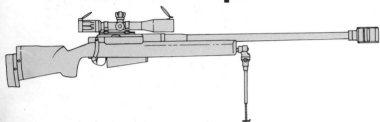

Specification
Cartridge: .50 Browning
(12.7×99)
Weight: 9.5 kg
(20 lb 15 oz)
Length: 1346 mm (53 in)
Barrel length: 736 mm
(29 in)
Magazine: 5-round box

Assessment
Reliability   ★★★★
Accuracy   ★★★★
Age   ★
Worldwide users   ★

Compare the size of the McMillan .50-calibre rifle (top) with the 7.62-mm Parker-Hale M85. McMillan developed a sniper rifle at the request of the US Navy SEALs.

McMillan is best known in the USA for its tough synthetic rifle stocks. These are fitted to the US Marine Corps M40A1 sniper rifles. Since 1986, the Marines sniper rifles have also been fitted with the same trigger actions as McMillan's own 'Signature' sporting rifles. When the US Navy SEALs began to experiment with .50-calibre rifles it requested McMillan to develop such a weapon. McMillan responded with the single-shot M87 ELR, which was soon followed by one with a five-round magazine. Both are conventional rifles with thumb safety and an adjustable trigger. A massive muzzle brake diverts the blast of gas sideways.

Steyr SSG

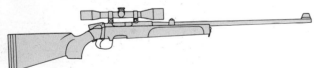

Specification
Cartridge: 7.62-mm
NATO
Weight: 4.6 kg
(10 lb 2 oz)
Length: 1140 mm (45 in)
Barrel length: 650 mm
(26 in)
Magazine: 5-round rotary
magazine

Assessment
Reliability   ★★★★★
Accuracy   ★★★★★
Age   ★★★
Worldwide users   ★★★

Detail of the trigger and bolt of the Steyr SSG sniper rifle. Popular in Europe among sports shooters as well as military forces, the SSG is an excellent weapon.

The Steyr-Mannlicher SSG 69 sniper rifle is used by the Austrian army and by several foreign military and police units. Using a Mannlicher rear-locking bolt, unlike most modern sniper rifles that employ Mauser-type forward-locking bolts, the SSG is an excellent and accurate weapon. The barrel is cold-forged – a method pioneered by Steyr in which the rifling is hammered into the bore using a mandrel. The five-round rotary magazine employed on Mannlicher's World War I-era rifles has been retained, although a 10-round box was also made. The latter is no longer in production due to changes in UIT competition shooting that reduced the demand from civilian sports shooters. The stock is synthetic and is adjustable to suit individual shooters. The standard military version of the SSG can produce 40 cm groups at 800 metres, and the heavy barrel match model can do even better.

Mauser sniper rifles

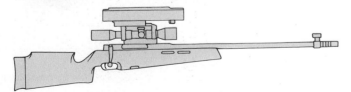

Specification
(Model 86)
Cartridge: 7.62-mm
NATO
Weight: 4.9 kg
(10 lb 13 oz)
Length: 1210 mm (47 in)
Barrel length: 650 or
730 mm (26 or 29 in) with
muzzle brake
Magazine: 9-round box

Assessment
Reliability   ★★★★★
Accuracy   ★★★★
Age   ★★★
Worldwide users   ★★★★

The Mauser SP66 and SP86 sniper rifles have been used by German police and military forces for many years and they have achieved considerable success on the export market. The profile shown here has the combination telescopic sight/ laser rangefinder attachment.

The Mauser SP66 sniper rifle is used by German forces and those of many other countries. A heavy barrel bolt-action rifle, it employs a variant of the traditional Mauser-type bolt used on so many rifles today. The bolt handle is at the front of the bolt, which allows the sniper to operate it without having to move his head and thus alter his position. This also allows the bolt to be a little shorter and the barrel slightly longer. The bolt design has been carefully worked to give a short lock time. The SP66 has an adjustable stock and a muzzle brake/flash suppressor. It has a contoured thumb aperture too, but the otherwise similar Mauser 86 reverts to a conventional butt. The latter is commonly seen with a combination telescopic sight and laser rangefinder.

Machine-guns have been the principal weapons of infantry sections since 1917. They vary from light machine-guns, only one step up from a rifle, to heavy weapons designed for sustained fire. General-purpose weapons designed to perform both roles are the most popular.

L7A2 General Purpose Machine Gun

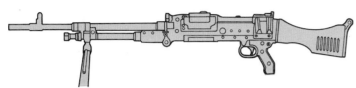

Specification
Cartridge: 7.62-mm NATO
Weight: 10.9 kg (24 lb)
Length: 1232 mm (48 in)
Cyclic rate of fire: 750–1000 rounds per minute
Effective range: 1200 m (1300 yd)

Assessment
Reliability   ★★★
Accuracy   ★★★★
Age   ★★★★
Worldwide users   ★★★★

The FN MAG, known to the British Army as the GPMG, is widely regarded as the best weapon of its type. It is reliable, accurate and extremely robust. Although the British Army is replacing it with the LSW, large numbers of GPMGs reappeared the moment troops were deployed to the Gulf.

The British Army's GPMG (General Purpose Machine Gun) is a development of the Belgian FN MAG machine-gun. The FN MAG is the most successful machine-gun design since World War II: a superb weapon that has been adopted by armies all over the world. The British Army has used the GPMG for some 30 years; each infantry section included a gun group, centred around a GPMG, and a rifle group equipped with 7.62-mm SLRs. Extremely reliable and highly accurate, the GPMG is equally useful in the sustained fire role. Fixed to a tripod, it can fire out to 1800 metres. Theoretically replaced in the infantry sections by the 5.56-mm LSW, many GPMGs came out of hiding to take part in the Gulf War. Whatever its theoretical advantages, the LSW is no substitute for a real machine-gun.

7.62-mm M60 GPMG

Specification
Cartridge: 7.62-mm×51
Weight: 10.5 kg (23 lb 2 oz)
Length: 1105 mm (43 in)
Cyclic rate of fire: 550 rounds per minute
Effective range: 1000 m (1100 yd)

Assessment
Reliability   ★★★
Accuracy   ★★★
Age   ★★★
Worldwide users   ★★★

The American M60 has been a problem for the US forces for many years. The Marines have now modified their M60s into acceptable weapons, but it remains astonishing that such a mediocre weapon should have remained in service for so long.

Although many design features were copied from earlier, successful machine-guns, like the German MG42, the M60 was obviously inferior to its contemporaries, the FN MAG and the Russian PK. The M60 was the standard US Army machine-gun throughout the Vietnam War, where it was known as 'the Pig'. By the time of the Gulf War the US had adopted FN's latest machine-gun, the 5.56-mm Minimi, to supplement the M60s. The Marine Corps had gone one better and had the M60 thoroughly redesigned: its M60E3s represent the best that can be achieved from this mediocre weapon.

7.62-mm PK GPMG

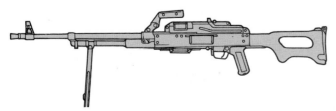

Specification
Cartridge: 7.62-mm×54R
Weight: 9 kg (19 lb 13 oz)
Length: 1160 mm (45 in)
Cyclic rate of fire: 690–720 rounds per minute
Effective range: 1000 m (1100 yd)

Assessment
Reliability   ★★★★
Accuracy   ★★★
Age   ★★★
Worldwide users   ★★★★

The PK GPMG is equivalent to the FN MAG or the M60. This effective weapon fires the old 7.62-mm rimmed cartridge, which was first used by the Russians in the 1890s

The Russian PK machine-gun was introduced in 1964 and was soon supplied to the Warsaw Pact allies and client-states around the world. It was used by the North Vietnamese during the Vietnam War and has been seen in almost every guerrilla war for the last 25 years. The PK series of weapons consists of a number of weapons for various applications, but the basic infantry gun is the PK or PKS; the former has a bipod and the latter a tripod mounting attachment. Still the standard infantry support machine-gun throughout the former Warsaw Pact countries, it is superior to the M60 but not the FN MAG.

7.62-mm RPK light machine-gun

Specification
Cartridge: 7.62-mm×39
Weight: 6 kg (13 lb 4 oz)
(including 40-round mag)
Length: 1035 mm (40 in)
Cyclic rate of fire: 600
rounds per minute
Effective range: 750 m
(820 yd)

Assessment
Reliability   ★★★★★
Accuracy   ★★★
Age   ★★★★
Worldwide users   ★★★★

An Iraqi soldier aims an RPK light machine-gun out of his bunker. This is little more than a heavy-barrelled Kalashnikov rifle. Simple and reliable, it cannot produce the volume of fire delivered by a GPMG.

The RPK is a light machine-gun rather than a general-purpose weapon; it fires from magazines, not belts, and its barrel cannot be changed. It cannot maintain the rate of fire required for the sustained fire role. Like the new British LSW (Light Support Weapon), the RPK provides each infantry section with a weapon that is more accurate at long range than those of a rifleman. Introduced in the mid-1960s, it equips all Russian and ex-Warsaw Pact armies, as well as many guerrilla movements. The 40-round banana-shaped magazine makes it more suited to firing from a foxhole or other cover.

7.62-mm Bren gun

Specification
Cartridge: 7.62-mm×51
Weight: 9.53 kg (21 lb)
Length: 1133 mm (45 in)
Cyclic rate of fire: 500
rounds per minute
Effective range: 600 m
(655 yd)

Assessment
Reliability   ★★★
Accuracy   ★★★★
Age   ★★★★★
Worldwide users   ★★★

The ultimate production version of the Bren gun is still in service with the British Army over 50 years after its introduction.

Over 50 years since the first one was made at Enfield, the famous Bren gun is still in limited service with the British forces. The original Bren guns served as section light machine-guns when the sustained fire role was performed by Vickers water-cooled weapons dating from before World War I. Originally chambered for the British .303-in cartridge, the Bren guns still in service are the L4A4 model which fires 7.62-mm NATO. They are used by British units all over the world, from infantry regiments serving with the ACE mobile force in Norway to the troops recently in action in the Gulf.

7.62-mm Heckler & Koch HK21 GPMG

Specification
Cartridge: 7.62-mm×51
Weight: 7.3 kg
(16 lb 1 oz)
Length: 1021 mm (40 in)
Cyclic rate of fire: 900
rounds per minute
Effective range: 1200 m
(1300 yd)

Assessment
Reliability   ★★★★
Accuracy   ★★★
Age   ★★★★
Worldwide users   ★

Heckler & Koch, now owned by British Aerospace, manufacture a fine series of machine-guns that have been widely exported. The HK21 is closely based on the G3 rifle.

The Heckler & Koch HK21 is a belt-fed general-purpose machine-gun. By the addition of an adaptor it can use any of the magazines used by H&K's G3 7.62-mm assault rifle. In fact the HK21 is closely-based on the rifle and can fire single shots as well as fully automatic. Unlike the M60, the HK21 has a quick and simple barrel-change facility. A recoil-booster allows the weapon to be used normally when firing blank cartridges, which is a useful training aid. Heckler & Koch have developed a whole family of machine-guns using the same basic operating systems. They are in service with many armies in Africa and Asia.

7.5-mm AA52 GPMG

Specification
Cartridge: 7.5-mm M/29
or 7.62-mm NATO
Weight: 10 kg (22 lb 1 oz)
Length: 1145 mm (45 in)
Cyclic rate of fire: 700
rounds per minute
Effective range: 800 m
(875 yd)

Assessment
Reliability   ★★
Accuracy   ★★★
Age   ★★★★
Worldwide users   ★

The AA52 is an unimpressive GPMG that remains in service with the French army and various French-supplied forces in Africa. It mangles the bullet cases as it ejects them.

This is the French equivalent to the FN MAG or M60, and was used by French troops during Operation Desert Storm. An uninspired design, it was designed primarily for cheap manufacture in the wake of the French defeat in Indo-China. Like the M60 the bipod is attached to the barrel, which is very inconvenient, and unlike the FN MAG it has to be carried cocked when a belt is in place. Originally chambered for the French 7.5-mm cartridge, it is no longer manufactured but remains in service both in France and with former French colonies.

vz 59 7.62-mm GPMG

The *vzor* (model) 59 machine-gun is produced in Czechoslovakia and continues the Czech tradition of high-quality infantry weapons. The Czech army version fires the Soviet 7.62 mm×54R cartridge and uses a non-disintegrating link metal belt, which is much better than the Soviet's own arrangement for their 7.62-mm PK machine-gun. With an eye to the export market, the Czechs also produce the vz 59 chambered for 7.62 mm NATO. With the collapse of the Warsaw Pact and the break-up of the Soviet Union, we can expect more NATO-calibre weapons to be produced by the Czechoslovakian arms industry.

Specification
Cartridge: 7.62-mm×54R or 7.62-mm×51
Weight: 8.67 kg (19 lb 2 oz)
Length: 1116 mm (44 in)
Cyclic rate of fire: 700–800 rounds per minute
Effective range: 1000 m (1100 yd)

Assessment
Reliability ★★★
Accuracy ★★★★
Age ★★★
Worldwide users ★

The vz 59 is a belt-fed only version of the belt- or magazine-fed vz 52. This in turn was a developed version of the pre-war ZB 26, which was also developed into the Bren gun. As with most Czech small arms, the vz 59 is a very well-made weapon.

7.62-mm MG 3 GPMG

The MG 3 is the latest version of the World War II German machine-gun, the MG42. Used by the German army and widely exported, it is an efficient weapon with a very high rate of fire which demands frequent barrel changes; when firing short bursts adding up to 250 rounds per minute, you must change the barrel after 150 rounds. The cyclic rate of fire depends on whether the gun is fitted with the 550-g or 950-g bolt. The original MG42's high rate of fire produced a distinctive sound, often described as being like ripping cloth. It was a sound feared by allied troops wherever they heard it.

Specification
Cartridge: 7.62-mm×51
Weight: 11.1 kg (24 lb 7 oz)
Length: 1225 mm (48 in)
Cyclic rate of fire: 1300 rounds per minute (light bolt); 800 rounds per minute (heavy bolt)
Effective range: 800 m (875 yd)

Assessment
Reliability ★★★
Accuracy ★★★
Age ★★★★
Worldwide users ★★★

Effective machine-guns have very long careers. The MG42 was the finest GPMG of its day, and was the Wehrmacht's standard MG at the end of World War II. Fifty years later the MG 3, now serving the Bundeswehr, is simply a modernised MG42.

SIG 710

The Swiss SIG 710 is a superbly engineered machine-gun but it has won few export orders, except for a couple of Latin American forces, including the Chilean police. Manufactured to very high standards, it has the best barrel change of any GPMG, even quicker than on the German MG 3 and far easier than that of the M60. It is the very quality of the SIG 710 that works against its export success, however. Such a high standard of manufacture comes at an equally high cost: like most Swiss personal weapons, the SIG 710 is very expensive.

Specification
Cartridge: 7.62-mm×51
Weight: 11 kg (24 lb 4 oz)
Length: 1143 mm (45 in)
Cyclic rate of fire: 800–950 rounds per minute
Effective range: 800 m (875 yd)

Assessment
Reliability ★★★★
Accuracy ★★★
Age ★★★
Worldwide users ★

The SIG 710 is a classic Swiss weapon. Highly effective, it nevertheless has not sold well. This is because the supremely high standard to which Swiss small arms are built comes with an equally high price tag.

FN Minimi

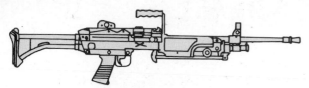

Specification
Cartridge: 5.56-mm×45
Weight: 6.875 kg
(15 lb 2 oz)
Length: 1040 mm (41 in)
Cyclic rate of fire: 750–
1000 rounds per minute
Effective range: 600 m
(695 yd)

Assessment
Reliability ★★★
Accuracy ★★★★
Age ★★
Worldwide users ★★

The FN Minimi is one of the most successful of the new generation of light machine-guns. Firing NATO standard 5.56-mm rounds, it can accept both belt and magazine feed. Here, a US Army gunner is firing belts from a clip-on plastic box.

Fabrique Nationale of Belgium produced one of the finest combat machine-guns ever in the shape of the FN MAG, so when they announced a light machine-gun designed to fire the new NATO standard 5.56-mm round it was clearly a weapon to watch. Using tried and tested mechanical systems, the Minimi is fed by either disintegrating link belts, standard M16 magazines or 200-round belts, which are supplied in sturdy plastic boxes that clamp directly onto the gun. This helps to keep out mud and dirt. The Minimi was selected by the US Army as the M249 Squad Automatic Weapon or SAW, and from 1984 it began replacing one M16 rifle in each infantry squad. With double the effective range of the M16, the M249 gives infantrymen formidable new firepower.

RPD

Specification
Cartridge: 7.62-mm×39
Weight: 7.1 kg
(15 lb 10 oz)
Length: 1036 mm (40 in)
Cyclic rate of fire: 700
rounds per minute
Effective range: 800 m
(875 yd)

Assessment
Reliability ★★★
Accuracy ★★★
Age ★★★★
Worldwide users ★★★★★

The RPD is typical of Russian small arms. Although less refined than contemporary Western designs, it can be relied upon to fire under most conditions.

The *Ruchnoi Pulemyot Degtyareva*, or Degtyarev light machine-gun dates back to the end of World War II. It was the first Russian machine-gun designed to fire the new intermediate power 7.62-mmx39 cartridge. It is belt-fed, usually from a 100-round drum. The RPD does not have a removable barrel so it is not suitable for sustained fire, but is an effective squad-support weapon as long as the rate of fire remains below 100 rounds per minute. It is a solid design and was manufactured in large numbers. It is now obsolete but is still used by most Russian-supported countries all over Asia and Africa.

M60E3

Specification
Cartridge: 7.62-mm×51
Weight: 8.61 kg (19 lb)
Length: 1067 mm (42 in)
Cyclic rate of fire: 550
rounds per minute
Effective range: 1000 m
(1100 yd)

Assessment
Reliability ★★★★
Accuracy ★★★
Age ★★★
Worldwide users ★★

The M60E3, as used by the US Marine Corps, is an effective weapon, intended mainly for heavyweight squad support. It is a pity that it took 20 years for the bugs to be ironed out of the original M60.

Although the M60 was the standard general-purpose machine-gun in US service, it was never entirely satisfactory. It quickly became known as the 'Pig', partly from affection but also out of irritation. Although powerful, it had several bad design features, and was never as reliable as the FN MAG or the PK. Many improvements have been built into the M60E3, however. This is a lightweight version of the M60 used extensively by the US Marine Corps. It has a new bipod mounted on the receiver rather than on the barrel, and a new carrying handle attached to the barrel rather than the receiver. These allow hot barrels to be changed without the need for asbestos gloves, which were essential when working with the old M60. The M60E3 retains all the capabilities of the original gun in a package that is over two kilograms lighter.

M2HB

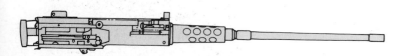

Specification
Cartridge: .50-cal
Browning (12.7-mm×99)
Weight: 39.1 kg
(86 lb 3 oz)
Length: 1653 mm (65 in)
Cyclic rate of fire: 450–
600 rounds per minute
Effective range: 2000 m
(2190 yd)

Assessment
Reliability ★★★★
Accuracy ★★★★
Age ★★★★★
Worldwide users ★★★★★

The M2HB is a wickedly potent heavy machine-gun, which has served for more than 70 years, with few other weapons approaching and none exceeding its effectiveness against personnel and vehicles.

The Browning .50-calibre heavy machine-gun has been one of the most fearsome battlefield weapons since its introduction over 70 years ago. The round is the heart of the weapon, and the big 'Fifty' is a prodigious man-stopper, also capable of penetrating vehicles, buildings, and in certain cases, even light armoured vehicles. The classic M2 or 'Ma Deuce' was developed from the original Browning M1921. It is available in a variety of models, all with similar mechanisms but with different barrels and mounts. The M2HB is the most numerous variant. It has a heavy barrel, and has been used on the ground and from vehicles against both ground targets and aircraft. It is still being manufactured, as troops in combat from the Falklands to the Gulf have found no substitute for its long-range power.

SUB-MACHINE GUNS No. 1

Evolved through necessity in the confined spaces of the trenches of World War I, the sub-machine gun has found a useful place in modern armies. Small, cheap and easily concealed, it is ideal for dealing with the urban terrors of the late 20th century.

Heckler & Koch MP5

Specification
Cartridge: 9-mm Parabellum
Weight: 3 kg (6 lb 10 oz)
Length: 490 mm (19 in) (stock folded)
Cyclic rate of fire: 800 rounds per minute
Magazine: 15- or 30-round box
Effective range: 200 m (220 yd)

Assessment
Reliability ★★★★★
Accuracy ★★★★★
Age ★★★
Worldwide users ★★★

A United States Air Force Security Police sergeant takes aim with his early model Heckler & Koch MP5 sub-machine gun. The MP5's accuracy makes it a highly effective weapon in the hands of trained security personnel.

The Heckler & Koch MP5 machine pistol has become one of the most widely used weapons of its type. When the SAS stormed the Iranian Embassy in London in 1981, TV viewers in the UK saw it in action for the first time. British airport police were also issued with the MP5 in 1986 following the terrorist attacks at Rome and Vienna. Firing from a closed bolt, the MP5 is probably the most accurate sub-machine gun in production today. It is manufactured in a number of variants, including silenced or cut-down weapons for clandestine operations, and is available with telescoping or fixed stocks. Although the MP5 is more complex and considerably more expensive than most other SMGs, its accuracy means that it is the favoured weapon of special operations and hostage rescue units around the world.

Sterling L2A3

Specification
Cartridge: 9-mm Parabellum
Weight: 3.5 kg (7 lb 11 oz)
Length: 480 mm (19 in) (stock folded)
Cyclic rate of fire: 550 rounds per minute
Magazine: 34-round box
Effective range: 150 m (165 yd)

Assessment
Reliability ★★★★
Accuracy ★★★
Age ★★★★★
Worldwide users ★★★★

Working out with the Sterling on the range teaches gunners that although its appearance might seem primitive, the high build-quality makes it easy and reliable to use under all conditions.

The Sterling was the British Army's standard sub-machine-gun since the 1950s. Although it looks like a typical cheap pressed steel weapon, it is in fact an extremely solid and well-constructed weapon, largely made out of machined parts. The high quality of its construction means that the Sterling is very reliable and performs well in adverse conditions. It is an obsolete design, however, since it does not have the wraparound bolt pioneered by the Czech CZ-25 and the Israeli Uzi; as a result its barrel is more than 6 cm shorter than the Uzi's. It has been replaced in the British Army by the SA80 Bullpup.

Uzi

Specification
Cartridge: 9-mm Parabellum
Weight: 4 kg (8 lb 13 oz)
Length: 470 mm (18 in) (stock folded)
Cyclic rate of fire: 600 rounds per minute
Magazine: 25-, 32- or 40-round box
Effective range: 200 m (220 yd)

Assessment
Reliability ★★★★★
Accuracy ★★★
Age ★★★★★
Worldwide users ★★★★

The Uzi, seen here in German Bundesgrenzschutz use, is one of the great post-war small-arms success stories. Designed for cheapness and ease of manufacture, the Uzi has proved a highly effective weapon, and is in service worldwide.

Although its design dates back nearly 40 years, the Uzi remains one of the best sub-machine guns available today. Developed at a time when Israel was beset by enemies yet had little in the way of manufacturing facilities, the gun is largely made from cheap pressed-steel parts. Based on the Czech Model 23, the Uzi features a bolt that wraps around the barrel. This means that although of short overall dimensions the Uzi has a barrel that is actually longer than that of more conventional weapons. The magazine's location in the pistol grip means that it is much easier to reload in the dark. Uzis have been sold widely over the years, and they have gained an enviable reputation for reliability.

Carl Gustav

Specification
Cartridge: 9-mm Parabellum
Weight: 4.2 kg (9 lb 4 oz) (loaded)
Length: 552 mm (22 in) (stock folded)
Cyclic rate of fire: 600 rounds per minute
Magazine: 36-round box

Assessment
Reliability	★★★★
Accuracy	★★★
Age	★★★★★
Worldwide users	★★

The Carl Gustav is a heavy piece of machinery, but it is easy to use, and reliable. These qualities made it popular with US Special Forces units in Vietnam in the 1960s. It is still a standard weapon with the Swedish army, for whom it was designed in the early 1940s.

The Kulspruta Pistol m/45 sub-machine gun is known as the Carl Gustav, after the Carl Gustavs Stads Gevärfactori, where it was manufactured for the Swedish army. Like many contemporary sub-machine guns of the 1940s and 1950s the Carl Gustav is a heavy weapon, solidly built from machined steel parts. Its double column magazine is noted for its reliability, and has been widely copied by other manufacturers. The Carl Gustav was used in South East Asia by US-supplied irregular troops and by US Army Special Forces, who developed a silenced variant for clandestine operations. Many Carl Gustavs were sold to Egypt, where it was also put into production as the 'Port Said'. It remains in service with the Swedish army, which uses a special high-velocity 9-mm round which, it is claimed, has greater range and penetration than any other type of sub-machine gun ammunition.

Steyr MPi 69

Specification
Cartridge: 9-mm Parabellum
Weight: 3.5 kg (7 lb 11 oz)
Length: 465 mm (18 in) (stock folded)
Cyclic rate of fire: 550 rounds per minute
Magazine: 25- or 32-round box
Effective range: 200 m (220 yd)

Assessment
Reliability	★★★
Accuracy	★★★★
Age	★★★
Worldwide users	★

An Austrian soldier holds his Steyr machine pistol as he throws a grenade. The Steyr's most unusual feature was the fact that it could only be cocked by tugging back on the permanently attached sling.

At first glance the Steyr MPi 69 looks like an Uzi clone, and in many ways it is. The Austrian sub-machine gun has a similar boxy body, and its magazine feeds through the pistol grip. It is somewhat different internally, however. The MPi 69 has a number of unusual features. It has no selector lever. A cross bolt safety has three positions: pressed to the right by the thumb it shows a white 'S' for safe. Pressed to the left, a red 'F' shows, releasing the trigger. First trigger pressure fires single-shot, and pulling the trigger all the way back gives full-auto fire. Early models were cocked by pulling back on the sling, but the later MPi 81 has a conventional cocking lever.

Beretta Model 12

Specification
Cartridge: 9-mm Parabellum
Weight: 3.8 kg (8 lb 6 oz)
Length: 420 mm (16 in) (stock folded)
Cyclic rate of fire: 550 rounds per minute
Magazine: 20-, 32- or 40-round box
Effective range: 200 m (220 yd)

Assessment
Reliability	★★★★
Accuracy	★★★★
Age	★★★★
Worldwide users	★★★

The Beretta Model 12 is in widespread use as a police and security firearm. Not as short as the Uzi, it is nevertheless a compact weapon which is extremely well made and as a result is very reliable.

Beretta sub-machine guns have always been superbly made, and were highly sought-after trophies in World War II. The Model 12, introduced in the late 1950s, was built to the same high standard, although for the first time stamped metal and plastic were used in the weapon's manufacture. Like the Uzi, the Model 12 uses a wraparound bolt to reduce the overall length of the gun, but it is a more conventional design, with the magazine housing ahead of the pistol grip. The Model 12 has been issued to Italian special operations units, and is a popular choice with protection and hostage rescue units around the world. It has been sold to many countries in North Africa, Latin America and the Far East.

Spectre

Specification
Cartridge: 9-mm Parabellum
Weight: 3.8 kg (8 lb 6 oz)
Length: 350 mm (14 in) (stock folded)
Cyclic rate of fire: 900 rounds per minute
Magazine: 30- or 50-round box
Effective range: 150 m (165 yd)

Assessment
Reliability	★★★★
Accuracy	★★★★
Age	★
Worldwide users	★

The Spectre is one of a new generation of personal weapons that hardly look like guns, or at least not like guns of the previous generation. They incorporate considerable advanced technology to maximise accuracy and firepower.

Urban terrorism has been a significant factor in Italian life for many years, and the Spectre has been developed specifically for counter-terrorism and unconventional warfare. It has a unique four-column 50-round magazine and fires from a closed bolt, making it more accurate than most other sub-machine guns. It has a double action facility: the weapon can be carried cocked with a round chambered, but with the hammer disengaged. Pulling the trigger engages the hammer rather like in a double action revolver, before releasing the bolt. Carrying the weapon cocked and yet safe means that you do not have to spend valuable moments cocking your weapon if you are ambushed by terrorists.

Sub-machine guns still have a place with modern armed forces. Despite the many advantages that the assault rifle has to offer in the SMG's place, the rifle is still a complex weapon that is too lengthy and powerful for effective use in the close-quarter fighting in which the sub-machine gun excels.

Jatimatic

Specification
Cartridge: 9-mm Parabellum
Weight: 1.95 kg (4 lb 5 oz) (gun and 20-round magazine)
Length: 375 mm (15 in)
Cyclic rate of fire: 650 rounds per minute
Magazine: 20- or 40-round box

Assessment
Reliability ★★★★
Accuracy ★★★★
Age ★
Worldwide users ★

Although not wildly successful on the international market, the Jatimatic machine pistol remains one of the few lightweight sub-machine guns that is fully controllable when fired fully automatically. It is currently built under licence in China.

The sub-machine gun has come a long way in its relatively short lifespan. The futuristic-looking Jatimatic from Finland is typical of modern weapons, if a little smaller than most. Largely made from pressed steel for economy in manufacture, the Jatimatic is not much bigger than a hand gun, and might best be described as a machine pistol. The weapon's 'bent' appearance stems from the fact that the bolt travels on an inclined plane angled up from the barrel. This also makes the weapon much simpler to control when firing full-auto. First trigger pressure gives single shots; further pressure against a spring stop produces automatic fire. The Jatimatic has a folding foregrip, which should be used whenever firing automatically. With a 20-round magazine the Jatimatic weighs less than two kilograms.

MAT -49

Specification
Cartridge: 9-mm Parabellum
Weight: 3.5 kg (7 lb 11 oz) (empty)
Length: 460 mm (18 in) (stock retracted)
Cyclic rate of fire: 400 rounds per minute
Magazine: 20- or 32-round box

Assessment
Reliability ★★★
Accuracy ★★★
Age ★★★★★
Worldwide users ★★

Entering service in 1949 and designed with colonial service in mind, the 9-mm MAT-49 is an extremely rugged design, manufactured from heavy-gauge steel stampings. It was used extensively in France's long, bloody colonial struggles in Indo-China and in Algeria.

In the years following World War II the French army was equipped with a variety of sub-machine guns, mainly of British and American origin. The variety of calibres was confusing, so a new 9-mm sub-machine gun was developed by the Manufacture d'Armes de Tulle. The MAT-49 is an extremely robust SMG that proved reliable in France's colonial wars in Indo-China and in Algeria. The magazine swings forward to lie under the barrel, which makes it convenient for paratroopers or vehicle crew, and it has a sliding wire stock similar to that of the American M3 'grease gun'. Unusually, the head of the bolt enters an extension of the chamber, producing a wrap-around barrel instead of a wrap-around bolt. The MAT-49 is still in widespread use with Francophone countries, but the FAMAS rifle has taken its place in French service.

Model 61 Skorpion

Specification
Cartridge: 7.65-mm (.32 ACP)
Weight: 2 kg (4 lb 6 oz) (loaded)
Length: 270 mm (11 in) (stock retracted)
Cyclic rate of fire: 840 rounds per minute
Magazine: 10- or 20-round box

Assessment
Reliability ★★★
Accuracy ★★
Age ★★★★
Worldwide users ★★

Stock fully extended, the Model 61 Skorpion can shoot with reasonable accuracy out to ranges of 200 metres. Its notably small size makes it eminently concealable, however, and it is most suited to clandestine, short-range operations.

Czechoslovakia has a long-established armaments industry. Even at the height of Soviet power the Czechs went their own way on weapon design. The Model 61 Skorpion was designed for use by tank crews, signallers and other personnel who can carry nothing much larger than a pistol but who have the need for more firepower than a pistol provides. Firing 7.65-mm ammunition, its small bolt would generate an unacceptably high rate of fire, so a spring-loaded weight is fitted into the butt as a rate reducer. However, the bouncing up and down this causes, added to the almost uncontrollable muzzle climb arising out of full-automatic fire through such a small weapon, means that the Skorpion sprays bullets about in a very alarming fashion. It is, as a result, a formidable close-quarters weapon, and its small size and ease of concealment make it a favourite of terrorist groups.

Steyr AUG 9 Para

Specification
Cartridge: 9-mm Parabellum
Weight: 3.8 kg (8 lb 6 oz) (loaded)
Length: 665 mm (26 in)
Cyclic rate of fire: 650–750 rounds per minute
Magazine: 25- or 32-round box

Assessment
Reliability	★★★★★
Accuracy	★★★★★
Age	★
Worldwide users	★

People have been predicting the end of the sub-machine gun for many years, most recently with the widespread introduction of the lightweight assault rifle. However, if you take an assault rifle and convert it to fire pistol rounds, it becomes indistinguishable from a sub-machine gun. Steyr AUG is a well-known assault rifle which can easily be converted into a 9 Para sub-machine gun because of its modular construction. The stock and receiver remain the same, but the barrel is changed, and the bolt mechanism is exchanged for an unlocked blowback bolt unit. The resulting weapon fires from a closed bolt, and its 420-mm barrel and optical sight give remarkable accuracy out to 200 metres.

The AUG system includes a 9-mm SMG in its range of weapons sharing common parts. However, since the 9-mm AUG Para is basically a modified assault rifle, it is far more accurate than most sub-machine guns.

FMK-3

Specification
Cartridge: 9-mm×19 Parabellum
Weight: 3.95 kg (8 lb 11 oz) (with 25-round magazine)
Length: 523 mm (21 in) (with butt retracted)
Cyclic rate of fire: 650 rounds per minute
Magazine: 40-round box

Assessment
Reliability	★★★
Accuracy	★★★
Age	★★★
Worldwide users	★

The FMK-3 is manufactured by Fabrica Militar de Armas Portatiles 'Domingo Matheu' of Argentina. It is a typical blowback-operated weapon of basic modern design. Manufactured from pressed steel components, it has a decidedly 'under-the-counter' appearance, but is nonetheless an effective weapon. The FMK-3 has a wrap-around bolt and the magazine is housed in the pistol grip in the fashion of the Israeli Uzi. Originally manufactured with a fixed plastic butt, it is now only available with a sliding wire butt, copied from the American M3 'grease gun'. A number of these weapons was used in the Falklands, and many captured examples have found their way into British regimental museums.

The FMK-3, also known as the PA-3DM, is a simple blowback weapon looking like a variant of the World War II American M3 'grease gun', but it copies a number of features from the Israeli Uzi.

9-mm F1

Specification
Cartridge: 9-mm×19 Parabellum
Weight: 4.3 kg (9 lb 8 oz) (with bayonet)
Length: 714 mm (28 in)
Cyclic rate of fire: 600–640 rounds per minute
Magazine: 34-round box

Assessment
Reliability	★★★★★
Accuracy	★★★★
Age	★★★★
Worldwide users	★

Replacing the very popular World War II vintage Owen Gun in Australian service, the F1 retains the uniquely Australian feature of a top-loading magazine. Similar but not identical to the Sterling, the F1 uses the same pistol grip as that used on the L1A1 self-loading rifle, and the cocking handle also duplicates the position and action of the FN design. A sling swivel bracket on the barrel shroud acts as a safety feature in preventing the hand getting too close to the muzzle, which is a common mishap with short-barrelled weapons. Simple and effective, the F1 in its prototype X3 form performed extremely well in the Mekong Delta during the Vietnam War.

The 9-mm F1 is instantly recognisable by its uniquely Australian top-loading magazine. Similar to, but not identical with, the British Sterling, the F1 is a tough, reliable, combat-tested sub-machine gun.

Star Z-84

Specification
Cartridge: 9-mm×19 Parabellum
Weight: 3 kg (6 lb 10 oz) (unloaded)
Length: 410 mm (16 in) (stock retracted)
Cyclic rate of fire: 600 rounds per minute
Magazine: 25-round box

Assessment
Reliability	★★★★
Accuracy	★★★★
Age	★
Worldwide users	★

Like many modern sub-machine guns, the Spanish Star Z-84 looks very like the Uzi. It is more than a Uzi clone, however, although it makes extensive use of steel stampings and has a similar wrap-around bolt. This cuts overall length while keeping the barrel as long as possible, hence maximising accuracy. There are no external moving parts; the cocking handle moves forward under spring power and remains still during firing. The Z-84 is highly water-resistant, and it can handle hollow-point and semi-jacketed ammunition as well as standard military full-metal-jacket rounds. These features make it an effective weapon for security and special operations troops.

Although it looks very like a clone of the ubiquitous Israeli Uzi, the Star Z-84 was designed for ease of manufacture and versatility in use. It currently equips Spanish special operations units.

Sub-machine guns that are currently in service include some elderly designs dating back to World War II, but these are just as lethal now as when they were first introduced.

Madsen sub-machine gun

Specification
Cartridge: 9-mm Parabellum
Weight: 3.17 kg (8 lb 2 oz)
Length: 794 mm (31 in) (stock extended); 523 mm (21 in) (stock retracted)
Cyclic rate of fire: 550 rounds per minute
Magazine: 32-round box

Assessment
Reliability	****
Accuracy	***
Age	*****
Worldwide users	***

The Danish Madsen 9-mm sub-machine gun was designed just after World War II. Adopted by the Danish army, it was also widely exported, and a version is still being manufactured in Brazil.

Work on the Danish Madsen sub-machine gun began only months after German forces occupying Denmark surrendered in 1945. Using the production techniques pioneered by the British with the Sten gun and the Soviets with the PPS, the Dansk Industri Syndicat produced a brutally simple weapon built mostly from sheet metal stampings. The Madsen Model 46 has a square receiver that swings into two longitudinal halves, held together by the barrel nut. Field stripping is simplicity itself, since by unscrewing the barrel nut you can open the receiver like a suitcase, hinged at the rear, and remove the working parts. Simple and reliable, the Madsen achieved considerable success on the export market and was adopted by military and paramilitary forces in South America and Asia. No longer made in Denmark, it is still in production under licence in Brazil.

Walther MP-K and MP-L

Specification
(MP-L)
Cartridge: 9-mm Parabellum
Weight: 3 kg (6 lb 10 oz) (empty); 3.6 kg (7 lb 15 oz) (loaded)
Length: 737 mm (29 in) (stock extended); 455 mm (18 in) (stock retracted)
Cyclic rate of fire: 550 rounds per minute
Magazine: 32-round box

Assessment
Reliability	***
Accuracy	***
Age	****
Worldwide users	***

The Walther 9-mm SMGs are conventional blowback weapons firing from an open bolt. Like the Madsen, they have been sold to many forces in South America.

Adopted by the West German police before the advent of the Heckler & Koch MP5, the Walther MP is made in two versions. The MP-K has a short (171-mm) barrel and the MP-L has a longer (257-mm) one. The former is more concealable, whereas the latter is more accurate and produces a higher muzzle velocity. Both models have been widely exported to armies and police forces in South America, including those of Brazil, Colombia, Mexico and Venezuela. Having a conventional blowback design, the Walther fires from an open bolt. The cocking handle can be secured to the bolt to close it manually if necessary. The wire stock folds forward so that the shoulder section can be used as a forward grip. Both models can be set for single-shot operation or fully automatic.

Thompson gun

Specification
Cartridge: .45 ACP
Weight: 4.8 kg (10 lb 9 oz) (empty); 5.37 kg (11 lb 13 oz) (loaded)
Length: 810 mm (32 in)
Cyclic rate of fire: 700 rounds per minute
Magazine: 20-round box

Assessment
Reliability	***
Accuracy	****
Age	*****
Worldwide users	*

A US Marine fires a Thompson gun during the battle for Okinawa in 1945. From Chicago to Belfast, the Pacific islands to the Balkans today, the Thompson gun has proved a popular and robust weapon.

The notorious 'gangster gun' of the 1920s and 1930s, widely used during World War II by American and Allied forces, the Thompson gun has occasionally been returned to production for civilian enthusiasts in the USA. But with the collapse of Yugoslavia the Thompson gun is back in the front line, since large numbers of these elderly sub-machine guns were still in Yugoslavian arsenals in 1991. The USA supplied the Communist guerrillas with them during World War II and more were acquired when President Tito secured arms concessions from both East and West at the same time. A heavy weapon chambered for the .45 ACP cartridge, the Thompson is a handsome and robust machine-gun. Its high standard of manufacture is a testimony to the craftsmanship of a bygone era.

M3

Specification
Cartridge: .45 ACP
Weight: 4.7 kg
(10 lb 6 oz) (loaded)
Length: 757 mm (26 in)
(stock extended); 579 mm
(23 in) (stock retracted)
Cyclic rate of fire: 450
rounds per minute
Magazine: 30-round box

Assessment
Reliability   ★★★
Accuracy   ★★★
Age   ★★★★★
Worldwide users ★

A US Marine fires an M3 sub-machine gun at North Vietnamese positions during the battle of Hue in 1968. Although officially classed as a reserve weapon by the 1960s, the M3 remained in limited service well into the 1970s.

The Thompson ceased manufacture during World War II once General Motors had the M3 sub-machine gun in volume production. The M3 was christened the 'Grease Gun' because it obviously looked more at home in a mechanic's tool box than a soldier's kit. Designed like the British Sten gun for rapid, low-cost manufacture, the M3 was a functional but ugly weapon. It had a very low rate of fire to help soldiers control the bucking recoil of the .45 cartridge, but it was never regarded with the same affection as the Thompson. Although General Motors was churning M3s out at a rate of 8,000 per week in 1944, production ceased at the end of the war with 650,000 manufactured compared with 1.4 million Thompsons.

PPS

Specification
Cartridge: 7.62-mm×25
Weight: 3.36 kg (7 lb 6
oz) (empty); 3.9 kg (8 lb 10
oz) (loaded)
Length: 820 mm (32 in)
(stock extended); 615 mm
(24 in) (stock retracted)
Cyclic rate of fire: 700
rounds per minute
Magazine: 35-round box

Assessment
Reliability   ★★★
Accuracy   ★★★
Age   ★★★★★
Worldwide users ★★

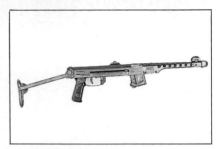

The PPS was designed and produced in the besieged city of Leningrad during World War II. It is a masterpiece of cut-price engineering.

This weapon is a remarkable example of Soviet ingenuity. It was designed by an engineer, A. I. Sudarev, in the besieged city of Leningrad (St Petersburg) in 1942. A major industrial centre, Leningrad was encircled by German and Finnish forces and was desperately short of weapons. Sudarev fashioned a very basic SMG from sheet metal stampings, held together by welds and rivets. Using the same stick magazine as existing Soviet SMGs and chambered for the same 7.62-mm×25 pistol round, the PPS was built in Leningrad and used by the city's garrison. It proved a sturdy and reliable weapon, and after the siege was lifted in 1943 production standards improved and the resulting PPS-43 was supplied to other Soviet units.

PPSh-41

Specification
Cartridge: 7.62-mm×25
Weight: 5.4 kg
(11 lb 14 oz) (loaded)
Length: 828 mm (32 in)
Cyclic rate of fire: 900
rounds per minute
Magazine: 35-round box
or 71-round drum

Assessment
Reliability   ★★★★★
Accuracy   ★★★★
Age   ★★★★★
Worldwide users ★★★

Firing the superb PPSh-41 with its 71-round drum magazine, the classic support position is to grip the underside of the large and heavy magazine.

One of the most famous weapons of World War II, the PPSh-41 was subsequently copied in China and became the main Communist infantry weapon in the Korean War. Remaining in reserve formations throughout the Warsaw Pact well into the 1960s, it was still being used in Beirut during the 1970s and also in Africa. With light recoil and reasonable accuracy at up to 150 metres, the PPSh-41 was extremely robust. The barrels were chrome-lined to offer some protection against the corrosive primers used on Soviet ammunition, although when demand was at its height, many PPSh barrels were made by cutting Mosin-Nagant rifle barrels in half! The PPSh had two types of magazine: a conventional single-stack 35-round box or a giant drum magazine capable of holding 71 rounds.

MAS Model 38

Specification
Cartridge: 7.65-mm
Weight: 2.87 kg (6 lb 5
oz) (empty); 3.4 kg (7 lb 8
oz) (loaded)
Length: 734 mm (29 in)
Cyclic rate of fire: 600
rounds per minute
Magazine: 32-round box

Assessment
Reliability   ★★★
Accuracy   ★★★★
Age   ★★★★★
Worldwide users ★

The curiously 'bent' silhouette of the MAS Model 38 results from an attempt to keep the barrel and sights in better alignment. It was used by French forces during the 1940s and 1950s, but it was soon replaced by the MAT 49.

The MAS (Manufacture d'Armes de St Etienne) Model 38 was in production when the French army was defeated in 1940, and the factory stayed in operation throughout the subsequent occupation. After 1945, when French forces were soon embroiled in guerrilla war in Indo-China, the MAS 38 was used alongside US-supplied Thompsons and its French successor, the MAT 49. The MAS Model 38 has a curious 'bent' profile because the barrel leaves the receiver at an angle. Inside, the breech block travels at an angle to the bore. Although accurate, it was chambered for the unique French 7.65-mm Long cartridge rather than the by-then popular 9-mm Parabellum. Some of those captured by the Viet Minh were reportedly converted to fire the Soviet 7.62-mm×25 pistol and SMG cartridge. In both forms the MAS Model 38 was used in small numbers by Communist forces in South East Asia during the 1960s.

Pistols are issued to a wide variety of soldiers. Many personnel need a small and handy means of self defence. Special Forces need a pistol as a back-up weapon — or sometimes as their only weapon during covert operations.

Browning High Power

Specification
Cartridge: 9-mm Parabellum
Muzzle velocity: 350 m (1150 ft) per second
Weight: 810 g (28 oz) (unloaded)
Overall gun length: 200 mm (8 in)
Barrel length: 130 mm (5 in)
Magazine capacity: 13

Assessment
Reliability	★★★★
Accuracy	★★★★
Age	★★★★★
Worldwide users	★★★★★

The Browning High Power is one of the most commonly encountered military handguns today. Used by the SAS in the storming of the Iranian Embassy, it dates from 1935 and was used in World War II by both Allied and German forces.

One of the most successful military pistols of all time, the Browning may be old but it remains in widespread use. Its large magazine capacity, simple design and 50-year combat record all count in its favour. Used by British forces since World War II, it is still in service, although in 1990 the Army ordered a limited purchase of SIG-Sauer pistols for Special Forces use. The Belgian company Fabrique National has developed several modernised versions of the High Power, but none has caught on like the original.

Colt .45 M1911A1

Specification
Cartridge: .45 ACP
Muzzle velocity: 253 m (830 ft) per second
Weight: 1130 g (40 oz) (unloaded)
Overall gun length: 220 mm (9 in)
Barrel length: 127 mm (5 in)
Magazine capacity: 7

Assessment
Reliability	★★★★
Accuracy	★★★★
Age	★★★★★
Worldwide users	★★★★★

Unlike most modern military handguns which are chambered for 9-mm Parabellum, the Colt M1911 fires the much more powerful .45 ACP cartridge. It remains extremely popular with sports shooters and numerous versions are still being manufactured.

Adopted by the US Army before World War I, the Colt was only recently replaced by the Beretta 92 9-mm. But production of the Beretta was behind schedule at the time of the Gulf War, so many units, especially the Marines, took their trusty .45s with them instead. The Colt M1911 has become the handgun by which all others are judged in the USA. Still enormously popular with sports shooters, its very powerful cartridge has the advantage over the 9-mm Parabellum round popular in Europe. The basic design has been widely modified for specialised sporting/combat pistols.

SIG-Sauer P220

Specification
Cartridge: 9-mm Parabellum
Muzzle velocity: 345 m (1130 ft) per second
Weight: 730 g (26 oz) (unloaded)
Overall gun length: 198 mm (8 in)
Barrel length: 112 mm (4 in)
Magazine capacity: 9

Assessment
Reliability	★★★★
Accuracy	★★★★
Age	★
Worldwide users	★

The SIG P220 was one of the first automatics to be fitted with a de-cocking lever and no safety. Simple to use, the first round is double-action while subsequent shots are single action. The SAS are now using SIGs in preference to Brownings.

The P220 is one of a series of high-quality automatic pistols produced by this Swiss/German company. Manufactured to a very high standard, SIG pistols have become popular with law enforcement organisations in the USA and Special Forces units worldwide. It employs the same sort of locking cam as the Browning, but locks into the slide by using the enlarged chamber of the barrel to engage a wide ejection slot in the slide; a simple idea and a robust arrangement. SIG pistols are relatively expensive but they have a good record of safety and reliability.

Makarov

Specification
Cartridge: 9-mm×18
Muzzle velocity: 315 m (1030 ft) per second
Weight: 663 g (23 oz) (unloaded)
Overall gun length: 160 mm (8 in)
Barrel length: 91 mm (4 in)
Magazine capacity: 8

Assessment
Reliability ★★★
Accuracy ★★★
Age ★★★★
Worldwide users ★★★★

The Russian army has never given much priority to handguns. The Makarov is an uninspired design issued to vehicle crew and officers.

The standard Russian service pistol since the 1950s, the small and handy Makarov is essentially a copy of the pre-war Walther PP. It fires the Russian 9-mmx18 pistol cartridge, which is less powerful than the 9-mm Parabellum. The trigger pull is usually awful, but on the other hand the weapons are well made and use high-quality steel. Makarovs have been supplied to most Russian allies and can be encountered all over the world. The Makarov is a very basic weapon, not comparable to a Browning, let alone a SIG. The Russian army has never considered the pistol to be a practical weapon.

Beretta 92F

Specification
Cartridge: 9-mm Parabellum
Muzzle velocity: 390 m (1280 ft) per second
Weight: 950 g (33 oz) (unloaded)
Overall gun length: 217 mm (9 in)
Barrel length: 125 mm (5 in)
Magazine capacity: 15

Assessment
Reliability ★★★★
Accuracy ★★★★
Age ★
Worldwide users ★

The Beretta 92 series of 9-mm pistols has been extremely successful, although the version built to US government specifications – the controversial M9 – has been dogged with problems as it enters service with the US forces.

This large-magazine-capacity 9-mm semi-automatic has become a controversial weapon since winning the protracted trials conducted by the US Army to select a replacement for the venerable Colt M1911A1. Adopted by the US Army under the designation M9, the Beretta has still not replaced the Colt, as deliveries are far behind schedule. A handsome and accurate gun, it was popularised in the USA by the movie *Lethal Weapon*. But the Beretta's future as a military weapon is still uncertain, and doubts have been voiced about its long-term durability.

CZ75

Specification
Cartridge: 9-mm Parabellum
Muzzle velocity: 340 m (1115 ft) per second
Weight: 980 g (34 oz) (unloaded)
Overall gun length: 203 mm (8 in)
Barrel length: 120 mm (5 in)
Magazine capacity: 15

Assessment
Reliability ★★★★
Accuracy ★★★★
Age ★★
Worldwide users ★

The Czech CZ75 was sold in the West during the early 1980s. Not patented, it was widely copied but the original weapon and the updated CZ85 are still selling well to sports shooters in the USA and Europe.

Produced in Czechoslovakia before the collapse of the Warsaw Pact, this well-made and well-designed handgun soon caught on with sports shooters in Europe and the USA. Unfortunately for the Czechs, they did not patent the weapon, and key features have been copied by weapons that have since achieved major commercial success. A sound combat pistol, the CZ75 has a surprisingly smooth double action and the improved CZ85 has ambidextrous controls and a better finish. The CZ75 is clear proof that Eastern European manufacture need not mean dodgy quality and the price tag is very attractive.

Steyr GB

Specification
Cartridge: 9-mm Parabellum
Muzzle velocity: (depending on cartridge) 360–420 m (1180–1380 ft) per second
Weight: 845 g (30 oz) (unloaded)
Overall gun length: 216 mm (9 in)
Barrel length: 136 mm (5 in)
Magazine capacity: 18

Assessment
Reliability ★★★★
Accuracy ★★★★
Age ★★
Worldwide users ★

The GB was popular with US Special Forces because it tolerated poor ammunition better than most guns: good news for soldiers behind the lines where the ammunition supply is uncertain.

The Steyr GB is an unusual pistol because it is gas-operated. The gas-delayed blowback action and its relatively large size absorb recoil excellently. The GB is issued with the now-common three-dot sighting system for rapid sight alignment, and they give a good clear picture. The enormous magazine capacity of the GB makes it a bulky weapon for concealed carry, but it does offer more than double the capacity of some earlier weapons. The Steyr is used by a few European law enforcement agencies.

New pistols are being introduced every year, but many older weapons are still encountered in the hands of irregular troops and the armies of the developing nations. In capable hands these are no less effective than many modern weapons.

Tokarev TT-33

Specification
Cartridge: 7.62-mm×25 Tokarev
Weight: 850 g (30 oz) (unloaded)
Length: 195 mm (8 in)
Barrel length: 116 mm (4 in)
Magazine: 8-round box

Assessment
Reliability	★★★★
Accuracy	★★★
Age	★★★★
Worldwide users	★★

The Tokarev is a very simple design, built for strength above all else. It has mediocre sights, no safety catch and fires a relatively light round, but will function in mud and snow, and can always double as a club.

Designed in the 1920s, this was the service pistol of the Soviet army from 1933 until the 1950s, when it was replaced by the Makarov. Using Browning's swinging-link locking system, the Tokarev is chambered for the Soviet 7.62-mm×25 cartridge, which is their designation for the old 7.63 Mauser Export round. The Tokarev is a typically robust Soviet design, able to take hard knocks but still keep functioning. It has no safety catch.

Walther P38

Specification
Cartridge: 9-mm Parabellum
Weight: 950 g (33 oz) (loaded)
Length: 219 mm (9 in)
Barrel length: 124 mm (5 in)
Magazine: 8-round box

Assessment
Reliability	★★★★
Accuracy	★★★★
Age	★★★
Worldwide users	★★

The Walther P38 introduced the double-action mechanism into military service. Used by German forces during World War II, it is still in production today, although its magazine capacity is small by modern standards.

One of the most influential military hand-guns of the 20th century, the P38 replaced the Luger just before World War II. The P38 was more tolerant of poor ammunition and harsh conditions than the Luger, and is still manufactured today under the designation P1. The Walther's double-action trigger mechanism allowed a fast, if relatively inaccurate, shot. This feature has become very popular since, and most modern service pistols have followed suit.

Luger

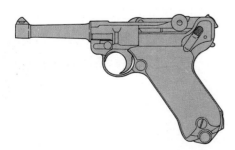

Specification
Cartridge: 9-mm Parabellum
Weight: 870 g (31 oz) (unloaded)
Length: 222 mm (9 in)
Barrel length: 103 mm (4 in)
Magazine: 8-round box

Assessment
Reliability	★★
Accuracy	★★★
Age	★★★★★
Worldwide users	★

The famous Luger pistol was manufactured in several calibres and with different barrel lengths. Its performance as a combat pistol leaves much to be desired, but its stylish design has won it many admirers.

One of the best known pistols of all time, the Luger was manufactured in numerous different versions and was used during both World Wars. It is a favourite collectors' piece today; as a combat pistol, it was always outranked by the Colt 1911. The toggle-link mechanism is sensitive to variations in ammunition quality, and many Lugers have a grim trigger pull. Copies of the Luger are still made in the USA as fun guns.

CZ38

Specification
Cartridge: 9-mm Short
Weight: 940 g (33 oz) (unloaded)
Length: 206 mm (8 in)
Barrel length: 118 mm (4 in)
Magazine: 8-round box

Assessment
Reliability ★★★
Accuracy ★
Age ★★★★
Worldwide users ★

This Czech design was a contemporary of the Tokarev, and it remains a classic example of how to get it wrong. It is 9-mm calibre but is a blowback design using the 9-mm Short cartridge, so its stopping power leaves much to be desired. The trigger mechanism only allowed self-cocking and had a very stiff pull. Fortunately the Czechs were so late in developing the CZ38 that their soldiers hardly saw it. All wartime production was taken by the German occupiers, which served them right.

The Czech CZ38 was a poor design chambered for the weak 9-mm Short cartridge that was due to be adopted just as the Germans invaded. Built to the Czechs' usual high standards, some 12,000 weapons were taken over by the Wehrmacht.

SACM Mle 35A

Specification
Cartridge: 7.65-mm Longue
Weight: 730 g (26 oz) (unloaded)
Length: 189 mm (7 in)
Barrel length: 109 mm (4 in)
Magazine: 8-round box

Assessment
Reliability ★★★
Accuracy ★★★
Age ★★★★
Worldwide users ★

This was the French army's service pistol from 1935, and the design was modified in 1950 to take 9-mm Parabellum. The Mle 35 was a sound-enough pistol, spoiled by the choice of cartridge, 7.65-mm Longue. This weak round was unique to the French army. Using a version of the Browning swinging-link locking system, the Mle 35 was manufactured in several versions. The Mle 50 redesign entered service in 1951 and can still be encountered.

The SACM (Sociéte Alsacienne de Construction Méchanique) 7.65-mm pistol won the French army contract for an automatic to replace the 8-mm Lebel revolver in 1935. The Modèle 50 is the same design but chambered for 9-mm Parabellum.

Lahti M35

Specification
Cartridge: 9-mm Parabellum
Weight: 1220 g (43 oz) (unloaded)
Length: 245 mm (10 in)
Barrel length: 105 mm (4 in)
Magazine: 8-round box

Assessment
Reliability ★★★★★
Accuracy ★★★★
Age ★★★★
Worldwide users ★★

Designed by Aimo Lahti, this Luger lookalike was built to withstand the very harsh conditions of the Finnish winter, and it will keep functioning in sub-zero temperatures. Although it resembles the Luger, the bolt actually moves inside the barrel extension and is locked by lugs underneath. Its exceptional arctic performance ensures its survival in the hands of the Finns and Swedes.

The Lahti M35 is extremely well sealed to prevent dirt and grit entering the mechanism. Carefully engineered to keep functioning in arctic conditions, it remains in service in Finland and Sweden.

Radom wz 35

Specification
Cartridge: 9-mm Parabellum
Weight: 1020 g (36 oz) (loaded)
Length: 197 mm (8 in)
Barrel length: 121 mm (5 in)
Magazine: 8-round box

Assessment
Reliability ★★★★
Accuracy ★★★★
Age ★★★
Worldwide users ★

Developed in 1935 – a good year for pistols – the Polish Radom ranks as one of the best 9-mm handguns. A single-action pistol that locks up like a Browning High Power, the Radom soaks up recoil very well and is a pleasant weapon to shoot. The grip safety is the only safety device. The hammer can be lowered onto a loaded chamber and then subsequently thumb-cocked. German forces used the Radom during World War II.

The Radom is also known as the WIS after its designers Wilneiwcyc and Skrzpinski. Original Polish weapons have the Polish eagle engraved on the slide; ones made during the German occupation are often poorly finished.

PISTOLS

While the design of Western military pistols has moved towards large-frame weapons with high magazine capacities, there is still a place for smaller handguns. For specialist units that need concealable weapons, there is a wide range of pistols available.

Heckler & Koch HK4

Specification
Cartridge: .22 LR, .25 ACP, .32 ACP or .380 ACP
Weight: 480 g (17 oz)
Length: 157 mm (6 in)
Barrel length: 85 mm (3 in)
Magazine: 8 rounds in .22 LR, .25 and .32 ACP; 7 rounds in .380 ACP

Assessment
Reliability ★★★★
Accuracy ★★★
Age ★★
Worldwide users ★

The Heckler & Koch HK4 is sold in four different calibres complete with barrels and springs, so the same gun can be quickly changed over to fire different ammunition.

The HK4 is one of the best blowback pistols ever designed. It is basically an updated version of the Mauser Model HSc 7.65-mm double-action auto introduced in 1940. The HK4 was sold as a four-calibre package all in one gun, so the weapon comes complete with barrels and springs for .22 LR, .25 ACP, .32 ACP and .380 ACP (9-mm Short). The .22 LR round is too small for self-defence, although the USSR makes extensive use of the PSM in 5.45-mm calibre, and Mossad, the Israeli secret service, has used .22 weapons to assassinate terrorist leaders.

Ruger Speed-Six

Specification
Cartridge: .357 Magnum or .38 Special
Weight: 940 g (33 oz) (70-mm barrel)
Length: 197 mm (8 in)
Barrel length: 70 or 102 mm (3 or 4 in)
Magazine: 6-round cylinder

Assessment
Reliability ★★★★★
Accuracy ★★★★
Age ★★★
Worldwide users ★★

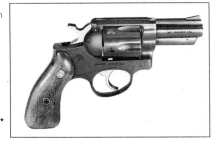

Ruger manufactures an excellent series of sports and law enforcement firearms, all built to exacting standards of strength and reliability. The Speed-Six popularised Rugers amongst police personnel.

There is now a plethora of pocket revolvers available in the USA intended for self-defence and as back-up weapons for law enforcement officers. The Ruger Speed-Six is a combat double-action weapon chambered for .357 Magnum, although many shooters will fire .38+P from it rather than endure the blast and recoil associated with this powerful cartridge. Ruger have recently launched an even smaller .357 Magnum revolver, although it is only supposed to fire the lighter 125-grain rounds.

Detonics Pocket 9

Specification
Cartridge: 9-mm Parabellum
Weight: 738 g (26 oz)
Length: 150 mm (6 in)
Barrel length: 76 mm (3 in)
Magazine: 6 rounds

Assessment
Reliability ★★★★
Accuracy ★★★
Age ★
Worldwide users ★

Detonics offer a wide range of 'pocket pistols' but in some serious calibres – 9-mm Parabellum and even .45 ACP. Note the absence of sights on this Pocket 9.

Detonics have specialised in producing small automatics in .380 ACP, 9-mm and .45. The Pocket 9 is a six-shot 9-mm auto that will fit in your pocket. Like several of the Detonics range it has no real sights since it is intended for point-blank range only. Very carefully put together, it has features that you would only usually find on larger pistols, such as double and single action, locked breech mechanism, ambidextrous safety catch and all-stainless-steel construction.

Tanfoglio GT32

Specification
Cartridge: .32 ACP
Weight: 740 g (26 oz)
Length: 170 mm (7 in)
Barrel length: 95 mm
(4 in)
Magazine: 7 rounds

Assessment
Reliability   ★ ★ ★ ★
Accuracy   ★ ★ ★
Age   ★ ★
Worldwide users   ★

The GT32 is an excellent little pistol chambered for 7.65-mm – a low-powered cartridge that has remained in widespread use throughout the century.

Tanfoglio are well known for their development of the CZ75 9-mm pistol, but the company also manufactures a full range of home-grown designs. The GT32 is a simple blowback .32-calibre semi-automatic pistol with several built-in safety features such as a magazine safety. The .32 ACP is a weak cartridge for serious self-defence, but it remains in widespread use in Europe and the USA.

Astra Constable

Specification
Cartridge: .380 ACP or
.22 LR
Weight: 1048 g (37 oz)
(.380); 793 g (28 oz)
(.22 LR)
Length: 168 mm (7 in)
Barrel length: 89 mm
(3 in)
Magazine: 7 rounds in
.380; 10 rounds in .22 LR

Assessment
Reliability   ★ ★ ★
Accuracy   ★ ★ ★
Age   ★ ★
Worldwide users   ★

The Astra Constable is typical of the small automatics chambered for 7.65-mm which are still in service with many European law enforcement agencies. The hammer can be lowered for a double-action first shot.

The Spanish company Astra produces several small automatics. This weapon is closely based on the classic Walther PP and is available in either .22 LR or .380 ACP. Like the Walther, it is a double-action blowback semi-automatic which shoots and handles very well. The pistol is easily concealed and can be carried hammer down to fire double action for the first shot, although it cannot be carried cocked and locked. A good little gun for the money.

Astra Falcon

Specification
Cartridge: .380 ACP or
.32 ACP
Weight: 668 g (23 oz)
(.380); 646 g (23 oz) (.32)
Length: 164 mm (6 in)
Barrel length: 98.5 mm
(4 in)
Magazine: 7 rounds in
.380; 10 rounds in .32

Assessment
Reliability   ★ ★ ★
Accuracy   ★ ★ ★
Age   ★ ★ ★ ★
Worldwide users   ★ ★ ★

The Astra Falcon is a classic of its kind: the 'air pistol' profile is typical of Astra's range of small-calibre automatic pistols.

This is the sole survivor in production of the design that made Astra famous. The pistol is of simple and robust design with external hammer and fixed sights, and has been distributed throughout Europe for civilian and police use, as well as being issued as a service pistol in Spain. Note the odd position of the magazine release in the grip. Unlike most modern blowback designs in this calibre, the Falcon is single action only.

Walther PPK

Specification
Cartridge: .22 LR,
6.35-mm, 7.65-mm or
9-mm Short (.380 ACP)
Weight: 568 g (20 oz)
Length: 155 mm (6 in)
Barrel length: 86 mm
(3 in)
Magazine: 7 rounds

Assessment
Reliability   ★ ★ ★
Accuracy   ★ ★ ★
Age   ★ ★ ★ ★ ★
Worldwide users   ★ ★ ★

Walther pistols pioneered the double-action/single-action trigger system for automatics. Safe and fast into action, the gun has been in production for over 60 years.

This well-made double-action blowback pistol appeared in 1931 and is available in several different calibres, all distinguished by a lack of stopping power. It had a reputation for reliability, which was badly dented in the UK when a police officer guarding Princess Anne had a stoppage on the first round during a kidnap attempt in the 1970s. This put the Metropolitan Police off automatic pistols for over 10 years. However, no-one else has had any complaints and the PPK will be around for some time to come.

PISTOLS

While the principles behind modern handguns have remained unchanged since the beginning of the 20th century, current designs are easier to use and far safer than their predecessors. These are some of Europe's most widely produced weapons, in service around the world.

Walther P5

Designed to meet the exacting safety requirements demanded by the German police, the P5 is a very handy weapon widely exported to the USA and South America and employed by German and Dutch police forces. You can fire it single action by cocking the hammer with your thumb or double action after releasing the de-cocking lever on the side.

Specification
Cartridge: 9-mm Parabellum
Weight: 795 g (28 oz)
Length: 180 mm (7 in)
Barrel length: 90 mm (4 in)
Magazine: 8-round box

Assessment
Reliability	★★★
Accuracy	★★★
Age	★★
Worldwide users	★★★

Walther's P5 was introduced in 1979, and is an updated version of the company's long-serving P38 design. It employs the same breech locking system and double-action trigger, but with revised safety arrangements.

Walther P88

The P88 looks radically different to previous Walther pistols because it employs a modified Colt-Browning locking system as opposed to the locking wedge used on the P38. It retains the double-action mechanism and de-cocking lever of the P5 and various safety features ensure that the firing pin cannot be pushed forwards by an accidental blow. The chunky grip is filled with a large capacity magazine which may give it more appeal to anyone anticipating a protracted firefight.

Specification
Cartridge: 9-mm Parabellum
Weight: 900 g (32 oz)
Length: 187 mm (7 in)
Barrel length: 102 mm (4 in)
Magazine: 15-round box

Assessment
Reliability	★★★
Accuracy	★★★
Age	★
Worldwide users	★

Walther's P88 falls into line with most other modern pistols, with its Colt-Browning locking system and large capacity magazine. It has many of the features called for by the US Army pistol competition, including ambidextrous safety and magazine release catches.

Browning DA

The Browning Double Action is derived by Fabrique Nationale from the famous FN Browning High Power, and retains many of the characteristics that have made the older pistol a best seller for half a century. The DA is designed to be fired left- or right-handed with a safety on both sides of the slide and a magazine release catch that can be reversed in seconds. The trigger guard has been reshaped to allow for a two-handed combat grip.

Specification
Cartridge: 9-mm Parabellum
Weight: 920 g (32 oz) (unloaded)
Length: 200 mm (8 in)
Barrel length: 118 mm (4 in)
Magazine: 14, plus one round chambered

Assessment
Reliability	★★★★
Accuracy	★★★★
Age	★
Worldwide users	★★

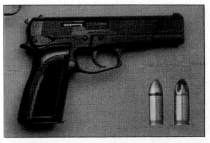

The Browning Double Action has some resemblance to the Browning High Power from which it was developed. But it is a much more modern design, with an ambidextrous de-cocking lever and reversible left or right side magazine release.

SIG-Sauer P226

Specification
Cartridge: 9-mm Parabellum
Weight: 750 g (27 oz)
Length: 196 mm (8 in)
Barrel length: 112 mm (4 in)
Magazine: 15-round box

Assessment
Reliability ★★★★★
Accuracy ★★★★★
Age ★★
Worldwide users ★★★

A new weapon combining parts from the P220 and P225, the P226 was developed for the infamous US joint services pistol trials (the longest-running show since *The Mousetrap*). It was beaten by the Beretta but has now been adopted by the FBI, who use with it Olin subsonic loads with 147-grain soft nose bullets. These do not overpenetrate like fully-jacketed 115-grain military loads, and still allow magazine capacity to be double that of a .45 pistol.

The SIG-Sauer P226 is a superbly-made pistol which was probably the best weapon tested in the US Army trials of the 1980s. However, quality comes at a price, and high cost ruled out its adoption for general service.

SIG-Sauer P228

Specification
Cartridge: 9-mm Parabellum
Weight: 830 g (30 oz)
Length: 180 mm (7 in)
Barrel length: 98 mm (4 in)
Magazine: 13-round box

Assessment
Reliability ★★★★★
Accuracy ★★★★
Age ★
Worldwide users ★

The latest in the family of pistols derived from the SIG P220, the P228 combines a P225 top unit and a shortened P226 frame and is chambered for 9-mm Parabellum. It has excellent three-dot combat sights, and an optional short trigger is on offer: this reduces the reach so that someone with small hands can manage it quite comfortably. Selective double action with trigger pulls of 5.5 kg (double action) and 4.4 kg (single action), it cannot be carried locked and cocked.

The SIG-Sauer P228 is the compact member of the P220 family. Small, but with a high magazine capacity, it offers all the quality of manufacture and reliability of earlier designs in a slightly smaller package.

Heckler & Koch P7

Specification
Cartridge: 9-mm Parabellum
Weight: 850 g (30 oz) (without magazine)
Length: 175 mm (7 in)
Barrel length: 105 mm (4 in)
Magazine: 8 or 13 rounds

Assessment
Reliability ★★★★
Accuracy ★★★★
Age ★★
Worldwide users ★★★

The prominent squeeze cocking device on the front of the grip cocks the pistol ready for the first shot and, when released, de-cocks the firing pin. There are three versions: the P7M13, with 13 rounds, and the P7M8 with eight rounds, which is easier to conceal. Most interesting is the P7M7, intended for the American market; this is chambered for .45 ACP and uses an artillery-style hydraulic recoil system.

The P7's design is a result of a German police requirement for a handgun which could be carried loaded with complete safety. The squared-off trigger guard helps with a two-handed firing grip.

Heckler & Koch P9

Specification
Cartridge: 9-mm Parabellum or .45 ACP
Weight: 880 g (31 oz) (magazine empty)
Length: 192 mm (8 in)
Barrel length: 102 mm (4 in)
Magazine: 9-round box (.45 ACP, 7 rounds)

Assessment
Reliability ★★★★
Accuracy ★★★
Age ★★★★
Worldwide users ★★★★

The P9 uses the famous Heckler & Koch roller-locked delayed blowback system originally developed for the G3 rifle. The P9 is single action, but the later P9S is double action. The gun is produced in .45 ACP for the American market and was briefly produced in 7.65-mm Parabellum. It is used by German and many other police forces and military units.

Intended mainly for police users, who prize reliability above all other features, the P9S is a robust weapon with few frills. Its nine-round magazine makes for a slim grip, producing a smaller, more easily concealable pistol.

COMBAT REVOLVERS

Although the self-loading pistol has become the standard military sidearm, the revolver remains a good weapon for security troops. Stronger, simpler and capable of firing more powerful rounds, the revolver is an ideal weapon for situations where reliability is more important than magazine capacity.

Webley Mk 4

Specification
Cartridge: .380 SAA ball
Weight: 767 g (27 oz)
Barrel length: 127 mm (5 in)
Cylinder: 6 rounds

Assessment
Reliability ★★★
Accuraoy ★★
Age ★★★★★
Worldwide users ★★★

The Webley .38 was supplied to almost every Commonwealth country after World War II and it can still be encountered all over the world.

After World War I, the British Army needed a smaller revolver than the .455 Webley then in service. The Enfield revolver was a scaled-down Webley, ordered instead of Webley's own .38-in Mk 4. Both were produced extensively during World War II, and after 1945 many found their way to the Empire, where they can still be found in use with Commonwealth and ex-Commonwealth military and police forces.

Ruger Police Service-Six

Specification
Cartridge: .357 Magnum
Weight: 935 g (33 oz) (with 70-mm barrel)
Barrel length: 70 or 102 mm (2³/₄ or 4 in)
Cylinder: 6 rounds

Assessment
Reliability ★★★★★
Accuracy ★★★
Age ★★★
Worldwide users ★★★

Ruger made its name in the revolver business with a series of powerful single-action weapons built to a very high standard. The Service-Six was adopted by some US law enforcement agencies.

Ruger produce a family of service revolvers based on the same exceptionally robust and safe design, utilising the transfer bar which prevents the weapon firing unless the trigger is pulled. The Service-Six and Speed-Six are both available in .38 Special or .357 Magnum models in blued steel or chrome finishes. The Service-Six is in service with the US armed forces, police and security services as the Model GS 32N Military Ruger revolver.

Ruger GP 100

Specification
Cartridge: .357 Magnum
Weight: 1162 g (41 oz) (with 102-mm barrel)
Barrel length: 102 or 152 mm (4 or 6 in)
Cylinder: 6 rounds

Assessment
Reliability ★★★★★
Accuracy ★★★★
Age ★
Worldwide users ★

Ruger introduced the GP 100 as a standard .357 Magnum aimed to challenge the Smith & Wesson 'L' frames that are so popular. The GP 100 performs well, although the cylinder release is an acquired taste.

This is Ruger's new offering in the police pistol market. The long ejector shroud gives a slightly muzzle-heavy feel that gives good point qualities and cuts down felt recoil; the composite grips of wood and rubber work very well; and the take-down has been improved, making the revolver even easier to strip and clean. The weapon is very accurate and has an exceptionally smooth double action straight out of the box.

Luigi Franchi RF 83 Service

Specification
Cartridge: .38 Special
Weight: 800 g (28 oz)
(with 152-mm barrel)
Barrel length: 102 or
152 mm (4 or 6 in)
Cylinder: 6 rounds

Assessment
Reliability   ★★★★
Accuracy   ★★★
Age   ★★
Worldwide users   ★

Looking remarkably similar to the Colt Python with its ventilated rib, the Franchi service .38 is only available in that calibre and will not take Magnum cartridges. Sustained use of +P loads is also questionable.

The Model RF 83 Service is a very good Colt Python copy with a 102-mm barrel and a smooth double action. The series also includes a 152-mm barrelled target version with adjustable sights which would also be suitable for police use. The only drawback with this series is that, like the Colt Diamondback, it will only fire .38 Specials, not .357 Magnums. The Franchi does not have any of the Ruger's innovative takedown system and relies on a conventional side plate for access to the lock work.

Colt Python

Specification
Cartridge: .357 Magnum
Weight: 980 g (34 oz)
(with 102-mm barrel)
Barrel length: 64 mm
(2¹/₂ in), 102 (4 in),
152 mm (6 in) or 203 mm
(8 in)
Cylinder: 6 rounds

Assessment
Reliability   ★★★★★
Accuracy   ★★★★
Age   ★★★★
Worldwide users   ★★

Colt's most successful post-war revolver, the Python, is an outstanding revolver, although its price tag restricts it to dedicated shooters. Finely-crafted weapons do not come cheap.

This is arguably the best production revolver in the world. It has an excellent double-action operation and the standard of workmanship is very high. The weapon is extremely heavy duty and will fire full-house .357 Magnum factory loads throughout its service life. The only real trouble is the price; many police forces simply cannot afford it.

Smith & Wesson Model 629

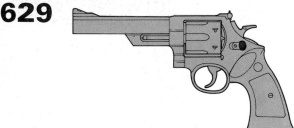

Specification
Cartridge: .44 Magnum
Weight: 1332 g (47 oz)
(with 152-mm barrel)
Barrel length: 102 (4 in),
152 mm (6 in), or 213 mm
(8³/₈ in)
Cylinder: 6 rounds

Assessment
Reliability   ★★★★★
Accuracy   ★★★★
Age   ★★
Worldwide users   ★

Smith & Wesson continues to dominate the .44 Magnum market. A popular hunting weapon, it is valued by a few police officers for its ability to penetrate an engine block.

Very few people would consider a .44 Magnum as a police revolver outside a 'Dirty Harry' film. The .44 Magnum Smith & Wesson double-action revolver is on issue to the Tennessee Police Department, but such field artillery would probably not go down well elsewhere. Stopping power is not a problem when firing a .44-calibre semi-jacketed hollowpoint bullet from a 152-mm barrel.

Colt Lawman Mk 5

Specification
Cartridge: .357 Magnum
Weight: 992 g (47 oz)
(with 102-mm barrel)
Barrel length: 51 or 102
mm (2 or 4 in)
Cylinder: 6 rounds

Assessment
Reliability   ★★★★
Accuracy   ★★★
Age   ★★★
Worldwide users   ★★★

The Lawman was a successful pistol in its time, but Colt's line of medium-frame revolvers has been eclipsed in recent years by Smith & Wesson and other manufacturers. Note the unshrouded ejector.

The Lawman is a medium-frame bull-barrelled .357 Magnum revolver with fixed sights. It handles well and has a good double action with a short hammer throw and it is obviously built for the police market as a more compact revolver than the Trooper Mk 5. The Colt Agent is shown below for comparison. The revolver is very solidly constructed and moderately priced, and is available in blue nickel or Colt Guard finishes in 51- or 102-mm barrel lengths.

SECURITY PISTOLS

No. 1

In the Western world military pistols are mostly chambered for the 9-mm Parabellum cartridge, which was selected as the NATO standard pistol and SMG round. However, there are many other cartridges available and guns to fire them. The future of the 9-mm round is by no means secure.

CZ52

Specification
Cartridge: 7.62-mm Tokarev
Weight: 960 g (34 oz)
Length: 209 mm (8 in)
Barrel length: 120 mm (5 in)
Magazine: 8-round detachable box

Assessment
Reliability	★★★
Accuracy	★★★
Age	★★★★
Worldwide users	★

The CZ52 is a remarkably comfortable weapon to shoot and pleasingly accurate too. Its complex internal workings do not seem to lead to any problems.

The USSR never adopted the 9-mm Parabellum round, preferring instead the 7.62-mmx25 cartridge fired by the TT-33 Tokarev. After World War II the USSR imposed its standard calibres on the Warsaw Pact in much the same way that the USA dominated NATO's formative years. The Czech army was provided with Tokarevs, which it regarded as crude and unsatisfactory, unworthy of the proud Czechoslovakian arms industry. Eská Zbrojovka promptly developed a new pistol chambered for the Soviet cartridge but offering much better performance. The result was the CZ52: a well balanced and comfortable pistol that employs an intricate system of recoil operation derived from the MG42 GPMG.

Glock 17

Specification
Cartridge: 9-mm Parabellum
Weight: 620 g (34 oz)
Length: 188 mm (7 in)
Barrel length: 114 mm (4 in)
Magazine: 17-round detachable box

Assessment
Reliability	★★★★★
Accuracy	★★★★
Age	★
Worldwide users	★★★

The 9-mm Glock pistol has become a market leader in only 10 years. Built with a plastic frame, it has only 33 parts and is highly reliable.

In 1983 an Austrian company that made entrenching tools was the surprise winner of the Austrian army's pistol trials. The innovative Glock pistol has since become a market leader in less than 10 years. With just 33 parts, it is astonishingly simple to maintain, and its pioneering use of a high-impact polymer frame raised a few eyebrows. Press reports that it was X-ray proof and thus a terrorist's dream were nonsense: it has a steel barrel and slide. Although it uses a conventional tilt-locking system, the Glock has a unique self-cocking mechanism that incorporates three internal safeties. There is no external safety catch. The trigger safety, firing-pin lock and trigger bar safeties keep the weapon safe until the trigger is pulled.

Glock 21

Specification
Cartridge: .45 ACP
Weight: 720 g (34 oz)
Length: 210 mm (8 in)
Barrel length: 116 mm (4 in)
Magazine: 13-round detachable box

Assessment
Reliability	★★★★
Accuracy	★★★★
Age	★
Worldwide users	★

The Glock 21 offers an unmatched combination of high magazine capacity and the renowned .45 ACP cartridge. It is otherwise identical in operation to the 9-mm model.

The creation of Glock Inc., based at Smyrna, Georgia, started one of the most dramatic success stories in recent firearms history. The Glock was well marketed and captured an increasing share of the civilian and law enforcement markets. But for many shooters, Americans especially, handguns are divided into two types – those that fire the famous .45 ACP cartridge and those that do not. Glock promptly redesigned the weapon and came up with the Model 21. With a high magazine capacity, good trigger action and simplicity of operation, the Glock 21 entered production in 1991. It is an excellent combat handgun and has already been trialled by the élite US Navy SEALs.

Glock 23

Specification
Cartridge: .40 S&W
Weight: 580 g (20 oz)
Length: 177 mm (7 in)
Barrel length: 102 mm (4 in)
Magazine: 13-round detachable box

Assessment
Reliability   ★★★★
Accuracy   ★★★★
Age   ★
Worldwide users   ★★

Law enforcement agencies in the USA have shown enormous interest in the new Smith & Wesson .40-cal cartridge. Glock introduced a .40 S&W version ahead of most of the competition.

Although sure of the demand for a .45-calibre Glock, Glock Inc. postponed its introduction to rush another version into gun shops across America. This was the Glock 23, which fires the increasingly popular .40 S&W cartridge. Glock Inc. moved so fast that it came close to beating Smith & Wesson at producing a gun to fire the Massachusetts company's own cartridge. The Model 23 is externally similar to the other Glock pistols and is well placed to collect large orders from US law enforcement agencies. The .40 S&W cartridge took the police market by storm and the Glock's simplicity of operation is popular with departments changing from revolvers to automatics.

Smith & Wesson 1006

Specification
Cartridge: 10-mm
Weight: 1070 g (38 oz)
Length: 216 mm (9 in)
Barrel length: 127 mm (5 in)
Magazine: 9-shot detachable box

Assessment
Reliability   ★★★★
Accuracy   ★★★★
Age   ★
Worldwide users   ★

The Smith & Wesson 1006 fires the powerful – some say too powerful – 10-mm cartridge. This offers excellent penetration but takes hard training to master.

The 10-mm cartridge was developed by practical pistol shooters in the USA who wanted a hard-hitting cartridge superior to the .45 ACP. The first pistol to fire it was the Bren 10 made by Dornaus & Dixon but, although prominent in the first series of 'Miami Vice', the company failed to deliver magazines with the guns, fell behind with production schedules and folded in 1985. Subsequent FBI interest in the 10-mm round led to collaborative work with Smith & Wesson and the introduction of the Model 1006 in 1990. With Novak sights, combat grips and double-action facility, it is a powerful handgun indeed. The FBI now uses the 1076, which has a de-cocking lever instead of a slide-mounted safety.

Smith & Wesson 4026

Specification
Cartridge: .40 S&W
Weight: 1070 g (38 oz)
Length: 190.5 mm (7 in)
Barrel length: 102 mm (4 in)
Magazine: 11-round detachable box

Assessment
Reliability   ★★★★
Accuracy   ★★★★
Age   ★
Worldwide users   ★★

Smith & Wesson now offers a variety of pistols chambered for its revolutionary .40 S&W cartridge. The 4026 is a handy pistol with all the characteristics of third generation S&W automatics.

Smith & Wesson's 'telephone number' numerical designations do describe the calibre and type of pistol to those who can remember the system. The 40 series all fire .40 S&W, the cartridge that captured the imagination of the gun-buying public in 1991. Developed from the '10-mm Lite' cartridge that appeared during the FBI's protracted research, .40 S&W offers a useful combination of high magazine capacity, excellent terminal ballistics and controllability. The 4026 is one of several Smith & Wesson automatics chambered for it: this one features a de-cocking lever, combat grips, Novak sights and a non-reflective steel finish.

Smith & Wesson 4506

Specification
Cartridge: .45 ACP
Weight: 980 g (34 oz)
Length: 143 mm (6 in)
Barrel length: 102 mm (4 in)
Magazine: 8-round detachable box

Assessment
Reliability   ★★★★
Accuracy   ★★★★
Age   ★
Worldwide users   ★★

Smith & Wesson rightly anticipated the continuing demand for new autos chambered for .45 ACP. The Model 4506 is a fine pistol, although it lacks the magazine capacity of the Glock equivalent.

The 4500 series of Smith & Wesson automatics includes six models, all chambered for .45 ACP. Smith & Wesson introduced a vast number of new models during the late 1980s and, while some are being discontinued already, the 4500 series is doing well. The different models offer the choice of double action with ambidextrous safety, double action with de-cocking lever or double action only. The large-frame 4506 is a pleasant gun to shoot, but its eight-round magazine capacity compares unfavourably with the Glock .45, and more polymer-frame, large-magazine-capacity .45s are entering production.

GRENADE LAUNCHERS No. 1

Grenade launchers are widely used by modern armies. Most are handheld single-shot weapons, usually fitted to a service rifle. The US and Russian armies have large automatic grenade launchers often fitted to armoured vehicles or helicopters.

Mk 19 40-mm

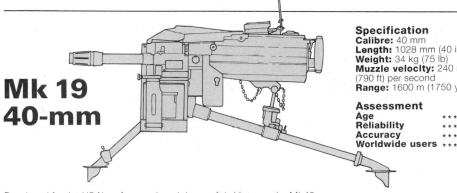

Specification
Calibre: 40 mm
Length: 1028 mm (40 in)
Weight: 34 kg (75 lb)
Muzzle velocity: 240 m (790 ft) per second
Range: 1600 m (1750 yd)

Assessment
Age   ★★★★
Reliability   ★★★
Accuracy   ★★★★
Worldwide users   ★★★

The Mk 19 grenade launcher is fitted to a wide variety of vehicles, including special forces high-mobility vehicles.

Developed for the US Navy for use aboard river craft in Vietnam, the Mk 19 entered service in 1967. Soon acquired by the US and Israeli armies, it had some reliability problems and an improved model was introduced in the late 1970s. The Mk 19 is an air-cooled, blowback-operated machine-gun that fires belted ammunition from an open bolt. The disintegrating link belt is unusual in that each link stays with the cartridge and is ejected with it.

AGS-17

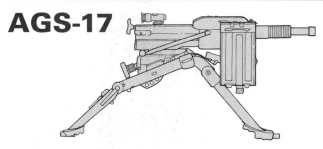

Specification
Calibre: 30 mm
Length: 840 mm (33 in)
Weight: 18 kg (39 lb 11 oz) (tripod 35 kg; 75 lb)
Muzzle velocity: unknown
Range: 1200 m (1300 yd)

Assessment
Age   ★★★
Reliability   ★★★★
Accuracy   ★★★
Worldwide users   ★★

The Soviet AGS-17 fires a smaller 30-mm grenade from a disintegrating link belt. A single-shot launcher also fires the same grenade from underneath Kalashnikov rifles.

The Plamya ('Flame') is a 30-mm grenade launcher introduced by the Soviet army in the mid-1970s and issued to the infantry companies of Motor Rifle regiments in sections of two. It is also fitted to Mi-8 'Hip' helicopters and has been seen on BTR-70 APCs. Extensively used in Afghanistan, where its high elevation enabled it to engage guerrillas firing down from the mountain peaks, the AGS-17 also became part of the Mujahideen armoury as some of them were captured. An automatic weapon like the US Mk 19, the AGS-17 is blowback operated. It is belt-fed from the right and ejects the empty cases through the bottom of the chamber.

Brunswick RAW

Specification
Calibre: 140 mm
Length: 305 mm (12 in)
Weight: 3.8 kg (8 lb 6 oz)
Muzzle velocity: 180 m (590 ft) per second
Range: 200 m (220 yd)

Assessment
Age   ★★
Reliability   ★★★★
Accuracy   ★★★
Worldwide users   ★★

The Brunswick RAW is a specialist assault weapon that fires an explosive charge against enemy strongpoints. Particularly useful in built-up areas, the RAW is used by the US Marines.

The RAW (Rifleman's Assault Weapon) is a novel device fitted to a standard M16 rifle. It launches a spherical projectile containing 1.27 kilograms of high explosive that 'pancakes' on striking the target, producing a spectacular effect against concrete structures or light armoured vehicles. It can blow a hole over 300 mm across in 200-mm thick reinforced concrete. This is far in excess of the capability of standard 40-mm grenades, but the RAW is a bulky weapon by comparison and is only intended for short-range urban combat. Although its internal rocket will propel the projectile to a maximum range of 2000 metres, its effective range is about 200 metres.

M79 grenade launcher

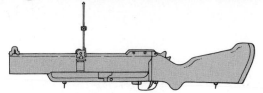

Specification
Calibre: 40 mm
Length: 738 mm (29 in)
Weight: 2.95 kg (6 lb 8 oz) (loaded)
Muzzle velocity: 76 m (245 ft) per second
Range: 150 m (165 yd)

Assessment
Age ★★★★★
Reliability ★★★★
Accuracy ★★★
Worldwide users ★★★★

A US soldier uses an M79 to launch CS gas grenades on a range in Vietnam. M79s were widely used in Vietnam, mainly firing HE and anti-personnel flechette rounds.

The M79 is a single-shot breech-loading weapon developed for the US Army during the 1950s. It was designed to fire spin-stabilised 40-mm grenades and entered service in 1961. Over 350,000 were manufactured over the next 10 years and it was extensively used in Vietnam. It was replaced by the M203, since a soldier equipped with an M79 could not carry a rifle as well. An interesting weapon to fire, owing to its incredibly high trajectory, the M79 is capable of surprising accuracy in the hands of an experienced shot. Widely exported, the M79 was used by British forces in the Falklands. Although replaced in the US armed forces, the M79 remains in service with several South American and Asian nations.

M203 40-mm grenade launcher

Specification
Calibre: 40 mm
Length: 380 mm (15 in)
Weight: 1.63 kg (3 lb 9 oz) (loaded)
Muzzle velocity: 75 m (245 ft) per second
Range: 400 m (440 yd)

Assessment
Age ★★★★
Reliability ★★★★
Accuracy ★★★★
Worldwide users ★★★★

This is the latest version of the famous M203 40-mm grenade launcher: the standard launcher tube fitted with a shoulder stock and used rather like the old M79.

Developed by the AAI Corporation in the late 1960s, the M203 replaced the M79 in the US armed forces during the 1970s; a prototype version was tested in combat during the Vietnam War. Fitted underneath an M16 rifle, the M203 provided an infantry squad with grenade-launching capability without sacrificing a rifle. A single-shot breech-loader, the M203 is worked like a pump-action shotgun and is able to deliver grenades with reasonable accuracy to over twice the effective range of an M79. The 1970s version could only be fitted to M16 rifles, but there is now a 'product-improved' M203 that is mounted on an interbar that can be clipped to almost any service rifle. It can also be fitted with a shoulder stock/pistol grip and used independently.

H&K 40-mm Granatpistole

Specification
Calibre: 40 mm
Length: 683 mm (27 in) (stock extended)
Weight: 2.3 kg (5 lb 1 oz)
Muzzle velocity: 75 m (245 ft) per second
Range: 350 m (380 yd)

Assessment
Age ★★★
Reliability ★★★
Accuracy ★★★
Worldwide users ★★

The German Heckler & Koch 40-mm grenade launcher is similar to the M79 but has a collapsable stock for handier operation. It can be fired with the stock collapsed.

Heckler & Koch have sold this single-shot break-action grenade launcher to the German army and several other military and paramilitary organisations. It has a retractable butt, collapsing to a very handy 463 mm, with fold-down sights as well. Grenades can be launched with or without the stock extended. It can fire on an almost flat trajectory as well as delivering high-angle fire. The barrel pivots when the cocking handle is fully withdrawn, permitting a fresh cartridge to be loaded. Spent cases are extracted manually. The sights are accurate to 100 metres in the lower position but must be raised for longer ranges.

CIS 40GL

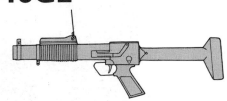

Specification
Calibre: 40 mm
Length: 655 mm (26 in)
Weight: 2.05 kg (4 lb 8 oz) (loaded)
Muzzle velocity: 71 m (230 ft) per second
Range: 350 m (380 yd)

Assessment
Age ★★
Reliability ★★★★
Accuracy ★★★★
Worldwide users ★★

The CIS 40-mm grenade launcher is a competitively-priced weapon built in Singapore. It fires a full range of projectiles and can be clipped underneath an assault rifle if required.

Chartered Industries of Singapore manufacture a wide range of infantry weapons, including this very competitive 40-mm grenade launcher. A shoulder-fired multi-purpose grenade launcher, it can be fired independently or can be attached to most service rifles. A single-shot breech-loading weapon, it consists of just four assemblies: receiver, barrel, leaf sight and buttstock or rifle adaptor. This helps ensure reliability as well as simplicity of manufacture and maintenance. It is loaded by depressing the charging lever on the left-hand side of the weapon, automatically unlocking the barrel, cocking the firing pin and applying the safety catch. The barrel swings out for easy loading and is swung back manually ready for launch.

MORTARS

Mortars are the infantry battalion's artillery. Organised as part of the battalion and providing close support to the riflemen, they have been used by most major armies since the middle of World War I. Modern mortars are much more effective than those of World War II, thanks to improved ammunition.

Brandt 120-mm rifled heavy mortar

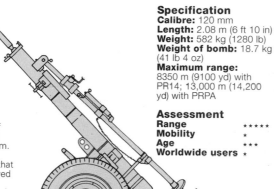

Specification
Calibre: 120 mm
Length: 2.08 m (6 ft 10 in)
Weight: 582 kg (1280 lb)
Weight of bomb: 18.7 kg (41 lb 4 oz)
Maximum range: 8350 m (9100 yd) with PR14; 13,000 m (14,200 yd) with PRPA

Assessment
Range	*****
Mobility	*
Age	***
Worldwide users	*

A Thomson Brandt 120-mm mortar being towed along a road by a VAB 4x4 APC. In service with the French army, these mortars have been widely exported.

Brandt manufactures a comprehensive range of mortars from man-portable 60-mm weapons to 120-mm mortars that require a truck to tow them. In addition to two conventional smoothbore 120-mm mortars, Brandt offers a rifled version that is effectively a light howitzer. Mounted and towed on a pair of road wheels, it can be brought into action in just 90 seconds by a well-trained crew. It fires a special type of pre-rifled projectile, primarily the standard PR14 HE bomb, which is similar in effect to a 105-mm artillery shell and can be fired much more rapidly. A rocket-assisted bomb offers a maximum range of 13000 metres.

Soltam heavy mortars

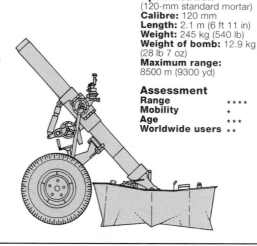

Specification
(120-mm standard mortar)
Calibre: 120 mm
Length: 2.1 m (6 ft 11 in)
Weight: 245 kg (540 lb)
Weight of bomb: 12.9 kg (28 lb 7 oz)
Maximum range: 8500 m (9300 yd)

Assessment
Range	****
Mobility	*
Age	***
Worldwide users	**

An Israeli mortar team in action during the Yom Kippur War. The Israelis make extensive use of heavy mortars, but operate most of them from APCs or half-track vehicles.

The Israeli company Soltam has provided the Israeli army and several foreign customers with several different 120-mm mortars and a vehicle-mounted 160-mm mortar. There is a 'light' 120-mm mortar that can be manhandled on the battlefield, although the weight of its ammunition remains a severe problem. The standard 120-mm mortar is designed to be towed by a jeep or light truck, but the Israeli Defence Force (IDF) is highly mechanised and mortars are more commonly fitted to converted M113 armoured personnel carriers. The 9600-metre range 160-mm mortar is fitted to modified M4 Super Sherman hulls or towed by truck. It requires a minimum crew of six and weighs 1700 kilograms when deployed for firing.

Soviet M43 160-mm mortar

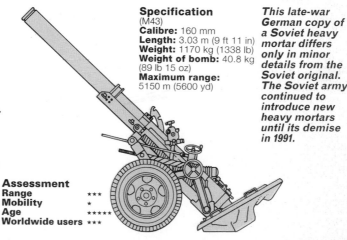

Specification
(M43)
Calibre: 160 mm
Length: 3.03 m (9 ft 11 in)
Weight: 1170 kg (1338 lb)
Weight of bomb: 40.8 kg (89 lb 15 oz)
Maximum range: 5150 m (5600 yd)

This late-war German copy of a Soviet heavy mortar differs only in minor details from the Soviet original. The Soviet army continued to introduce new heavy mortars until its demise in 1991.

The Soviet army made extensive use of heavy mortars during World War II. Cheap to manufacture, sturdy and reliable, they were also simple to operate. The M1943 was the heaviest mortar employed by Soviet forces and it was widely exported to Warsaw Pact armies during the 1950s. A larger modernised version, the M-160, was introduced in 1953 and used until the demise of the Soviet military. The Indian Army used them in 1971 and they have also been in action in most Arab-Israeli conflicts. A giant 240-mm mortar was also produced in 1952 with an improved self-propelled version entering service in 1980. The latter has an automatic loading system.

Assessment
Range	***
Mobility	*
Age	*****
Worldwide users	***

M1937 82-mm mortar

While Soviet motor rifle battalions were primarily equipped with the M1943 120-mm mortar, naval infantry and airborne forces retained the pre-war 82-mm weapon. This has the advantage of being man-portable and, supplied to left-wing forces all over the world, it has been used in countless guerrilla campaigns since World War II. Some users effected modifications – the North Vietnamese created a delayed-action fuse for use against American forces – but the ammunition was otherwise unchanged since the 1930s. Post-war versions incorporated some extra features, including a lightening tripod and a safety device that prevented a second bomb being loaded before the first one had been fired.

Specification
Calibre: 82 mm
Length: 1.22 m (4 ft)
Weight: 56 kg (124 lb)
Weight of bomb: 3 kg (6 lb 10 oz)
Maximum range: 3000 m (3280 yd)

Assessment
Range ★★★
Mobility ★★★
Age ★★★★★
Worldwide users ★★★★★

The standard Soviet mortar during World War II was this 120-mm weapon, which was widely exported after 1945. The lighter 82-mm mortar was also supplied to foreign armies, especially guerrilla forces.

L16 81-mm mortar

The British Army's standard mortar is designed to fire the 81-mm ammunition of most NATO countries as well as British bombs. Widely exported and even in service with the US Army, the L16 is man-portable with a three-man crew. It was a vital weapon during the Falklands war when British forces were desperately short of artillery. The barrel is thicker than that of many similar weapons and it has fins to help dissipate the heat generated by rapid firing. It performs so well that the British Army no longer uses heavy mortars, preferring the hail of fire that is possible from the L16. Mechanised battalions have FV 432s converted to self-propelled mortar carriers.

Specification
Calibre: 81 mm
Length: 1.23 m (4 ft)
Weight: 37.8 kg (83 lb 5 oz)
Weight of bomb: 4.2 kg (9 lb 4 oz)
Maximum range: 5650 m (6200 yd)

Assessment
Range ★★★
Mobility ★★★★
Age ★★★
Worldwide users ★★★★★

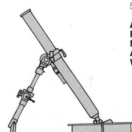

A mortar team from Britain's 5 Airborne brigade goes into action. The British army's L16 81-mm mortar has proved a great success and has even been purchased by the US Army.

US 60-mm mortars

The US Army discovered that its 81-mm mortars were too heavy for jungle operations in Vietnam. They were highly effective in static fire bases, but carrying them and their ammunition demanded too much manpower when infantry companies ventured into the trackless rainforest. Some units reverted to using the obsolete M19 60-mm mortar, which was much lighter and handier, and an infantry company could carry a great deal more ammunition for it. The M19 is a simple muzzle-loading weapon but is trigger-fired. A new weapon was developed in 1970 for infantry and airborne forces: the M224. This can be fired without a bipod and has special multi-fuse ammunition, offering the choice of high or low airburst and detonation on contact or delayed detonation.

Specification
(M19)
Calibre: 60 mm
Length: 0.819 m (2 ft 8 in)
Weight: 19.1 kg (42 lb 2 oz)
Weight of bomb: 1.46 kg (3 lb 3 oz)
Maximum range: 2100 m (2300 yd)

Assessment
Range ★★
Mobility ★★★★★
Age ★★★★★
Worldwide users ★★★

US forces made widespread use of 60-mm mortars during World War II. They enjoyed a new lease of life thanks to the Vietnam War when standard mortars proved too heavy for jungle fighting.

M30 107-mm mortar

While the British Army abandoned its 4.2-in mortars after World War II, the US Army has retained these heavy weapons, although they have been substantially improved. Weighing over 300 kilograms in action, they are too heavy for infantry use and are usually mounted in armoured personnel carriers or fired from fixed defensive positions. The 107-mm mortar was widely used during the Vietnam War and has been supplied to numerous other armies. A muzzle-loading drop-fired mortar, it is rifled and fires semi-fixed ammunition. The choice of bombs includes HE, smoke, illumination and gas (CS or a lethal type). Despite the weight of the projectiles, the M30 can fire 18 bombs in its first minute of fire; sustained rate is three or four rounds per minute.

Specification
Calibre: 107.7 mm
Length: 1.52 m (4 ft 11 in)
Weight: 305 kg (672 lb)
Weight of bomb: 12.2 kg (26 lb 14 oz)
Maximum range: 6800 m (7400 yd)

Assessment
Range ★★★★
Mobility ★★
Age ★★★★★
Worldwide users ★★★★

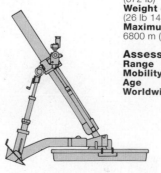

A US Army 107-mm mortar fires with a deafening noise. These heavy mortars are best suited to vehicle mounts and are usually fired from a specialist version of the M113 APC.

COMBAT SHOTGUNS No. 1

As a close-quarter weapon, the shotgun has few equals. Modified sporting guns have been used in battle in the past, but now, for the first time, purely military shotguns are being developed.

Franchi SPAS-12

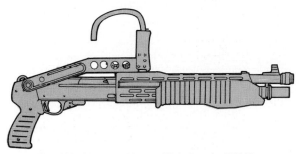

Franchi had been working on this before the RHINO programme appeared; that merely speeded things up. And since 1979 this has been the one to beat, since it produced all sorts of innovations – semi-automatic or pump-action selectable at the press of a button, one-handed operation by using a special elbow hook on the folding stock, a shot diverter to give excellent lateral short-range spread, and a general air of combat efficiency which no shotgun ever had before. Somewhat bulky on first acquaintance, but a practical and efficient weapon.

Specification
Cartridge: 12-gauge 2³/₄-in
Weight: 4.2 kg (9 lb 4 oz)
Length: 930 mm (36 in) (stock extended); 710 mm (28 in) (folded)
Cyclic rate of fire: semi-automatic only, 240 rounds per minute
Magazine: 7 rounds

Assessment
Reliability ★★★★★
Accuracy ★★★
Age ★
Worldwide users ★★

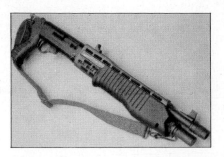

The Franchi SPAS-12 is an impressive looking piece of equipment. This is a big plus in police and security work, where it can overawe a felon and lead to an arrest without any exchange of fire.

Beretta RS 202P M2

This weapon is a direct development of the conventional pump-action RS 200P military and police shotgun. It is easy to strip and fire, and is capable of firing a wide range of 12-gauge ammunition including rifle slug and tear gas out to 100 metres. The weapon is fitted with a 'Mobilchoke' variable choke and shot expander, a barrel jacket and rapid aiming sights.

Specification
Cartridge: 12-gauge
Weight: 3.4 kg (7 lb 8 oz)
Length: 1030 mm (40 in) (stock extended)
Cyclic rate of fire: pump-action only
Magazine: 6 rounds in tubular magazine

Assessment
Reliability ★★★★★
Accuracy ★★★★
Age ★
Worldwide users ★

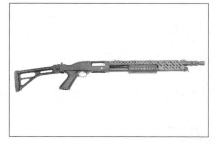

In spite of its high-tech appearance, the Beretta RS 202 is a conventional pump-action shotgun. It can fire a variety of ammunition, however, and can be used to great effect in situations from riot control to close-quarter battle.

Smith & Wesson AS

'AS' means Assault Shotgun, and this weapon is designed along the lines of an assault rifle. It comes in three variations: AS-1 is semi-auto, AS-2 is semi-auto plus a three-round burst, and AS-3 fires full-auto at 375 rounds a minute. All use short recoil operation with a rotating bolt which has 12 lugs and is therefore strong enough to fire the special CAWS ammunition. Feed is from a 10-shot box magazine, and the weapon is built from massive alloy forgings and plastic. The long barrel makes it very accurate, and the three-round burst is rather more practical than the full-automatic option.

Specification
Cartridge: 12-gauge 2³/₄- or 3-in Magnum or CAWS
Weight: 4.42 kg (9 lb 12 oz) (unloaded)
Length: 1054 mm (41 in)
Cyclic rate of fire: 375 rounds per minute
Magazine: 10 rounds

Assessment
Reliability ★★★★
Accuracy ★★★
Age ★
Worldwide users ★

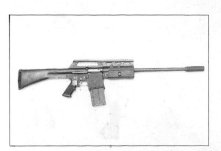

Looking very different from earlier shotguns, the Smith & Wesson AS series are combat weapons, pure and simple. The full-auto AS-3 can put out an awesome amount of firepower.

Remington 870

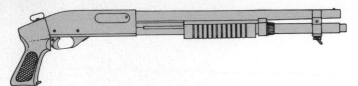

Specification
Cartridge: 12-gauge 2³/₄-in
Weight: 3.6 kg (7 lb 15 oz)
Length: 1060 mm (42 in)
Cyclic rate of fire: pump-action only
Magazine: 7 rounds in tubular magazine

Assessment
Reliability	★★★★★
Accuracy	★★
Age	★★★★
Worldwide users	★★★★

The Remington 870 is one of the most widely used military shotguns in the world. This example is in the hands of a Marine security patrol aboard a US Navy carrier.

The Model 870 is one of the most widely manufactured shotguns of all time, being produced in sporting and hunting versions as well as in dedicated police and security variants. When the US Marine Corps conducted trials to find a combat shotgun in the mid-1960s, it was decided that the reliability of the 870's pump-action gave it the edge over the semi-automatic weapons then available. The Model 870 has a seven-round tubular magazine, and can fire a wide variety of ammunition ranging from light shot and riot rounds to heavy buckshot and flechettes. Its primary function in Marine hands is for use in boarding parties, and as a security weapon aboard ship.

Striker

Specification
Cartridge: 12-gauge 2³/₄-in
Weight: 4.2 kg (9 lb 4 oz) (unloaded)
Length: 780 mm (31 in) (stock extended); 500 mm (20 in) (folded)
Cyclic rate of fire: single shot, double-action only
Magazine: 12-shot cylinder

Assessment
Reliability	★★★★★
Accuracy	★★
Age	★
Worldwide users	★

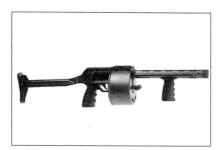

South Africa's UN-embargoed arms industry has produced a number of interesting weapons. The Striker is a fairly successful attempt to increase the firepower for shotgun users.

This was designed in South Africa, and is now being marketed around the world by an Israeli licensee. A very simple and robust revolver-type weapon, there is very little to go wrong with it, and it has been adopted by a number of police forces. The 12-shot cylinder makes it rather bulky, but it is more comfortable to use than you might think.

Pancor Jackhammer

Specification
Cartridge: 12-gauge 2³/₄-in
Weight: 4.57 kg (10 lb)
Length: 762 mm (30 in)
Cyclic rate of fire: 240 rounds per minute
Magazine: 10-shot cylinder

Assessment
Reliability	★★★★
Accuracy	★★★★
Age	★
Worldwide users	★

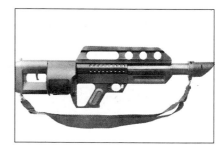

The Pancor Jackhammer is another high-tech combat shotgun. The magazine behind the trigger or 'bullpup' configuration reduces weapon length and makes it easier to use in confined spaces.

The Jackhammer is another revolver-type weapon, but with some differences. The cylinder is completely removable and is not reloaded: merely dropped out when fired and replaced with a new loaded 'ammo cassette', as the makers call it. The circumference is grooved rather like the old Webley-Fosbery revolver, and a gas piston with a stud on it drives the cylinder around. It will fire full-automatic at 240 rounds per minute, and the makers are developing high-performance ammunition to give it a lethal range in excess of any other shotgun. An American weapon, this could well step into the gap left by the CAWS programme.

Olin/HK CAWS

Specification
Cartridge: 12-gauge 3-in belted
Weight: 4.3 kg (9 lb 8 oz) (unloaded)
Length: 764 mm (30 in)
Cyclic rate of fire: (selective fire) no data available
Magazine: 10 rounds

Assessment
Reliability	★★★★
Accuracy	★★★★
Age	★
Worldwide users	★

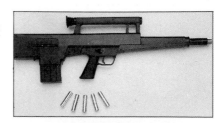

The US Army's CAWS programme has seen shotgun development pushed into the 21st century. The Olin/HK Close Assault Weapon System, using revolutionary new ammunition, has some claim to being the most advanced shotgun ever built.

The US Joint Services Small Arms Program decided in 1979 that there was a requirement for a RHINO (Repeating Hand-held Improved Non-rifled Ordnance). In short, what was required was an improved shotgun with no restraints placed on design other than the amount of felt recoil. Olin started the ball rolling by designing a cartridge with hit probability and penetration significantly better than existing shotgun rounds, and then developed a three-inch brass belted round capable of firing conventional ball bearing or flechettes out to 150 metres. The weapon was then designed around the cartridge by H&K.

SILENCED WEAPONS

Very few silenced weapons are genuinely silent. The large 'cans' on their muzzles are more properly described as suppressors. They do have a military role, however, particularly in clandestine and special operations.

Silenced Ruger Mk II

Specification
Cartridge: .22LR
Weight: 1.43 kg
(3 lb 2 oz)
Length: 342 mm (13 in)
Muzzle velocity: 246 m
(807 ft) per second (with
standard ammunition); 194
m (635 ft) (with subsonic)
Magazine: 9-round box

Assessment
Reliability	★★★
Accuracy	★★★
Age	★★★★
Worldwide users	★★★★

The Ruger Mk II target pistol is a very popular weapon, manufactured in large numbers and very easy to use. In its silenced form it makes an ideal close-range clandestine weapon.

Rifles and long arms are not the only weapons which use silencers. Silenced pistols à la James Bond do have a place in military affairs. They are smaller and more unobtrusive, easy to hide and more useful at close quarters. Silenced pistols come in a variety of shapes and sizes. The Ruger Mk II .22LR target pistol is a popular choice for suppression, being accurate and robust. It is used by such diverse groups as local pest-control officers, the US Navy SEALs and Israel's Mossad secret intelligence service. The latest versions are almost totally silent, and are accurate to 70 metres and more.

Heckler & Koch MP5 SD

Specification
Cartridge: 9-mm
Parabellum
Weight: 3.62 kg (8 lb)
Length: 780 mm (31 in)
Muzzle velocity: 285 m
(935 ft) per second
Cyclic rate of fire: 800
rounds per minute
Magazine: 30-round box

Assessment
Reliability	★★★★
Accuracy	★★★★
Age	★★
Worldwide users	★★★

Heckler & Koch's MP5 is the weapon of choice for many of the world's elite forces. The suppressed version has all the accuracy and reliability of the original, but does its job much more quietly.

This is the silenced version of the MP5. It has the same mechanism but the barrel has 30 3-mm diameter holes. It fires standard 9-mm ammunition but the silencer reduces the muzzle velocity to subsonic speed. The muzzle report sounds rather like the air brake on a lorry: you can hear it up to 100 metres away but it is not recognisable as a gunshot unless you fire bursts. Single-shot accuracy is excellent within 100 metres and the silencer requires no special maintenance, just rinsing with a cleaning agent.

9-mm L34A1 Sterling SMG

Specification
Cartridge: 9-mm
Parabellum
Weight: 4.31 kg (9 lb 8
oz) (loaded)
Length: 864 mm (34 in)
(stock extended)
Muzzle velocity: c.300
m (980 ft) per second
Cyclic rate of fire: 515–
565 rounds per minute
Magazine: 34-round box

Assessment
Reliability	★★★★★
Accuracy	★★★
Age	★★★★
Worldwide users	★★★

As with many such weapons, the suppressor on the Sterling SMG makes its effect by slowing down the bullets to subsonic speed and so drastically reducing the noise.

Also firing standard 9-mm ammunition, the L34A1 is the British Army's designation for the silenced version of the Sterling SMG, which is no longer in service. The barrel has 72 holes drilled in it which disperses the propellant gases, producing a subsonic muzzle velocity. This also reduces the pressure on the bolt, which is therefore lightened, and only one return spring is used. Mechanical noise is inaudible over 30 metres away and the sound cannot be recognised as a gunshot at over 50 metres.

Type 64 sub-machine gun

Specification
Cartridge: 7.62-mm×25
Weight: 3.4 kg (7 lb 8 oz)
(unloaded)
Length: 843 mm (33 in)
(stock extended)
Muzzle velocity: 513 m
(1640 ft) per second
Cyclic rate of fire: 1315
rounds per minute
Magazine: 30-round box

Assessment
Reliability   ★★★
Accuracy   ★★★
Age   ★★★★
Worldwide users   ★

This unusual weapon was produced by the Chinese and is remarkable in being a purpose-built silenced weapon: most silenced guns are conversions of existing weapons. It is blowback-actuated, using the 7.62-mm×25 pistol cartridge, so a Chinese assassin needs to be close to his target and able to place his shots very accurately. The design is an interesting combination: the bolt action is a copy of that on the Soviet PPS-43, the trigger copies that of the Bren gun, and the mechanism follows the design of pre-war Czech machine-guns bought by the Nationalists in the 1930s.

Designed specifically as a silenced weapon, the Type 64 fires the weak 7.62-mm×25 pistol round through a Maxim-type suppressor. This combination is only of value in very close-range covert or assassination operations.

De Lisle carbine

Specification
Cartridge: .45 ACP
Weight: 3.74 kg
(8 lb 4 oz)
Length: 895 mm (35 in)
Muzzle velocity: 253 m
(830 ft) per second
Magazine: 7-round box

Assessment
Reliability   ★★★★★
Accuracy   ★★★★★
Age   ★★★★★
Worldwide users   ★★

This is the quietest silenced weapon ever developed. Accurate to 400 metres, it outranges all silenced sub-machine guns. Developed for British commandos in World War II, it combines the action of the Lee-Enfield rifle with the .45 ACP pistol cartridge. The large silencer makes the weapon truly silent and the heavy bullet is an accurate round. Its only drawback is that, being bolt action, a second shot requires you to work the bolt to chamber the next round. But for the silent headshot at over 100 metres, the De Lisle is unbeatable.

Possibly the quietest-firing weapon ever produced, the De Lisle carbine only suffers from its use of a noisy bolt action. This could give the firer's position away if more than one shot was needed.

9-mm Suppressed AUG

Specification
Cartridge: 9-mm
Parabellum
Weight: 3.3 kg (7 lb 4 oz)
(without suppressor)
Length: depends on the
suppressor used
Muzzle velocity: c.380
m (1250 ft) per second
Cyclic rate of fire: 650–
750 rounds per minute
Magazine: 25- or 32-
round box

Assessment
Reliability   ★★★★
Accuracy   ★★★★
Age   ★
Worldwide users   ★

Steyr-Mannlicher offer the AUG fitted with a suppressor. As explained above, these reduce the velocity of the propellant gases to subsonic speed so there is no loud muzzle report. However, the bullets' velocity is not reduced, so the sound wave generated by supersonic rounds is still present. The suppressed AUG has a standard optical sight and can produce 125-mm groups at 100 metres. Its bullpup configuration allows a 420-mm barrel in a conveniently short weapon. Full silencing is only possible with subsonic ammunition.

The Austrian AUG is a true weapon system, interchangeable parts allowing it to be used as a sub-machine gun, rifle, or light machine-gun. Steyr-Mannlicher offer a suppressor for use with the 9-mm sub-machine gun variant.

Vaime Super Silenced Rifle Mk 2

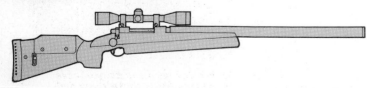

Specification
Cartridge: 7.62-mm×51
subsonic
Weight: 4.1 kg (9 lb)
(without scope)
Length: 1180 mm (46 in)
Muzzle velocity: 320 m
(1050 ft) per second
Magazine: 10-round box

Assessment
Reliability   ★★★★★
Accuracy   ★★★★
Age   ★
Worldwide users   ★

This Finnish purpose-built sniper rifle has been developed for police and military use. A bolt-action rifle, it fires subsonic 7.62-mm×51 ammunition with a muzzle velocity of 320 metres per second: the result is no recoil, a trajectory like a rainbow and a maximum effective range of about 200 metres. They also offer a similar rifle chambered for .22LR for training or situations where over-penetration is a serious problem. In emergencies the Mk 2 can fire 7.62-mm NATO without suffering any harm, but the bullet will be heard as it travels at over twice the speed of sound.

Vaime of Finland are experienced manufacturers of suppressed weapons, producing both rifles with integrally silenced barrels and detachable silencers that can be fitted to almost any modern firearm.

ATTACK HELICOPTERS No. 1

Armed helicopters have come a long way since their combat debut in the 1950s. They now bristle with advanced optical and electronic equipment and carry a wide variety of lethal weaponry, ranging from machine-guns and cannon to long-range, tank-busting guided missiles.

McDonnell Douglas AH-64 Apache

Specification
Length overall: 17.76 m (58 ft 3 In)
Rotor diameter: 14.63 m (48 ft)
Maximum cruising speed: 155 knots
Range: 482 km (300 miles)
Standard weapon load: M230 30-mm Chain Gun; 16×Hellfire anti-tank missiles

Assessment
Manoeuvrability ★★★
All-weather capability ★★★★★
Versatility ★★
Worldwide users ★

The preponderance of Soviet armour on the Central Front at the height of the Cold War meant that the US Army needed advanced weapon systems to even the odds. The McDonnell Douglas AH-64 Apache entered service in the 1980s as the world's most sophisticated battlefield helicopter. Heavily armoured to survive in the hostile skies over a Soviet tank army, the Apache is equipped with night vision, target acquisition and designation systems to enable it to fly and fight in all weathers, day or night. It is armed with Hellfire missiles that can lock on to and destroy any known tank, and for softer targets it is also equipped with 2.75-inch rockets and an extremely accurate 30-mm Chain Gun. It is the most expensive combat helicopter ever built, but it proved in the Gulf that it is reliable and, above all, deadly to the enemy.

Designed to fight and survive in the hostile modern battlefield, the McDonnell Douglas Helicopters AH-64 Apache is the most sophisticated and the most expensive attack helicopter ever built. It was money well spent: in the Gulf the Apache proved to be a reliable and supremely effective tank and vehicle destroyer.

Bell AH-1 HueyCobra

Specification
Length overall: 16.18 m (53 ft)
Rotor diameter: 13.41 m (44 ft)
Maximum cruising speed: 123 knots
Range: 507 km (315 miles)
Standard weapon load: 8×TOW anti-tank missiles; 1×3-barrelled 20-mm cannon; 2×unguided rocket or cannon pods

Assessment
Manoeuvrability ★★★
All-weather capability ★
Versatility ★
Worldwide users ★★★★

The Bell AH-1 HueyCobra gunship was one of the weapons most feared by the Viet Cong during the Vietnam War. It was the first dedicated attack helicopter to enter production, marrying the engine and rotors of the well-proven UH-1 Huey to a slender new fuselage which introduced the now classic two-man tandem cockpit to front-line service. The snake-like form of the AH-1 belies its fearsome punch, in the shape of a devastating 20-mm Gatling gun beneath the nose and TOW anti-armour missiles or cannon pods or rocket pods beneath the helicopter's stub wings. It is limited in some respects, having no bad-weather or night-fighting capability, but nevertheless the Cobra remains a potent fighting machine nearly a quarter of a century after its combat debut.

The Bell Model 209 was developed from the ubiquitous UH-1 Huey in the mid-1960s. It was the pioneering gunship helicopter, which established the tandem cockpit which has since become standard on helicopters of this type. Still in service, it remains a highly effective clear air weapon.

Bell AH-1T Sea Cobra

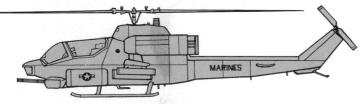

Specification
Length overall: 17.68 m (58 ft)
Rotor diameter: 14.63 m (48 ft)
Maximum cruising speed: 189 knots
Range: 635 km (395 miles)
Standard weapon load: 8×TOW or Hellfire anti-tank missiles; 3-barrelled 20-mm cannon; up to 76× 2.75-in unguided rockets or 16×5-in Zuni rockets or cannon pods or 2×AIM-9L Sidewinder missiles

Assessment
Manoeuvrability ★★★
All-weather capability ★★★
Versatility ★★★
Worldwide users ★★

The US Marines were quick to see the value of the helicopter gunship for close-support. The Corps evaluated the Army's AH-1G HueyCobra, and decided to adopt the type but with some significant improvements. The biggest difference between the AH-1G and the Marines' AH-1J was the addition of a second engine to improve reliability in over-water operations. The AH-1T developed in the late 1970s has more powerful engines and upgraded transmission together with a slightly lengthened tail boom with increased fuel capacity, and more efficient main and tail rotors. The latest twin-engined variant is the AH-1W Super Cobra. This has more powerful engines, and can be armed with Hellfire laser-guided anti-tank missiles and Sidewinder or Stinger air-to-air missiles.

Marine Cobras are distinguishable from Army AH-1s by their rounded, fighter style cockpit canopies rather than the flat panes of the land-based version. They also have larger engine compartments, for the twin engines that the Marine Corps specified for extra safety on overwater operations.

Agusta A 129 Mangusta

The A 129 is a light tank-busting helicopter developed for the Italian army. Taking a lead from US Army gunships, the Mangusta (Mongoose) has separate tandem cockpits for the pilot and co-pilot/gunner. The Mangusta is a very fast and manoeuvrable weapon system, with full day, night and bad-weather fighting abilities. Like its namesake in the animal kingdom, the Mangusta has a powerful bite for its size. Mid-mounted stub wings each have a pair of weapons stations. In the anti-tank role the armament of eight TOW missiles can be supplemented by a mix of pods for 12.7-mm machine-guns, 20-mm cannon, or air-to-ground rockets. The Mangusta was to form the basis for a co-operative attack helicopter design for the British, Italian and Dutch armies, but like so many international weapons systems it has fallen by the wayside.

Specification
Length overall: 14.29 m (46 ft 10 in)
Rotor diameter: 11.9 m (39 ft)
Maximum cruising speed: 140 knots
Range: not quoted
Standard weapon load: 8×TOW anti-tank missiles; 2×rocket or 20-mm cannon pods

Assessment
Manoeuvrability ★★★
All-weather capability ★★★★
Versatility ★★
Worldwide users ★

The Mangusta has a number of advanced features but it cannot carry as many weapons as a machine like the AH-64 Apache. It is more strictly comparable with the AH-1 Cobra, but the Italian machine has far better all-weather capability.

Mil Mi-24 'Hind'

The Mil Mi-24's primary mission is to provide support to troops on the ground. Russian offensive tactics call for a headlong advance, in which the 'Hind' is used as a flying tank. It has a small frontal area and is armoured against the fire of infantry weapons; characteristics that are of great value in its role as an assault helicopter. Its formidable armament includes a 12.7-mm Gatling-type machine-gun or twin 23-mm cannon, and there are four pylons for stores such as bombs, rocket pods or chemical weapons. The 'Hind' is also equipped with launch rails for anti-tank guided weapons.

Specification
Length overall: 21.5 m (70 ft)
Rotor diameter: 17 m (55 ft 9 in)
Maximum cruising speed: 159 knots
Range: 750 km (460 miles)
Standard weapon load: 4×UV-32-57 rocket pods; 4×AT-6 'Spiral' anti-tank missiles; 1×4-barrelled 12.7-mm cannon

Assessment
Manoeuvrability ★★★
All-weather capability ★
Versatility ★★★
Worldwide users ★★★★★

The Mil Mi-24 is a large machine with good speed, heavy armament, and high-speed agility. At the low speeds required by modern anti-tank tactics it is less of a bargain, however.

Mil Mi-28 'Havoc'

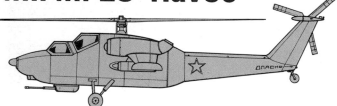

Although the 'Hind' is equipped to combat armoured vehicles, it is not ideal for the purpose. Western anti-tank helicopters are designed to operate from a hover or behind cover, and the Russians have followed suit. The Mil Mi-28 'Havoc' uses 'Hind' components but is smaller, quieter and more manoeuvrable. Like the 'Hind', it can mount a variety of weapons, but in its main anti-armour role it will carry up to 16 laser-guided AT-6 'Spiral' missiles. It has the classic two-man gunship layout and, like the American Apache, is heavily armoured and carries a 30-mm cannon beneath the cockpit.

Specification
(estimated)
Length overall: (excluding rotors) 17.4 m (57 ft)
Rotor diameter: 17 m (55 ft 9 in)
Maximum cruising speed: 162 knots
Range: 240 km (150 miles)
Probable weapon load: various rocket pods; guided anti-tank missiles

Assessment
Defensive systems/ armour ★★★★★
Firepower ★★★★★
Versatility ★★
Worldwide users ★

The 'Havoc' is the Russian's version of the Apache. It is a potent machine but has had development problems and is unlikely to enter general service until the mid- to late 1990s.

Kamov Ka-34 'Hokum'

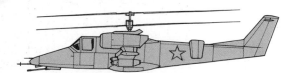

The Kamov 'Hokum' is an advanced, highly manoeuvrable close-support and air-combat helicopter, with twin counter-rotating rotors, capable of high speeds and with a powerful punch. First reports indicated that it would hunt helicopters as well as tanks, though it is also thought to be tasked with "supporting combined arms offensives into enemy territory". Since Kamov helicopters are used extensively by the Russian navy, it is likely that the 'Hokum' will also be based afloat, acting as an escort to the heavily armed and armoured Kamov Ka-29TB 'Helix-B' combat transport helicopters.

Specification
(estimated)
Length overall: (excluding rotors, probe and gun) 13.5 m (44 ft 3 in)
Rotor diameter: 15 m (49 ft)
Maximum cruising speed: 189 knots
Range: 250 km (155 miles)
Probable weapon load: 2×rocket pods and 4×missiles

Assessment
Defensive systems/ armour ★★★
Firepower ★★★
Versatility ★★
Worldwide users ★

The 'Hokum' attack helicopter. Its armament includes a nose-mounted gun turret and wing-mounted air-to-air missiles.

ATTACK HELICOPTERS No. 2

Many helicopters can be used in several different roles. Many light and manoeuvrable reconnaissance helicopters can be fitted with missiles to become budget anti-tank helicopters. Some transport helicopters, like the Soviet Mi-8, make very powerful attack helicopters.

Mil Mi-8 'Hip-E'

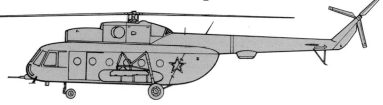

Specification
Length overall: 25.24 m (83 ft)
Rotor diameter: 21.29 m (69 ft 10 in)
Maximum cruising speed: 122 knots
Range: 445 km (275 miles)

Assessment
Manoeuvrability ★★★
Role equipment ★★★★★
Speed ★★★
Worldwide users ★★★★★

Russia has manufactured an estimated 13,000 Mi-8 'Hip' helicopters. It has a large troop compartment and can carry a potent rocket and missile armament.

The Mi-8 is the world's most heavily-armed helicopter, able to carry six UV-32-57 rocket pods, which contain a total of 192 57-mm rockets. The Mi-8 also carries four AT-2 'Swatter' or six AT-3 'Sagger' anti-tank missiles, and has a 12.7-mm machine-gun in the nose. Widely exported, the Mi-8 was supplied to the Warsaw Pact countries, Angola, Cuba, India, Peru and many Russian allies. In Afghanistan it was used to deliver supplies to isolated mountain-top positions, and also to carry troops into battle during airborne assaults. The Mi-8 is one of the most successful of Russian machines.

Westland Lynx AH.Mk 1

Specification
Length overall: 15.16 m (49 ft)
Rotor diameter: 12.8 m (42 ft)
Maximum cruising speed: 140 knots
Range: 180 km (112 miles)

Assessment
Manoeuvrability ★★★★
Role equipment ★★★★
Speed ★★★★★
Worldwide users ★

The British Army's Westland Lynx helicopters are armed with American TOW wire-guided anti-tank missiles with an effective range of 3750 metres. The warhead will penetrate all known Soviet tanks.

The Lynx is the British Army's attack helicopter. Fast, highly manoeuvrable and well equipped, it carries eight American TOW anti-tank missiles. Unlike the heavily-armoured AH-64 Apache or Mi-24 'Hind', the Lynx is not built to take damage, and it relies on its performance and the skill of its crew to avoid being hit. Army Lynxes work closely with Gazelle reconnaissance helicopters that locate enemy forces and identify useful firing positions for their armed brethren. Night and all-weather capability is to be added to the roof-mounted sight, and the possibility of acquiring the US Hellfire missile would greatly improve Lynx's capability.

Aérospatiale SA 342 Gazelle

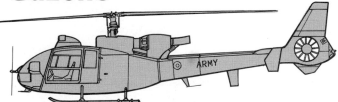

Specification
Length overall: 11.97 m (39 ft 3 in)
Rotor diameter: 10.5 m (34 ft 5 in)
Maximum cruising speed: 140 knots
Range: 360 km (220 miles)

Assessment
Manoeuvrability ★★★★★
Role equipment ★★★★
Speed ★★★
Worldwide users ★★★

The Gazelle is light and very fast. Used for reconnaissance by the British Army, it serves as a gunship in other forces, fitted with a variety of anti-tank missiles.

The Gazelle is one of the fastest military helicopters, and its incredible agility is ruthlessly exploited by the Army Air Corps. Flying a few feet above the ground, they fly around forestry blocks rather than over them. Gazelles work with the CVR(T)s of the recce troops, probing ahead and around British battle groups, and giving the commander up-to-the-minute intelligence on the enemy forces. The Gazelle is used by many armies, and has seen action in the Middle East and the Falklands. Some operators have fitted Gazelles with HOT, TOW or 'Sagger' anti-tank missiles.

Aérospatiale Alouette III

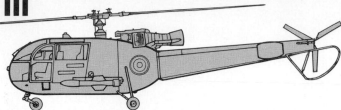

Specification
Length overall: 12.05 m
(39 ft 6 in)
Rotor diameter: 10.2 m
(33 ft 5 in)
Maximum cruising speed: 100 knots
Range: 495 km
(310 miles)

Assessment
Manoeuvrability ★★
Role equipment ★★
Speed ★
Worldwide users ★★★★

The Alouette III was developed as an advanced version of the smaller Alouette II, with a new and larger cabin and improved equipment. Overall performance is substantially better, and the Alouette III has been widely exported, both as a light attack helicopter and for reconnaissance. It saw action in the Middle East and the Rhodesian War, and with the South African Defence Force in Namibia and Angola. Alouettes have been fitted with all manner of weapons, from anti-tank missiles to the sideways-firing 20-mm cannon mounted on some Rhodesian aircraft.

The Alouette III has seen a great deal of action in southern Africa where it was used by the SADF and the Rhodesians. Also used by Syria and Iraq, the Alouette can carry a wide selection of weapons.

MBB BO 105

Specification
Length overall: 11.86 m
(38 ft 11 in)
Rotor diameter: 9.84 m
(32 ft 3 in)
Maximum cruising speed: 119 knots
Range: 570 km
(350 miles)

Assessment
Manoeuvrability ★★★★★
Role equipment ★★★★
Speed ★★★
Worldwide users ★★

The BO 105 is a small and highly manoeuvrable helicopter that forms the backbone of the German army's anti-tank helicopter units. It has been widely exported: Sweden and Spain both employ BO 105s with TOW anti-tank missiles. Iraq used the BO 105 during the Iran-Iraq War. The rigid, hingeless titanium rotor head of the BO 105 confers astonishing agility, and the aircraft has even been looped and rolled without incident. Although most BO 105s are equipped with anti-tank missiles, Spain has fitted some with 20-mm cannon for escort duties.

The German MBB BO 105 was used by Iraq during its war with Iran. This extremely manoeuvrable helicopter is armed with TOW anti-tank missiles.

McDonnell Douglas Defender

Specification
Length overall: 9.4 m
(30 ft 10 in)
Rotor diameter: 8.03 m
(26 ft 4 in)
Maximum cruising speed: 119 knots
Range: 428 km
(265 miles)

Assessment
Manoeuvrability ★★★★★
Role equipment ★★★★
Speed ★★★
Worldwide users ★★★★

Vast numbers of OH-6 and Model 500 helicopters are in service worldwide, including unarmed reconnaissance versions and anti-tank and gunship variants. The OH-6 was used as a light scout helicopter during the Vietnam War, often fitted with a Minigun for good measure. These remain in service, although OH-58 Kiowas have largely replaced them. The US Special Forces use two versions of the Model 530, and they accompanied US troops to the Persian Gulf operations to protect oil tankers from Iranian attacks.

Introduced during the Vietnam War, the versatile McDonnell Douglas Defender is manufactured in several versions and has been widely exported.

Bell Kiowa

Specification
Length overall: 12.49 m
(41 ft)
Rotor diameter: 10.77 m
(35 ft 4 in)
Maximum cruising speed: 120 knots
Range: 491 km
(305 miles)

Assessment
Manoeuvrability ★★★
Role equipment ★★★★
Speed ★★★
Worldwide users ★★★★★

The US Army's OH-58 Kiowa is a military version of the Bell Jet Ranger, the most successful civil helicopter in the world. The Army acquired 2,200 OH-58s between 1968 and 1973, largely because the unit cost of the OH-6 had risen unacceptably. The Kiowa served alongside the OH-6 in the Vietnam War, and has been exported to Australia, Austria and several other nations. Italy manufactures the Jet Ranger under licence for both civil and military users. The current OH-58D version has new avionics and instruments, a four-bladed rotor and a mast-mounted sight.

The Bell OH-58 Kiowa was adopted by the US Army during the Vietnam War partly because of cost overruns on the OH-6. Used for reconnaissance or as an attack helicopter, weapon fits include 7.62- or 20-mm Miniguns, plus anti-tank missiles.

TRANSPORT HELICOPTERS No. 1

The transport helicopter has become one of the most indispensable items in modern mobile warfare. It carries everything from troops and vital supplies to ice-cream and mail, and it does it at much greater speed than any truck can.

Aérospatiale Super Puma

The Puma was a product of the Anglo-French Westland/Aérospatiale consortium. First flying in 1965, the Puma went on to form the backbone of British and French helicopter support forces. Fast and agile, the Puma has seen combat from South Africa to the Gulf. Aérospatiale then went on to develop the vastly improved Super Puma. This incorporates new engines, uprated transmissions and new rotor blades, the improvements giving better performance and increased load capacity. The Super Puma is much tougher than its predecessor, and has entered service with a number of air arms around the world.

Specification
Length overall: 14.76 m (48 ft 5 in)
Rotor diameter: 15.6 m (51 ft 2 in)
Maximum cruising speed: 151 knots
Range: 635 km (395 miles)
Load: 25 troops or 4500 kg (4 tons 960 lb) underslung

Assessment
Manoeuvrability ★★★★★
Robustness ★★★★
Versatility ★★★★
Worldwide users ★★★

French troops make an assault landing from an Aérospatiale AS 332 Super Puma. The Puma's speed and agility mean that it can be used in the front-line role as well as a logistics support helicopter.

Boeing Helicopters CH-47 Chinook

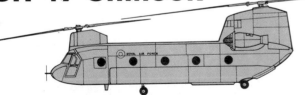

Looking like a larger and more powerful version of the CH-46, Vertol's Model 114 was to become one of the most successful and versatile battlefield mobility helicopters ever built. The US Army ordered the helicopter as the CH-47 Chinook, and the first production models were delivered by what was then the Boeing Vertol company in late 1962. The Chinook built up an unrivalled reputation during the Vietnam War, and it has been sold to air arms around the world, seeing operational use from the Falklands to the Persian Gulf. Boeing Vertol became Boeing Helicopters in the 1980s, but whatever the name the company continued developing the Chinook. The current CH-47D is considerably more powerful and capable than previous models.

Specification
Length overall: 30.18 m (98 ft 11 in)
Rotor diameter: 18.29 m (60 ft)
Maximum cruising speed: 138 knots
Range: 370 km (230 miles)
Load: 44+ troops or 12,700 kg (12 tons 1120 lb) underslung

Assessment
Manoeuvrability ★★★
Robustness ★★★
Versatility ★★★★★
Worldwide users ★★★★★

An RAF Chinook flies in formation with a similar helicopter operated by the Spanish army. The CH-47 is one of the West's premier medium- and heavy-lift helicopters, and has been proved in action from the South Atlantic to the desert.

Boeing Vertol CH-46D Sea Knight

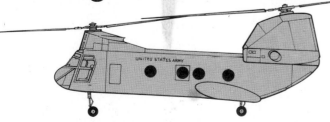

Twin-rotor helicopters were a speciality of the pioneering Piasecki Helicopter Corporation. Piasecki became Vertol in the mid-1950s, and one of the new company's first products was a Model 107, which flew in April 1958. It was one of the earliest turbine-powered helicopters, and although US Army interest soon waned in favour of the larger Model 114, the Model 107 was ordered in large numbers by the US Navy. Known as the CH-46D Sea Knight, its primary Navy role was in the vertical replenishment of vessels at sea. The CH-46 is also important to the US Marine Corps, as its primary assault transport helicopter. The Sea Knight has been updated several times in its long career, and it remains an important front-line helicopter, which was used extensively in the Gulf.

Specification
Length overall: 25.40 m (83 ft 4 in)
Rotor diameter: 12.54 m (41 ft 2 in)
Maximum cruising speed: 140 knots
Range: 380 km (240 miles)
Load: 25 troops or 4535 kg (4 tons 1040 lb) underslung

Assessment
Manoeuvrability ★★★
Robustness ★★★
Versatility ★★★
Worldwide users ★★

A US Navy CH-46 Sea Knight comes in to land aboard a replenishment ship. The CH-46 is one of the US Navy's most important support helicopters, and plays an equally important role as Marine Corps assault transport.

Sikorsky CH-53E Super Stallion

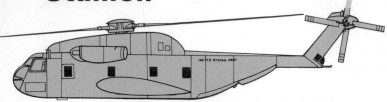

Specification
Length overall: 30.18 m (98 ft 11 in)
Rotor diameter: 24.08 m (79 ft)
Maximum cruising speed: 150 knots
Range: 2075 km (1290 miles)
Load: 55 troops or 16,329 kg (16 tons) underslung

Assessment
Manoeuvrability ★★★★
Robustness ★★★
Versatility ★★★★★
Worldwide users ★★

The three-engined Sikorsky S-80 Super Stallion is the largest and most powerful helicopter produced outside the Soviet Union. Developed from the Sikorsky S-65 built in the 1960s for the US Navy and Marine Corps, the Super Stallion first flew in the mid-1970s, and it entered service as the CH-53E in 1981. Used by the Marines as a heavy assault helicopter, it can carry 55 troops or underslung loads of 16 tonnes. It is used by the US Navy for vertical replenishment and for the recovery of damaged aircraft. The Navy uses the same airframe for airborne minesweeping; designated MH-53E, it was given the name Sea Dragon. The only other user of the Super Stallion to date is the Japanese Defence Agency.

This Sikorsky CH-53E Super Stallion has landed on the broad fantail of a US Navy battleship. Such a large helicopter needs an equally large landing area in order to operate successfully at sea.

Westland Commando Mk 2

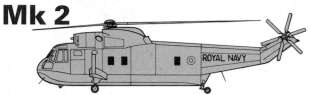

Specification
Length overall: 22.15 m (72 ft 8 in)
Rotor diameter: 18.90 m (62 ft)
Maximum cruising speed: 112 knots
Range: 445 km (275 miles)
Load: 28 troops or 3628 kg (3 tons 1280 lb) underslung

Assessment
Manoeuvrability ★★★★
Robustness ★★★
Versatility ★★★★
Worldwide users ★★

The Sikorsky S-61 helicopter has been around since 1959, serving in many civil and military forms, but most notably as the Sea King ASW and rescue helicopter. Westland Helicopters took out a licence to build the aircraft in 1959, and it entered service with the Royal Navy in 1964. The Commando is a dedicated support derivative of the Sea King, with optimised payloads, ranges and endurance for tactical troop transport, logistic support and cargo transport. It can also be used for air-to-air surface attack and for search and rescue. The Commando is used by the Royal Navy to support the Royal Marines, and it has also been acquired by Egypt and Qatar.

The Westland Commando is a member of the long-serving Sikorsky Sea King family. Larger than the anti-submarine warfare variants of the Sea King, the Commando is optimised as an assault helicopter.

Mil Mi-6 'Hook'

Specification
Length overall: 41.74 m (136 ft 11 in)
Rotor diameter: 35 m (115 ft)
Maximum cruising speed: 135 knots
Range: 620 km (385 miles)
Load: 70 troops or 8000 kg (7 tons 1950 lb) underslung

Assessment
Manoeuvrability ★★
Robustness ★★★★★
Versatility ★★
Worldwide users ★★

First flying in 1957, the Mil Mi-6 was by far the largest helicopter of its time, and remains the largest series-produced helicopter in the world, although the Mil Mi-26 introduced in the late 1970s is heavier and more powerful. Given the NATO reporting name of 'Hook', the Mil Mi-6 is used for civil and military purposes, and in spite of its less than dynamic manoeuvrability it remains an immensely capable helicopter. The 'Hook' is in service with a number of former Russian client states ranging from Algeria to Vietnam, and it remains in service in both civil and military versions in Russia.

Mil Mi-6 'Hooks' come in to land at a mountain pass high in central Asia. Two such helicopters can deliver 140 fully-equipped troops, or nearly 20 tonnes of cargo.

Mil Mi-26 'Halo'

Specification
Length overall: 40.03 m (131 ft 3 in)
Rotor diameter: 32 m (105 ft)
Maximum cruising speed: 137 knots
Range: 800 km (500 miles)
Load: 90 troops or 20,000 kg (19 tons 1520 lb) underslung

Assessment
Manoeuvrability ★★
Robustness ★★★★★
Versatility ★★
Worldwide users ★

Marginally smaller than the 'Hook' but with a payload half again as large, the Mil Mi-26 'Halo' is the heaviest, most powerful helicopter in the world. Its clamshell rear loading doors open onto a cargo hold with the size and carrying capacity of the C-130 Hercules transport aircraft. It was the first helicopter in the world to be equipped with an eight-blade main rotor, and it has been fitted with sophisticated avionics and navigation systems, allowing for auto-hover as well as day and night operations. The 'Halo' is currently in service with the Soviet armed forces and with India.

The Mil Mi-26 'Halo' is the heaviest and most powerful military helicopter in the world, but it has other uses. This Mi-26 is seen dropping tonnes of sand over Chernobyl during the desperate attempts to clear up after the disastrous reactor accident.

TRANSPORT HELICOPTERS No. 2

While the range of utility helicopters available to modern armies continues to increase, many older helicopters remain in service around the world. The collapse of the USSR also leaves many military helicopters (and their pilots) available for work elsewhere.

Sikorsky S-55 Whirlwind

Manufactured under licence by Westland as the Whirlwind, the Sikorsksy S-55 was originally ordered by the US Air Force. The prototype flew in 1949, and successive versions were adopted by the USAF, US Navy, US Marines and the US Coast Guard. The US Army operated it under the designation H-19 and called it the Chickasaw. The US Marines also used it as a troop transport, while ASW and SAR (Search And Rescue) variants were flown by the US and Royal Navies. Most USAF H-19s were also operated in the SAR role. In the USA, Sikorsky manufactured a total of about 1,300 S-55s in civil as well as military versions. Westland built 437 Whirlwinds, including some civil types and some for the Queen's Flight. They were also built in Japan and France in limited numbers.

Specification
Length overall: 12.88 m (42 ft 3 in)
Rotor diameter: 16.15 m (53 ft)
Maximum cruising speed: 80 knots
Range: 579 km (360 miles)
Load: 1200 kg (1 ton 405 lb)

Assessment
Manoeuvrability ★★★
Robustness ★★★
Versatility ★★★
Worldwide users ★★★★

The Sikorsky S-55 was used in many roles by British and US forces. It was manufactured under licence in the UK by Westland and saw action with the British Army in the Middle East and Borneo.

Mil Mi-2 'Hoplite'

The Mi-2 is still used as a training helicopter, but its front-line service is over. It was basically a Mi-1 with twin turbines instead of a piston engine. These gave a 50 per cent increase in power while weighing only about half as much. First flown in 1962, the Mi-2 was manufactured in Poland by PZL as part of the Comecon system, whereby Eastern European industry was directed from Moscow. Later helicopters, however, were always built in Russia, so the Mi-2 remains the only Soviet helicopter never manufactured in Russia. Production continued until the demise of the Warsaw Pact.

Specification
Length overall: 11.9 m (39 ft)
Rotor diameter: 14.56 m (47 ft 10 in)
Maximum cruising speed: 103 knots
Range: 240 km (150 miles)
Load: 1500 kg (1 ton 1075 lb)

Assessment
Manoeuvrability ★★
Robustness ★★★
Versatility ★★
Worldwide users ★★★★

The Mi-2 is still used for training in Russia and some former Warsaw Pact nations. Unusually for a Soviet design, it was manufactured in Poland but not in the USSR.

Mil Mi-4 'Hound'

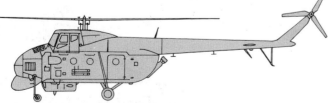

Known to NATO as the 'Hound', it was one of the largest helicopters in the world when it entered service in 1953. It was built in enormous numbers and formed the backbone of Warsaw Pact helicopter forces for many years. The Soviets demonstrated the Mi-4 as an assault helicopter as early as the 1956 Tushino Air Display and, fitted with a machine-gun in the nose and rocket pods on outriggers, it became the USSR's first armed helicopter. Some were fitted with a search radar and used by the Black Sea and Baltic Fleets. The Mi-4 was supplied to China and manufactured there as the H-5. While the Mi-4's days as an assault helicopter were numbered after the introduction of the Mi-8, some were fitted with ECM equipment and used to jam enemy communications.

Specification
Length overall: 16.79 m (55 ft)
Rotor diameter: 21 m (68 ft 11 in)
Maximum cruising speed: 86 knots
Range: 590 km (370 miles)
Load: 2500 kg (2 tons 1030 lb)

Assessment
Manoeuvrability ★★
Robustness ★★★★
Versatility ★★★
Worldwide users ★★★★★

The shape of the Mi-4 is similar to that of contemporary Sikorsky designs, but its much larger dimensions give it a significantly greater load-carrying capacity. This one is in service with KGB border troops.

Westland Wessex

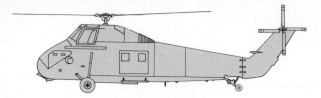

Specification
Length overall: 14.7 m
(48 ft 3 in)
Rotor diameter: 17 m
(55 ft 9 in)
**Maximum cruising
speed:** 105 knots
Range: 628 km
(385 miles)
Load: 2100 kg
(1 ton 2170 lb)

Assessment
Manoeuvrability ★★
Robustness ★★★★
Versatility ★★★★
Worldwide users ★

*A Westland Wessex takes part in
rescue operations following the
Argentine air strike on British forces
landing at Bluff Cove during the
Falklands war.*

Based on the Sikorsky S-58 of the 1950s, the Westland Wessex was built under
licence for the Fleet Air Arm as an anti-submarine helicopter. The Wessex HAS
(Helicopter Anti-Submarine) Mk 1 entered service in 1960, but the RAF was soon
interested and in 1962 it adopted a version equipped to carry 16 troops. Further
ASW versions followed, and the Royal Navy ordered the final Wessex variant,
the Wessex HU.Mk 5, as an assault helicopter for the Royal Marines. These
operated from the aircraft carriers that were converted to helicopter-operating
'commando carriers'. The HU.Mk 5s played a vital role in the Falklands campaign,
where their ability to operate in foul weather conditions was tested to the limit.

Aérospatiale SA321 Super Frelon

The Frelon (Hornet) was a transport helicopter built by Sud Aviation that first flew
in 1959. Aérospatiale developed a larger helicopter that became the largest
European-designed helicopter to be manufactured in quantity. Initially flown by
the French navy as an ASW helicopter, the Super Frelon entered service in 1965.
It was touted as a civil aircraft but attracted little interest. However, France was
supplying large quantities of equipment to the state of Israel at the time and the
Israelis ordered the Super Frelon as an assault helicopter. The SADF (South
African Defence Force) also ordered it for the same purpose, and it has seen
combat in both the Middle East and southern Africa. Other export customers
include Libya, China and Iran.

Specification
Length overall: 19.4 m
(63 ft 8 in)
Rotor diameter: 18.9 m
(62 ft)
**Maximum cruising
speed:** 149 knots
Range: 820 km
(510 miles)
Load: 6700 kg
(6 tons 1330 lb)

*The French Super Frelon was used in
action by the SADF (South African
Defence Force) in Namibia and
Angola during the guerrilla wars of
the 1980s.*

Sikorsky UH-60 Black Hawk

Selected in 1972 to replace the popular Bell UH-1, the UH-60 is the US Army's
standard utility helicopter. In service since 1978, it is now used in a wide number
of variants, including electronic warfare, rescue and long-range special forces
versions. Built primarily as an assault helicopter, it incorporates some of the
lessons learned in Vietnam. It is extremely robust and armoured to withstand
hits from small arms fire up to 7.62-mm calibre. With accommodation for a crew
of three and 11 fully-equipped troops, the UH-60 has an external cargo hook that
can take a 3629-kilogram load. It can serve as a casualty evacuation helicopter
with four stretchers replacing the cabin seats.

Specification
Length overall: 19.7 m
(64 ft 7 in)
Rotor diameter: 16.3 m
(53 ft 6 in)
**Maximum cruising
speed:** 147 knots
Range: 600 km
(372 miles)
Load: 4200 kg
(4 tons 290 lb)

Assessment
Manoeuvrability ★★★★
Robustness ★★★★★
Versatility ★★★★
Worldwide users ★★★

*The Sikorsky UH-60 Black Hawk was
used in enormous numbers during the
Gulf War when the US 101st Airborne
Division made its dramatic helicopter
assault.*

Bell UH-1 Iroquois

Employed in vast numbers during the Vietnam War, the UH-1 served in a
multitude of roles. Using the UH-1, the US Army pioneered the art of large-scale
helicopter assaults with the same helicopter providing the transports ('slicks')
and the gunships ('hogs'). The same UH-1 also served to move the wounded
back from remote landing zones to base hospitals and to fly special forces and
CIA mercenaries on secret missions to Cambodia and Laos. In addition to its
service with the US Army, Navy, Marines, Air Force and intelligence agencies,
the UH-1 was exported to some 60 countries. It has also been manufactured in
China, Germany, Italy, Japan and Taiwan. British forces captured some UH-1s
from Argentina during the Falklands war.

Specification
Length overall: 17.6 m
(57 ft 9 in)
Rotor diameter: 14.6 m
(48 ft)
**Maximum cruising
speed:** 110 knots
Range: 512 km
(320 miles)
Load: 1950 kg
(1 ton 2060 lb)

Assessment
Manoeuvrability ★★★★
Robustness ★★★
Versatility ★★★
Worldwide users ★★★★★

*The Bell UH-1, universally known as
the 'Huey', was a familiar sight in the
Vietnam War where it served as troop
transport, gunship, command
platform and casualty evacuation
aircraft.*

MARITIME HELICOPTERS No.1

Helicopters are an important asset to modern warships. Long used for hunting submarines, they proved their value in defeating fast attack craft during the Gulf War. Helicopters are also used for targeting over-the-horizon missile attacks, allowing their parent warship to launch strikes from a position of relative safety.

Westland Sea King HAS.Mk 5

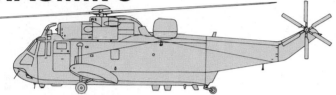

The HAS.Mk 5 is the anti-submarine/search-and-rescue version of this long-serving helicopter, delivered to the Royal Navy during the 1980s. Using dipping sonar or sonobuoys, it is able to monitor signals from sonobuoys delivered by RAF Nimrod aircraft as well. It is designed to remain on station about 185 kilometres from its ship for long periods, working with Nimrods to attack enemy submarines. Its primary ASW (anti-submarine warfare) armament is either four Mk 46 or Stingray homing torpedoes. Four Mk 11 depth charges can be carried instead.

Specification
Crew: 4
Range: 1102 km (685 miles)
Cruise speed: 110 knots
Sensors: Type 195 dipping sonar, AW 391 radar and ESM (electronic support measures)
Armament: 4×Mk 46 or Stingray torpedoes, or 4×Mk 11 depth charges, or 2×Sea Eagle air-to-surface missiles

Assessment
Submarine detection ★★★★
Submarine killing ★★★★
Anti-ship capability ★★★★
Range ★★★★

A Royal Navy Sea King helicopter lowers its dipping sonar into the water. If it detects an enemy submarine it can attack with a variety of torpedoes or depth charges.

Westland Lynx HAS.Mk 3

During the Gulf War, Royal Navy Lynx helicopters used BAe Sea Skua semi-active homing missiles to destroy a force of Iraqi and captured Kuwaiti fast attack craft. Although the Lynx has mainly been used for ASW in the North Atlantic, its success at destroying fast attack craft is significant. Missile-armed fast attack craft are a common Third World navy weapon and perhaps the main future threat to Royal Navy surface ships. The Lynx is much smaller than the Sea King and can be operated by frigates, but its range is shorter.

Specification
Crew: 2
Range: 533 km (330 miles)
Cruise speed: 125 knots
Sensors: Sea Spray radar, SSQ-947B sonobuoys, MAD (magnetic anomaly detector) and ESM
Armament: 4×Sea Skua missiles, or 2×Mk 46 or Stingray torpedoes, or 2×Mk 11 depth charges

Assessment
Submarine detection ★★★
Submarine killing ★★★
Anti-ship capability ★★★★
Range ★★

The Westland Lynx made an impressive combat debut during the Gulf War, sinking many Iraqi fast attack craft.

Westland/Agusta EH.101 Merlin

This is an ASW helicopter developed for the Royal Navy and the Italian navy in a collaborative venture that began in 1980. Known as Merlin to the British, it is intended for Type 23 frigates, Royal Fleet auxiliaries and any 'Invincible' class carriers that survive the defence cuts. Its main advantage over existing helicopters is a much increased range and the ability to carry larger anti-surface missiles if required. The Royal Navy is understood to be interested in purchasing 50, and other sales will include the Italian and Canadian navies and a different version for the British Army.

Specification
Crew: 3
Range: 1945 km (1210 miles)
Cruise speed: 150 knots
Sensors: Blue Kestrel radar, HISOS 2 sonar, up to 32 sonobuoys, MAD, ESM
Armament: 4×A 244 or Stingray torpedoes or Mk 11 depth charges, or 2×AM.39 Exocet missiles

Assessment
Submarine detection ★★★★
Submarine killing ★★★★
Anti-ship capability ★★★★
Range ★★★★★

The Westland/Agusta EH.101 offers a substantially increased range and can carry air-to-surface missiles such as the AM.39 Exocet as an alternative weapons fit.

Kaman SH-2 Seasprite

Specification
Crew: 3
Range: 361 km
(220 miles)
Cruise speed: 120 knots
Sensors: LN-66 radar,
MAD and up to 15
sonobuoys
Armament: one or two
Mk 46 torpedoes

Assessment
Submarine detection	**
Submarine killing	***
Anti-ship capability	–
Range	*

A Kaman Seasprite coming in to land on the deck of a US Navy warship. The SH-2 has relatively short range and lighter armament than the latest Western naval helicopters.

Kaman is a major subcontractor to aircraft manufacturers and NASA. It was founded by Charles Kaman, an expert in composite materials whose other claim to fame was designing the Ovation guitar. The Kaman Seasprite first flew in 1959, but was put back into production in 1981 and modified to Mk I LAMPS (Light Airborne Multi-Purpose System) standard. Intended to provide frigates with an ASW helicopter, SH-2s have served on destroyers, cruisers and even on battleships. Short-ranged and lightly armed, the SH-2 must stay in radar line-of-sight to its parent ship to use sonobuoys. Carrying two torpedoes reduces its range to 326 kilometres. The alternative scheme is to fit a drop-tank and a single torpedo, which increases the range to 394 kilometres.

Sikorsky SH-60B Seahawk

Specification
Crew: 3
Range: 740 km
(465 miles)
Cruise speed: 100 knots
Sensors: AN/APS-124
radar, FLIR camera, MAD,
ESM, blip enhancer and
25 sonobuoys
Armament: 2×Mk 46 or
Mk 50 torpedoes or
Penguin missiles, or
1×Mk 57 nuclear depth
charge

Assessment
Submarine detection	****
Submarine killing	****
Anti-ship capability	****
Range	***

The SH-60 Seahawk can fire Penguin anti-ship missiles as an alternative to its usual homing torpedo/depth charge armament. Drop-tanks can be used to extend its range.

The naval version of the Black Hawk, this won the US Navy's competition for a LAMPS Mk III helicopter. Able to stay on station for nearly an hour longer than a LAMPS I helicopter, the SH-60B is also capable of engaging surface vessels. It can be fitted with the Norwegian-designed Penguin air-to-surface missile, which has a range of 30-40 kilometres. The SH-60's range can be extended by the use of a drop-tank that adds another 122 kilometres. This can be substituted for a torpedo or depth charge, trading range for armament. SH-60s were used by US naval forces during the Gulf War, primarily for search-and-rescue, since Iraq had no submarines.

Aérospatiale SA 321 Super Frelon

Specification
Crew: 5
Range: 733 km
(455 miles)
Cruise speed: 135 knots
Sensors: ORB-31D radar,
HS-12 dipping sonar and
MAD; Libyan and Chinese
ASW Frelons have ORB-32
radar
Armament: 4×Mk 46, L4
or Murene torpedoes;
alternatively 2×AM.39
Exocets and ORB-31 radar
can be fitted

Assessment
Submarine detection	**
Submarine killing	***
Anti-ship capability	***
Range	***

The large and heavily-armed Super Frelon has been sold by France to several countries including Libya, but only a few were manufactured as dedicated anti-submarine helicopters.

The large and heavily-armed Super Frelon was developed during the early 1960s and is used by the French navy in the ASW role. Super Frelons operate in groups of three or four, with one carrying detection equipment and guiding the armed helicopters onto their targets. With four-hour endurance, the Super Frelon is also used to escort French nuclear submarines to sea, guarding the SSBNs while they transit the Bay of Biscay. The French have exported the Frelon to several countries, including Libya, communist China, Iran and South Africa, but most are for use as military transports. Only 24 dedicated ASW versions were built.

Kamov Ka-25 'Hormone'

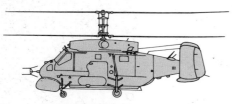

Specification
('Hormone-A')
Crew: 3
Range: 359 km
(220 miles)
Cruise speed: 105 knots
Sensors: dipping sonar,
three sonobuoys, MAD,
'mushroom' radar and
possibly FLIR fitted to
some aircraft
Armament: 2×E45-75A
torpedoes, or 1×B-1 depth
charge or nuclear depth
charge

Assessment
Submarine detection	*
Submarine killing	**
Anti-ship capability	–
Range	*

The once powerful Soviet navy took Kamov Ka-25s to sea aboard a wide variety of warships. Unable to use its dipping sonar in poor visibility and with a short range, the Ka-25 compares badly with Western equivalents.

The Soviets built some 460 Ka-25s between 1966 and 1975 and they were the mainstay of the Soviet fleet's helicopter force. Embarked on all surface warships from frigates to dedicated helicopter carriers, there are three main versions. 'Hormone-A' is the standard ASW model, 'Hormone-B' is for over-the-horizon targeting and is fitted with 'Big Bulge' radar, ESM and a data-link, and 'Hormone-C' is the utility/search-and-rescue model. The use of three-blade co-axial rotors (no tail rotor) makes it a very compact helicopter – an important consideration given the amount of equipment crammed into most Soviet warships. With no automatic hover facility, the Ka-25 cannot use its dipping sonar at night or in poor weather conditions.

McDonnell Douglas F-15 Eagle

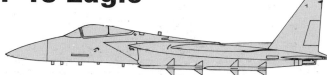

The F-15 Eagle has been the West's premier air-defence fighter for more than 15 years. First flying in July 1972, it has built up an unparalleled combat record in the hands of the Israelis in the 1982 war over Lebanon, and as the anti-Saddam coalition's star MiG-killer during the Gulf War. Big, powerful and with outstanding manoeuvrability, the F-15 can carry a significant weapons load over great distances. Indeed, with a full load of conformal tanks and drop tanks, it can operate over intercontinental distances. Nearly 1,000 F-15s have been produced, and are in service with the US Air Force, the Israeli Heyl Ha'Avir, the Royal Saudi air force and Japan's air self-defence force. The original single- and two-seat F-15A and B, respectively, were followed into service by the F-15C and F-15D, which became the standard production models In June 1979. The F-15 has also formed the basis for the F-15E strike fighter, which is probably the most capable ground-attack aircraft in service today.

Specification
Type: (F-15C) single-seat air-superiority fighter
Dimensions: wing span 13.05 m (42 ft 10 in); length 19.43 m (63 ft 9 in)
Performance: max. speed 1450 km/h (900 mph) at low level; Mach 2.5 at altitude; max. ferry range 5750 km (3570 miles)
Armament: 4×medium-range radar-guided missiles plus 4×short-range infra-red homing missiles, or 8×AIM-120 AMRAAM missiles, plus 1×6-barrelled 20-mm rotary cannon

Assessment
Performance ★★★★
Range ★★★★★
Age ★★★★
Worldwide users ★★

The McDonnell Douglas F-15 Eagle has been the West's premier air-defence fighter for nearly two decades, and it remains one of the most capable fighters in the world. It was the anti-Saddam coalition's top MiG-killer during the Gulf War.

General Dynamics F-16 Fighting Falcon

The US Air Force in the early 1970s had a requirement for a lightweight fighter to be built in large numbers for fair-weather use. The F-16 Fighting Falcon was designed to meet the requirement, first flying in February 1974. The Falcon has evolved considerably over the years, and is now a multi-role aircraft with superb manoeuvrability that is equally at home in a dogfight or in a ground-attack mission. The F-16 has become the standard fighter in many free-world air forces, with more than 3,500 in service with some 20 countries, from Bahrain to Venezuela. In US Air Force service, the F-16 is largely used as a ground-attack and close-support machine. However, 270 early examples operated by the Air National Guard have been modified for the air-defence role, replacing old Convair F-106 fighters in the protection of the air space of the United States.

Specification
Type: (F-16C) single-seat multi-purpose fighter
Dimensions: wing span 10.01 m (32 ft 10 in); length 15.03 m (49 ft 4 in)
Performance: max. speed c. Mach 2 at 10,000 m (32,800 ft); ferry range with drop tanks 3900 km (2400 miles)
Armament: air-air role usually 2×AIM-9 Sidewinders and 2×AIM-7 Sparrows, or 6×AIM-120 AMRAAM missiles, plus 1×6-barrelled Vulcan 20-mm rotary cannon

Assessment
Performance ★★★★
Range ★★★
Age ★★★
Worldwide users ★★★★★

The General Dynamics F-16 Fighting Falcon was designed as a lightweight multi-purpose fighter. Highly manoeuvrable, it is a superb dogfight machine, and later versions have been fitted with some longer-range combat capability.

Lockheed F-22

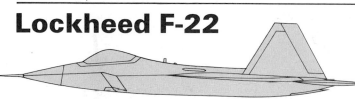

The length of time it takes to develop a modern fighter meant that the McDonnell Douglas F-15 Eagle had not been in large-scale service for more than about five years before the US Air Force was looking for a replacement. The new aircraft, which was to become known as the Advanced Tactical Fighter, or the ATF, was to incorporate the then new stealth low-observability technology, and was to have radically new engines that were able to drive the machine at supersonic speeds economically, without afterburning. Two projects came to the fore in the late 1980s. The eventual winner of the competition was the F-22, developed by Lockheed, General Dynamics and Boeing. The YF-22 is even larger than the F-15, but with thrust-vectoring engine-exhausting highly-advanced engines it is even more manoeuvrable, and careful attention to low-observable technology means that it has a much lower radar signature. The unit cost of the F-22, due to enter service in the year 2000, is about $61 million per fighter.

Specification
Type: (Lockheed F-22) single-seat ATF
Dimensions: wing span 13.11 m (43 ft); length 19.56 m (64 ft 2 in)
Performance: max. speed, supercruise without afterburning, Mach 1.6 at 9000 m (29,500 ft); 1480 km/h (920 mph) at sea level
Armament: 8×AIM-9 Sidewinders or AIM-120 AMRAAM missiles in 3 internal bays, plus 1 long-barrelled Vulcan 20-mm rotary cannon

Assessment
Performance ★★★★★
Range ★★★★
Age ★
Worldwide users –

The Lockheed F-22 Lightning II is a huge machine, but its advanced design, new engines and stealth construction give it an unmatched performance at combat speeds, together with low observability in the infra-red and radar spectra.

Panavia Tornado Air Defence Variant

The main threat to British airspace at the height of the Cold War was seen to come from Soviet long-range bombers operating over the Atlantic and the North Sea. The further out that intruders could be intercepted, the safer the country would be. From the start of the multi-national project which was to evolve into the Tornado, the RAF was considering a variant with long-range radar and missiles optimised for making intercepts of enemy bombers hundreds of kilometres out to sea. Development was protracted, but the Air Defence Variant of the Tornado entered service in 1984. The Tornado F.Mk 2 and its successor, the F.Mk 3, share 80 per cent of their components with the standard Tornado. The most obvious difference is that the ADV has a stretched fuselage. Designed as a long-range interceptor, the ADV Tornado has only limited capability as an air superiority fighter, but it has been exported to Saudi Arabia, and both British and Saudi planes were used to fly combat air patrols during the Gulf War.

Specification
Type: (F.Mk3) two-seat all-weather interceptor
Dimensions: wing span 14 m (46 ft) (spread) 8.6 m (28 ft 3 in) (swept); length 16.72 m (54 ft 10 in)
Performance: Mach 2.2 at altitude; 1480 km/h (920 mph) low level; combat radius 800 km (500 miles); ferry range 4000 km (2500 miles)
Armament: 4×Sky Flash missiles, 2×Sidewinders, or 6×AIM-120 AMRAAMs, plus one Mauser 27-mm cannon

Assessment
Performance   ★★★★
Range   ★★★★★
Age   ★★
Worldwide users   ★★

The air-defence versions of the Panavia Tornado are not dogfighters, although they are reasonably agile. They are, however, supremely capable long-range interceptors, with high speed and good range, and they can loiter far from home for long periods.

Eurofighter EFA

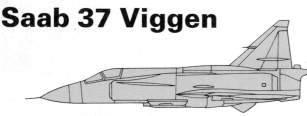

The immense cost of developing a state-of-the-art fighter means that few nations can go it alone. In 1983, the air staffs of Britain, France, Germany, Italy and Spain issued a joint requirement for a single-seat, highly-agile fighter which would have a secondary ground-attack capability. The French withdrew to pursue their own projects in 1985, but the rest continued with what was to become the European Fighter Aircraft. Although not incorporating wholesale new technology like the American ATF, the EFA does utilise carbon-fibre composite construction designed for low observability. Fly-by-wire controls and advanced avionics ensure that the EFA will be a considerable advance on current generation aircraft, and its radar should give snap-up, look-down shoot-down, and multi-target engagement capability.

Specification
Type: (European Fighter Aircraft) advanced single-seater air-defence/air-superiority fighter
Dimensions: wing span 10.5 m (34 ft 5 in); length 14.5 m (47 ft 8 in)
Performance: (estimated): max. speed more than Mach 1.8; combat radius 550 km (340 miles)
Armament: 4×advanced, medium-range missiles and 4×short-range, plus one Mauser 27-mm cannon

Assessment
Performance   ★★★★★
Range   ★★★
Age   ★
Worldwide users   –

The European Fighter Aircraft is a highly-advanced design. Although it does not look as revolutionary as the American F-22, it still offers a considerably enhanced performance over anything in service in Europe today.

Saab 37 Viggen

Since the end of World War II, the independent Swedish aviation industry has produced a number of technologically-advanced aircraft designs well able to match anything else in the world. The Saab Viggen (Thunderbolt) was dramatically different to anything else when it first flew in the late 1960s. The Viggen is a true multi-role aircraft, being used for attack, reconnaissance, training and interception missions. All versions of the Viggen share the then unique double delta canard configuration, although now, some 25 years after that first flight, such layouts are becoming increasingly common. The JA 37 is the interceptor variant of the Viggen, and was the last to enter service. It has an engine of increased power, and is fitted with an advanced Ericsson pulse-Doppler radar for search and acquisition of targets.

Specification
Type: (Saab JA 37 Viggen) single-seat interceptor
Dimensions: wing span 10.6 m (34 ft 9 in); length including probe 16.4 m (53 ft 10 in)
Performance: max. speed Mach 2+ at altitude; Mach 1.2 at low level; hi-lo-hi combat radius more than 1000 km (620 miles)
Armament: 2×Sky Flash missiles, 6×Sidewinders, plus one Oerlikon 30-mm KCA cannon

Assessment
Performance   ★★★★
Range   ★★★★
Age   ★★★★★
Worldwide users   ★

Saab's Viggen fighter was the first high-performance fighter equipped with 'canard' foreplanes to enter service. Over 20 years later, many advanced fighters feature a similar layout.

JAS 39 Gripen

The JAS 39 Gripen (Griffon) is an advanced multi-purpose fighter intended to replace the Saab 37 Viggen in Swedish service. Considerably smaller and lighter than the Viggen, it shares the canard wing layout with the earlier fighter, as well as with the multi-national EFA and the French Rafale. Like the Viggen, the JAS 39 has excellent short-field capability, being able to operate off straight stretches of road. In spite of its advanced fly-by-wire design and composite construction, the Gripen is intended to be simple to keep in operation, even when being looked after by conscripts with a minimum of maintenance training. When the first prototype crashed, the development programme came under pressure, but for the moment it continues, and the first operational units are expected to be formed in the mid-1990s.

Specification
Type: lightweight single-seat multi-role fighter
Dimensions: wing span 8 m (26 ft 3 in); length 14.1 m (46 ft 3 in)
Performance: max. speed c. Mach 1.2/1.8 at low/high altitude;
Armament: 2×infra-red dogfight missiles on wingtip rails, plus combination of up to 5 short-/medium-range missiles, plus one Mauser 27-mm cannon

Assessment
Performance   ★★★★
Range   ★★★★
Age   ★
Worldwide users   –

The JAS 39 Gripen has been designed to replace the Viggen. It is a tiny fighter, but still manages a performance to match larger aircraft being built elsewhere.

AIR SUPERIORITY FIGHTERS No. 2

The end of the Cold War will not mean an end to the development of fighter aircraft. The machines listed here, once front-line machines in NATO and Warsaw Pact forces, have already been sold to countries all over the world — and may yet be used against their former owners.

Mikoyan Gurevich MiG-21

Entering service with the Soviet air force in 1959, the distinctive delta-winged MiG-21 is the most widely-manufactured fighter of modern times. Total production exceeded 15,000, with no less than 15 major variants featuring improved powerplants, upgraded avionics or better armament. Large numbers of MiG-21s were supplied to Arab air forces and used in the Arab-Israeli wars, which were a poor showcase for Soviet military technology. Pitted against the intensively-trained Israeli pilots and their more capable aircraft, the MiG-21 performed poorly. However, the MiG-21 remained in service with the Warsaw Pact until its dissolution. China still builds copies designated the F-7 and this continues to be improved.

Specification
Type: single-seat multi-role fighter
Dimensions: wing span 7.15 m (23 ft 6 in); length 15.1 m (49 ft 6 in)
Performance: max. speed Mach 2.15 at altitude; max. range 1100 km (685 miles)
Armament: 1×twin-barrelled 23-mm cannon, 1500 kg (1 ton 1075 lb) of ordnance on 4 wing pylons or 4×AA-2 'Aphid' air-to-air missiles

Assessment
Performance ★★★
Range ★★
Age ★★★★
Worldwide users ★★★★

The MiG-21 is one of the most widely exported Soviet aircraft, and a version is still manufactured in China. This example belongs to the Indian air force.

Mikoyan Gurevich MiG-25

Given the NATO reporting name 'Foxbat', the MiG-25 was designed to intercept the US B-70 bomber that was to have been capable of Mach 3. The B-70 was never built however, so the Soviets were left with a long-range interceptor capable of astonishing speed and a phenomenal rate of climb. A MiG-25 can take off and climb to an altitude of 35000 metres (114,000 ft) in a little over four minutes. NATO had its first detailed look at the MiG-25 when a Soviet pilot defected to Japan with one in September 1976. This exposed its 1950s-era radar and other features that dispelled much of the mythology built up by some Western analysts since the first sightings of the 'Foxbat' in 1967. This fast but unmanoeuvrable interceptor has also been deployed as a high altitude reconnaissance platform.

Specification
Type: single-seat all-weather interceptor
Dimensions: wing span 13.95 m (45 ft 9 in); length 23.82 m (78 ft 2 in)
Performance: max. speed Mach 3.2; max. range 2250 km (1400 miles)
Armament: 4×air-to-air missiles (usually AA-6 'Acrid')

Assessment
Performance ★★★★
Range ★★★★
Age ★★★
Worldwide users ★★

The MiG-25 was designed to intercept very fast bombers at great altitudes. It survives today as a long-range interceptor and reconnaissance platform.

Mikoyan Gurevich MiG-29

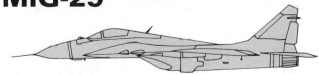

By the late 1970s Western analysts had identified a new fighter under development for the Soviet air force. The twin-finned air superiority fighter now known as the MiG-29 first flew in 1977 and entered service with Soviet fighter regiments in 1983. Like contemporary Soviet submarines, the USSR's new fighter benefited from stolen Western technology, including radar systems and long-range air-to-air missiles. In contrast to the primitive electronics of the MiG-25, the MiG-29 has a radar system comparable to some Western machines. Like the post-Vietnam generation of US fighters, it is an agile aircraft capable of violent manoeuvring in a dog-fight. Subsequently supplied to India, Syria, Iraq, Cuba and Afghanistan, as well as Czechoslovakia, East Germany and Yugoslavia, the MiG-29 is turning into a useful export for the new Russian Republic.

Specification
Type: single-seat all-weather interceptor
Dimensions: wing span 11.5 m (37 ft 9 in); length 17.2 m (56 ft 5 in)
Performance: max. speed Mach 2.3; max. range 2300 km (1400 miles)
Armament: one 23-mm cannon, plus 4 or 6 air-to-air missiles on underwing pylons

Assessment
Performance ★★★★
Range ★★★★
Age ★★
Worldwide users ★★★

The MiG-29 follows the design of US aircraft such as the F-18 Hornet. Highly manoeuvrable, it is currently being offered for export on very favourable terms by the cash-strapped Russian government.

Dassault-Breguet Mirage III

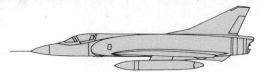

A contemporary of the MiG-21, the Dassault-Breguet Mirage III entered service with the French air force in 1960. Since then it has been sold to more than 20 countries and it has seen combat from the Middle East to southern Africa and South America. It was the principal fighter of the Israeli air force for many years – so much so that when France suspended deliveries in 1967 Israel developed a copy, the IAI Dagger – later used by Argentina in the Falklands war. Argentina also used Mirage III interceptors during that campaign, but kept them back to defend mainland bases after the famous 'Black Buck' bombing raid. Since 1960 there have been many versions of the Mirage III, including reconnaissance aircraft, fighter-bombers and the clear-weather day fighter, the Mirage 5.

Specification
Type: single-seat fighter bomber
Dimensions: wing span 8.22 m (26 ft 11 in); length 15.03 m (49 ft 4 in)
Performance: max. speed Mach 2.2; max. range 2400 km (1500 miles)
Armament: 2×30-mm cannon plus 3×454 kg (1000 lb) bombs or equivalent stores, or 1×R530 and 2×Matra Magic air-to-air missiles

Assessment
Performance ★★★★
Range ★★★★
Age ★★★★
Worldwide users ★★★★

The Argentine air force had over a dozen Mirage IIIs available during the Falklands campaign, but they refused to hazard them in dogfights with Royal Navy Sea Harriers.

Northrop F-5E

The Northrop F-5 'Freedom Fighter' first flew in 1959. Unusually for a military aircraft, it has proved a tremendous success on the export market. Over 30 countries have flown the F-5 and total production ran to some 2700 machines. The improved F-5E Tiger II was introduced in 1972. Featuring uprated engines and much better avionics, this version attracted equally strong interest around the world, and some 20 air forces acquired Tiger IIs by the mid-1980s. Relatively cheap and easy to operate, the F-5 may lack all-weather capability, but it is a robust aircraft and very agile in capable hands.

Specification
Type: single-seat light tactical fighter
Dimensions: wing span 8.13 m (26 ft 8 in); length 14.68 m (48 ft 2 in)
Performance: max. speed 1734 km/h (1100 mph); max. range 1600 km (1000 miles)
Armament: 2×20-mm cannon and up to 3174 kg (3 tons 280 lb) of ordnance

Assessment
Performance ★★★
Range ★★★
Age ★★★★
Worldwide users ★★★★

The Northrop F-5 has been sold to many US allies. These F-5s are flown by the US Navy 'Aggressors' to simulate Russian aircraft in training missions.

McDonnell-Douglas F-4 Phantom II

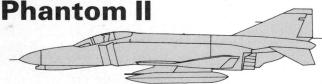

Designed as a multi-role attack aircraft, the F-4 entered service with the US Navy as a long-range interceptor armed with air-to-air missiles but no guns. Flown by the USAF, Marine Corps and US Navy, the Phantom saw extensive action during the Vietnam War, which cruelly exposed the limitations of an all-missile armament. This led to the F-4E fighter version, which features a 20-mm rotary-barrel cannon and a slatted wing for better manoeuvrability when carrying heavy loads. The F-4 was widely exported and customers included the RAF and Royal Navy, which operated Phantoms from HMS *Ark Royal*. The F-4 played a key role in Israel's victorious air wars with Syria and Egypt, both as a fighter and in suppressing the Arab SAM sites that caused so much damage in the early days of the Yom Kippur War. F-4 variants include dedicated reconnaissance and electronic warfare aircraft.

Specification
Type: two-seat multi-role fighter
Dimensions: wing span 11.71 m (38 ft 5 in); length 19.2 m (63 ft)
Performance: max. speed Mach 2.27; max. range 2817 km (1750 miles)
Armament: one 20-mm rotary cannon, plus 4×Sparrow air-to-air missiles and up to 7258 kg (7 tons 320 lb) of ordnance

Assessment
Performance ★★★★
Range ★★★★
Age ★★★★
Worldwide users ★★★★

A Phantom prepares to take off from a US carrier off Vietnam. This twin-seat multi-role aircraft has achieved great success on land and sea from South East Asia to the Middle East.

Dassault-Breguet Mirage F1

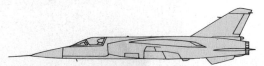

Within a year of the Mirage III entering service with the French air force, Dassault-Breguet was developing a successor. First flying in 1966, the Mirage F1 has 40 per cent more internal fuel than the Mirage III and a better wing design that improves manoeuvrability and enables it to take off from shorter runways. The French air force ordered the Mirage F1 for its interceptor squadrons, and the first F1s entered service in 1973. The F1 proved a very popular export, with over 500 of them sold abroad in the first 10 years of production. The Mirage F1 has seen combat in the Persian Gulf, where Iraqi Mirage F1s played an important role in the attacks on tankers during the late 1980s. There are several versions now operational – all-weather interceptors, fighter-bombers and dedicated reconnaissance aircraft.

Specification
Type: single-seat all-weather interceptor/fighter-bomber
Dimensions: wing span 8.4 m (27 ft 7 in); length 15 m (49 ft)
Performance: max. speed 2350 km/h (1460 mph); max. range 1300 km (810 miles)
Armament: 2×30-mm cannon, 2×air-to-air missiles (AIM-9 or Matra Magic), plus 4000 kg (3 tons 2105 lb) of ordnance

Assessment
Performance ★★★★
Range ★★★★
Age ★★★★
Worldwide users ★★★★

A French air force Mirage F1 takes part in a strike against Iraqi forces during the Gulf War. Some 500 Mirage F1s have been exported to many countries, ironically including Iraq.

GROUND ATTACK AIRCRAFT No. 1

The aerial bombardment of the Iraqi ground forces played a key role in the Allied victory in the Gulf War. It was the latest demonstration of the enormous power of fighter/ground-attack aircraft armed with bombs, rockets and guided missiles.

Sukhoi Su-22M-4 'Fitter-K'

Specification
Length overall: 19.2 m (63 ft)
Wing span: 10.6 m (34 ft 9 in); (spread) 14 m (46 ft)
Maximum speed at sea level: (estimated) 695 knots
Combat radius lo-lo-lo: (estimated) 360 km (220 miles)
Maximum weapon load: 3000 kg (2 tons 2120 lb)
Take-off distance: (clean) 610 m (2000 ft)

Assessment
Manoeuvrability ★★★
Rough field
  capability ★★★
Versatility ★★★
Robustness ★★★★

The 'Fitter' is a robust aircraft used by Russian forces and allied nations including Libya. It is handicapped by a relatively light weapon load and very short range.

The last of the 'Fitter' series, the backbone of Russian ground attack squadrons since the 1960s, the 'Fitter-K' is designed to operate from forward airfields. Known as the *Strizh* (Martlet), it has a short range compared to most ground attack aircraft. It can carry four rocket pods – each 32x57-mm folding fin rockets – or four air-to-air missiles, or bombs. Or It may carry a wide range of guided weapons from the AS-7 'Kerry' command-guided missile to the AS-9 'Kyle' anti-radar missile. Due to problems in Afghanistan with shoulder-fired heat-seeking missiles, the 'Fitter-Ks' have chaff and flare dispensers.

Sukhoi Su-25 'Frogfoot'

Specification
Length overall: 14.5 m (47 ft 8 in)
Wing span: 15.5 m (50 ft 10 in)
Maximum speed at sea level: (estimated) 475 knots
Combat radius lo-lo-lo: (estimated) 544 km (340 miles)
Maximum weapon load: 4000 kg (3 tons 2105 lb)
Take-off distance: (estimated) 472 m (1550 ft)

Assessment
Manoeuvrability ★★★★
Rough field
  capability ★★★★
Versatility ★
Robustness ★★★★

An Su-25 of the Czechoslovakian air force displays the eight underwing weapons pylons that can carry a wide assortment of ordnance. Su-25s were used alongside Mi-8 and Mi-24 helicopter gunships in Afghanistan.

This is the Russian equivalent of the US A-10. It is designed to survive hits from anti-aircraft fire and can carry a heavy bomb load. Known as the *Grach* (Rook) to the Russians, it proved much stronger than the Su-17 in Afghanistan, but poor navigation and sensor systems made precision attacks difficult. It has no auto-pilot, no all-weather and no night-attack capabilities. Russian pilots have criticised its short range and inadequate electronic counter-measures. Its turbojet, however, give it superior speed to the A-10 and a shorter take-off run, and it is highly manoeuvrable, but tiring, to fly.

Mikoyan Gurevich MiG-27 'Flogger'

Specification
Length overall: 16 m (52 ft 6 in)
Wing span: 8.17 m (26 ft 10 in); (spread) 14.25 m (46 ft 9 in)
Maximum speed at sea level: (estimated) 725 knots
Combat radius lo-lo-lo: (estimated) 390 km (240 miles)
Maximum weapon load: 2200 kg (2 tons 400 lb)
Take-off distance: (clean) 2200 m (7200 ft)

Assessment
Manoeuvrability ★★★
Rough field
  capability ★★★
Versatility ★★
Robustness ★★★★★

The Russian MiG-27 has been widely exported and has seen action from the Middle East to southern Africa. In the 1980s, its arrival in Angola caused problems for South Africa.

The air forces of the ex-Warsaw Pact nations and Russia include a high proportion of MiG-23s/27s. The aircraft is available in two main versions: a long-range, all-weather interceptor, or a dedicated ground attack aircraft. In continuous production for nearly 20 years, there are numerous sub-variants with different engines and equipment. The MiG-27 'Flogger-J' has an armoured cockpit and can carry gun or rocket pods, bombs or guided missiles. Export versions of the MiG-23 and MiG-27, fitted with inferior electronic equipment, have been supplied to numerous Russian allies.

British Aerospace Harrier

Specification
Length overall: 14.27 m (46 ft 10 in)
Wing span: 7.7 m (25 ft 3 in)
Maximum speed at sea level: 634 knots
Combat radius lo-lo-lo: 370 km (230 miles) (with 1360-kg (1 ton 800 lb) external load)
Maximum weapon load: 3630 kg (3 tons 1600 lb)
Take-off distance: vertical, or up to 300 m (980 ft) at max. weight

Assessment
Manoeuvrability	★★★★★
Rough field capability	★★★★★
Versatility	★★★★★
Robustness	★★

In service for over 20 years, the Harrier was the first V/STOL (Vertical/Short Take-Off-Landing) combat aircraft. Designed to fight from improvised sltes rather than vulnerable airfields, successive versions of the Harrier culminated in the GR.Mk 5, with updated avionics and a more powerful engine. The US Marine Corps adopted a much-modified version, designated AV-8, which fought in close support of the Marine ground units during the Gulf War. Harriers can carry a full range of laser-guided bombs, rockets and missiles.

From the Falklands to the Gulf War, the remarkable Harrier has performed very well. Incredibly manoeuvrable, its ability to operate from improvised airstrips is unsurpassed.

SEPECAT Jaguar

Specification
Length overall: 16.83 m (55 ft 3 in)
Wing span: 8.69 m (28 ft 6 in)
Maximum speed at sea level: 729 knots
Combat radius lo-lo-lo: 917 km (570 miles)
Maximum weapon load: 4763 kg (4 tons 1550 lb)
Take-off distance: 565 m (1850 ft)

Assessment
Manoeuvrability	★★
Rough field capability	★★★★
Versatility	★★★
Robustness	★★★

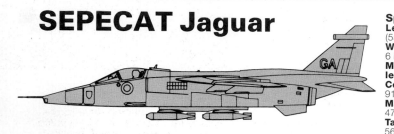

The Anglo-French Jaguar was designed from the outset for operation at high speed and very low level. Its Rolls-Royce Turboméca Adour turbofans give it a much greater range than other ground attack aircraft. Modern avionics, including the Ferranti NAVWASS (Navigation and Weapons Aiming Sub-System), enable the Jaguar to attack in all weathers. The Jaguar entered French service in 1972 and deliveries to the RAF were complete by 1978. French Jaguars saw limited combat in Chad, but the Jaguar did not see major action until the Gulf War. RAF Jaguars deployed to the Gulf were fitted with overwing pylons for AIM-9L air-to-air missiles.

The ageing Jaguar finally saw action in a major conflict when British and French forces deployed them to the Gulf. It carries a laser rangefinder but requires another aircraft to designate targets for laser-guided munitions.

Fairchild A-10

Specification
Length overall: 16.26 m (53 ft 4 in)
Wing span: 17.53 m (57 ft 6 in)
Maximum speed at sea level: 381 knots
Combat radius lo-lo-lo: 463 km (290 miles)
Maximum weapon load: 7257 kg (7 tons 320 lb)
Take-off distance: (clean) 1219 m (4000 ft)

Assessment
Manoeuvrability	★★★★
Rough field capability	★★
Robustness	★★★★
Worldwide users	★

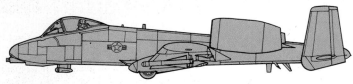

The Fairchild A-10 has few rivals as a close support aircraft. Heavily armoured and very manoeuvrable at low level, it carries a formidable weapons load and its devastating combination of guided missiles and 30-mm cannon proved very effective during the Gulf War. The A-10 is very slow, and doubts that it could perform such a role against heavy Soviet air defences have led the US Air Force to order their withdrawal from Europe. However, their success against the Iraqis has led to calls for the US Army to take them over. The Air Force's A-10s already fight in conjunction with US Army AH-64 helicopter gunships.

The distinctive A-10 is armed with a 30-mm cannon in its nose. Firing armour-piercing shells tipped with depleted uranium, it can knock out any tank in existence. A-10s also carry laser- or TV-guided missiles.

General Dynamics F-16C

Specification
Length overall: 15.09 m (49 ft 4 in)
Wing span: 10.01 m (32 ft 10 in)
Maximum speed at sea level: 793 knots
Combat radius lo-lo-lo: 547 km (340 miles)
Maximum weapon load: 5443 kg (5 tons 800 lb)
Take-off distance: 365 m (1200 ft)

Assessment
Manoeuvrability	★★★★★
Rough field capability	★★
Versatility	★★★
Robustness	★★★

The US Air Force developed a ground-attack version of this agile fighter aircraft to replace the A-10. Capable of over twice the speed of the lumbering 'Warthog', the F-16 is better equipped to fight in poor weather conditions and carries superior electronic countermeasures. But the F-16 can only operate from prepared runways, and is much less able to survive battle damage. Nevertheless, the F-16's good range and respectable weapon load make it a dangerous enemy.

The F-16 is an outstanding and highly manoeuvrable fighter that can also double as a ground attack aircraft. Its only weakness is its inability to operate from rough airstrips.

Air power used to be divided between strategic and tactical applications, but that distinction has now blurred. Fighters designed for deep interdiction are often equally capable of battlefield support.

General Dynamics F-111

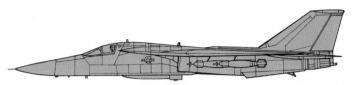

Specification
Length overall: 22.4 m (73 ft 6 in)
Wing span: 19.2 m (63 ft)
Maximum speed at sea level: 793 knots
Combat radius hi-lo-hi: 1480 km (920 miles)
Maximum weapon load: 11,340 kg (11 tons 360 lb)
Take-off distance: 914 m (3000 ft)

Assessment
Manoeuvrability ✭✭✭
Rough field capability ✭
Robustness ✭✭✭
Range ✭✭✭✭✭

Designed in the 1960s, the General Dynamics F-111 was the first supersonic fighter-bomber with the ability to make low-level precision bombing attacks by day or night, whatever the weather. Known as the 'Aardvark' because of its droop-snooted silhouette, the swing-wing F-111 entered service prematurely over Vietnam in 1968, and a number of aircraft were lost. By 1972, however, it had matured into a highly effective interdictor and strike aircraft. In 1986 F-111s based in England struck at Colonel Gaddafi's Libya, and in 1991 the F-111 was one of the anti-Saddam coalition's most important aircraft. Nearly a quarter of a century after its first combat flight, the F-111 remains a highly potent warplane, with capabilities possibly matched but not bettered by later designs like the multi-national Tornado and the Soviet Su-24 'Fencer'.

The F-111 is one of the oldest all-weather fighter bombers still flying, but it is possible that it remains the most potent aircraft of its type in the world today. It was one of the most important aircraft used in the Gulf War.

Vought A-7 Corsair II

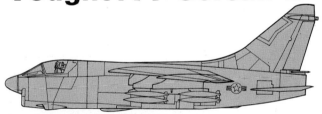

Specification
Length overall: 14.06 m (46 ft)
Wing span: 11.81 m (38 ft 9 in)
Maximum speed at sea level: 606 knots
Combat radius lo-lo-lo: 1432 km (890 miles)
Maximum weapon load: 9072 kg (8 tons 2080 lb)
Take-off distance: 1524 m (4900 ft) (with maximum load)

Assessment
Manoeuvrability ✭✭
Rough field capability ✭
Robustness ✭✭
Range ✭✭✭✭

Commonly known as the 'Sluf', or 'Short Little Ugly F✱✱✱er', the Vought A-7 Corsair II was designed in the 1960s for the US Navy as a carrier-borne light attack aircraft. Derived from, but differing considerably from, the F-8 Crusader fighter, it was intended to replace the A-4 Skyhawk. In the event, the A-7 was much more than a light attack machine, its huge bomb load and highly effective bombing system leading to its adoption by the US Air Force. It was replaced in US Air Force service by the Fairchild A-10, which is much more the dedicated close-support aircraft, but the last US Navy A-7 squadrons remained in service long enough to participate with some effect in the Gulf War, after having seen combat over Vietnam, the Lebanon, Grenada, in the confrontation with Libya, and in Panama.

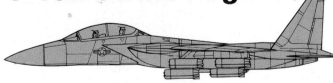

Of the same vintage as the F-111, the Vought A-7 Corsair II is now almost out of service with the US forces. However, countries which manage to obtain used examples of the Corsair will be acquiring a potent combat aircraft, capable of carrying a very heavy warload.

McDonnell Douglas F-15E Strike Eagle

Specification
Length overall: 19.43 m (63 ft 9 in)
Wing span: 13.05 m (42 ft 10 in)
Maximum speed at sea level: 790 knots
Combat radius hi-lo-hi: 1200 km (750 miles)
Maximum weapon load: 10,659 kg (10 tons 1100 lb)
Take-off distance: not released

Assessment
Manoeuvrability ✭✭✭✭✭
Rough field capability ✭✭
Robustness ✭✭
Range ✭✭✭

The two-seat F-15E is a logical development of the single-seat air-superiority F-15. It retains the fighter's phenomenal performance, being supremely fast and agile, but there the similarity ends. The F-15E is a superb all-weather interdiction and strike aircraft, with a huge weapons load. It is packed with advanced avionics, with automatic terrain-following flight controls, laser-enhanced inertial navigation, high resolution radar, and all-weather LANTIRN and wide-field infra-red targeting pods. The modern all-glass cockpit has a wide-angle head-up display and numerous CRT displays for the pilot and weapons system officer. F-15Es became operational in 1989, and two squadrons of this type were used to great effect during the Gulf War, making precision attacks on strategic targets deep inside Iraq.

The McDonnell Douglas F-15E retains most of the original fighter's superb performance, but it is equipped with advanced avionics which enable the ground-attack Eagle to deliver huge loads of bombs with pinpoint accuracy.

Panavia Tornado GR.Mk 1

The tri-national Tornado went through a 10-year development before entering service in the early 1980s. Designed to undertake a variety of missions, it is most often tasked with low-level interdiction. The Tornado relies heavily on its advanced avionics and terrain-following radar to fly at high speed and ultra-low level in all weathers, minimising the chances of detection by the enemy, before delivering a wide range of weapons with pinpoint accuracy. Tornado's combat debut came in the Gulf War, when RAF, Saudi and Italian aircraft were heavily involved in the attack on Saddam Hussein's Iraq. Low-level tactics proved costly, with combat losses of six British and one Italian aircraft. Once it became clear that Iraqi aircraft and missiles offered little danger, the Tornados switched to medium altitude attacks.

Specification
Length overall: 16.72 m (58 ft 2 in)
Wing span: 13.91 m (45 ft 8 in) (fully spread)
Maximum speed at sea level: 800 knots
Combat radius hi-lo-hi: 1390 km (865 miles)
Maximum weapon load: 9000 kg (8 tons 1900 lb)
Take-off distance: 885 m (2900 ft)

Assessment
Manoeuvrability   ★★★★
Rough field capability   ★★★
Robustness   ★★★★
Range   ★★★★

The Tornado is a mainstay of Western defence, serving in large numbers with the British, German and Italian air forces. Like the F-111, the Tornado is an all-weather, day-night aircraft, and was heavily involved in the Gulf War.

Sukhoi Su-24 'Fencer'

Designed from the outset as an all-weather, low-level attack aircraft, the Sukhoi Su-24 'Fencer' bears a resemblance to the American F-111, although the Soviet jet is somewhat smaller. Entering service after the F-111, but before the Tornado, the 'Fencer' is comparable in performance with the two premier Western interdictors, being somewhat faster and with better rough-field capability, but having less advanced avionics and attack systems. At least 500 attack 'Fencers' have been built. The type is also used for maritime strike/reconnaissance and for electronic jamming/Sigint/reconnaissance. The eight weapons pylons beneath the Su-24's fuselage, wing gloves and outer wing panels can carry a wide variety of weaponry, ranging from tactical and defence-suppression bombs and missiles through to nuclear weapons.

Specification
Length overall: 21.29 m (69 ft 10 in)
Wing span: 17.5 m (57 ft 5 in)
Maximum speed at sea level: 790 knots
Combat radius hi-lo-hi: 950+ km (590+ miles)
Maximum weapon load: 11,000 kg (10 tons 1860 lb)
Take-off distance: 762 m (2500 ft) (estimated)

Assessment
Manoeuvrability   ★★★
Rough field capability   ★★★★
Robustness   ★★★★
Range   ★★★

The Sukhoi Su-24 'Fencer' is a large, capable Soviet attack aircraft that bears a resemblance in form and function to the American F-111. Iraq operated Su-24s, but their crews fled to Iran rather than fight in the Gulf.

Mikoyan-Gurevich MiG-27 'Flogger-J'

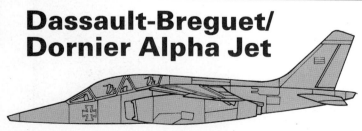

The Russian MiG-27 'Flogger-J' is the most advanced of the MiG-23 and MiG-27 family. MiG-27s differ from MiG-23s in that they do not have variable geometry air intakes, so that they have lower supersonic performance. However, such speeds are a luxury on a ground attack fighter, and what the 'Flogger-J' does have is a laser range-finder and a laser-designator, which give the aircraft the ability to use precision-guided munitions. Compared with Western fighters the 'Flogger-J' has a short range, poor weapons load, and might have reliability problems, but it is sturdy and cheap.

Specification
Length overall: 16 m (52 ft 6 in)
Wing span: 8.17 m (26 ft 10 in) (swept); 14.25 m (46 ft 9 in) (spread)
Maximum speed at sea level: 725 knots (estimated)
Combat radius hi-lo-hi: 390 km (240 miles) (estimated)
Maximum weapon load: 4500 kg (4 tons 960 lb) (estimated)
Take-off distance: 2200 m (7200 ft) (clean)

Assessment
Manoeuvrability   ★★★
Rough field capability   ★★★★
Robustness   ★★★★
Range   ★

The MiG-27 'Flogger-J' is a ground attack version of the hugely successful MiG-23 swing-wing fighter. Like all MiG designs it is a sturdy aircraft, but it carries a smaller weapons load than Western equivalents.

Dassault-Breguet/ Dornier Alpha Jet

State-of-the-art ground attack and strike aircraft do not come cheap, and for many air forces the capabilities of the Tornado or the Strike Eagle would be wasted. However, there are much less expensive aircraft, often designed for different purposes, which are capable of undertaking ground attack missions in lower threat environments. The Dassault-Breguet/Dornier Alpha Jet is a Franco-German advanced trainer which was designed to have a secondary attack role. Indeed, German Alpha Jets are flown almost exclusively as single-seat close-support, weapons trainer or battlefield reconnaissance aircraft. Weapons load and avionics do not match those of more advanced jets, but the Alpha Jet is manoeuvrable, easy to fly and simple to maintain. The Alpha Jet has been sold to a number of countries in Africa and the Middle East.

Specification
Length overall: 13.23 m (43 ft 5 in)
Wing span: 9.11 m (29 ft 11 in)
Maximum speed at sea level: 540 knots
Combat radius lo-lo-lo: 390 km (240 miles)
Maximum weapon load: 2500 kg (2 tons 1030 lb)
Take-off distance: 370 m (1200 ft)

Assessment
Manoeuvrability   ★★★
Rough field capability   ★
Robustness   ★
Range   ★

The Alpha Jet shows that an aircraft need not be a technological marvel to be an effective warplane. Simple, cheap and easy to maintain, the Alpha Jet is perfectly suited to lower intensity warfare.

BOMBERS

The bomber has been a vital part of air warfare for more than 70 years. The heavy bomber reached its peak in the 1950s. Since then the number of bombers has declined, but at the same time individual aircraft and air-launched weapons have become vastly more effective.

Boeing B-52 Stratofortress

The Boeing B-52 Stratofortress entered service in 1952 as a high-level strategic bomber, but the development of the surface-to-air missile made high-altitude missions very risky. From the early 1960s, the B-52's strategic mission was transformed into one of low-level penetration. The B-52 was used as a conventional bomber in Vietnam and the Gulf. It survives in the shape of the B-52G and the B-52H, although the G-model is gradually being withdrawn from service as the USA cuts its strategic forces following the relaxation of East-West tensions. Both types have been considerably upgraded in their offensive and defensive electronics, and while they are still able to deliver vast quantities of free-fall conventional weapons, they now carry a primary armament of nuclear missiles. The B-52H can carry up to 20 AGM-86B air-launched cruise missiles.

Specification
(Boeing B-52H)
Type: six-seat strategic bomber
Dimensions: length 47.85 m (157 ft); span 56.39 m (185 ft); height 12.4 m (40 ft)
Performance: max. speed 1014 km/h (630 mph) at 40,000 ft (12,200 m); range 12,000+ km (7450+ miles)
Armament: one 20-mm cannon in remote-controlled radar-directed tail turret, plus 20×ALCM or up to 24,000 kg (23 tons 1400 lb) of disposable stores carried internally or externally

Assessment
Size   *****
Range   *****
Payload *****
Stealth *

*Known to its crews as the BUFF, or Big Ugly Fat F*****, the B-52 has been in service for more than 30 years.*

Rockwell B-1B

The Rockwell B-1B entered service in 1986 as a replacement for the B-52, and in spite of continued problems with its defensive electronics suite it is considerably more capable than its predecessor. The origins of the type lie in a Mach 2.2 high-altitude bomber, which first flew as the B-1A in 1974. This was cancelled by President Carter in 1977, but the project was revived as the B-1B under President Reagan. The B-1B was optimised for low-level, high subsonic speed operations, with Mach 1.25 dash capability. The airframe and landing gear remained unchanged, but the powerplant and engine nacelles were considerably modified. Other modifications included the incorporation of radar-absorbent materials to reduce the aircraft's already low radar cross-section. Current strength of the B-1B force is 97 aircraft, which will serve alongside 95 B-52H bombers through the 1990s.

Specification
(Rockwell B-1B)
Type: four-seat supersonic strategic bomber
Dimensions: length 44.81 m (147 ft); span 41.67 m (136 ft 8 in); and 23.84 m (78 ft 2 in) (swept); height 10.25 m (33 ft 7 in)
Performance: max. speed 1330 km/h (825 mph); range 10,400 km (6500 miles)
Armament: 20×ALCM or up to 29,000 kg (28 tons 1200 lb) of missiles or free-fall bombs carried internally and externally

Assessment
Size   *****
Range   *****
Payload *****
Stealth ****

Although the subject of considerable criticism, the B-1B Lancer is still one of the most potent warplanes in the world.

Northrop B-2

The Northrop B-2 is an extremely bold attempt to produce a strategic bomber with sufficient 'stealth' to avoid detection by an enemy's electromagnetic and infra-red sensors, except at very close range. Success in that aim will restore the bomber's ability to make attacks at medium or high level, with all the advantages of improved range and economy and lessened crew fatigue that this gives. First flown in July 1989, the B-2 uses a high proportion of composite materials in its construction. It is a flying wing design, with leading edges swept at 40 degrees, trailing edges in a 'W' layout and no vertical surfaces. Although succeeding in many of its aims, the B-2 is extremely expensive, and Congress has cut the USAF's purchase of the bomber from the 132 aircraft requested to a token 20-strong force.

Specification
(Northrop B-2)
Type: two-/three-seat strategic bomber
Dimensions: length 21.03 m (69 ft); span 54.43 m (178 ft 6 in); height 5.18 m (17 ft)
Performance: max. speed 770 km/h (480 mph); range 12,250 km (7600 miles)
Armament: 16 Advanced Cruise Missiles or up to 22,500 kg (22 tons 300 lb) of stores carried internally

Assessment
Size   ****
Range   *****
Payload *****
Stealth *****

With the withdrawal of funding for any more than 20 B-2s, it has become the world's most expensive aeroplane.

Tupolev Tu-16 'Badger'

The Tupolev Tu-16 'Badger' was one of the first jet-powered bombers. When it entered service late in 1953 it represented a truly remarkable advance in terms of payload, speed and range, although it was soon surpassed by later designs. Long Range Aviation operated nearly 300 'Badgers' right up to the dissolution of the Soviet Union, and the air forces of the Commonwealth of Independent States will no doubt continue to do so for many years to come. Although a fair proportion of this total is tasked with electronic warfare and refuelling, there is still a sizable force of 'Badger-A' bombers still active. The CIS's naval air arm also operates the Tu-16 in the strike role. China is the other major operator, building a copy of the 'Badger' known as the Xian H-6. More than 100 are currently in service with the air force of the People's Liberation Army.

Specification
(Tupolev Tu-16 'Badger-G')
Type: six-seat medium bomber
Dimensions: length 34.8 m (114 ft); span 32.99 m (108 ft); height 10.36 m (34 ft)
Performance: max. speed 1050 km/h (650 mph); range 7200 km (4500 miles)
Armament: seven 23-mm cannon and up to 9000 kg (8 tons 1900 lb) of disposable stores

Assessment
Size	***
Range	***
Payload	***
Stealth	*

The Tupolev Tu-16 has been in front-line service for nearly 40 years.

Tupolev Tu-95/142 'Bear'

The Tu-95 'Bear' first flew in 1954 and entered service little more than a year later. It is one of the classic post-war aircraft designs, with jet-type performance provided by four extremely powerful turboprops, each driving massive contra-rotating propellers and mounted on swept flying surfaces. 'Bears' were initially operated by Long Range Aviation, which was the Soviet strategic air force. The Soviet Navy also used the 'Bear' as a long-range maritime-reconnaissance and ASW aircraft. The successors to the Soviet Union still operate about 125 'Bears' in the strategic role. The original 'Bear-A' is a strategic bomber, with a 20-tonne payload of free-fall weapons. 'Bear-Bs' and 'Bear-Gs' are missile carriers, while the latest 'Bear-H' is a dedicated long-range cruise missile carrier, armed with 10 AS-15 'Kent' air-launched cruise missiles.

Specification
(Tupolev Tu-142K 'Bear-H')
Type: 10-seat strategic bomber
Dimensions: length 48 m (157 ft 5 in); span 51.1 m (167 ft 7 in); height 12.12 m (39 ft 9 in)
Performance: max. speed 1000 km/h (620 mph); range 16,500 km (10,250 miles)
Armament: 2×NR-23 23-mm cannon in the tail, plus up to 10×AS-15 'Kent' air-launched cruise missiles or 11,000 kg (10 tons 1860 lb) of stores carried internally and externally

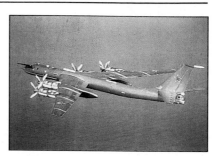

Assessment
Size	*****
Range	*****
Payload	****
Stealth	*

Archaic though it may seem, the propeller-driven Tupolev 'Bear' remains an effective warplane.

Tupolev Tu-160 'Blackjack'

First flown in 1982, the Tupolev Tu-160 'Blackjack' is a counterpart to the American B-1B. Both share a similar configuration, but the Soviet-designed bomber is about 30 per cent larger and considerably faster. Its unrefuelled combat radius of 7300 km is estimated on a mission profile of subsonic high-altitude cruise, transsonic penetration at low altitude, supersonic attack and departure, followed by a subsonic return at high altitude. The 'Blackjack' has a conventional or nuclear free-fall bombing capability, but it has more often been associated with the AS-15 'Kent' cruise missile. The 'Blackjack' is an extremely expensive aircraft, so with the current economic crisis affecting the former Soviet Union, together with the relaxation in international tension, it is unlikely that more than the 25 bombers currently in service will be completed.

Specification
(Tupolev Tu-160 'Blackjack')
Type: four-seat strategic supersonic bomber
Dimensions: length 53.9 m (176 ft 10 in); span 55.5 m (182 ft) (spread) and 33.75 m (110 ft 8 in) (swept); height 12.8 m (42 ft)
Performance: max. speed 2230 km/h (1380 mph); range 14,600 km (9000 miles)
Armament: up to 16,500 kg (16 tons 500 lb) of free-fall bombs, air-to-surface missiles or air-launched cruise missiles carried internally

Assessment
Size	*****
Range	*****
Payload	*****
Stealth	****

The Tu-160 'Blackjack' is the largest bomber in the world, but it is very expensive.

Dassault Mirage IV

The Dassault Mirage IV medium-range bomber is by far the largest of the fighters and ground attack aircraft in the distinctive Mirage series of delta-wing warplanes. First flying in 1959 and entering service in 1964, the Mirage IV is of the same general configuration as the Mirage III fighter, but is nearly 10 metres longer. As part of France's nuclear deterrent, the Mirage IVs were dispersed on top security bases around the country. One bomber was always ready to go at 15-minutes' notice, and the rest of the three-squadron force was maintained at 80 per cent readiness. The Mirage IV was fitted with assisted take-off booster rockets to ensure a fast response if a scramble order came. The Mirage IV force is now reduced in size, and has been retasked as a reconnaissance asset, but the aircraft retain their bombing capability.

Specification
(Dassault Mirage IV A)
Type: two-seat supersonic medium bomber
Dimensions: length 23.5 m (77 ft); span 11.85 m (38 ft 11 in); height 5.4 m (17 ft 9 in)
Performance: max. dash speed 2340 km/h (1450 mph); range 2500 km (1500 miles)
Armament: one free-fall nuclear bomb or up to 7250 kg (7 tons 320 lb) of disposable stores

Assessment
Size	**
Range	**
Payload	***
Stealth	**

A Mirage IV armed with an Air-Sol-Moyenne-Porte nuclear missile.

BOMBERS No.2

The bomber aircraft operated by the world's air forces are a mixture of new and old; some bombers from the 1950s are still in service while others are retired or are now flying as tankers. New designs continue to enter service.

Ilyushin Il-28 'Beagle'

Specification
Type: 3-seat light bomber
Dimensions: length 17.6 m (57 ft 9 in); span 21.4 m (70 ft); height 7.65 m (25 ft)
Performance: max. speed 900 km/h (560 mph) at 15,000 ft (4500 ft); range 2180 km (1350 miles) at 33,000 ft (10,000 m)
Armament: internal bay for 3000 kg (2 tons 2120 lb) of bombs or two torpedoes, and two 23-mm cannon in nose, plus two in tail turret

Assessment
Size ★★★
Range ★★
Payload ★
Stealth ★

This was the first jet bomber to enter service with the Soviet air force and it was also supplied to the newly-created air fleets of the Warsaw Pact countries. Designed in the late 1940s, the Il-28 was powered by Rolls-Royce turbojets supplied by Britain just before relations with our wartime ally cooled completely. With manual bomb-aiming and even a manned tail turret, the Il-28 was very much a jet-powered World War II bomber, but over 1,000 were built and eventually exported to Soviet allies in the Arab world like Syria and Yemen. Nigeria used Il-28s in the Biafran War. China manufactured its own Il-28s as the B-5 bomber and continued using the type long after the Soviet and Warsaw Pact aircraft had been retired.

The Soviet Ilyushin Il-28 bomber was built with British help just after World War II. Although retired from front-line service with the Warsaw Pact in the 1970s, it remained operational in communist China.

Tupolev Tu-22 'Blinder'

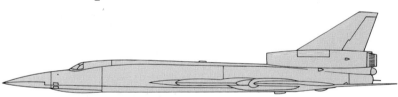

Specification
Type: supersonic bomber and reconnaissance aircraft
Dimensions: length 40.5 m (133 ft); span 27.7 m (90 ft 10 in); height 10.6 m (34 ft 9 in)
Performance: max. speed 1480 km/h (920 mph); max. range with bomb load 3100 km (1900 miles)
Armament: one AS-4 missile ('Blinder-B') or 9000 kg (8 tons 1920 lb) of bombs ('Blinder-A'), plus two 23-mm cannon in remotely-controlled tail barbette

Assessment
Size ★★★★
Range ★★★
Payload ★★★
Stealth ★

Developed in the 1950s, the Tu-22 was the successor to the Tu-16 high-altitude supersonic bomber. Carrying a similar payload to only a slightly greater range, the Tu-22 offered no real increase in capability, although it was reportedly designed for KGB-controlled high-altitude reconnaissance missions as well as bombing. With a high accident rate, even by Soviet standards, and poor reliability, the Tu-22 was not a success and only about 200 were built, not enough to replace the Tu-16s which were kept in service well into the 1970s. The main production version was known to NATO as the 'Blinder-B' and carried air-to-surface missiles; about 70 'Blinder-C' reconnaissance and electronic warfare aircraft were also used. A few were exported to Iraq and Libya.

Unreliable and prone to accidents, the Tupolev Tu-22 'Blinder' was not built in sufficient numbers to replace the ageing Tu-16 'Badgers'. It was supplied in limited numbers to Iraq and Libya.

Tu-22M 'Backfire'

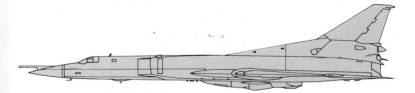

Specification
Type: strategic bomber and maritime strike aircraft
Dimensions: length 39.6 m (130 ft); span 34.3 m (112 ft 6 in) (spread) and 23.4 m (77 ft) (swept); height 10.8 m (35 ft 5 in)
Performance: max. speed at high altitude c. 2000 km/h (1240 mph); range 5000 km (3100 miles)
Armament: 2×AS-4 missiles or 12,000 kg (11 tons 1800 lb) of bombs, plus 2×twin 23-mm guns

Assessment
Size ★★★★★
Range ★★★★★
Payload ★★★
Stealth ★

Designated the Tu-22M for political reasons (the Soviets tried to present this new aircraft as a development of the existing Tu-22), the variable geometry 'Backfire' bomber was introduced in the mid-1970s. The USA, then embroiled in the SALT talks, classified it as a strategic bomber, while the USSR disagreed, claiming it lacked the range. In fact the 'Backfire' may have been intended for intercontinental operations but ultimately failed to achieve the necessary performance. Whatever its origins, the 'Backfire' entered service with both the Soviet navy and air force, and as a long-range maritime bomber armed with cruise missiles it was seen as a major threat to NATO's Atlantic lifeline. At the time of its collapse in 1991 the USSR had 370 'Backfires' with the air force and 160 with the navy.

Probably intended to be an intercontinental bomber, the 'Backfire' was more feared as a long-range maritime strike aircraft. Carrying massive air-to-surface missiles, they were regarded by NATO commanders as a serious threat in the North Atlantic.

BAC Canberra

Entering service with RAF Bomber Command in 1951, the Canberra outperformed contemporary fighters. Even when carrying its full 2722-kilogram bomb load it was very manoeuvrable. Equipped for visual bombing only, due to problems with the radar system, the Canberra was soon modified as a reconnaissance platform, and several RAF aircraft penetrated Soviet airspace until the communist air defences made this too risky. A total of 27 variants was reached and the Canberra was exported all over the world. A dozen air forces were still flying them into the 1980s. Ethiopia used Canberras in its war with Somalia in 1977-78, Rhodesia used them in its civil war and Chilean PR.Mk 9s were very active during the Falklands campaign.

Specification
Type: three-seat light bomber
Dimensions: length 19.96 m (65 ft 5 in); span 19.51 m (64 ft); height 4.75 m (15 ft 7 in)
Performance: max. speed 973 km/h (600 mph) at 40,000 ft (12,200 m); range 1779 km (1100 miles)
Armament: 2722 kg (2 tons 1520 lb) of bombs in internal bay, plus 2×454-kg (1000-lb) bombs on pylons

Assessment
Size	★★★
Range	★★
Payload	★
Stealth	★

The Canberra was an outstanding light bomber built during the 1950s and flown by many air forces. Argentina used Canberras against the British Task Force in 1982.

Hawker Siddeley Buccaneer

Developed to a Royal Navy specification during the 1950s, the Buccaneer entered service with the Fleet Air Arm in January 1962. Thirty years later some of the RAF's surviving Buccaneers took part in the Gulf War to provide laser designation for the Tornados. They flew over 200 sorties and dropped 48 bombs in an unexpected finale to a very long career. The RAF began to operate Buccaneers in 1970 as successive British governments ate away at the Royal Navy's carrier strength. The Buccaneer is subsonic but is able to carry a massive weapon load with little loss of performance: a fully-loaded Buccaneer is faster than a fully-loaded F-4 Phantom and far more fuel efficient.

Specification
Type: two-seat low-level bomber
Dimensions: length 19.93 m (65 ft 5 in); span 13.4 m (44 ft); height 4.95 m (16 ft)
Performance: max. speed at low level with full bomb load 1110 km/h (690 mph); max. range 998 km (620 miles)
Armament: 7257 kg (7 tons 320 lb) of bombs or stores

Assessment
Size	★★★
Range	★
Payload	★★
Stealth	★

Originally built for the Royal Navy, the Buccaneers were transferred to the RAF when the British government stopped the Navy operating aircraft carriers. It was a superb low-level bomber.

Avro Vulcan

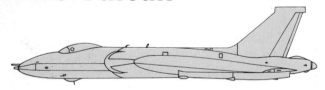

In 1982, the RAF established a new world record for long-range bombing missions when Avro Vulcans attacked targets on the Falklands from their base at Ascension Island over 12870 kilometres away. These distinctive delta-shaped aircraft were on the brink of retirement and left RAF service shortly afterwards. The last flying example will probably be grounded by the end of 1992 due to its high operating cost. Avro Vulcans entered service in 1957 as part of the RAF's 'V' bomber force, Britain's nuclear deterrent. After the Royal Navy's SSBNs became operational in the early 1960s the Vulcans were switched to low-level attack missions and their all white (anti-flash) colour scheme was replaced with grey/green camouflage.

Specification
Type: five-seat strategic bomber
Dimensions: length 32.16 m (105 ft 5 in); span 33.83 m (111 ft); height 8.28 m (27 ft 2 in)
Performance: max. speed 1043 km/h (650 mph) at 40,000 ft (12,200 m); max. range 7400 km (4600 miles)
Armament: 21,454-kg (21-tons 260-lb) bomb load

Assessment
Size	★★★★★
Range	★★★★★
Payload	★★★★★
Stealth	★★

The majestic Avro Vulcan holds the world record for long-distance bombing sorties after the 'Black Buck' missions of the Falklands war.

Mirage 2000N

The Mirage 2000 was selected in 1975 to be the French air force's main combat aircraft by the end of the 1980s. This multi-role aircraft was to be a single-seat interceptor, fighter-bomber, reconnaissance platform or two-seater low-altitude strike aircraft. The two-seat Mirage 2000N entered operational service in 1988 and its primary role was to launch the ASMP nuclear missile. With terrain-following radar and extensive ECM fit, the Mirage 2000N is intended for low-level penetration of enemy airspace and it carries two Matra Magic missiles for self-defence. In wartime it would operate below at well under 300 ft.

Specification
Type: two-seat strike aircraft
Dimensions: length 14.55 m (47 ft 8 in); span 9.13 m (30 ft); height 5.15 m (16 ft 11 in)
Performance: max. speed at low level 1110 km/h (690 mph); max. range 1480 km (920 miles)
Armament: one ASMP medium-range nuclear missile

Assessment
Size	★★
Range	★★
Payload	★
Stealth	★★★

The French air force acquired the Mirage 2000N to deliver the ASMP air-launched nuclear missile. It is capable of other low-level attack missions and carries a variety of electronic countermeasures equipment.

MARITIME PATROL AIRCRAFT No.1

Although there was once a duel between a Zeppelin and a submarine in World War I, it was not until World War II that aircraft became a serious threat to warships. Today, specialist aircraft range far across the oceans to monitor naval activity and above all to track potentially hostile submarines.

Lockheed P-2 Neptune

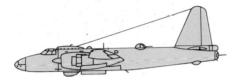

Specification
Cruise speed: 180 knots
Range: 3500 km (2200 miles)
Payload: 3630 kg (3 tons 1600 lb)
Armament: eight 454-kg (1000-lb) bombs, or two Mk 46 torpedoes, or 12 depth charges. Could also carry 5-in Zuni rockets

Assessment
Age ★★★★★
Range ★★
Weapon load ★★
Worldwide users ★

The US Navy operated P-2 Neptunes from 1947 until the early 1980s. In the Vietnam War they were used for coastal patrols and as gunships. The Argentine navy used two Neptunes during the Falklands war.

Developed during World War II, the Lockheed Neptune entered service with the US Navy in 1947. It was widely exported; Argentina, Australia, Brazil, Japan, the Netherlands, Portugal and the UK all operated the Neptune. The production line was in operation for over 30 years. Argentina's two surviving Neptunes were used to search for the British Task Force during the Falklands war and one guided in the Etendard attack that sank HMS *Sheffield*. However, both broke down in the middle of the war, illustrating the danger of relying on ageing aircraft in combat. All Neptunes were retired during the 1980s except for Japan's more modern force of locally-built P-2Js.

Lockheed P-3 Orion

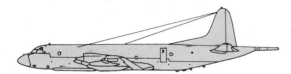

Specification
Cruise speed: 328 knots
Range: 8105 km (5000 miles)
Payload: 9070 kg (8 tons 2000 lb)
Armament: eight Mk 46 324-mm homing torpedoes plus four Harpoon, or four Mk 46 torpedoes and one Mk 101 nuclear depth charge

Assessment
Age ★★★★
Range ★★★★
Weapon load ★★★★★
Worldwide users ★★★★

The P-3 is the US Navy's current maritime patrol aircraft, and it can remain on station for up to seven hours. It can be equipped to attack surface ships as well as hunt and sink submarines.

Lockheed followed the Neptune with this even more successful aircraft. It has been the backbone of the US Navy's shore-based anti-submarine patrol forces for over 20 years. Seventeen-hour patrols across the Atlantic or Pacific enable it to cover vast areas of ocean. It can fly quickly to and from its patrol area, yet loiter for up to seven hours 1850 kilometres away from its base. Carrying a MAD (Magnetic Anomaly Detector), search radar and 87 or more sonobuoys, the Orion can search for submarines and attack with homing torpedoes or depth charges. Later versions are able to carry Harpoon anti-ship missiles too.

Dassault-Breguet Atlantic

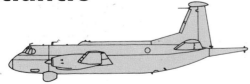

Specification
Cruise speed: 355 knots
Range: 5888 km (3600 miles)
Payload: 6500 kg (6 tons 900 lb)
Armament: 12 depth charges, or four L4, or eight Mk 46 homing torpedoes

Assessment
Age ★★★★
Range ★★★★
Weapon load ★★★
Worldwide users ★★★

A Dassault-Breguet Atlantic of the German navy. This aircraft is yet another example of a NATO joint project that half the members withdrew from.

In 1958, all 15 NATO countries approved a design for a common maritime patrol aircraft to be manufactured by a multinational consortium. However, the US Navy adopted the Orion instead and the British and Belgians withdrew from the programme also. The aircraft they rejected was the Dassault-Breguet Atlantic, but it is in service today with France, Germany and Italy. Although primarily used for anti-submarine duties, the Atlantic can carry AS-12 or Martel missiles for use against surface targets.

British Aerospace Nimrod

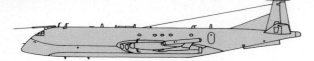

Specification
Cruise speed: 500 knots
Range: 9265 km (4500 miles)
Payload: 6120 kg (6 tons)
Armament: up to nine Stingray homing torpedoes, or four AIM-9L IR-homing missiles

Assessment
Age	★★★
Range	★★★★★
Weapon load	★★★
Worldwide users	★

With a large payload and tremendous endurance, the Nimrod has proved very successful. Several bold sorties near the Argentine coast in 1982 showed the way was clear for a landing on the Falklands.

With careful use of inflight refuelling from aircraft based on Ascension Island, RAF Nimrods flew several missions during the Falklands war that set new records for long-range reconnaissance missions. Adopted in 1968 and upgraded from 1979, the British Aerospace Nimrods were even fitted with air-to-air missiles in 1982 when operating close to the Argentine coast. Although primarily equipped for ASW, the Nimrod's long-range Searchwater radar enables a single aircraft to sweep vast stretches of sea for enemy shipping. Having also acquired Harpoon missiles, the Nimrod can attack warships too.

Tupolev Tu-16 'Badger'

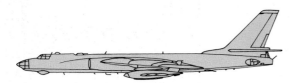

Specification
Cruise speed: 535 knots
Range: 5700 km (3500 miles)
Payload: 8000 kg (7 tons 1950 lb)
Armament: ('Badger-G') two AS-5 'Kelt' missiles, or one AS-2 'Kipper'; some versions have up to seven 23-mm cannon

Assessment
Age	★★★★★
Range	★★★
Weapon load	★★★★
Worldwide users	★

The Soviets operated a vast fleet of Tu-16 'Badgers' in a variety of maritime roles. The Soviet navy remained dependent on land-based air support until the collapse of the USSR.

This Soviet supersonic bomber first flew in 1952 and 'Badger-A' bombers entered service with the Soviet air force two years later. Over 300 were still operating with AV-MF (Soviet naval aviation) when the communist regime collapsed. The 'Badger' is a versatile beast and is used for maritime reconnaissance, electronic countermeasures and electronic intelligence gathering as well as bombing missions. The maritime strike aircraft variants all carry very large air-to-surface missiles which have enormous warheads and ranges of up to 350 kilometres.

Tupolev Tu-142 'Bear'

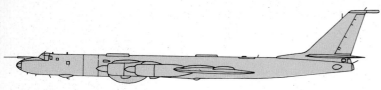

Specification
Cruise speed: 500 knots
Range: 16000 km (9900 miles)
Payload: unknown
Armament: (ASW) eight 450-mm anti-submarine homing torpedoes, or eight depth charges; ('Bear-G') two AS-4 anti-ship missiles. Some have twin 23-mm cannon in rear

Assessment
Age	★★★★★
Range	★★★★★
Weapon load	★★★
Worldwide users	★

The 'Bear' is a well-known visitor to NATO naval exercises and for many years was frequently found loitering over the North Atlantic and testing the UK's air defences.

This is the final maritime version of an aircraft originally introduced as a strategic bomber in the early 1950s. Powered by four turboprop engines, driving contra-rotating four-blade propellers 18 ft across, the 'Bear' is one of the world's noisiest military aircraft. It was also one of the most visible, and Soviet 'Bears' flew long patrols across all major oceans. They monitored the US coast from a base in Cuba, and they even observed the British Task Force off the Falklands, flying from Angola. Throughout the 1980s they operated from the former US base at Cam Ranh in Vietnam.

Ilyushin Il-38 'May'

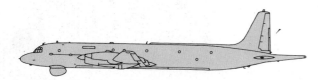

Specification
Cruise speed: 380 knots
Range: 7200 km (4500 miles)
Payload: 6000 kg (5 tons 2000 lb)
Armament: six 450-mm anti-submarine homing torpedoes, or six depth charges

Assessment
Age	★★★
Range	★★★★
Weapon load	★★★
Worldwide users	★★

The Il-38 is an anti-submarine aircraft based on an airliner. It is one of the few Russian maritime aircraft to have been exported. Production ended in the 1970s.

The ASW aircraft is based on the Ilyushin Il-18 turboprop passenger aircraft and was first flown in 1967. Used for long-range maritime reconnaissance, as well as anti-submarine duties, the Il-38 used to rove over the Mediterranean and the Atlantic and Indian Oceans from Russian bases in friendly countries. The Indian Navy bought six Il-38s, but no other Russian ally or client was supplied with this aircraft. In 1991 Russian naval aviation was believed to be operating about 50 or so Il-38s.

TACTICAL TRANSPORT AIRCRAFT No.1

Although sometimes disparagingly called 'trash haulers' by more glamorous members of the aviation community, modern tactical transport aircraft have become vital and highly flexible cogs in the military wheel.

McDonnell Douglas C-17A

The massive C-17 can fulfil two seemingly conflicting roles, since it is both strategic transport and tactical airlifter. Capable of moving vast loads over intercontinental distances, it can also deliver these massive cargoes to semi-prepared airfields close to the battle area. The C-17 is able to carry up to 105 fully-equipped paratroops, but its main strengths are as a cargo lifter. Its 78-tonne payload can be made up from air-droppable pallets, or five-ton trucks loaded two abreast, or three Apache helicopters, or an M1A1 Abrams tank. The C-17 has had a somewhat chequered career, having been cancelled and put into production again, and even now, with the first example flying, its future is far from certain.

Specification
Wing span: 52.2 m (171 ft 3 in)
Maximum speed: 350 knots
Maximum range: 4445 km (2800 miles) (with maximum payload)
Maximum load: 78,108 kg (76 tons 1950 lb)

Assessment
Manoeuvrability ★★★★
Versatility ★★★★★
Robustness ★★★★★
Worldwide users ★

The Gulf War showed how urgently the USAF needs C-17s, but the current round of defence cuts still threaten the programme.

Lockheed C-130 Hercules

What can be said about the Hercules? In service with nearly 60 nations, and the pioneer of modern tactical assault, the Lockheed C-130 is regarded as one of the world's most important military aircraft, and performs its role so well that, even after over 30 years in service, there is no replacement in sight.

Specification
Wing span: 40.41 m (132 ft 6in)
Maximum speed: 325 knots
Maximum range: 3791 km (2350 miles) (with maximum payload)
Maximum load: 19,356 kg (19 tons)

Assessment
Manoeuvrability ★★★★
Versatility ★★★★★
Robustness ★★★★★
Worldwide users ★★★★★

In service since the 1960s, the Lockeed C-130 is used in an astonishing variety of roles.

Lockheed C-141 StarLifter

Specification
Wing span: 48.74 m (159 ft 10in)
Maximum speed: 492 knots
Maximum range: 4725 km (2900 miles) (with maximum payload)
Maximum load: 41,222 kg (40 tons 1300 lb)

Assessment
Manoeuvrability ★★
Versatility ★★
Robustness ★★★
Worldwide users ★★★

The much larger StarLifter, the Hercules' big brother, is used more for long-range transport, but a measure of rough field performance allows its use on some theatre missions. Its main asset is its speed, which allows it to make rapid long-distance flights at little notice.

The Lockheed C-141 StarLifter is used by the US 82nd Airborne Division to make parachute landings over very great distances, and it also serves as a general-purpose transport.

Antonov An-12 'Cub'

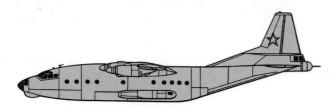

Specification
Wing span: 38 m (125 ft)
Maximum speed: 419 knots
Maximum range: 3600 km (2250 miles) (with maximum payload)
Maximum load: 20,000 kg (19 tons 1500 lb)

Assessment
Manoeuvrability ★★★
Versatility ★★★★
Robustness ★★★★
Worldwide users ★★★★

The Antonov An-12 is the Soviet equivalent to the Hercules. Widely used in Afghanistan, An-12s dropping flares to avoid guerrilla missiles caused frequent fires around Kabul.

The An-12 is a direct Soviet Hercules equivalent, resembling it in layout as well as role. As with the Hercules, the An-12 has been used for several different roles, such as tactical jamming and electronic reconnaissance. It has been supplied to most Soviet allies and satellite nations.

Ilyushin Il-76 'Candid'

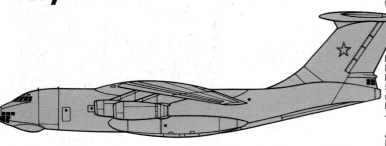

Specification
Wing span: 50.5 m (165 ft 8 in)

Maximum speed: 459 knots
Maximum range: 5000 km (3100 miles) (with maximum payload)
Maximum load: 48,000 kg (47 tons 550 lb)

Assessment
Manoeuvrability ★★★
Versatility ★★
Robustness ★★★
Worldwide users ★★★

Also extensively used in Afghanistan, the Il-76 serves in several roles. Iraq used it as the platform for an airborne early warning system.

Designed to replace the An-12 in service, the Il-76 is a four-jet transport which combines the advantages of a rough field transport with the speed of jets. Used widely in Afghanistan, the Il-76 is fitted with an array of countermeasures such as decoy flares to deter attacks from the ground. It appears to not be as manoeuvrable as either the An-12 or C-130.

Transall C-160

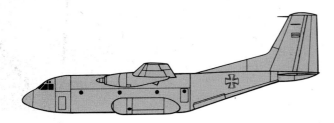

Specification
Wing span: 40 m (131 ft)
Maximum speed: 277 knots
Maximum range: 1850 km (1150 miles) (with maximum payload)
Maximum load: 16,000 kg (15 tons 1680 lb)

Assessment
Manoeuvrability ★★★★
Versatility ★★★
Robustness ★★★
Worldwide users ★★

The Transall C-160 was adopted by France and Germany instead of the Hercules. It also reached South Africa and is used by SADF airborne forces.

France and West Germany elected to 'go it alone' in terms of a tactical transport, building the C-160 jointly rather than buying Hercules. Although slightly smaller, the Transall fills the role admirably. In French service, it has recently adopted the inflight-refuelling, electronic reconnaissance and radio relay roles.

Aeritalia G222

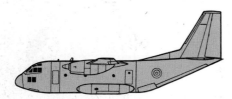

Specification
Wing span: 28.7 m (94 ft)
Maximum speed: 291 knots
Maximum range: 1370 km (850 miles) (with maximum payload)
Maximum load: 9000 kg (8 tons 1920 lb)

Assessment
Manoeuvrability ★★★★★
Versatility ★★
Robustness ★★★★
Worldwide users ★★★

The G222 can operate from very small airstrips and is used by the Italians as a supplement for their larger C-130s. Aeritalia has exported the G222 in a number of different configurations...

To complement its Hercules fleet, Italy builds the G222 as a small tactical transport with even better short field performance. Another main attribute is the type's agility, which is phenomenal for a transport. Overseas sales have been made to several nations, and a number of roles such as reconnaissance, navaid calibration and firefighting have been adopted.

CARRIER AIRCRAFT

Modern carrier aircraft have to do all that their land-based equivalents do, but they have to do it in a very hostile environment, without any kind of landmarks to help with navigation, from an airfield that is not only moving through the sea but which is also rolling and bouncing up and down!

Grumman F-14 Tomcat

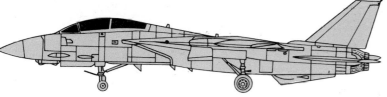

The Grumman F-14 Tomcat is an extremely capable fleet defence fighter. Two combat squadrons out of the five in the standard carrier air wing are Tomcat-equipped, one of them operating F-14s with TARPS reconnaissance pods. The F-14 first flew in 1970. It uses the powerplant, radar, fire-control system and missiles designed for the abortive F-111B fighter, and like the F-111 it is equipped with variable-geometry wings. The F-14A entered fleet service in 1972, and its combination of AWG-9 radar and AIM-54 Phoenix missile gave it unmatched long-range combat ability. A typical weapon load is four Phoenix missiles, two AIM-7 Sparrow medium-range missiles and two short-range Sidewinders.

Specification
Dimensions: wing span 19.55 m (64 ft) (spread) and 11.65 m (38 ft 3 in) (swept); length 19.1 m (62 ft 8 in)
Performance: max. sped 2517 km/h (1560 mph); combat range 3250 km (2000 miles)
Weapon load: one 20-mm cannon, up to 6 long- or medium-range AAMs plus 2×AIM-9 missiles, or 6577 kg (6 tons 1050 lb) of ordnance

Assessment
Performance ★★★★
Range ★★★★★
Age ★★★★
Worldwide users ★★

The Tomcat has been upgraded twice, the F-14B having more powerful engines and the F-14D adding more capable radar and a considerably enhanced electronic fit.

McDonnell Douglas F/A-18 Hornet

The McDonnell Douglas F/A-18 Hornet entered service late in 1983. Its airframe is not designed for extreme speed, but for manoeuvrability and flawless handling right through the flight envelope. The Hornet incorporates very advanced electronics to enable the pilot to perform complex tasks without the aid of a second crewmember. The F/A-18 has seven hardpoints for a large and highly varied weapon load. The aircraft also has a fast-firing 20-mm cannon and wingtip rails for AIM-9 Sidewinder dogfight missiles. The original F/A-18A was partnered by the combat-capable F/A-18B conversion and proficiency trainer. These two models have been succeeded by the much improved F/A-18C and F/A-18D. The two-seat D model pioneered the type's night-attack capability.

Specification
Dimensions: wing span 11.43 m (37 ft 6 in); length 17.07 m (56 ft)
Performance: max. speed 1920 km/h (1200 mph); combat range 1500 km (930 miles)
Weapon load: one 20-mm cannon, and up to 7715 kg (7 tons 1320 lb) of disposable stores

Assessment
Performance ★★★★★
Range ★★★
Age ★★★
Worldwide users ★★★

The Hornet will become the backbone of US Navy carrier wings in the 1990s, serving as a fighter and light attack aircraft, and with a stretched variant entering service to replace the Grumman A-6.

Grumman A-6 Intruder

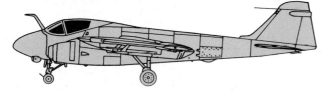

The original requirement for the Grumman A-6 Intruder dates back to the end of the 1950s, when the US Navy saw the need for a subsonic 'bomb truck'. The aircraft was to have advanced electronics so that weapons could be delivered by day or night, whatever the weather. The Intruder first flew in 1963, and by the end of the 1960s was in all-weather action in the skies over Vietnam. Deliveries of the current A-6E variant, with more effective and reliable electronics, began in 1972. Some aircraft were newly built, while others were converted A-6As. In-service modification began in 1979, with the addition of the TRAM package to enable precision-guided munitions to be used effectively. The Target Recognition and Attack, Multi-sensor package comprises a stabilised chin turret with a FLIR sensor and a laser system.

Specification
Dimensions: wing span 16.15 m (53 ft); length 16.69 m (54 ft 9 in)
Performance: max. speed 1040 km/h (645 mph); combat range with maximum weapon load 1700 km (1100 miles)
Weapon load: up to 8200 kg (8 tons 160 lb) of disposable stores

Assessment
Performance ★★★
Range ★★★★
Age ★★★★★
Worldwide users ★

The A-6 remains an effective aircraft in spite of its age. The basic airframe has also been used for the EA-6 electronic warfare aircraft and the KA-6 tanker.

Lockheed S-3 Viking

An aircraft carrier is a prime target for a submarine, and it makes sense to protect such an important resource from the submarine threat. Each US Navy carrier has an anti-submarine warfare squadron equipped with 10 Lockheed S-3 Viking aircraft. The Viking is a sophisticated machine, packing the electronic capabilities of the large four-engined P-3 Orion into a much smaller airframe. It has an adequate warload, carries enough fuel for long patrols, and is jet-powered for high transit speeds to and from the operational area. The Viking entered service in the mid-1970s, and the S-3 force began to be upgraded to S-3B standard from 1987. The S-3B has a completely revised mission electronics suite which promises greater versatility.

Specification
Dimensions: wing span 20.93 m (68 ft 8 in); length 16.26 m (53 ft 4 in)
Performance: max. speed 834 km/h (520 mph); combat range 3700 km (2300 miles)
Weapon load: up to 3200 kg (3 tons 340 lb) of disposable stores

Assessment
Performance ★★★
Range ★★★★★
Age ★★★
Worldwide users ★

The S-3B has a comprehensive electronics fit, with some added attack capabilities. Vikings can now operate with the Harpoon missile, giving the S-3 a long-range anti-ship strike capability.

Grumman E-2 Hawkeye

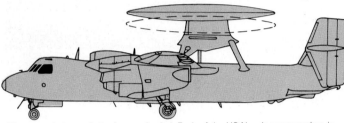

The control of a carrier's airspace is vital. Each of the US Navy's supercarriers is equipped with four or five Grumman E-2 Hawkeye airborne early warning and control aircraft. The Hawkeye is easily identifiable. It is the only propeller-driven plane serving aboard US Navy carriers, but above all it has a huge radome to house its radar antennas. The current E-2C is fitted with the advanced APS-139 radar system. Each aircraft's systems operators can monitor up to 600 air and surface targets out to a range of nearly 400 kilometres, and with passive ESM systems can extend the detection range to beyond 800 kilometres.

Specification
Dimensions: wing span 24.56 m (80 ft 8 in); length 17.54 m (57 ft 6 in)
Performance: max. speed 600 km/h (375 mph); combat range 2600 km (1600 miles)
Weapon load: none

Assessment
Performance ★★
Range ★★★★
Age ★★★★
Worldwide users ★★

The E-2 can control as many as 30 simultaneous fighter interceptions, as well as providing guidance for a number of other missions. These include co-ordinating combat air patrol and providing early warning of surface ship attack.

British Aerospace Sea Harrier FRS.Mk 2

Britain's unique Harrier ground attack fighter was adapted for naval use in the 1970s, for use aboard the Royal Navy's helicopter carriers and through-deck cruisers. It proved its worth in the Falklands, when Sea Harriers knocked out around 30 Argentine aircraft in air combat without loss. The FRS.Mk 2 is an updated Sea Harrier, which first flew in 1988. Fitted with the Blue Vixen multi-mode pulse-Doppler radar, the new model is designed to carry the Hughes AIM-120 AMRAAM weapon system. This advanced missile gives the Sea Harrier beyond-visual-range and multiple-target-kill capability. The radar has 11 operational modes for air-to-air and air-to-surface attack. Integrating the radar into the Harrier's small airframe required a number of changes.

Specification
Dimensions: wing span 8.3 m (27 ft 3 in); length 14.1 m (46 ft 3 in)
Performance: max. speed 1185 km/h (735 mph); combat range 1500 km (930 miles)
Weapon load: two 30-mm cannon and 3600 kg (3 tons 1200 lb) of disposable stores

Assessment
Performance ★★★
Range ★★★
Age ★★
Worldwide users ★

The Sea Harrier FRS.Mk 1 has more electronics than the original fighter, and to accommodate the extra equipment the aircraft has a fuselage plug which stretches its length by 35 centimetres.

Dassault-Breguet Super Etendard

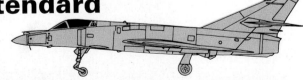

Developed from the 1950s vintage Etendard ship-board attack aircraft, the Dassault-Breguet Super Etendard is a multi-role fighter equipped for interception, but which is primarily tasked with maritime strike/attack. The aircraft is fitted with an inertial navigation system to help the pilot find his way over the featureless ocean. The Super Etendard's primary strike weapon is the highly successful AM.39 Exocet anti-ship missile, and for self-defence it carries the Matra Magic heat-seeking air-to-air missile. Etendards were used in the Iran-Iraq war, when five aircraft loaned to the Iraqis sank a number of tankers in the Gulf. Argentina is the only other operator of Super Etendards. The Argentine navy took advantage of the Royal Navy's lack of airborne early warning during the Falklands war, when their aircraft used Exocets to sink HMS *Sheffield* and the container ship *Atlantic Conveyor*.

Specification
Dimensions: wing span 9.6 m (31 ft 6 in); length 14.3 m (46 ft 3 in)
Performance: max. speed 1200 km/h (745 mph); combat range 1300 km (810 miles)
Weapon load: two 30-mm cannon and 2100 kg (2 tons 150 lb) of disposable stores

Assessment
Performance ★★★
Range ★★★
Age ★★★
Worldwide users ★★

The Super Etendard armed with the best-selling AM.39 Exocet missile is a potent anti-ship weapon, as the Royal Navy discovered at the hands of the Argentines during the Falklands war.

Airborne early warning (AEW) aircraft can monitor enemy activity over an enormous area. An aircraft flying at 30,000 ft and fitted with surveillance radar can detect targets at nearly 400 kilometres. Some AEW aircraft also serve as airborne command posts, directing friendly forces from their lofty vantage point.

Grumman E-2 Hawkeye

Entering service with the US Navy in 1964, the Grumman E-2 provides the airborne early warning for the US carrier Task Forces. With an endurance of some six hours, the E-2 can scan vast stretches of ocean with its APS-96 search radar, alerting the carriers to threats from sea or air. Improved electronics and computer systems resulted in the E-2B, introduced in 1970. Three years later the US Navy received its first E-2Cs. These had greatly enhanced sensors, including the APS-125 search radar, and computers that can monitor up to 250 targets simultaneously as well as control up to 30 friendly aircraft on interception missions. The E-2 Hawkeye has been exported to Israel, where it played a key role in defeating the Syrian air force over Lebanon in 1982.

Specification
Type: airborne early warning and control aircraft
Dimensions: length 17.54 m (57 ft 6 in); span 24.5 m (80 ft); height 5.58 m (18 ft 4 in)
Weights: empty 17,091 kg (17 tons 1800 lb); maximum take-off 23,392 kg (23 tons)
Performance: maximum speed 602 km/h (375 mph); range 2583 km (1600 miles) (for ferrying)

Assessment
Sensors ★★★
Range ★★★
Age ★★★★
Worldwide users ★★★

The Grumman E-2 provides vital airborne early warning for the US Navy, detecting enemy aircraft before they can threaten the US aircraft carriers.

E-3 Sentry

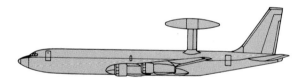

One of the most distinctive military aircraft in service, the E-3 is a Boeing 707 airliner fitted with a massive rotodome mounted on two struts above the fuselage. It is also referred to by the name of its radar and computer system, AWACS (Airborne Warning And Control System). The powerful Westinghouse APY-1 search radar, allied to command and control systems, enables a single E-3 to monitor an enormous area and vector friendly fighter aircraft to intercept targets. A squadron of E-3s, under direct NATO control, operated over western Europe ready to detect incoming Warsaw Pact aircraft, and 20 E-3s operated from Saudi Arabia during Operation Desert Storm. The E-3 was also exported to Saudi Arabia and, belatedly, to the UK after the failure of the British Nimrod AEW aircraft.

Specification
Type: airborne early warning and control aircraft
Dimensions: length 46.6 m (152 ft 10 in); span 44.42 m (145 ft 8 in); height 12.93 m (42 ft 5 in)
Weights: empty 78,019 kg (76 tons 1770 lb); maximum take-off 147,417 kg (145 tons)
Performance: maximum speed 853 km/h (530 mph); range 1610 km (1000 miles) (6 hours on station)

Assessment
Sensors ★★★★★
Range ★★★★★
Age ★★
Worldwide users ★★

The Boeing E-3 Sentry houses the long-range AWACS (Airborne Warning And Control System) radar and communications equipment that was developed to co-ordinate US and NATO air forces against Warsaw Pact air attack.

Boeing E-4

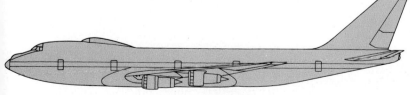

The United States SAC (Strategic Air Command) maintained its ability to fight a nuclear war with four airborne command posts bristling with communications systems and able to remain in the air for up to 72 hours with inflight refuelling. One was always kept at Andrews Air Force Base outside Washington DC, standing by to be boarded by the President if the worst came to the worst. Based on a Boeing 747 airliner, the first E-4 flew in 1973. Two years later the E-4B was introduced, featuring more advanced communications equipment and accommodation for a larger 'battle staff'. Its electronic systems were 'hardened' to protect them from the EMP (electro-magnetic pulse) produced by nuclear explosions.

Specification
Type: airborne command post
Dimensions: length 70.5 m (231 ft); span 59.6 m (195 ft 6 in); height 19.3 m (63 ft)
Weights: empty 172,368 kg (169 tons 1450 lb); maximum take-off 352,901 kg (347 tons 730 lb)
Performance: maximum speed 978 km/h (610 mph); range 10,460 km (6500 miles)

Assessment
Sensors ★★★
Range ★★★★★
Age ★★★
Worldwide users ★

The Boeing E-4 is an airborne command post built to allow the US President to control his forces during a nuclear war. Communications centres on the ground were prime targets for Soviet missiles.

EC-130 Hercules

Specialist electronic warfare and command versions of the C-130 were first introduced during the Vietnam War. Delivering and monitoring ground sensors deployed along the 'Macnamara line' and electronic eavesdropping over North Vietnam, these early Elint (electronic intelligence) aircraft were converted back to cargo carriers after the war. However, a dedicated electronic intelligence gatherer was being developed, and the EC-130H entered service with the 41st Electronic Countermeasures Squadron in 1982. There are now four discrete versions in service providing command and control facilities, monitoring enemy radio traffic and sensors, as well as engaging in psychological warfare. All types were active during the Gulf War, feeding intelligence data to the allied command and jamming Iraqi communications.

Specification
Type: electronic warfare aircraft
Dimensions: length 29.79 m (97 ft 9 in); span 40.41 m (145 ft 8 in); height 11.66 m (38 ft 3 in)
Weights: empty 33,064 kg (32 tons 1200 lb)
Performance: maximum speed 592 km/h (370 mph); range 3895 km (2400 miles)

Assessment
Sensors ★★★★
Range ★★★★
Age ★★★★
Worldwide users ★★

The Lockheed EC-130 of the US Coast Guard. The Hercules serves in an astonishing variety of roles, including electronic warfare, airborne early warning and psychological warfare.

Tupolev Tu-126 'Moss'

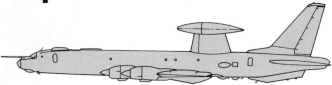

Throughout the Cold War the USSR remained behind its Western enemies in electronic equipment. The Soviets introduced the Tupolev Tu-126 in the late 1960s for airborne early warning missions, basing a large rotodome on a modified Tu-114 turboprop airliner. The Soviet air force relied heavily on ground-based direction and radar stations and the arrival of the Tu-126 did not alter this. US sources estimated that only about a dozen of this aircraft were operational throughout the 1980s and the performance of its radar was regarded as inferior to American equivalents. The only point in its favour was its powerful jamming equipment. The Tu-126 was replaced by the Ilyushin Il-76 during the last years of the USSR.

Specification
Type: airborne early warning aircraft
Dimensions: length 57.3 m (188 ft); span 51.2 m (167 ft 7 in); height 11.58 m (38 ft)
Weights: empty 90,720 kg (89 tons 640 lb); maximum take-off 165,550 kg (163 tons)
Performance: maximum speed 740 km/h (460 mph)

Assessment
Sensors ★★
Range ★★★★
Age ★★★★
Worldwide users ★

The Tupolev Tu-126, designated 'Moss' by NATO, is based on a turboprop airliner. Its radar system is primitive, but it does carry powerful jamming equipment.

Ilyushin Il-76

Allotted the NATO reporting name 'Mainstay', the Ilyushin Il-76 was developed during the 1970s to replace the Tu-126. Based on the Il-76 'Candid' turbofan-powered tactical transport, the 'Mainstay' has a large rotodome and a lengthened fuselage. It has a far better electronic and sensor fit than the Tu-126, and fitted with a new IFF system and a comprehensive ECM suite, the Il-76 is equipped for inflight refuelling to achieve maximum endurance. Intended to direct Soviet fighter aircraft over battlefields in Europe or Asia, the Il-76 controlled MiG-29 and MiG-31 interceptors. It was estimated that at least 12 were in service by 1990, with an annual production rate of five machines per year. Whether Russia can maintain this force or continue manufacture remains to be seen.

Specification
Type: airborne early warning aircraft
Dimensions: length 46.59 m (152 ft 10 in); span 50.5 m (165 ft 8 in); height 14.75 m (48 ft 5 in)
Weights: empty 75,000 kg (73 tons 1815 lb); maximum take-off 170,000 kg (167 tons 700 lb)
Performance: maximum speed 800 km/h (500 mph); range 6400 km (4000 miles)

Assessment
Sensors ★★★
Range ★★★★
Age ★★
Worldwide users ★

The Ilyushin Il-76 was built to co-ordinate Soviet air force operations in a major war. Fitted with good electronic countermeasures equipment, it has much better radar than the Tu-126.

Avro Shackleton AEW.Mk 2

It is shameful to record that Britain, a country once in the forefront of radar technology, failed to put an airborne early warning aircraft into service with the RAF until the 1970s. When it finally did, the aircraft and its radar were both hopelessly out of date. By taking the AEW radar systems from obsolete Fairey Gannet carrier aircraft and adding them to ageing Shackleton maritime patrol/ASW aircraft, the RAF created a squadron of 12 Shackleton AEW.Mk 2s. Gamely operated by No. 8 Squadron based at Kinloss in Scotland, this bizarre unit continued well into the 1980s, although half of the force was retired in the 1981 defence cuts. Meanwhile, the government invested vast sums of money in an AEW version of the Nimrod, which ultimately failed to work. Eventually the Boeing E-3 was ordered instead and the gap in the UK's air defences was finally closed.

Specification
Type: airborne early warning aircraft
Dimensions: length 26.59 m (87 ft 3 in); span 36.58 m (120 ft); height 5.1 m (16 ft 9 in)
Weights: empty 25,855 kg (28 tons); maximum take-off 44,453 kg (43 tons 1700 lb)
Performance: maximum speed 439 km/h (270 mph); range 6437 km (4000 miles)

Assessment
Sensors ★
Range ★★★★
Age ★★★★★
Worldwide users ★

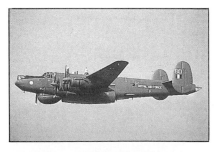

The RAF was obliged to operate ancient Shackletons with geriatric electronics as a makeshift AEW force well into the 1980s while the government funded an AEW version of the BAe Nimrod.

AAMs

Air-to-air missiles either use radar to find their targets or they home in on the heat from the aircraft's engines. Radar guidance allows aircraft to engage at longer ranges, often at targets too far away to see. Effective electronic identification systems are essential if blue-on-blue tragedies are to be avoided.

AA-6 'Acrid'

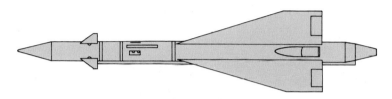

Specification
Length: 6.2 m (20 ft 4 in)
Launch weight: 460 kg (1015 lb)
Warhead: 50 kg (110 lb)
Fuse: radar and active-laser
Range: 30 km (19 miles)

Assessment
Range ★★
Warhead ★★★★
Reliability ★★★
Worldwide users ★★★★

The AA-6 'Acrid' narrowed the technological gap between Russian and NATO air forces in the 1970s. It was first seen on the MiG-25 'Foxbat' high-altitude interceptor.

Developed during the 1960s, the 'Acrid' missiles can be fitted with either infra-red or radar guidance and is designed for high-altitude interception. NATO regarded it as the first of a new generation of Russian missiles introduced to replace their previously relatively crude weapons, which continued to be used by Arab air forces in their lopsided battles with Israel. The 'Acrid' entered service during the 1970s and armed many front-line Russian aircraft such as the MiG-25 'Foxbat'. This usually carried four missiles, two with semi-active radar guidance and two with infra-red.

AA-9 'Amos'

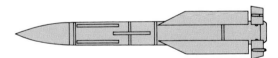

Specification
Length: 4.3 m (14 ft)
Launch weight: 450 kg (1000 lb)
Warhead: unknown
Fuse: active-radar
Range: 100 km (62 miles)

Assessment
Range ★★★★
Warhead ★★★★★
Reliability ★★★
Worldwide users ★

The AA-9 'Amos' may be based on the American Phoenix missile, which was sold to Iran, before the revolution in 1979, for use with the Shah's F-14 Tomcats.

Developed during the 1970s to replace the AA-6, the 'Amos' is a very long-range weapon, possibly designed to engage NATO's vital AEW (airborne early warning) aircraft. First seen fitted to a MiG-31 'Foxhound' over the Norwegian Sea in 1985, the 'Amos' bears a close resemblance to the American AIM-54 Phoenix. Its appearance is radically different from all other Russian air-to-air weapons and it may well have been developed from stolen technology. The MiG-31's radar has a reported range of 270 kilometres, and the 'Amos' is believed to be capable of hitting targets up to 100 kilometres away.

AA-10 'Alamo'

Specification
('Alamo C')
Length: 4.6 m (15 ft)
Launch weight: 240 kg (530 lb)
Warhead: 30 kg (66 lb)
Fuse: active-radar
Range: 35 km (22 miles)

Assessment
Range ★★
Warhead ★★★
Reliability ★★★
Worldwide users ★★

The AA-10 'Alamo' represents a substantial advance for Soviet air-to-air weapons. It is the main armament of the MiG-29 fighter and may yet see action over Europe as Serbian forces operate MiG-29s.

First publicly identified in 1986, the 'Alamo' has been manufactured in at least three versions: two with radar guidance and one with infra-red. Fitted to the Sukhoi Su-27 'Flanker' and the MiG-29 'Fulcrum', the 'Alamo A' uses semi-active radar-homing and is believed to have a range of 25 kilometres. 'Alamo C' is longer, heavier and has a range of 35 kilometres. The infra-red-homing variant, 'Alamo B', is sensitive enough to pick out its target from any angle and is not restricted to the target's rear arc like many earlier heat-seeking weapons. It is rumoured that the AA-10 has been supplied to Yugoslavia for use with their MiG-29s.

Skyflash

Specification
Length: 3.66 m (12 ft)
Launch weight: 195 kg
(430 lb)
Warhead: 30 kg (66 lb)
Fuse: active-radar
Range: 40 km (25 miles)

Assessment
Range   ★★
Warhead   ★★★
Reliability   ★★★★★
Worldwide users   ★★

Skyflash is a British development of the US AIM-7 Sparrow radar-guided missile. It is carried by RAF Tornados.

Skyflash is a British development of the American AIM-7 Sparrow and looks very similar. Indeed, from the start of the programme in 1973 it was intended to be interchangeable so that aircraft could fire either missile. Skyflash's radar seeker has a better performance against low-flying aircraft and was designed to find its target despite enemy ECM (electronic countermeasures). Fitted to RAF Tornados, the Skyflash has also been bought by Sweden, and since 1988 British Aerospace has been working with Thomson-CSF on a version with an active-radar seeker.

AIM-7 Sparrow

Specification
(AIM-7P)
Length: 3.66 m (12 ft)
Launch weight: 230 kg
(500 lb)
Warhead: 39 kg (86 lb)
Fuse: active-radar
Range: 45 km (28 miles)

Assessment
Range   ★★★
Warhead   ★★★
Reliability   ★★★★★
Worldwide users   ★★★★★

The AIM-7 Sparrow has been continually improved since its introduction nearly 40 years ago. It is also employed by many navies as a ship-launched SAM.

The AIM-7A beam-riding radar-guided missile entered service in 1956 and has been continually improved since then. The AIM-7C semi-active radar-guided version entered service in 1958; the AIM-7E appeared in 1962 and was used during the Vietnam War, and a ship-launched variant, the RIM-7H, is in widespread use. The longer-range AIM-7F was introduced in 1975, followed by the AIM-7M, which has improved capability against low-flying targets and better ECCM (electronic counter countermeasures). The AIM-7P is designed to intercept sea-skimming anti-ship missiles and cruise missiles, and the latest model, the AIM-7R, has a multi-mode infra-red semi-active-radar seeker to defeat enemy jamming.

AIM-54 Phoenix

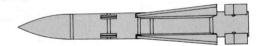

Specification
(AIM-54C)
Length: 3.96 m (13 ft)
Launch weight: 454 kg
(1000 lb)
Warhead: 60 kg (132 lb)
Fuse: active-radar
Range: 150 km (93 miles)

Assessment
Range   ★★★★★
Warhead   ★★★★★
Reliability   ★★★★★
Worldwide users   ★

The AIM-54 is the fastest radar-guided air-to-air missile in service and no other missile can match its enormous range. US Navy F-14 Tomcats can carry six of them.

This very long-range missile is the primary armament of the US Navy's F-14 Tomcat interceptors. It was intended to allow US aircraft carriers to defeat enemy air attacks as far away from the fleet as possible. Development work began in 1960 and the first deliveries to the US Navy took place in 1974. An improved version, the AIM-54C, was tested from 1979-85 and entered service from 1989. Further development continues. The F-14 can carry up to six AIM-54s and can launch and control all of them against multiple targets. Using semi-active radar-homing with mid-course updates, the AIM-54 uses an active radar to guide it through the final stage of its interception.

AIM-120A AMRAAM

Specification
Length: 3.65 m (12 ft)
Launch weight: 157 kg
(346 lb)
Warhead: 22 kg (48 lb)
Fuse: active-radar
Range: 50 km (31 miles)

Assessment
Range   ★★★
Warhead   ★★
Reliability   ★★★★★
Worldwide users   ★

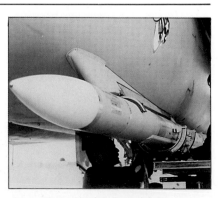

The AMRAAM is intended as a replacement for the ageing AIM-7 Sparrow, and it can be modified for use with most modern fighters.

The AMRAAM (Advanced Medium-Range Air-to-Air Missile) was developed as a joint programme by the US Navy and US Air Force. Designed to replace the AIM-7, AMRAAM is faster, longer-ranged and even less susceptible to enemy ECM. The first production version, AIM-120A, entered service with the US Air Force in 1991. AMRAAM is designed to be fired from the F-14, F-15, F-16 and F-18. It could be modified to be launched by the Tornado F3, Sea Harrier and the controversial EFA (European Fighter Aircraft) depending on the level of European interest.

While aircraft can use radar-guided missiles at long range, closer targets are better dealt with by 'fire-and-forget' heat-seeking weapons that home in without further assistance from the launching aircraft.

R550 Matra Magic

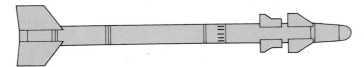

Specification
(Magic Mk 1)
Length: 2.72 m (8 ft 11 in)
Launch weight: 89 kg (196 lb)
Warhead: 13 kg (28 lb 10 oz)
Fuse: IR
Range: 3000 m (1 mile 1500 yd)

Assessment
Range   ★★★
Reliability   ★★★
Accuracy   ★★★
Worldwide users ★★★

The R550 Matra Magic is an early type of heat-seeking missile limited to attacking enemy aircraft from astern.

Manufactured in France from the early 1970s until 1984, the Matra Magic Mk 1 can be fired from weapons pylons designed for the American AIM-9 Sidewinder series of air-to-air missiles. Magic Mk 1's infra-red detector is not sufficiently sensitive to allow attacks from the beam or ahead, so it is limited to engagement from the target's rear arc only. Magic 2, introduced in 1985, has an improved detector which provides all-aspect capability. Magic Mk 1s were used by the Argentine air force during the 1982 Falklands war and were often fired head on with predictable inaccuracy.

AIM-4 Falcon

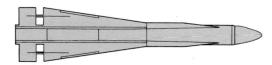

Specification
(AIM-4D)
Length: 2.02 m (6 ft 8 in)
Launch weight: 61 kg (135 lb)
Warhead: 12 kg (26 lb 7 oz)
Fuse: active-radar
Range: 3000 m (1 mile 1500 yd)

Assessment
Range   ★★★
Reliability   ★★★
Accuracy   ★★★
Worldwide users ★★

The AIM-4 Falcon was the first guided anti-aircraft missile to enter service. It was retained for many years by the US Air National Guard.

The US Air Force received its first AIM-4 Falcon missiles in 1954. It was the first guided air-to-air missile to enter service and was designed to shoot down large bombers. Produced in both infra-red and radar-homing versions, the Falcon was carried by a variety of aircraft, including the F-101 Voodoo, F-102 Delta Dagger, J35 Draken and Mirage III. It has continued to be employed by the US Air National Guard aircraft long after the US Air Force has replaced it. The AIM-4 series was acquired by Finland, Sweden and Switzerland, and the production total exceeded 50,000 by the time manufacture ceased in the late 1960s.

AIM-9 Sidewinder

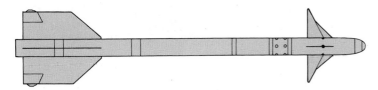

Specification
(AIM-9L)
Length: 2.87 m (9 ft 5 in)
Launch weight: 87 kg (192 lb)
Warhead: 9.5 kg (20 lb 15 oz)
Fuse: laser
Range: 8000 m (5 miles)

Assessment
Range   ★★★★★
Reliability   ★★★★★
Accuracy   ★★★★★
Worldwide users ★★★★

The AIM-9 Sidewinder is probably the most widely used air-to-air missile in the Western world. Built in many different versions, the latest type can attack from head on, unlike earlier IR-homing weapons.

Developed just after World War II, the AIM-9 Sidewinder entered service with the USAF in 1956 and became the first guided air-to-air missile to be used in combat when Nationalist Chinese F-86s downed several MiG-15s over the Formosa straits in 1958. The basic design was copied abroad – most significantly by the USSR – and modified for use as a surface-to-air missile: the US Army's MIM-72 Chaparral. A succession of improved versions followed, with later models better able to discriminate between aircraft and other heat sources. The most important breakthrough was the AIM-9L, which can engage from abeam or ahead of its target and was used to great effect by Royal Navy Sea Harriers during the Falklands campaign.

Shafrir

Specification
Length: 2.6 m (8 ft 6 in)
Launch weight: 95 kg (209 lb)
Warhead: 11 kg (24 lb 4 oz)
Fuse: unknown
Range: 3000 m (1 mile 1500 yd)

Assessment
Range   ★★★
Reliability   ★★★★
Accuracy   ★★★★
Worldwide users ★★

The Shafrir was the Israeli air force's first 'homegrown' air-to-air missile. First used in combat during the 1970s, it was also used by Argentine aircraft during the Falklands war.

With its unique dependence on air power for national survival, Israel was quick off the mark to develop its own air-to-air missile. Work began on the Shafrir infra-red-homing missile in 1961 and it was in operational service by 1969. Restricted to engagements against the rear arc of the target, the Shafrir was superior to contemporary AIM-9s and the Soviet copy which needed to be launched from almost directly astern if it was to home in properly. The Shafrir achieved hits even when fired from almost beam on. In 1982 it was used to deadly effect by the Israelis against Syrian fighters over Lebanon. In the same year it performed poorly over the South Atlantic, when Argentine aircraft repeatedly launched from outside its effective range or from head on.

Python

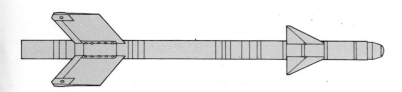

Specification
Length: 3 m (9 ft 11 in)
Launch weight: 120 kg (264 lb)
Warhead: 11 kg (24 lb 4 oz)
Fuse: laser
Range: 5000 m (3 miles)

Assessment
Range   ★★★★
Reliability   ★★★★★
Accuracy   ★★★★★
Worldwide users ★

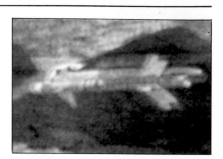

The Python is the replacement for Shafrir: a far more capable missile able to attack aircraft from all angles and not restricted to the 'hot spot' behind the tailpipe.

Also used in the massacre of the Syrian air force over Lebanon in 1982, the Python was developed from the Shafrir. It has all-aspect capability and carries a more effective warhead, after the Israeli air force expressed concern about the number of Shafrirs that failed to cause the complete destruction of their targets. The Python is better able to discriminate between the target aircraft and flares, or other countermeasures designed to throw it off. It is believed that the Python has been exported to China and South Africa.

AA-2 'Atoll'

Specification
Length: 2.83 m (9 ft 4 in)
Launch weight: 75 kg (165 lb)
Warhead: 11 kg (24 lb 4 oz)
Fuse: IR
Range: 3000 m (1 mile 1500 yd)

Assessment
Range   ★★
Reliability   ★★
Accuracy   ★★
Worldwide users ★★★★★

The Soviets achieved their first air-to-air missile by copying a captured AIM-9. Widely used in the Middle East and Vietnam, the AA-2 'Atoll' was exported to most Soviet allies.

The most widely-used air-to-air missile in the communist world, the AA-2 was copied from the US AIM-9 after a Sidewinder warhead lodged in the tailpipe of a Chinese MiG-15 during a battle over the Formosa straits in 1958. The MiG landed safely and the remains of the missile were rushed to the USSR. Three years later the Soviet air force received its first infra-red-homing missiles, which were allotted the NATO reporting name 'Atoll'. It took another 10 years for the Soviets to introduce a version with semi-active radar homing. The AA-2 is obsolete today, but has seen extensive combat in the Arab-Israeli wars and was supplied to Warsaw Pact forces and Soviet allies throughout Africa and Asia.

AA-8 'Aphid'

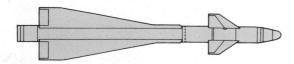

Specification
Length: 2.08 m (6 ft 10 in)
Launch weight: 65 kg (143 lb)
Warhead: 6 kg (13 lb 4 oz)
Fuse: active-radar
Range: 3000 m (1 mile 1500 yd)

Assessment
Range   ★★★
Reliability   ★★★
Accuracy   ★★★
Worldwide users ★★★★

The AA-8 'Aphid' was the standard 'dogfighting' air-to-air missile of the Soviet air force in its final form. A small, short-ranged missile, which is also fitted to helicopter gunships.

Developed during the late 1960s, the AA-8 'Aphid' was the Soviets' replacement for the AA-2 and it entered service during the mid-1970s. It is believed to have been in production until the final collapse of the USSR in 1991. The 'Aphid' is smaller than most air-to-air missiles and is designed for short-range engagements in which its manoeuvrability is paramount. The 'Aphid' is credited with all-aspect capability, although it may be restricted to beam on and rear arc attacks. Fitted to aircraft including the MiG-21 and all later MiGs, as well as the Su-17, -21 and -27, the 'Aphid' is also mounted on Mi-24 'Hind-Ds' and 'Hind-Es'.

AIR-TO-SURFACE MISSILES

Guided missiles were launched from aircraft as early as 1915, but none were very effective until World War II, when German guided anti-ship missiles achieved some success. Today, they are a key aerial weapon system. Guided weapons are vastly more expensive than 'iron' bombs, but they are so much more accurate that they are well worth the cost.

AS-4 'Kitchen'

The USSR developed a series of very large air-to-surface missiles during the 1950s; the nuclear-tipped AS-3 weighed no less than 11 tonnes. AS-4 'Kitchen' is the NATO designation for a medium-range missile that was first seen carried by Tu-22 'Blinder' bombers in 1961. Later fitted to the Tu-22 'Blinder' and Tu-22M 'Backfire', the 'Kitchen' carries either a nuclear or a conventional warhead. Several different versions were introduced; the last variant which appeared in the 1970s is believed to have a radar seeker which allows the missile to home in on surveillance radar sets aboard warships or land sites.

Specification
Length: 11.3 m (37 ft)
Body diameter: 1 m (3 ft 3 in)
Wing span: 3 m (9 ft 11 in)
Overall weight: 5900 kg (5 tons 1800 lb)
Warhead: 1000-kg (2200-lb) HE or 350-kiloton nuclear
Guidance: inertial with active or passive radar
Range: 400 km (250 miles)

Assessment
Age ★★★★★
Accuracy ★★
Reliability ★★
Worldwide users ★★

The Soviets manufactured a series of enormous air-to-ground missiles which made up for lack of accuracy with massive warheads.

AS-7 'Kerry'

The Soviets were well behind the USA in the deployment of tactical guided missiles. The AS-7 'Kerry' was the first Soviet air-to-surface missile designed for use by fighter-bombers against ground targets on the battlefield. Developed during the 1960s and introduced circa 1972 the 'Kerry' is handicapped by its relatively short range and the primitive guidance system. Once launched from an aircraft such as the MiG-21 or Su-17, the missile is radio guided by the pilot. Observing the bright flare in the missile's tail, he steers it onto the target using a joystick – all while flying his own aircraft, which is quite probably under fire. The later AS-10 'Karen' is the same basic missile but with semi-active laser guidance.

Specification
Length: 3.53 m (11 ft 7 in)
Body diameter: 0.275 m (11 in)
Wing span: 0.79 m (2 ft 7 in)
Overall weight: 287 kg (633 lb)
Warhead: 110-kg (240-lb) hollow-charge HE
Guidance: radio command
Range: 5 km (3 miles)

Assessment
Age ★★★★★
Accuracy ★
Reliability ★★
Worldwide users ★★★

Sukhoi Su-17 bombers are capable of firing the AS-7 and AS-10 guided missiles. The 'Kerry' relied on radio-command guidance and was not likely to be accurate under combat conditions.

Apache

The Apache missile is a joint Franco-German project designed to be launched from aircraft such as the F-4, F-15, F-16 and F-18, as well as the Mirage F1, the Mirage 2000 and the Tornado. It is described as a CWS (container weapon system) and is really a cross between a cruise missile and a weapons dispenser. Instead of a warhead the Apache carries over 700 kilograms of sub-munitions in the centre of the body section. These can be runway-cratering devices, anti-tank bomblets or 'intelligent' mines. Many targets can be engaged more effectively with a profusion of small bombs rather than a single, large warhead, and the Apache may represent the first of a new generation of air-launched weapons.

Specification
Length: 5.1 m (16 ft 9 in)
Body dimensions: 0.48 m (19 in) wide; 0.63 m (25 in) high
Wing span: 2.53 m (8 ft 3 in)
Overall weight: 1230 kg (1 ton 470 lb))
Warhead: variable payload
Guidance: inertial with updates and active radar
Range: 150 km (93 miles)

Assessment
Age ★
Accuracy ★★★★
Reliability ★★★
Worldwide users ★

The Apache CWS (container weapon system) can deliver up to 700 kilograms of sub-munitions such as mines or bomblets. Its long range allows aircraft to attack from relative safety.

AS 30

Specification
Length: 3.65 m (12 ft)
Body diameter: 0.342 m (13 in)
Wing span: 1 m (3 ft 3 in)
Overall weight: 520 kg (1150 lb)
Warhead: 240-kg (530-lb) HE
Guidance: semi-active laser
Range: 10 km (6 miles)

Assessment
Age   ★★★
Accuracy   ★★★
Reliability   ★★★
Worldwide users ★★★

During the Gulf War, the French air force deployed 27 SEPECAT Jaguars which fired a total of 60 AS 30L missiles, achieving an 80 per cent hit rate.

The first version of this tactical missile appeared in 1960 and employed the same manual radio guidance as the Russian 'Kerry' (q.v.). However, the AS 30L, which was developed in the 1980s, has semi-active laser guidance and the launching aircraft is able to manoeuvre after releasing the weapon. The target designator pod uses a TV camera for daylight operation and an infra-red thermal imager at night. The warhead has a delayed impact fuse, which allows the warhead to detonate after penetrating the target. The AS 30L was exported to several countries in the Middle East, including Iraq.

AGM-65 Shrike

Specification
Length: 3.05 m (9 ft 11 in)
Body diameter: 0.203 m (8 in)
Wing span: 0.91 m (2 ft 11 in)
Overall weight: 177 kg (390 lb)
Warhead: 66-kg (145-lb) HE fragmentation
Guidance: passive radar
Range: 12 km (7 miles)

Assessment
Age   ★★★★
Accuracy   ★★★
Reliability   ★★★
Worldwide users ★★★

The Shrike missile homes in on enemy radar systems, forcing them to switch off or risk destruction. First used to suppress North Vietnamese defences, it was used by the RAF in the Falklands.

Introduced by the US Air Force during the mid-1960s, the Shrike is based on components from the AIM-7 Sparrow radar-guided missile. The Shrike is guided by passive radar homing with up to 12 different homing head assemblies tuned to various wavebands. Homing in on enemy radar emissions, the Shrike first saw operational service in Vietnam. The Israeli air force has used Shrikes extensively against Arab SAM batteries and – after some hasty modification – the RAF's Avro Vulcans fired two Shrikes against the Argentine long-range radar station established at Port Stanley in 1982.

ALARM

Specification
Length: 4.3 m (14 ft)
Body diameter: 0.224 m (9 in)
Wing span: 0.72 m (2 ft 4 in)
Overall weight: 268 kg (590 lb)
Warhead: undisclosed
Guidance: passive radar
Range: 45 km (28 miles)

Assessment
Age   ★
Accuracy   ★★★★
Reliability   ★★★★
Worldwide users ★

ALARM is the British replacement for Shrike and appeared just in time for the Gulf War. About 120 ALARMs were fired during RAF attacks on Iraqi targets.

Entering service just a few weeks before the coalition air strikes against Iraq began, the ALARM (Air-Launched Anti-Radar Missile) was introduced to replace the RAF's Shrike and Martel missiles. Over a hundred ALARMs were expended in the Gulf War; RAF Tornado GR.Mk 1s can carry up to nine. ALARM has a useful capability to loiter, deploying a parachute and descending slowly over the target area in the hope that the enemy will resume radar emissions. If a set is switched on again, ALARM jettisons the parachute and dives onto the target. ALARM is also designed to be ripple-fired, onboard processors ensuring that the missiles engage separate targets.

AGM-65 Maverick

Specification
Length: 2.49 m (8 ft 4 in)
Body diameter: 0.305 m (12 in)
Wing span: 0.72 m (28 in)
Overall weight: 210–307 kg (462–677 lb)
Warhead: 57-kg (125-lb) HE (AGM-65A/B/D) or 136 kg (300 lb) (AGM-65E/F/G)
Guidance: TV (AGM-65A/B), IIR (AGM-65 D/F/G), semi-active laser (AGM-65E)
Range: 3 km (2 miles) (AGM-65A), 8 km (5 miles) (AGM-65B), 20 km (12 miles) (AGM-65D/E), 25 km (15 miles) (AGM-65F/G)

Assessment
Age   ★★★★
Accuracy   ★★★★
Reliability   ★★★★

The Maverick missile has been manufactured in six main versions with different guidance systems and warheads. It was the primary armament of the USAF's A-10 ground attack aircraft and can also be launched from helicopters.

Developed by the Hughes Aircraft Company during the 1960s, the Maverick missile was introduced in 1972 as a TV-guided weapon intended to attack hardened targets. Infra-red and laser-guided versions followed, and the later Maverick variants are fitted with special warheads better able to penetrate reinforced concrete. The US Air Force, Navy and Marine Corps have all sponsored different versions of the Maverick on their respective fixed-wing aircraft. Trials in 1990 demonstrated the feasibility of firing Maverick from helicopters, and it can also be fitted to the AH-64 or AH-1 gunships.

AIR-TO-SURFACE MISSILES No. 2

The collapse of the USSR will probably lead to the latest generation of Soviet missiles being exported to any regime with ready cash. Meanwhile, some important Western systems are being terminated due to the end of the Cold War.

AGM-136 Tacit Rainbow

Developed during the early 1980s under the codename Tacit Rainbow, the AGM-136 is a long-range anti-radar missile. Propelled by a turbofan, it is launched by bombers such as the B-52, F-111 or A-6 and can engage targets up to 90 kilometres away. Tacit Rainbow's main advantage is its excellent loiter time which allows the launching aircraft to send the missile on ahead where it will circle, waiting for any enemy radar transmissions. If the enemy switch on their set the missile locks on and attacks, leaving its parent aircraft free to continue with its mission. There have been trials with the MRLS for a ground-launched version. However, the AGM-136 programme was terminated in 1990, although the final test flights continued into 1991. The USAF has stated that it would like to use the electronics and the engine in other missiles.

Specification
Length: 2.54 m (8 ft 4 in)
Body diameter: 0.686 m (27 in)
Wing span: 1.56 m (5 ft 2 in)
Overall weight: 227 kg (500 lb)
Warhead: 18 kg (39 lb 11 oz)
Guidance: passive radar homing
Range: 90 km (56 miles)

Assessment
Age ★★
Accuracy ★★★★
Reliability ★★★★
Worldwide users ★

Tacit Rainbow was cancelled by the USAF in 1990, but it was a promising anti-radar missile capable of loitering for 45 minutes or more, ready to attack as soon as the enemy switched on their sets.

AGM-88 HARM

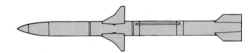

HARM (High-speed Anti-Radar Missile) was developed to replace the AGM-45 Shrike anti-radar missile. HARM is capable of dealing with higher radar frequencies and is less vulnerable to the traditional countermeasure: switching off the radar set once missile launch has been detected. HARM can store the bearing of the target and is able to attack successfully even if the radar system is shut down. HARM entered service with the USAF in 1983 and was employed three years later during the US bombing raids on Libya. HARM was widely used during the 1991 Gulf War. It can be carried by the A-6 Intruder, F-4 Phantom, F-16 Falcon, F-18 Hornet, F-111 Aardvark and the Tornado. The latest model is designed to attack frequency agile radar targets.

Specification
Length: 4.17 m (13 ft 8 in)
Body diameter: 0.254 m (10 in)
Wing span: 1.13 m (3 ft 9 in)
Overall weight: 361 kg (800 lb)
Warhead: 66 kg (145 lb)
Guidance: passive radar homing
Range: 25 km (15 miles)

Assessment
Age ★★★★
Accuracy ★★★★
Reliability ★★★★
Worldwide users ★★★

HARM is the USAF and US Navy's standard anti-radar missile and has seen action against Libya and during the Gulf War.

AGM-114 Hellfire

The Hellfire (Helicopter-launched Semi-active Laser Fire-and-Forget) missile was developed during the 1970s to enable US Army helicopters to attack massed Soviet tank formations. It entered service in 1985 and was extensively used by AH-64 Apache gunships during the Gulf War, inflicting enormous damage on Iraqi vehicle columns and fixed defences. It is guided by a laser-seeking device, homing in on the laser energy reflected by a target that is being 'painted' with a laser designator. Hellfire is also cleared for use by the the US Army's OH-58D Kiowas and AH-1W SuperCobras, as well as the US Marine Corps AH-1J Sea Cobras. It can also be fitted to the Westland Lynx and the UH-1 and UH-60. Recent developments have included a tandem warhead and a digital autopilot that could more than double the missile's speed from about 300 knots to over Mach 1.

Specification
(AGM-114A)
Length: 1.63 m (5 ft 5 in)
Body diameter: 0.178 m (7 in)
Wing span: 0.33 m (13 in)
Overall weight: 46 kg (101 lb)
Warhead: 8-kg (17-lb 10-oz) shaped charge
Guidance: semi-active laser
Range: 8 km (5 miles)

Assessment
Age ★★★
Accuracy ★★★★
Reliability ★★★★
Worldwide users ★★

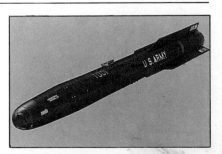

The Hellfire anti-tank missile is the primary weapon of the AH-64 helicopter gunship and is just one of the reasons that an AH-64 costs more than the tanks it is designed to kill. A single hit will destroy any known tank.

AGM-86 ALCM

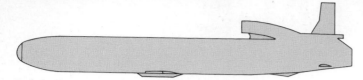

Specification
Length: 6.32 m (20 ft 9 in)
Body diameter: 0.693 m (27 in)
Wing span: 3.65 m (12 ft)
Overall weight: 1458 kg (975 lb)
Warhead: 200-kiloton nuclear
Guidance: inertial with Tercom
Range: 2500 km (1600 miles)

Assessment
Age   **
Accuracy   *****
Reliability   ****
Worldwide users   *

The ALCM (Air-Launched Cruise Missile) was developed as a strategic weapon system. USAF bombers equipped with cruise missiles would be able to attack targets deep inside the USSR without needing to penetrate Soviet airspace and suffer inevitable losses from missiles and interceptors. The ALCM has a range of 2500 kilometres. During the 1980s the B-52G Stratofortress bombers were successfully modified to carry six cruise missiles on underwing weapons points. The B-52H fleet can carry another eight in a specially-designed rotary launcher in the bomb bay. The controversial B-1B bomber carries no less than 14 cruise missiles under the fuselage, as well as eight internally. The ALCM is inertially guided with terrain-contour matching for maximum accuracy. A radar altimeter maintains the missile's low altitude.

Until the Gulf War it was not widely known that the Air-Launched Cruise Missile had a conventional warhead. ALCMs had been part of the USAF's nuclear arsenal.

RB04

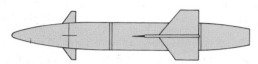

Specification
Length: 4.45 m (14 ft 7 in)
Body diameter: 0.50 m (20 in)
Wing span: 2.0 m (6 ft 7 in)
Overall weight: 600 kg (1320 lb)
Warhead: HE semi-armour piercing
Guidance: inertial/terminal active radar homing
Range: 30 km (19 miles)

Assessment
Age   ****
Accuracy   ****
Reliability   ***
Worldwide users   **

The RB04 is a medium-range radar-guided missile designed and manufactured by the Swedish Saab company for use with the Saab AJ37 Viggen fighter-bomber. Introduced during the 1960s, the RB04 missile has been steadily improved with versions designated RB04A, -B, -C, -D and now RB04E. It was part of the Swedish defensive preparations designed to make any Soviet assault on the country as expensive as possible. AJ37 Viggens were planned to attack Soviet landing craft with RB04s should such an invasion ever have taken place. Although mid-course guidance is inertial, terminal active radar guidance enables the RB04 to home in on a target ship in the last stage of its flight. Flying at about 20 metres above the water, it descends to a few metres above the waves just before impact.

The RB04 is a sea-skimming radar-guided anti-ship missile associated with the Saab Viggen fighter-bomber flown by the Swedish air force.

AS-10 'Karen'

Specification
Length: 3.75 m (12 ft 4 in)
Body diameter: 0.275 m (11 in)
Wing span: 0.82 m (32 in)
Overall weight: 305 kg (672 lb)
Warhead: 110 kg (240 lb)
Guidance: semi-active laser
Range: 10 km (6 miles)

Assessment
Age   ***
Accuracy   ***
Reliability   ***
Worldwide users   ***

The Soviet Union followed the US and European lead in developing guided weapons for its ground-attack aircraft. The missile designated by NATO as the AS-10 (reporting name 'Karen') is reported to be called the Kh-25 in the Soviet/Russian forces. It was developed during the late 1960s and is believed to have entered service in the mid-1970s. It is associated with the MiG-27 'Flogger', Su-17 'Fitter', Su-24 'Fencer' and the Su-25 'Frogfoot' that was widely used during the occupation of Afghanistan. An earlier model, NATO reporting name 'Kerry', is radio-command guided, whereas the AS-10 has semi-active radar homing. There is a third variant now identified – the AS-12 'Kegler' passive radar-homing missile. All three are operated by the Russian forces today.

The AS-10 'Karen' was used extensively by the Soviet air force during the occupation of Afghanistan. A semi-active laser-homing weapon, it can be used against ground or naval targets.

AS-14 'Kedge'

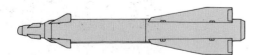

Specification
Length: 3.84 m (12 ft 7 in)
Body diameter: 0.380 m (15 in)
Wing span: 1.15 m (3 ft 9 in)
Overall weight: 660 kg (1450 lb)
Warhead: 250 kg (550 lb)
Guidance: semi-active laser
Range: 12 km (7 miles)

Assessment
Age   **
Accuracy   ***
Reliability   ***
Worldwide users   **

The AS-14 'Kedge' (NATO designation and reporting name) is believed to have entered service with the Soviet forces in 1980. Seen with TV- or semi-active laser guidance, the AS-14 is carried by the same ground attack aircraft as the AS-10 described above. Unlike the AS-10, it is known to have been cleared for carriage by at least one Western aircraft: the Mirage F1. Just as the French supplied Iraq with Exocet anti-ship missiles during the mid-1980s, the USSR sold Saddam Hussein a consignment of AS-14s for use with his Su-17s and Mirages. The AS-14 uses a 250-kilogram bomb as its warhead, the missile body and wings fitting around it. The aircraft launching an AS-14 carries a laser designator pod to illuminate the target. The Iraqis modified a French designator that increased the weapon's range from 8 to 12 kilometres.

The AS-14 'Kedge' is another modern Soviet laser-guided missile now being offered for export by Russia. Some were sold to Iraq during the 1980s and used against Iran.

Following the collapse of the USSR many of Russia's latest missiles are being offered for export at very competitive prices. Minor powers can now acquire military technology that was only previously available to the superpowers and their allies.

AS-9 'Kyle'

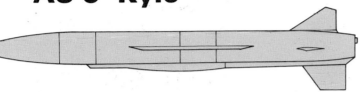

The AS-9 'Kyle' is the NATO designation for this large anti-radar missile that entered service with the Soviet air force in the early 1970s. It has a similar shape to the AS-4 'Kitchen' air-to-surface missile and it has been observed on many different Soviet aircraft. These include the Su-17, Su-20, Su-22 and Su-24 ground attack aircraft and the Tu-16 and Tu-22 bombers. MiG-27 fighter-bombers and MiG-25Es have also been fitted with AS-9. The missile is designed to attack the fire-control radars of enemy surface-to-air missile batteries. Flying at high altitude, it makes a steep dive on to the target. In two decades of service the AS-9 has been widely exported, supplied to several Warsaw Pact air forces as well as traditional allies such as Libya, Syria, Iraq and Vietnam. The Iraqis developed their own version, designated Nisan 28.

Specification
Length: 6 m (19 ft 9 in)
Body diameter: 0.430 m (16 in)
Wing span: 1.4 m (4 ft 7 in)
Overall weight: 715 kg (1570 lb)
Warhead: 150 kg (330 lb)
Guidance: passive radar
Range: 90 km (56 miles)

Assessment
Age ★★★★
Accuracy ★★★
Reliability ★★★
Worldwide users ★★★★★

The AS-9 'Kyle' is carried by the full range of Sukhoi strike aircraft and is widely used by former Warsaw Pact air forces as well as by Russia. The AS-9 was also used by Iraq.

AS-11 'Kilter'

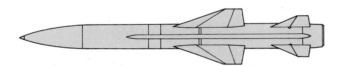

The AS-11 'Kilter' is the NATO designation for this Russian anti-radar missile that entered service in the 1970s. Smaller than the AS-9 'Kyle', the 'Kilter' is carried by a similar range of aircraft plus the Su-25 'Frogfoot'. Homing in on the radar emissions of its target, the AS-11 probably has different seeker heads for different radar frequencies. It was supplied to Bulgaria and former Czechoslovakia before the demise of the Warsaw Pact, and exported to North Korea and possibly some Middle East countries. It is one of the missiles that Russia has been actively promoting at several international arms fairs.

Specification
Length: 4.8 m (15 ft 9 in)
Body diameter: 0.380 m (15 in)
Wing span: 1.2 m (3 ft 11 in)
Overall weight: 650 kg (1430 lb)
Warhead: 150 kg (330 lb)
Guidance: passive radar
Range: 70 km (43 miles)

Assessment
Age ★★★
Accuracy ★★★
Reliability ★★★
Worldwide users ★★★★

The later AS-11 anti-radar missile is associated with the Sukhoi Su-25 'Frogfoot' ground attack aircraft, and has also been exported to several Middle Eastern countries.

Aérospatiale AS 11

The French AS 11 missile was one of the earliest helicopter-launched anti-tank missiles. Nord-Aviation had developed a wire-guided anti-tank missile as early as 1952; designated the SS 10, it paved the way for the first generation of guided tactical missiles. Its successor was the SS 11 and the AS 11, the air-launched variant. Launched from helicopters such as the Alouette or Westland Scout, it is powered by a sustainer motor that gives 20 seconds of power and a maximum range of 3000 metres. Two flares in the rear of the missile help the operator see where it is going. He controls its flight with a small joystick that transmits signals to the jet deflector in the missile's tail via steel wires that uncoil in flight. Later versions of the AS 11 had infra-red guidance and the operator only had to keep the target in his sights for the missile to strike it. Production ceased in 1984 with the AS 11 in service with seven NATO countries, as well as in the Middle East and South America.

Specification
Length: 1.21 m (4 ft)
Body diameter: 0.164 m (6 in)
Wing span: 0.50 m (20 in)
Overall weight: 30 kg (66 lb)
Warhead: 4.5 kg (9 lb 15 oz)
Guidance: wire guided
Range: 3 km (2 miles)

Assessment
Age ★★★★★
Accuracy ★★
Reliability ★★★
Worldwide users ★★★★★

The Aérospatiale AS 11 is seen here fitted to a French army Alouette III helicopter. One of the first wire-guided anti-tank missiles, the AS 11 was widely used by NATO forces.

Aérospatiale AS 12

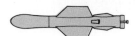

Specification
Length: 1.87 m (6 ft 2 in)
Body diameter: 0.180 m (7 in)
Wing span: 0.65 m (26 in)
Overall weight: 76 kg (165 lb)
Warhead: 30 kg (66 lb)
Guidance: wire guided
Range: 5 km (3 miles)

Assessment
Age   ★★★★
Accuracy   ★★★
Reliability   ★★★
Worldwide users ★★★★★

An AS 12 is launched from a Royal Navy Westland Wasp. Note the two wires trailing behind and the guidance flares burning in the rear of the missile. The bar in the top right of the picture is the helicopter's rotor blade.

The AS 12 is the air-launched version of the SS 12 anti-tank missile, introduced in 1960 for the French navy's Etendard bombers and Super Frélon helicopters. It was soon in service with maritime patrol aircraft, including the Lockheed SP-2 Neptune and Breguet Atlantique as well as other helicopters. Exported to many countries, it was one of several weapons in service with both sides during the Falklands war. Royal Navy Westland Wasps used AS 12s to cripple the Argentine submarine *Santa Fe*, preventing the boat from submerging when it was caught off South Georgia. The Royal Navy has since replaced its AS 12s with Sea Skua but, although production ceased in 1982, the AS 12 remains in use in the Middle East and South America. The French navy has replaced it with the AS 15

Aérospatiale AS 15TT

Specification
Length: 2.3 m (7 ft 7 in)
Body diameter: 0.180 m (7 in)
Wing span: 0.53 m (21 in)
Overall weight: 96 kg (211 lb)
Warhead: 30 kg (66 lb)
Guidance: radar command
Range: 15 km (9 miles)

Assessment
Age   ★
Accuracy   ★★★★
Reliability   ★★★★
Worldwide users ★★

The 15000-metre range AS 15TT is carried by the Super Puma naval helicopter. Largely financed by Saudi Arabia, the AS 15TT was acquired by Saudi forces and saw service in the Gulf War.

The AS 15TT (*Tous Temps* – all weather) is the latest version of the tactical guided missile series that began with the AS 11. Entering service with the French navy in 1985, the AS 15TT no longer relies on unreeling a wire behind it to receive commands from the operator. It is radar guided; both the missile and the target are tracked by the launching helicopter's Thomson-CSF Agrion 15 radar. A radar altimeter keeps the missile about 15 metres above the water surface, making it a difficult target to detect on radar and hard to shoot down. At about 300 metres short of the target, the missile descends to an altitude of two metres to strike the target as close to the waterline as possible. Cleared for use by the SA 365 Dauphin and AS 332 Super Puma, the AS 15TT was developed with some financial assistance from Saudi Arabia and was used by Saudi forces during the Gulf War.

AS 37 Martel

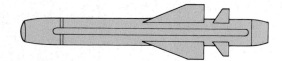

Specification
Length: 4.2 m (13 ft 10 in)
Body diameter: 0.40 m (16 in)
Wing span: 1.2 m (3 ft 11 in)
Overall weight: 535 kg (1180 lb)
Warhead: 150 kg (330 lb)
Guidance: passive radar
Range: 55 km (34 miles)

Assessment
Age   ★★★
Accuracy   ★★★★
Reliability   ★★★★
Worldwide users ★★

A Martel anti-radar missile carried by a Blackburn Buccaneer. The anti-radar version has a pointed nose; the TV-guided type has a flat one containing the camera lens.

In 1964 when the Royal Navy still operated full-size aircraft carriers, Britain and France collaborated on a new naval air-to-surface missile. There were two versions: a TV-guided one produced in the UK and an anti-radar type developed in France. The missiles entered service in 1970. France only used the anti-radar version but the British adopted both. The AS 37 anti-radar missile was designed to be launched at high altitude and there were three homing heads available, each designed to home in on different radar frequencies. The TV-guided version, designated the AJ 168, had a range of 20 kilometres and was 300 mm shorter. It approached the target at about 300 metres, relaying a TV image to the launch aircraft so the operator could steer it on to the target. The AJ 168 had a semi-armour-piercing warhead that exploded inside the target's hull. The Royal Navy replaced Martel with the Sea Eagle and France has now adopted ARMAT.

ARMAT

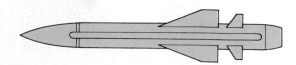

Specification
Length: 4.15 m (13 ft 7 in)
Body diameter: 0.40 m (16 in)
Wing span: 1.2 m (3 ft 11 in)
Overall weight: 550 kg (1200 lb)
Warhead: 150 kg (330 lb)
Guidance: inertial/passive radar
Range: 90 km (56 miles)

Assessment
Age   ★★
Accuracy   ★★★★
Reliability   ★★★★
Worldwide users ★★

ARMAT is a modern anti-radar missile sold all over the world by France. It has been bought by Iraq, Egypt, Kuwait and several other nations. With long range and the ability to attack even if the target radar shuts down, it is a very effective weapon.

ARMAT is a French anti-radar missile that employs the same airframe as the AS 37 but with a new passive radar seeker and updated electronics. The anti-radar missiles of the 1970s were all vulnerable to electronic countermeasures and generally went ballistic if the target radar was turned off. ARMAT is designed to resist enemy jamming and to attack even if the target radar shuts down. Entering service with the French air force in 1984, ARMAT was soon supplied to Iraq and used against Iranian radars from French-supplied Mirage F1s. ARMAT has been exported to Kuwait and Egypt. It is also cleared for use by the Mirage III and Mirage 2000, as well as the SEPECAT Jaguar and Dassault Atlantique maritime patrol aircraft.

The incredible range of air-delivered ordnance now in service enables air forces to attack targets with weapons specifically designed to deal with them. With the soaring cost of modern strike aircraft, 'smart' weapons are now regarded as essential.

BL755 cluster bomb

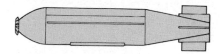

The BL755 is manufactured by Hunting Engineering in the UK and was adopted by the RAF in the early 1970s. The bomb contains seven internal bays, each holding 21 bomblets. These are ejected by gas pressure from a cartridge that is fired after the bomb is released. The bomblets are thrown out in an even pattern and their flight is controlled in two ways: the original type had pop-out tail fins, while the No. 2 bomblet is parachute-retarded. Both have a shaped-charge warhead that will penetrate 250 mm of armour plate, enough to defeat the top armour of most Main Battle Tanks. On detonation each bomblet splinters into approximately 2,000 fragments, providing a deadly anti-personnel effect and causing great damage to soft vehicles, radar installations, AAA batteries and other targets. BL755 is designed for release during very low-level attacks.

Specification
Length: 2.45 m (8 ft)
Body diameter: 0.419 m (16 in)
Wing span: 0.566 m (22 in)
Overall weight: 277 kg (610 lb)
Guidance: none
Range: none

Assessment
Age ★★★
Accuracy ★★★★
Reliability ★★★★
Worldwide users ★★★★

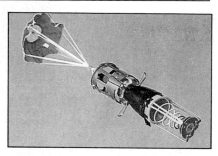

The sub-munitions delivered by the BL755 cluster bomb can penetrate the top armour of most Main Battle Tanks. The small parachute gives the bomblet an almost vertical trajectory.

Hades area denial weapon system

The BL755's bomb body is also used to deliver a very different sub-munition to the shaped-charge bomblets of the original system. Hades uses the same body as BL755 but is loaded with 49 HB876 delayed-action bombs originally developed for the JP233 runway-cratering dispenser. After release, a gas cartridge fires and ejects the HB876 bombs in a wide pattern. The bombs are parachute-retarded to reduce the force of impact. Once on the ground, the bomb is armed and spring-loaded steel legs are activated, turning the bomb upright. There it remains until its sensors or a time fuse detonates the device. On detonation it fires a high-velocity slug and a shower of lethal fragments. The slug is designed to be sufficiently powerful to disable most conventional mine-clearing ploughs. Hades is designed to attack crossroads, river crossings or other fixed points where a scattering of mines will cause maximum difficulty.

Specification
Length: 2.45 m (8 ft)
Body diameter: 0.419 m (16 in)
Wing span: 0.566 m (22 in)
Overall weight: 259 kg (570 lb)
Guidance: none
Range: none

Assessment
Age ★★
Accuracy ★★★★
Reliability ★★★★
Worldwide users ★★★

A Hades cluster bomb spreads its sub-munitions in a wide pattern as the gas cartridge inside detonates. It delivers delayed-action bomblets derived from the JP233 system.

BLG 66 Belouga

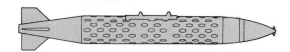

The BLG 66 is a cluster bomb developed by Matra for the French air force, and it entered service in the early 1980s. It was used by French aircraft against Libyan-backed forces in Chad and again during the Gulf War. It can carry a wide variety of sub-munitions, including delayed-action bomblets, fragmentation devices and hollow-charge weapons for attacking armoured forces. The bomb's body contains 19 rings, each housing eight sub-munitions; the bomb is parachute-retarded to allow the aircraft to attack from as low as 60 metres. The bomblets are also parachute-retarded, released either in a high-density pattern (circa 5000 m²) or a low-density pattern (circa 10000 m²). The bomblets descend vertically, maximising their effect against vehicles.

Specification
Length: 3.3 m (10 ft 10 in)
Body diameter: 0.366 m (14 in)
Wing span: 0.55 m (22 in)
Overall weight: 305 kg (672 lb)
Guidance: none
Range: none

Assessment
Age ★★
Accuracy ★★★★
Reliability ★★★★
Worldwide users ★★

The French Belouga cluster bomb has been used by the French air force against Libyan and Chadian forces, as well as during the Gulf War. It can be delivered from very low altitude.

BM 400

Specification
Length: 3.2 m (10 ft 6 in)
Body diameter: 0.320 m
(13 in)
Wing span: 0.40 m
(16 in)
Overall weight: 390 kg
(860 lb)
Guidance: none
Range: up to 10 km (6
miles)

Assessment
Age   ★★
Accuracy   ★★★★
Reliability   ★★★★
Worldwide users ★

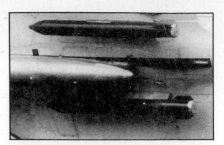

The French BM 400 bomb can be fitted with a booster rocket that gives it a useful stand-off capability. Each bomb contains three fragmentation sub-munitions.

The BM 400 was developed by Thomson Brandt as a private venture and it was adopted by the French air force in the late 1980s. It offers a major advantage over the Belouga system: the BM 400 can be fitted with a booster rocket, giving it a stand-off range of approximately 10000 metres. The BM 400 contains three fragmentation sub-units which separate in succession after the bomb is released. The sub-units are parachute-retarded, slowing and descending vertically towards the target. The sub-units explode when they strike the ground, delivering either around 800 fragments or around 1,500 depending on the type of sub-munition selected. The choice is between 800 fragments capable of penetrating 17 mm of steel 50 metres away from the detonation point, or 1,500 smaller fragments that can penetrate 12 mm of steel. Two BM 400s have a lethal zone of about 600×100 metres.

Paveway

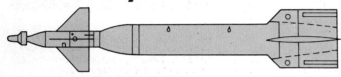

Specification
(GBU-10 Mk 84
2000-lb bomb)
Length: 4.32 m (14 ft 2 in)
Body diameter: 0.457 m
(18 in)
Wing span: 1.16 m
(3 ft 9 in)
Overall weight: 953 kg
(2100 lb)
Guidance: laser
Range: 18 km (11 miles)

Assessment
Age   ★★★★
Accuracy   ★★★★
Reliability   ★★★★
Worldwide users ★★★★

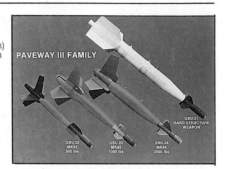

The Paveway family of guided bombs has continued to expand since its debut in the Vietnam War.

Paveway is a laser guidance assembly that can be fitted to standard, unguided bombs. First fitted to US Mk 117 340-kilogram demolition bombs, it was tested in the 1960s for use in Vietnam, where US aircraft were suffering heavy losses from North Vietnamese air defence systems. Paveway was used in action for the first time in 1971 and it was soon applied to many other varieties of bomb. In all cases the target has to be illuminated with a laser and the bomb glides towards the reflected laser energy with its onboard computer adjusting the tail fins to keep it on course. It can be used at night and in poor visibility providing the cloud base is not below 760 metres. Paveway requires no modification to the aircraft delivering it and allows the aircraft to release its ordnance some distance away from the target, thus running a lower risk from ground fire.

GBU-15

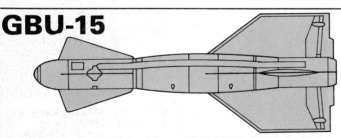

Specification
Length: 3.94 m (12 ft 11
in)
Body diameter: 0.460 m
(18 in)
Wing span: 1.50 m
(4 ft 11 in)
Overall weight: 1111 kg
(1 ton 2200 lb)
Guidance: TV or IIR
Range: 80 km (50 miles)

Assessment
Age   ★★★
Accuracy   ★★★★
Reliability   ★★★★
Worldwide users ★★

An F-4 Phantom drops a GBU-15 glide bomb – a heavy bunker buster reserved for well-protected point targets during the Gulf War.

Like the GBU-10, the GBU-15 also delivers a Mk 84 2,000-lb (904-kilogram) bomb in a glide attack, controlled by a computerised guidance system. However, the GBU-15 uses TV or IIR (imaging infra-red) seekers to find its target. The controlling aircraft must have a data-link pod and associated control equipment. The seeker relays an image to a TV screen in the cockpit and its course is guided by a hand controller. The data-link system enables the GBU-15 to be fired without any lock-on since the course corrections can only be transmitted just before impact. Several aircraft can deliver GBU-15s at long range, having them controlled by another orbiting closer to the target. Depending on the launching aircraft's speed and altitude, the GBU-15's range can be as far as 80 kilometres or it can be dropped from as close as 1500 metres.

Mk 82 Snakeye

Specification
Length: 2.21 m (7 ft 3 in)
Body diameter: 0.273 m
(11 in)
Wing span: 0.38 m (15 in)
Overall weight: 241 kg
(530 lb)
Guidance: none
Range: none

Assessment
Age   ★★★★★
Accuracy   ★★★
Reliability   ★★★★★
Worldwide users ★★★★★

The US Mk 82 227-kilogram bomb has been widely copied since the 1950s. The Snakeye attachment consists of folding fins that spring out when the bomb is dropped, decelerating the bomb and allowing the aircraft to escape the effects of its explosion.

The Mk 82 500-lb (227-kilogram) bomb was designed for the USAF and US Navy shortly after World War II as a general-purpose weapon for delivery by high-speed aircraft. This low-drag design has been widely imitated since and it is used by many bomb-manufacturing nations today. Its long, slim, aerodynamically-shaped body suits it to fast aircraft and it can be fused in a variety of ways. The Snakeye attachment consists of four blades that flip out from the back of the bomb, providing a sudden braking effect. This allows the bomb to fuse properly, even if delivered at very low level. Without such an attachment, a bomb dropped in such circumstances will probably not detonate properly – as demonstrated by the Argentine air force during its attacks on the British Task Force in 1982. The Mk 82 is one of the most commonly-encountered 'iron' bombs in the world and is still in production in the USA.

SUPERCARRIERS No.1

There is no greater concentration of fighting power than in a modern aircraft carrier. Its air wing contains fighters, bombers and ASW aircraft in a multi-role, multi-weapon, go-anywhere force.

'Forrestal' class

The four 'Forrestal' class carriers were completely reconfigured before construction. They were the first carriers built specifically for jet aircraft operations. The **Forrestal** (CV-59) was commissioned in 1955, followed by the **Saratoga** (CV-60), **Ranger** (CV-61) and **Independence** (CV-62) between 1956 and 1959. They were the first of the modern supercarriers, their expansive flight decks and huge hangars being suitable for handling larger and higher performance aircraft than any previous vessel. *Forrestal* becomes the US Navy's training carrier in 1992; *Ranger* might soon be paid off; while the modernised *Saratoga* and *Independence* are to remain in service until the end of the century.

Specification
(USS *Forrestal*)
Dimensions: length 331 m (1085 ft); flight deck width 76.8 m (250 ft)
Full load displacement: 80,520 tonnes (79,250 tons)
Speed: 33 knots
Range: 22,000 km (13,670 miles) at 20 knots
Armament: three octuple Sea Sparrow launchers and three 20-mm Phalanx CIWS
Air wing: 84 aircraft
Crew: 5179

Assessment
Size   ★★★★★
Air group   ★★★★★
Fighting power   ★★★★★
Combat persistence   ★★★★

The USS **Forrestal,** *launched in the early 1950s, was the first of the supercarriers. Larger and vastly more capable than any preceding aviation vessel, the vessel served as the prototype for all succeeding US Navy carriers. The* **Forrestal** *has now become the US Navy's training carrier.*

'Kitty Hawk' class

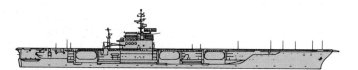

Built to an improved 'Forrestal' design, the 'Kitty Hawk' class carriers are the **Kitty Hawk** (CV-63), **Constellation** (CV-64) and the **America** (CV-66). The *John F. Kennedy* (CV-67) is different enough to be treated as a separate sub-class. The first two were commissioned in 1961, having originally been ordered as the fifth and sixth of the 'Forrestal' class. The most obvious difference from the 'Forrestals' is that they carry their islands further aft and the deck-edge elevators have been repositioned, allowing for more efficient aircraft handling. The *America*, entering service in 1965, was built as a conventionally-powered carrier for reasons of economy, since the preceding *Enterprise* had proved extremely costly.

Specification
(USS *Kitty Hawk*)
Dimensions: length 323.6 m (1060 ft); flight deck width 76.8 m (250 ft)
Full load displacement: 82,425 tonnes (81,123 tons)
Speed: 32 knots
Range: 22,000 km (13,670 miles) at 20 knots
Armament: three octuple Sea Sparrow launchers and three 20-mm Phalanx CIWS
Air wing: 84 aircraft
Crew: 5340

Assessment
Size   ★★★★★
Air group   ★★★★★
Fighting power   ★★★★★
Combat persistence   ★★★★

The 'Kitty Hawk' class carriers were built to an improved 'Forrestal' design, with a repositioned island allowing for more effective aircraft handling on deck. The **Constellation,** *seen here, made eight combat tours to Vietnam.*

USS *Enterprise*

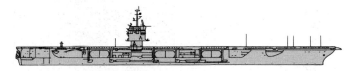

The USS *Enterprise* (CVN-65), laid down in 1958 and launched in 1960, was the most astonishing vessel of its time and by far the largest warship in the world. Powered by eight nuclear reactors, it is an enlarged version of the 'Forrestal' design. However, being nuclear-powered, it does not need to carry its own fuel oil and so has more room for aviation fuel and weapons. In 1963, *Enterprise* and the similarly powered cruisers *Long Beach* and *Bainbridge* made a non-stop voyage round the world to demonstrate the viability of nuclear power. The *Enterprise* is no longer in service.

Specification
(USS *Enterprise*)
Dimensions: length 342.3 m (1120 ft); flight deck width 76.8 m (250 ft)
Full load displacement: 95,480 tonnes (93,970 tons)
Speed: 33 knots
Range: 750,000 km (470,000 miles) at 20 knots
Armament: three octuple Sea Sparrow launchers and three 20-mm Phalanx CIWS
Air wing: 86 aircraft
Crew: 5765

Assessment
Size   ★★★★★
Air group   ★★★★★
Fighting power   ★★★★★
Combat persistence   ★★★★★

Easily the largest warship built up to that time, the **Enterprise** *and its nuclear powerplant took the carrier into new realms of combat capability.* **Enterprise,** *seen here entering San Francisco Bay in 1982, had undergone a major refit in the three preceding years.*

USS *John F. Kennedy*

Specification
(USS *John F. Kennedy*)
Dimensions: length
320.6 m (1050 ft); flight
deck width 76.8 m (250 ft)
Full load displacement:
82,300 tonnes (81,000
tons)
Speed: 33 knots
Range: 22,000 km
(13,670 miles) at 20 knots
Armament: three octuple
Sea Sparrow launchers
and three 20-mm Phalanx
CIWS
Air wing: 84 aircraft
Crew: 5279

Assessment
Size ★★★★★
Air group ★★★★★
Fighting power ★★★★★
Combat
persistence ★★★★

Built to a modified 'Kitty Hawk' design, the USS John F. Kennedy is identifiable by its outward-canted funnel and the more sharply-angled contours of its deck forward of numbers three and four catapults.

The USS **John F. Kennedy** (CV-67) is ostensibly the fourth carrier of the 'Kitty Hawk' class. In the mid-1960s, when the carrier was being funded, it was clear that the US Navy wanted a nuclear-powered vessel. However, the Secretary of Defense of the time was Robert S. MacNamara, who refused the Navy's request on the grounds of cost. Thus, the vessel was laid down as a conventionally-powered carrier. Nevertheless, the *Kennedy* incorporated a number of new features that had been learned from operational experience with the *Enterprise*, including better underwater protection, an outward-canted funnel and revised forward flight deck contours.

'Nimitz' class

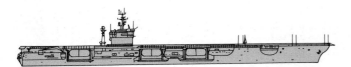

Specification
(USS *Abraham Lincoln*)
Dimensions: length
332.9 m (1092 ft); flight
deck width 76.8 m (250 ft)
Full load displacement:
103,640 tonnes (102,000
tons)
Speed: 35+ knots
Range: 1,850,000 km
(1,150,000 miles) at 20
knots
Armament: three octuple
Sea Sparrow launchers
and four 20-mm Phalanx
CIWS
Air wing: 87 aircraft
Crew: 6054

The first three 'Nimitz' class carriers, the USS **Nimitz** (CVN-68), **Dwight D. Eisenhower** (CVN-69) and **Carl Vinson** (CVN-70) were originally designed as replacements for the World War II-designed 'Midway' class carriers. Commissioned in 1975, 1977 and 1982, respectively, they differ from the earlier nuclear-powered *Enterprise* by having much more powerful reactors, two doing the job of eight. As a result, they have more internal space which is used to increase the amount of aviation fuel and ordnance carried. The basic design is once again a development of the tried and tested 'Forrestal' layout, and they carry the standard US Navy air wing. Three further carriers, the USS **Theodore Roosevelt** (CVN-71), **Abraham Lincoln** (CVN-72) and **George Washington** (CVN-73) have been built to an improved 'Nimitz' design, with Kevlar armour and full-load displacement taken to beyond 100,000 tons.

Assessment
Size ★★★★★
Air group ★★★★★
Fighting power ★★★★★
Combat
persistence ★★★★★

Nimitz and Eisenhower are seen during a changeover of the Indian Ocean battle group.

Admiral Kuznetsov

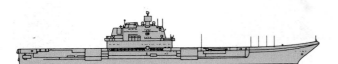

Specification
Dimensions: length
304.5 m (1000 ft); flight
deck width 70 m (230 ft)
Full load displacement:
68,580 tonnes (67,500
tons)
Speed: 32 knots
Range: probably 20,000
km (12,430 miles) at 18
knots
Armament: 12×SS-N-19
long-range anti-ship
missiles, 4×SA-N-9 vertical
launch systems, each with
48 missiles, 8×twin 30-
mm/octuple SS-N-11
combined CIWS, 6×ADG-6
30-mm CIWS and 2×RBU
1000 ASW rocket
launchers
Air wing: 24 fixed-wing
aircraft and 18 helicopters
Crew: 2100

The Soviet navy has been developing an aviation capability since the early 1960s, starting with helicopter-carrying cruisers and passing through the V/STOL aircraft carriers such as the *Kiev* until the launch of its first vessel capable of operating conventional take-off aircraft. The **Admiral Kuznetsov**, which in the past has also been known as the *Leonid Brezhnev* and the *Tbilisi*, is marginally smaller than the US Navy's *Forrestal*. It carries a much smaller air wing than American carriers, launching them with the assistance of a 'ski-jump' rather than catapults. A larger carrier is under construction, and this is expected to be closer in capability to the US Navy's supercarriers.

Assessment
Size ★★★★
Air group ★★★
Fighting power ★★★★
Combat
persistence ★★★

The first genuine Soviet carrier went to sea in 1989 under the name of Tbilisi.

'Clemenceau' class

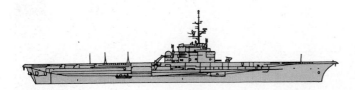

Specification
(*Clemenceau*)
Dimensions: length
265 m (870 ft); flight deck
width 29.5 m (85 ft)
Full load displacement:
33,300 tonnes (32,780
tons)
Speed: 32 knots
Range: 13,800 km (8600
miles) at 18 knots
Armament: two octuple
Crotale SAM launchers and
four 100-mm dual-purpose
cannon
Air wing: 35–40 aircraft
Crew: 1689

Assessment
Size ★★★
Air group ★★★
Fighting power ★★★
Combat
persistence ★★

The **Clemenceau** was the first carrier designed as such to be completed in France. Built in the late 1950s and commissioned in 1961, she incorporated all of the advances in carrier design developed up to that time. The *Clemenceau* was joined in commission in 1963 by the **Foch**. Similar in size and capability to the modernised 'Essex' class carriers of the US Navy, the 'Clemenceau' will continue in service to the end of the century. By that time, the French navy will be operating a new carrier in the shape of the nuclear-powered *Charles de Gaulle*. Far less capable than the US Navy's giant carriers, *Clemenceau* is nevertheless more than a match for most other fighting ships.

Designed in the late 1950s, the Clemenceau and Foch are smaller and far less capable than the American supercarriers. They are due to be replaced in the late 1990s by the nuclear-powered Charles de Gaulle.

V/STOL AND LIGHT CARRIERS No.1

Aircraft carriers operating conventional take-off and landing aircraft are phenomenally expensive to build and operate, so many navies wishing to take air power to sea are taking an alternative and cheaper route: light carriers with V/STOL fixed-wing aircraft and helicopter air groups.

'Kiev' class

Soviet planning for a hybrid cruiser/carrier probably started in the 1960s. At that time all Soviet naval assets were subordinated to their submarine force, and the new carriers were designed to provide air defence to ASW task forces intended to destroy NATO hunter-killer submarines. **Kiev**, the first of a four-ship class, was commissioned in October 1976 after extensive trials. From the bridge forwards, the 'Kievs' are heavy cruisers, with a significant ASW, anti-surface ship and anti-aircraft missile fit. The after portion of the vessels are devoted to air power, with a fully-angled flight deck with six or seven landing spots for its air group of Kamov helicopters and Yak-38 'Forger' VTOL fighters. A typical air group might consist of a dozen 'Forgers' and 22 Kamov Ka-25 'Hormones' or Ka-27 'Helix' helicopters. Most of the latter are ASW helicopters, but two or three will be equipped to give mid-course, over the horizon guidance to the carrier's long-range missiles. The **Admiral Gorshkov** is the last of the class and was built to a modified design.

Specification
(*Admiral Gorshkov*)
Dimensions: length 274 m (900 ft); flight deck width 47.2 m (155 ft)
Full load displacement: 41,660 tonnes (41,000 tons)
Speed: 32 knots
Range: 21,000 km (13,000 miles) at 18 knots
Armament: 12×SS-N-12 'Sandbox' long-range surface-to-surface missiles with 24 reloads; 4×sextuple vertical launchers for SA-N-9 short-/medium-range SAMs with 192 missiles; 2×100-mm dual-purpose guns; 6×30-mm 6-barrel close-in weapon systems
Crew: 2400

Assessment	
Size	★★★★
Air group	★★★
Fighting power	★★★
Versatility	★★★

Much larger than other light carriers, the 'Kiev' class are more like hybrid carrier/cruisers.

'Invincible' class

The imminent demise of Britain's fixed-wing carrier fleet in the 1960s led to the Admiralty planning a 12,500-ton command cruiser carrying six Westland Sea King helicopters. Refinement of the concept led to the 19,500-ton 'through-deck cruiser', a light carrier in all but name, but so called to avoid political repercussions. Sufficient space was reserved from the outset for the new carriers to operate naval versions of the RAF's V/STOL Harrier then being developed. HMS **Invincible** was the first of a three-ship class, entering service in July 1980. The original air group was to consist of nine Sea Kings and five Sea Harriers, but during the Falklands war the aircraft complement rose to 11 Harriers, eight Sea Kings and two Lynx helicopters. An innovation which was to more than prove its worth was the 'ski-jump' ramp, which allowed Harriers to take off with much heavier fuel and weapon loads.

Specification
(HMS *Ark Royal*)
Dimensions: length 209.1 m (685 ft); flight deck width 36 m (118 ft)
Full load displacement: 20,900 tonnes (20,600 tons)
Speed: 28 knots
Range: 8000 km (5000 miles) at 18 knots
Armament: one twin Sea Dart medium-range SAM launcher with 36 missiles, and 2×20-mm Phalanx CIWS (to be replaced by 3×30-mm Goalkeeper CIWS)
Crew: 1032

Assessment	
Size	★★★
Air group	★★★
Fighting power	★★★
Versatility	★★★★

The British 'Invincible' class carriers were designed primarily as anti-submarine platforms.

Giuseppe Garibaldi

Originating from an Italian navy requirement for a gas-turbine-powered helicopter carrier, the **Giuseppe Garibaldi** was ordered in 1977, and launched in 1983. The design was modified during construction to allow for the operation of fixed-wing V/STOL fighters. Smaller than the British 'Invincibles', the *Garibaldi* is designed to act as a fleet flagship, to operate at the head of an ASW task force, or to provide air and ASW cover to merchant convoys. In emergencies, the carrier can also carry up to 600 troops for short periods. Primary strike power is provided by 16 or 18 aircraft, with varying proportions of McDonnell Douglas/BAe AV-8B Harrier IIs and EH.101 helicopters. The *Giuseppe Garibaldi* carries a wider range of weapons than its British equivalents, although not as many as the very much larger 'Kiev' class.

Specification
(*Giuseppe Garibaldi*)
Dimensions: length 180 m (590 ft); flight deck width 33.4 m (109 ft)
Full load displacement: 13,585 tonnes (13,370 tons)
Speed: 30 knots
Range: 11,250 km (6990 miles) at 20 knots
Armament: 4×Teseo Mk 2 surface-to-surface missiles; 2×octuple Albatros SAM launchers with 48 missiles; 3×twin dual-purpose 40-mm cannon; 2×triple 324-mm lightwight torpedo tubes
Crew: 825

Assessment	
Size	★★
Air group	★★★
Fighting power	★★★
Versatility	★★★★

The Giuseppe Garibaldi packs a considerable punch into a relatively small package.

Principe de Asturias

Specification
(*Principe de Asturias*)
Dimensions: length
196 m (640 ft); flight deck
width 24.3 m (80 ft)
Full load displacement:
17,000 tonnes (16,700
tons)
Speed: 26 knots
Range: 10,500 km (6500
miles) at 20 knots
Armament: 4×Meroka
12-barrelled CIWS
Crew: 765

Assessment
Size   ★★★
Air group   ★★★
Fighting power   ★★★
Versatility   ★★★

The design of the Principe de Asturias is based on that of the US Navy's abortive Sea Control Ship project of the 1970s, modified to include such features as a 'ski-jump' take-off ramp and deck-edge elevators.

Spain has operated aviation ships since the 1960s, initially with the light carrier *Dedalo*, which was formerly the US Navy's World War II light carrier *Cabot*. The *Dedalo* has been replaced as the Spanish navy's fleet flagship by the **Principe de Asturias**. The design is basically that of the US Navy's abortive Sea Control Ship of the 1970s, considerably modified and refined to enable V/STOL aircraft to be carried. The *Principe de Asturias* has a 12° 'ski-jump' ramp fitted at the bow, which enables the AV-8B Harrier IIs of the air group to take off with greater fighting loads. Depending on the mission, the carrier can operate with up to 12 Harriers, or 10 Sea King or Sea Hawk helicopters, plus four AB.212 utility helicopters. A fully digital command and control system is fitted, enabling the *Principe de Asturias* to be used as a flag vessel.

Minas Gerais

Specification
(*Minas Gerais*)
Dimensions: length
212 m (695 ft); flight deck
width 36.4 m (119 ft)
Full load displacement:
20,210 tonnes (19,890
tons)
Speed: 24 knots
Range: 19,000 km
(11,800 miles) at 14 knots
Armament: two
quadruple and one twin
40-mm cannon
Crew: 1300

Assessment
Size   ★★★
Air group   ★
Fighting power   ★★
Versatility   ★★

Dating back to the last years of World War II, the Minas Gerais is too small to act as a conventional carrier. It is now largely an ASW-dedicated vessel, with secondary helicopter assault capabilities.

The **Minas Gerais** started life in 1945 as the Royal Navy's 'Colossus' class light fleet carrier HMS *Vengeance*. Loaned to the Australian navy in the mid-1950s, she was purchased and given her present name by Brazil in 1955. Comprehensively refitted in the Netherlands, the *Minas Gerais* received new weapons, a steam catapult, an angled flight deck, a new island superstructure and new American radar. Used from the start for anti-submarine warfare, the *Minas Gerais* originally shipped an air group of eight Grumman S-2 Trackers, four Sea Kings and four or five utility helicopters. Given a refit between 1976 and 1981, the carrier entered the 1990s with an unchanged air group, but there is some doubt as to the future of the fixed-wing Trackers. Currently undergoing another refit, there are tentative plans to replace the *Minas Gerais* with a larger conventional carrier.

25° de Mayo

Specification
(*25° de Mayo*)
Dimensions: length
212 m (695 ft); flight deck
width 40.6 m (133 ft)
Full load displacement:
20,220 tonnes (19,900
tons)
Speed: 24 knots
Range: 19,500 km
(12,120 miles) at 14 knots
Armament: nine Bofors
40-mm dual-purpose
cannon
Crew: 1500

Assessment
Size   ★★★
Air group   ★★★
Fighting power   ★★★
Versatility   ★★

A McDonnell Douglas A-4 Skyhawk comes in to land on the Argentine navy's only carrier. Shipping conventional take-off and landing aircraft, it lacks the flexibility of V/STOL-equipped vessels.

Originally a sister ship to the Brazilian *Minas Gerais*, the **25° de Mayo** was completed as the Royal Navy's 'Colossus' class carrier HMS *Venerable*, which was sold to the Netherlands in 1948 as the *Karel Doorman* and acquired by Argentina in 1968. In 1980, the *25° de Mayo* underwent a further refit to increase the strength of the flight deck and allow more aircraft parking space. The carrier supported the original Argentine landings on the Falklands, but was not used to any great extent during the Falklands war. A major refit planned for the late 1980s was to re-engine the carrier, which had suffered from a notoriously unreliable powerplant, but lack of funds postponed that refit. The carrier's current air group includes 12 Super Etendard strike fighters, six Grumman Tracker ASW aircraft, four SH-3D Sea King ASW and one utility helicopter.

Viraat

Specification
(INS *Viraat*)
Dimensions: length
227 m (745 ft); flight deck
width 48.8 m (160 ft)
Full load displacement:
29,160 tonnes (28,700
tons)
Speed: 28 knots
Range: 10,000 km (6200
miles) at 20 knots
Armament: two
quadruple Sea Cat short-
range SAM launchers and
some Russian-supplied
six-barrelled 30-mm CIWS
may be fitted
Crew: 1350

Assessment
Size   ★★★★
Air group   ★★★★
Fighting power   ★★★
Versatility   ★★★

As HMS Hermes, the INS Viraat performed well in the Falklands. It is one of the largest of the light carriers, capable of carrying a potent air group almost as powerful as that carried by the much larger 'Kiev' class.

The Indian carrier **Viraat** has a somewhat convoluted design and service history. Originally HMS *Hermes*, she was laid down in 1944 as one of the Royal Navy's 'Centaur' class of light fleet carriers. Incomplete at the end of World War II, the vessel remained on the stocks for a decade. New developments in carrier design meant that the vessel which entered service in the late 1950s was equipped with an angled flight deck. In 1971 the *Hermes* was recommissioned as a commando carrier, and then in the late 1970s as an interim V/STOL carrier. After serving as the flagship of the Royal Navy's task force during the Falklands war, the *Hermes* was sold to India in May 1986. After a major refit, the carrier, now renamed *Viraat*, was commissioned into the Indian Navy in 1987. The current air group includes 12 or 18 Sea Harrier V/STOL fighters and seven or eight Sea King or Kamov 'Hormone' ASW helicopters. In emergencies, the *Viraat* can operate up to 30 Harriers.

AIRCRAFT CARRIERS

Some aircraft carriers built during or just after World War II are only now retiring from service. But while veteran US carriers saw action off Korea and Vietnam, the British carrier fleet was destroyed by the Labour government in 1966.

'Intrepid' class

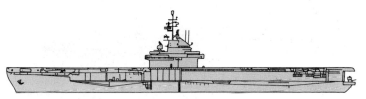

USS *Intrepid* was one of many World War II 'Essex' class aircraft carriers to be extensively modified during the 1950s so that it could operate jet aircraft. After wartime service that included surviving Japanese suicide 'kamikaze' aircraft attacks, the *Intrepid* served off Korea. In the 1960s with a much improved air group, USS *Intrepid* made three tours off Vietnam, operating up to 80 aircraft. Unable to operate the next generation of carrier aircraft, the old carrier served as an anti-submarine carrier into the 1970s. USS *Intrepid* paid off in 1974 and is now preserved as a museum in New York. One sister ship, **USS** *Lexington*, continued to serve as a training ship until 1992, when it was replaced by USS *Forrestal.*

Specification
Dimensions: length 272 m (890 ft); beam 31 m (102 ft)
Standard displacement: 31,070 tonnes (30,580 tons)
Speed: 29 knots
Armament: four 127-mm DP guns
Crew: 3545

Assessment
Size ★★★
Air group ★★★★
Fighting power ★★★★
Combat persistence ★★★★

USS Intrepid *underway in the North Atlantic during the 1970s. After three tours of duty off Vietnam, this World War II aircraft carrier continued to serve as an anti-submarine carrier until becoming a museum ship in New York.*

'Midway' class

Three 'Midway' class aircraft carriers joined the US Navy at the end of World War II, and they were refitted during the 1950s to operate jet aircraft. The largest warships built for the US Navy during World War II, these were the first to be too large to pass through the Panama Canal. USS **Midway** was further modernised in the 1960s, although similar improvements to sister ships **Coral Sea** and **Franklin D. Roosevelt** were not funded. All three served off Vietnam, but *Franklin D. Roosevelt* was stricken in 1977 and broken up. *Coral Sea* did not decommission until 1990. *Midway* continued to operate from Japan, the only US carrier to be based overseas, until recently relieved by USS *Independence*. The final air group aboard *Midway* was typically 36 F-18s, 18 A-6s, four EA-6s and four E-2s, plus some KA-6 tankers.

Specification
Dimensions: length 307 m (1000 ft); beam 43 m (141 ft)
Standard displacement: 51,800 tonnes (51,000 tons)
Speed: 30 knots
Armament: two octuple launchers for Sea Sparrow SAMs and two Phalanx 20-mm CIWS
Crew: 4360

Assessment
Size ★★★★★
Air group ★★★★★
Fighting power ★★★★★
Combat persistence ★★★★★

The 'Midway' class aircraft carrier USS Coral Sea *finally decommissioned in 1990, after nearly 40 years of service. These 51,000-ton vessels were the first warships built for the US Navy that were too large to use the Panama Canal.*

'Moskva' class

The 'Moskva' class are hybrid helicopter carriers/missile cruisers which were intended to spearhead Soviet anti-submarine operations. Laid down in the early 1960s, when the potential of NATO nuclear submarines was becoming a serious concern to the Soviets, the **Moskva** and **Leningrad** were the first of a planned 12-strong class. However, their poor sea-keeping and small air group of only 14 Kamov Ka-25 helicopters did not provide much aerial support for a Soviet surface squadron. No more were built and the 'Kiev' class aircraft carriers followed instead. Commissioned in 1967 and 1968, *Moskva* and *Leningrad* were frequently seen on overseas deployments to the Mediterranean, Indian Ocean and North Atlantic. They will probably be put into reserve or even scrapped soon.

Specification
Dimensions: length 191 m (625 ft); beam 34 m (111 ft)
Standard displacement: 15,140 tonnes (14,900 tons)
Speed: 31 knots
Armament: two twin SA-N-3 launchers, one SUW-N-1 anti-submarine missile launcher, two RBU 6000 12-tube anti-submarine mortars and four 57-mm DP guns
Crew: 850

Assessment
Size ★★
Air group ★
Fighting power ★★
Combat persistence ★★★

Moskva *was one of only two helicopter carriers to be completed out of a planned class of 12. Unimpressive sea boats, these carriers had a small air group of primitive ASW helicopters and were soon followed by the 'Kiev' class.*

'Colossus' class

The British 'Colossus' class aircraft carriers saw a great deal of service after World War II. In December 1945, **HMS Ocean** became the first aircraft carrier to receive landings by a jet aircraft. Five 'Colossus' class carriers were employed by the Royal Navy off Korea, where a propeller-driven Sea Fury fighter from *Ocean* shot down a MiG-15 fighter in 1952. Of the 10 built, one was sold to France, one to Brazil and two to Argentina. One of the latter, **Veinticinco de Mayo**, served during the Falklands war against the Royal Navy. **Glory**, **Ocean** and **Theseus** were scrapped in 1961-62. **Triumph** survived as a repair ship until placed in reserve in 1975; she was scrapped in 1981-82.

Specification
Dimensions: length 211 m (695 ft); beam 24 m (80 ft)
Standard displacement: 13,400 tonnes (13,190 tons)
Speed: 25 knots
Armament: 17 40-mm Bofors anti-aircraft guns
Crew: up to 1500, depending on air group

Assessment
Size ★★
Air group ★★
Fighting power ★★★
Combat persistence ★★★

HMS Colossus steams to Korea, where British and Commonwealth troops were fighting as part of the UN forces in 1952. On deck are propeller-driven Sea Fury fighters; one from HMS Ocean shot down a MiG-15 that year.

HMS *Ark Royal*

Near sister of HMS *Eagle*, **Ark Royal**'s completion was delayed by the addition of steam catapults, a 5½-degree angled flight deck and other modern features. She underwent a £30-million refit from 1967-70 and became Britain's last real aircraft carrier thanks to the Wilson government's monstrous folly: the decision announced on 22 February 1966 to cancel a new 50,000-ton carrier. *Ark Royal* remained in service until 1978, with an air group consisting of 12 F-4 Phantoms, 14 Buccaneers, four Sea Gannet AEW aircraft and six Wessex ASW helicopters. Her latter days dogged by engineering problems, *Ark Royal* was finally taken out of service in 1978 and scrapped in 1980. Two years later, the Royal Navy fought exactly the sort of war she was built for.

Specification
(post-1967 refit)
Dimensions: length 275 m (902 ft); beam 34 m (112 ft)
Standard displacement: 43,700 tonnes (43,000 tons)
Speed: 31 knots
Armament: none, but fitted for four quadruple Sea Cat SAM launchers
Crew: 2637

Assessment
Size ★★★★
Air group ★★★★
Fighting power ★★★★
Combat persistence ★★★★

HMS Ark Royal as completed. Refitted from 1967-70, she became Britain's last genuine aircraft carrier to remain operational and was not scrapped until two years before the Falklands war.

HMS *Bulwark*

Bulwark and **Albion** were 'Centaur' class aircraft carriers built to incorporate the lessons of World War II carrier operations. They took part in the attack on Egypt in 1956, but were then converted to helicopter carriers in 1959-60 and 1961-62, respectively. Carrying 700-900 Royal Marines and embarking 16 Westland Wessex helicopters, they served off Aden and during the crisis with Indonesia in 1966. *Albion* was scrapped in 1972 and *Bulwark* placed in reserve in 1976. However, she was recommissioned in 1979 as an anti-submarine helicopter carrier, releasing HMS *Hermes* from the amphibious warfare role. *Bulwark* paid off in 1981, once *Invincible* was operational, and was in too bad a state of repair to be recommissioned for the Falklands war a year later. She was scrapped in 1984.

Specification
Dimensions: length 225 m (738 ft); beam 27 m (88 ft)
Standard displacement: 22,660 tonnes (22,300 tons)
Speed: 28 knots
Armament: three twin and two single 40-mm anti-aircraft guns
Crew: 1035, plus 900 Royal Marines

Assessment
Size ★★
Air group ★
Fighting power ★★
Combat persistence ★★

HMS Albion undergoes full power trials before sailing for the Far East in 1965. After conversion to a Commando Carrier, Albion could carry 900 Royal Marines and a squadron of Wessex transport helicopters.

HMS *Eagle*

HMS Eagle trialled F-4 Phantoms for the Fleet Air Arm, but she ended her days as a source of spares to keep HMS Ark Royal operational for as long as possible.

Commissioned in 1952, 10 years after she was laid down at Harland and Wolff, **Eagle** was reconstructed from 1959-64 at a cost of £31 million. The ship that emerged was a very capable carrier with a powerful air group, modern anti-aircraft armament and even NBC protection. Deployed to the Far East for the Indonesian confrontation, *Eagle* also served off Mozambique during the Royal Navy's blockade of Rhodesia. In 1969, *Eagle* trialled the F-4 Phantom for the Fleet Air Arm and embarked her first ASW helicopter squadron. However, she became another victim of the Wilson Labour government and her career was cut short, paying off in January 1972 to become a source of spares for HMS *Ark Royal*.

Specification
Dimensions: length 247 m (807 ft); beam 34 m (112 ft)
Standard displacement: 44,800 tonnes (44,100 tons)
Speed: 31 knots
Armament: six quadruple Sea Cat SAM launchers and four twin 4.5-in guns
Crew: 2750, including full air group

Assessment
Size ★★★★
Air group ★★★
Fighting power ★★★★
Combat persistence ★★★★

CRUISERS

For most of naval history, cruisers have been fast and powerful warships designed for independent action far from the fleet. Today, however, the cruiser designation is used for expensive missile-armed vessels capable of operating in high-threat areas as important parts of task forces.

'Leahy' class

The 'Leahy' class were the first American warships primarily armed with missiles, with a pair of twin 76-mm guns added almost as an afterthought. Their main armament was the Terrier surface-to-air system, and a limited ASW capability was provided by an eight-round ASROC launcher. The class' fighting power has seen a considerable upgrade since the vessels entered service in the mid-1960s. Terrier has been replaced by the long-range variant of the latest Standard SM-2 missile, eight Harpoon anti-ship missiles have been added and two Phalanx close-in weapon systems have taken the place of the twin 76-mm gun mounts. The 'Leahys' were designed as fleet escorts, whose role was to provide air defence to fast task forces. Known as frigates under the post-war US Navy nomenclature, they were redesigned as cruisers in 1975. One nuclear-powered equivalent to the 'Leahys' was built, in the shape of the slightly larger USS *Bainbridge*.

Specification
Dimensions: length 162.5 m (533 ft); beam 16.6 m (54 ft 6 in)
Displacement: 8335 tonnes (8203 tons)
Speed: 33 knots
Armament: two quadruple Harpoon SSM launchers, two twin Mk 10 Standard SAM launchers with 80 missiles, one octuple ASROC ASW missile launcher, two 20-mm CIWS and two triple tubes for lightweight ASW torpedoes
Aircraft: platform only
Crew: 441

Assessment
Versatility ★★★★
Firepower ★★★★
Age ★★★★
Worldwide users ★

In service for 30 years, the 'Leahy' class carry a mixed ASW and anti-surface ship armament.

'Belknap' class

Originally intended as a relatively cheap guided missile destroyer, the 'Belknap' design evolved into a more capable vessel based on the 'Leahy' design. Being a single-ended missile ship with one rather than two twin launchers, the 'Belknap' carries fewer missiles than the preceding 'Leahys'. However, each of the vessels in the class is fitted with a 127-mm gun and a helicopter deck and hangar in place of the stern missile launcher, greatly increasing the type's ASW and surface warfare capability. 'Belknap' class cruisers were used in combat in Vietnam, serving as fleet air defence to the carriers on Yankee Station in the Gulf of Tonkin, and acting as forward air controllers to fighters attacking North Vietnam. The USS *Truxton* is the nuclear equivalent to the 'Belknaps', having a similar armament fit.

Specification
Dimensions: length 166.7 m (547 ft); beam 16.7 m (54 ft 9 in)
Displacement: 8330 tonnes (8200 tons)
Speed: 33 knots
Armament: two quadruple Harpoon SSM launchers, Standard SAM and ASROC ASW missiles fired by one twin Mk 10 launcher with 40 missiles, one 127-mm gun, two 20-mm CIWS and two triple tubes for lightweight ASW torpedoes
Aircraft: one SH-2F LAMPS I ASW helicopter
Crew: 497

Assessment
Versatility ★★★★
Firepower ★★★★
Age ★★★★
Worldwide users ★

Flagship of the Sixth Fleet, Belknap has Kevlar armour over some vital spaces.

'Virginia' class

After the one-off nuclear-powered cruisers of the 1960s, the US Navy built the two 'California' class cruisers in the 1970s. These were followed by the four 'Virginia' class cruisers. Originally intended to be nuclear counterparts to the 'Spruance' guided missile destroyers, the 'Virginias' emerged as improved 'Californias'. Stark, spare-looking vessels, the 'Virginias' act as fast area defence SAM escorts to nuclear-powered carriers. Although primarily AAW vessels, the 'Virginias' had some ASW capability, thanks to the helicopters they carried in helicopter hangars below their fantail flight decks. The class has lost its helicopter handling capacity, carrying in its place the armoured box launchers for Tomahawk cruise missiles. These, when added to the Harpoon missiles and two fast-firing 127-mm guns with which each of the class is armed, give the 'Virginias' considerable surface action capability.

Specification
Dimensions: length 178.3 m (585 ft); beam 19.2 m (63 ft)
Displacement: 11,480 tonnes (11,300 tons)
Speed: over 33 knots
Armament: eight Tomahawk cruise missiles, eight Harpoon SSMs, Standard SAM and ASROC ASW missiles fired from two twin Mk 26 launchers with 68 missiles, two 127-mm guns, two 20-mm CIWS and two triple tubes for lightweight ASW torpedoes
Aircraft: none
Crew: 624

Assessment
Versatility ★★★★
Firepower ★★★★
Age ★★★
Worldwide users ★

With cruise missiles, Harpoon and ASW systems, the nuclear-powered 'Virginias' are very capable warships.

'Ticonderoga' class

The 'Ticonderoga' design was originally intended as a minimum cost platform for the Aegis air defence system. Based on the 'Spruance' class destroyer hull, the 'Ticonderogas' have emerged as extremely costly vessels which, nevertheless, offer value for money since they are the most capable air defence ships ever commissioned. The SPY-1 radars of the Aegis system have the ability to track hundreds of targets simultaneously, and extensive computerisation makes for very fast reaction times. The Mk 41 vertical launch system can accommodate Standard SAMs, ASROC, or Tomahawk cruise missiles, allowing for a very flexible weapon fit. Unlike previous air defence cruisers, the 'Ticonderogas' also have an effective ASW capability, thanks to the SH-60 LAMPS III helicopters they carry.

Specification
Dimensions: length 172.8 m (567 ft); beam 16.8 m (55 ft 2 in)
Displacement: 9620 tonnes (9466 tons)
Speed: over 30 knots
Armament: two 61-round Mk 41 vertical launch systems holding variable combinations of Standard, ASROC and Tomahawk cruise missiles, two quadruple Harpoon SSM launchers, two 127-mm guns, two 20-mm CIWS and two triple tubes for lightweight ASW torpedoes
Aircraft: two SH-60B LAMPS III helicopters
Crew: 358

Assessment
Versatility ★★★★★
Firepower ★★★★★
Age ★★
Worldwide users ★

The 'Ticonderoga' class are the most effective air defence warships in service.

'Nikolayev' class

The evolution of the modern missile cruiser in the Soviet navy could be traced from the 'Kynda' class of the early 1960s, which introduced the characteristic pyramidal superstructure to carry a multitude of sensors, through the 'Kresta I' and 'Kresta II' classes of the 1970s, with a more efficient hull form and heavier ASW weaponry, to the larger 'Kara' – now renamed 'Nikolayev' – class, which was a gas-turbine-powered refinement of the 'Kresta II'. Equipped to act as leaders of anti-submarine task groups, the 'Nikolayevs' have more effective anti-aircraft defences than preceding vessels.

Specification
Dimensions: length 173.2 m (568 ft); beam 18.6 m (61 ft)
Displacement: 10,060 tonnes (9900 tons)
Speed: 34 knots
Armament: eight SS-N-14 'Silex' ASW missiles, two twin SA-N-3 'Goblet' SAM launchers with 72 missiles, two twin SA-N-4 'Gecko' SAM launchers with 40 missiles, two twin 76-mm guns, four 30-mm CIWS, two quintuple tubes for heavyweight torpedoes, four multi-barrel ASW mortars
Aircraft: one Kamov Ka-25 'Hormone' ASW helicopter
Crew: 540

Assessment
Versatility ★★★★
Firepower ★★★★
Age ★★★
Worldwide users ★

The former 'Karas' have more SAMs than previous cruisers.

'Ushakov' class

In December 1977, the USSR launched the largest non-carrier surface combatant built since World War II. Designated as a missile carrier by the Soviets, the *Kirov* (now renamed the *Ushakov*) has been called a battle cruiser because of its size and very heavy armament. Three of these powerful warships have been built, with a fourth under construction. Similar in concept to the abortive US Navy functions, from serving as a fleet flagship, through providing a carrier screen in high-threat environments, to independent action at the head of a surface action group.

Specification
Dimensions: length 252 m (830 ft); beam 28.5 m (93 ft 6 in)
Displacement: 24,690 tonnes (24,300 tons)
Speed: 33 knots
Armament: 20×SS-N-19 SSMs, 12 octuple SA-N-6 'Grumble' vertical SAM launchers, 2 twin SA-N-4 'Gecko' SAM launchers with 40 missiles, 2 octuple SA-N-9 vertical SAM launchers, 1 twin 130-mm gun, 8×30-mm CIWS, 2 quintuple tubes for heavyweight torpedoes, 3 multi-barrel ASW mortars
Aircraft: three Kamov Ka-27 'Helix' ASW helicopters
Crew: 840

Assessment
Versatility ★★★★★
Firepower ★★★★★
Age ★★★
Worldwide users ★

The former 'Kirov' class are the largest cruisers in the Russian fleet.

'Slava' class

Falling midway between the massive 'Kirovs' and the 'Sovremenny' class destroyers, the 'Slava' class surface action cruisers make a powerful addition to the former Soviet fleet now controlled by Russia. 'Slavas' are being built at the same yard that built the 'Kara' class cruisers, and the hull appears to be a stretched version of the earlier design. First deployed in 1983, the 'Slava' class was intended to contest vital sea areas like the North Atlantic's GIUK gap, with a primary task of attacking carrier battle groups. Each cruiser carries 16 SS-N-12 'Sandbox' missiles. These potent weapons have a range of 550 kilometres and carry a nuclear or a 500-kilogram high-explosive warhead.

Specification
Dimensions: length 186 m (610 ft); beam 20.8 m (65 ft)
Displacement: 11,380 tonnes (11,200 tons)
Speed: 34 knots
Armament: 16×SS-N-12 long-range SSMs, 2 twin SA-N-4 'Gecko' SAM launchers with 40 missiles and 8 octuple SA-N-6 'Grumble' vertical SAM launchers, 1 twin 130-mm gun, 6×30-mm CIWS, 2 quintuple tubes for heavyweight torpedoes, 2 multi-barrel ASW mortars
Aircraft: one Kamov Ka-27 'Helix' ASW helicopter
Crew: 505

Assessment
Versatility ★★★★
Firepower ★★★★★
Age ★★
Worldwide users ★

The 'Sandbox' missiles of the 'Slava' class can reach targets up to 550 kilometres away.

MODERN DESTROYERS

Warships are classified with names that were originally coined for ship types that have long vanished. The 'destroyers' that first appeared at the beginning of this century were gunboats built to sink enemy torpedo boats. Modern destroyers are general-purpose warships, but at what point a 'frigate' becomes a 'destroyer' is interpreted differently from navy to navy.

Type 42 class

The 14 Type 42 class destroyers were commissioned between 1976 and 1985, and were built in three batches of six, four and four vessels. Batch 3 Type 42s were enlarged to alleviate some of the difficulties encountered with the earlier ships. Seven Type 42s served in the Falklands war: five in the Royal Navy (of which *Sheffield* and *Coventry* were sunk) and two (*Santissima Trinidad* and *Hercules*) with the Argentine fleet. The latter were built for the Argentines by Vickers during the 1970s. The Type 42's primary weapon is the long-range Sea Dart SAM, with a range of 40 kilometres, that scored seven kills from 18 launches during the war. However, the lack of a close-range defence proved to be a major liability.

Specification
Dimensions: length 154 m (505 ft); beam 16.8 m (55 ft)
Displacement: 4165 tonnes (4100 tons)
Speed: 29 knots
Armament: 1 twin Sea Dart SAM launcher with 22 missiles, 1×4.5-in gun, 4×20-mm Oerlikon AA guns, 2 triple 324-mm torpedo tubes with 6 Stingray guided torpedoes
Aircraft: one Lynx HAS.3 helicopter
Crew: 253

HMS Sheffield was lost to an Exocet missile attack during the Falklands war. Both sides operated Type 42 destroyers during that conflict.

'Arleigh Burke' class

The latest destroyers to join the US Navy, the 'Arleigh Burke' class incorporate many recent technological developments. They have 'quietened' propulsion to reduce acoustic signature, a 'stealth'-modified superstructure to reduce radar signature and 130 tons of Kevlar armour over vital spaces. With a towed array sonar, ASROC, Harpoon and Tomahawk cruise missiles, these large destroyers are versatile and well armed. The only drawback to attract attention is the lack of a hangar for a helicopter. There is an aft heli-pad and provision for refuelling and re-arming LAMPS helicopters, but because there is no hangar there is no on-board helicopter.

Specification
Dimensions: length 154 m (505 ft); beam 20 m (65 ft)
Displacement: 6730 tonnes (6625 tons)
Speed: 31 knots
Armament: 2 Mk 41 vertical launch systems with 29 missiles forward and 61 aft (Tomahawk and ASROC ASW missiles, and SM-2 MR SAMs), 2 Mk 141 quadruple Harpoon SSM launchers with 4 Harpoons each, 2 Mk 32 triple 324-mm torpedo tubes with Mk 46 anti-submarine torpedoes, 1×5-in gun and 2×20-mm Phalanx CIWS
Aircraft: none, but can refuel/re-arm helicopters
Crew: 303

Assessment		
Anti-air	★★★	*The state-of-the-art. 'Arleigh Burke' class destroyer.*
Anti-ship	★★★★★	
Anti-sub	★★★	
Damage capacity	★★★★★	

'Spruance' class

The 31-ship 'Spruance' class destroyers were commissioned between 1975 and 1983. Regarded as the last word in ASW surface ships at the time, they are being modernised with the addition of the Mk 41 vertical launch system, which allows them to carry Tomahawk cruise missiles and Standard SM-2 MR SAMs. Highly manoeuvrable, the 'Spruance' class carry a passive towed array for submarine detection and have hangar facilities to operate a LAMPS III helicopter. The first major US warships to have gas turbine propulsion, they also have noise reduction features and limited Kevlar protection on vital spaces.

Specification
Dimensions: length 171 m (560 ft); beam 16.8 m (55 ft)
Displacement: 5920 tonnes (5830 tons)
Speed: 33 knots
Armament: 1 Mk 16 octuple launcher with 24 ASROC missiles, 1 Mk 29 launcher with 8 Sea Sparrow SAMs, 8 Harpoon SSMs, 2×5-in DP guns, 2×20-mm Phalanx CIWS, 2 triple 324-mm torpedo tubes with Mk 46 torpedoes
Aircraft: one LAMPS III helicopter
Crew: 324

Assessment		
Anti-air	★★★	*The 'Spruance' class destroyer*
Anti-ship	★★★★	*USS Elliot.*
Anti-sub	★★★★★	
Damage capacity	★★★	

'Charles F. Adams' class

The first units of the 'Charles F. Adams' class were laid down in 1958 and in total 23 were built. The German and Canadian navies each bought three modified versions and they are still operational. Many of the US Navy's 'Charles F. Adams' destroyers were decommissioned in the last three years, and some may yet be traded or sold to minor navies. All the US ships were going to be modernised during the 1980s, but only seven actually received the 'DDG upgrade', which included improved sonar and gunnery control radar. Since then all have been withdrawn from service.

Specification
Dimensions: length 133 m (436 ft); beam 14.3 m (47 ft)
Displacement: 3420 tonnes (3370 tons)
Speed: 31 knots
Armament: 1 Mk 11 launcher on DDG 2-14 with 36×SM-1 MR SAMs and 6 Harpoon SSMs, 1 Mk 13 launcher on DDG 15-24 with 36×SM-1 MR SAMs and 4 Harpoon SSMs, 2 octuple ASROC launchers with 8 missiles each and 4 reloads, and 2 Mk 32 triple 324-mm torpedo tubes with Mk 46 torpedoes
Aircraft: none
Crew: 361

Assessment	
Anti-air	★★★★
Anti-ship	★★★
Anti-sub	★★★★
Damage capacity	★★

DDG-2 USS Charles F. Adams underway in the Atlantic in 1978.

'Kashin' class

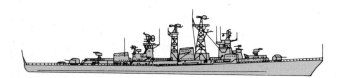

Destroyers of the 'Kashin', now renamed the 'Komsomolets Ukrainyy', class entered service from 1963 to 1972. Primarily designed for ASW, their main weapons were SET-65 533-mm homing anti-submarine torpedoes and ASW mortars. Five ships were modified during the 1970s with four SS-N-2 'Styx' SSMs, four 30-mm 'Gatling' CIWS gun systems and variable-depth sonar. Five modified versions were built for India during 1980–88, while some of the unmodified destroyers have been laid up or, in the case of the *Smely*, transferred to Poland. *Provorny* was used to test the SS-N-7 'Gadfly' SAM.

Specification
(Modified 'Kashin')
Dimensions: length 147 m (482 ft); beam 15.8 m (52 ft)
Displacement: 4013 tonnes (3950 tons)
Speed: 35 knots
Armament: 2 twin 76-mm guns, 4×30-mm CIWS, 2 twin launchers for SA-N-1 'Goa' SAMs, 1 quintuple 533-mm torpedo tube bank with 5×SET-65 homing torpedoes, 2×RBU 6000 12-tube ASW mortars and 4 single SS-N-2 'Styx' SSM launchers (no reloads)
Aircraft: none
Crew: 320

Assessment	
Anti-air	★★★
Anti-ship	★★
Anti-sub	★★★
Damage capacity	★★★

Fifteen 'Kashin' class destroyers remain in service with the former Soviet navy.

'Udaloy' class

The destroyers of the 'Sovremenny' class were commissioned between 1980 and 1992, and a total of 17 are currently in service. They are primarily equipped for surface action, thus complementing the mainly ASW armament of the 'Udaloy' class. Their main weapon is the SS-N-22 'Sunburn' SSM, which has a range of 120 kilometres and carries a massive 500-kg warhead. A single hit from this missile would cripple most surface ships of a similar size. Air defence is provided by 44 SA-N-7 'Gadfly' missiles, and the four 130-mm automatic guns are dual-purpose air/surface weapons.

Specification
Dimensions: length 163.45 m (536 ft); beam 19.3 m (63 ft 4 in)
Displacement: 6807 tonnes (6700 tons)
Speed: 30 knots
Armament: 2 quadruple SA-N-9 SAM launchers, 2 quadruple SS-N-14 A/S missile launchers, 2 quadruple 533-mm torpedo tubes with SET-65 homing torpedoes, 2×100-mm automatic guns, 4×30-mm CIWS
Aircraft: two Ka-27 'Helix' helicopters
Crew: 249

Assessment	
Anti-air	★★★★
Anti-ship	★
Anti-sub	★★★★
Damage capacity	★★★

The 'Udaloy' class are much more capable ships, armed with SS-N-14 'Silex' missiles.

'Sovremenny' class

The 13 units of the 'Sovremenny' class were commissioned between 1980 and 1992. Four more were laid down during 1987-88 and their future remains uncertain. The Soviet navy designated the 'Udaloys' as 'anti-submarine vessels' but classified the 'Sovremennys' as destroyers. They are primarily equipped for surface action, thus complementing the mainly ASW armament of the 'Udaloy' class. Their main weapon is the SS-N-22 'Sunburn' SSM, which has a range of 120 kilometres and carries a massive 500-kilogram warhead. A single hit from this missile would cripple most surface ships of a similar size. Air defence is provided by 44 SA-N-7 'Gadfly' missiles, and the four 130-mm automatic guns are dual-purpose air/surface weapons.

Specification
Dimensions: length 156 m (512 ft); beam 17.3 m (56 ft 9 in)
Displacement: 6604 tonnes (6500 tons)
Speed: 32 knots
Armament: 2 quadruple SS-N-22 launchers (8 missiles, no reloads), 2×SA-N-7 launchers with 44 missiles, 4×130-mm automatic DP guns, 4×30-mm CIWS and 2 twin 533-mm torpedo tubes with 4 Type 53 homing torpedoes
Aircraft: one Ka-25 'Hormone' or one Ka-27 'Helix' helicopter
Crew: 364

Assessment	
Anti-air	★★★★
Anti-ship	★★★★
Anti-sub	★★
Damage capacity	★★★

The 'Sovremenny' class are primarily intended for surface action.

The following vessels are classified as destroyers in the English-speaking naval world. However, like the Soviet fleet the French navy has its own classification system which seeks a more descriptive designation for its warships.

Chilean destroyers

Four ex-Royal Navy 'County' class destroyers were transferred to Chile during the 1980s. As the country's most modern surface warships they bear some of the most honoured Chilean naval names. All are named after famous Chilean naval officers, but in a departure from traditional practice the ranks are not used. *Blanco Encalada* and *Cochrane* (formerly HMS *Fife* and HMS *Antrim*) have been substantially modified with a long flight deck to operate a pair of Super Pumas. *Prat* and *Latorre* (once HMS *Norfolk* and HMS *Glamorgan*) look much as they did in British service. *Latorre* was supplied with 40-mm guns instead of the Sea Cat missiles damaged during the Falklands war.

Specification
Dimensions: length 158.7 m (520 ft); beam 16.5 m (54 ft)
Displacement: 5530 tonnes (5440 tons)
Speed: 30 knots
Armament: 4 Exocet SSMs, 1 Sea Slug SAM launcher (*Prat* and *Latorre* only), 2 Sea Cat launchers (not *Latorre*), 2×4.5-in guns, 2×40-mm guns and 2×20-mm guns, and two triple 324-mm torpedo tubes with Mk 44 homing torpedoes
Aircraft: 1×SA 319 Alouette helicopter (*Prat* and *Latorre*); 2×NAS 332 Super Puma helicopters (*Blanco*, *Encalada* and *Cochrane*)
Crew: 470

Assessment	
Anti-air	★★★
Anti-ship	★★★
Anti-sub	★★★
Damage capacity	★★★★★

This is Falklands veteran HMS Glamorgan, which was renamed Latorre.

'Allen M. Sumner' class

The US Navy commissioned over 50 of these destroyers between 1944 and 1945. Based on the successful 'Fletcher' class, the 'Sumners' were larger and more heavily armed and they remained in service longer. The 'Sumner' class survived until the early 1970s, when they were sold off to allied navies. Today they are operated by Brazil (four), Greece (one), Iran (two), Korea (two), Taiwan (two) and Turkey (one). Armament and sensor fits vary from navy to navy. The Taiwanese destroyers have locally-made SSMs, most others have improved anti-aircraft weapons varying from Bofors guns to the 20-mm Vulcan cannon fitted to the Korean ships. All except the Taiwanese and Turkish ships carry a helicopter.

Specification
(Brazilian *Espiritu Santo*)
Dimensions: length 114.8 m (376 ft); beam 12.5 m (41 ft)
Displacement: 2235 tonnes (2200 tons)
Speed: 30 knots
Armament: 6 Mk 38 5-in guns, 2 triple 324-mm torpedo tubes with Mk 32 A/S homing torpedoes and 2 Hedgehog A/S mortars
Aircraft: one Bell JetRanger helicopter
Crew: 274

Assessment	
Anti-air	★★
Anti-ship	★★
Anti-sub	★★★
Damage capacity	★★

The Brazilian destroyer Rio Grande do Norte was formerly USS Strong. The US Navy commissioned vast numbers of destroyers during World War II and many were sold to allied navies during the 1960s.

'Audace' class

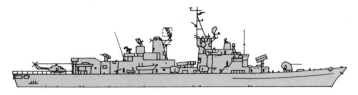

Commissioned in 1972, the Italian navy's two 'Audace' class destroyers have proved highly successful and formed the basis for the 'Animoso' class currently completing. They ship a powerful general-purpose armament, including Otomat SSMs, Standard SAMs and homing anti-submarine (A/S) torpedoes. Both are fitted with stabilisers and their pair of AB 212 ASW helicopters provide over-the-horizon guidance for the Otomats as well as good anti-submarine capability. As originally built they had two OTO-Melara 5-in guns, but the 'B' turret was removed during modernisation and replaced by an octuple SAM launcher firing Aspide semi-active radar-homing missiles. They also had two twin 21-in torpedo tubes in transom mounts, but these have been removed.

Specification
Dimensions: length 136.6 m (448 ft); beam 14.2 m (46 ft)
Displacement: 3660 tonnes (3600 tons)
Speed: 33 knots
Armament: 8 Otomat SSMs, 1 Mk 13 launcher with 40 Standard SM-1 SAMs, 1 octuple launcher for Aspide SAMs, 1×5-in gun, 4 Super Rapid 76-mm guns and 2 triple 324-mm torpedo tubes with Mk 32 guided A/S torpedoes
Aircraft: two AB 212 ASW helicopters
Crew: 380

Assessment	
Anti-air	★★★★★
Anti-ship	★★★★★
Anti-sub	★★★★
Damage capacity	★★★

Audace at sea during the 1970s. This has proved a very successful design.

'Georges Leygues'class

Designated *Frégates* or *Escourteurs d'Escadre*, these vessels were originally known as the C-70 *Frégates anti-sousmarines* when laid down in the mid-1970s. The French classifications express their purpose better than the catch-all phrase 'destroyer', but they are larger than most ships classed as frigate and the authoritative *Jane's Fighting Ships* rates them as destroyers. With two Lynx helicopters able to carry AS12 anti-ship missiles or a powerful anti-submarine fit and a comprehensive weapon fit themselves, the 'Georges Leygues' class are versatile warships. They are also large enough to accept new weapons systems in due course; OTO-Melara Matra anti-submarine missiles are planned in due course. The last three ships of the seven-ship series have towed arrays, and the others may receive them in mid-life refits.

Specification
Dimensions: length 139 m (456 ft); beam 14 m (46 ft)
Displacement: 3890 tonnes (3830 tons)
Speed: 30 knots
Armament: 4 Exocet SSMs, 1 octuple Crotale SAM launcher, 1×100-mm gun, 2 Oerlikon 20-mm AA guns and 2 torpedo tubes with 10 ECAN L5 guided A/S torpedoes
Aircraft: two Lynx HAS.Mk 2 helicopters
Crew: 218

Assessment
Anti-air   ★★★★
Anti-ship   ★★★★
Anti-sub   ★★★★
Damage capacity ★★★

The 'Georges Leygues' destroyers are capable anti-submarine vessels that are also well equipped for surface action. This is the **Dupleix.**

'Tourville' class

Still rated as 'anti-submarine frigates' the 'Tourville' class are large enough for destroyers, let alone frigates. In fact they have carried 'D' pennants since their commissioning in the mid-1970s. Shipping a powerful anti-surface and anti-submarine armament, the three 'Tourville' class ships are very capable warships, all currently serving with the French Atlantic squadron. Refits are scheduled for the mid-1990s, which will extend their service lives into the first decade of the next century. Towed arrays, OTO-Melara Matra anti-submarine missiles and Murene torpedoes will probably be added if the planned refits go ahead.

Specification
Dimensions: length 152.8 m (501 ft); beam 16 m (52 ft)
Displacement: 4654 tonnes (4580 tons)
Speed: 32 knots
Armament: 6 Exocet SSMs, 1 octuple Crotale SAM launcher, 1 Malafon launcher with 13 missiles (delivering an L4 acoustic A/S torpedo), 2×100-mm guns, 2×20-mm guns and 2 torpedo tubes with 10×L5 guided A/S torpedoes
Aircraft: two Lynx helicopters with AS12 missiles or Mk 46 torpedoes
Crew: 301

Assessment
Anti-air   ★★★★
Anti-ship   ★★★★★
Anti-sub   ★★★★
Damage capacity ★★★★

De Grasse off Norfolk, Virginia, for the bicentennial celebrations in 1981.

'Suffren' class

Designated *Frégates lance-missiles* by the French navy, the two ships of the 'Suffren' class are distinguished by the massive spherical radomes of their DRBI 23 D band air search radar sets. *Suffren*, commissioned in 1967, and *Duquesne*, in 1970, both ship a mixed armament of anti-surface and anti-submarine weapons on relatively large hulls. Equipped with stabilisers, they have the reputation of excellent sea-boats. Both serve with the French Mediterranean squadron. *Suffren* underwent a major refit in 1988-89, which involved extensive modernisation of her sensors, fire-control systems and ECCM. *Duquesne* received similar treatment in 1991-92.

Specification
Dimensions: length 157.6 m (5171 ft); beam 15.5 m (51 ft)
Displacement: 5170 tonnes (5090 tons)
Speed: 34 knots
Armament: 4 Exocet SSMs, 1 twin ECAN Ruelle Masurca SAM launcher, 1 Malafon launcher with 13 missiles (delivering 1×L4 homing A/S torpedo), 2×100-mm guns, 6 Oerlikon 20-mm guns and 2 twin launchers for L5 guided A/S torpedoes
Aircraft: none
Crew: 355

Assessment
Anti-air   ★★★
Anti-ship   ★★★
Anti-sub   ★★
Damage capacity ★★★★★

Suffren is instantly recognisable thanks to the massive dome of its air search radar.

'Hamburg' class

The three units of the 'Hamburg' class were commissioned in 1964–65 and carry a mixed anti-surface and anti-submarine armament. As constructed they were little advanced from World War II ships, with four 100-mm guns, anti-submarine mortars and standard 533-mm torpedo tubes. They were modernised in the late 1970s with four Exocet missiles mounted in place of the 'X' turret and Breda 40-mm guns instead of the old-style Bofors guns. Nevertheless, their anti-aircraft armament was weak by modern standards. The destroyers of the 'Hamburg' class are no longer in service.

Specification
Dimensions: length 133.7 m (438 ft); beam 13.4 m (44 ft)
Displacement: 3394 tonnes (3340 tons)
Speed: 34 knots
Armament: 4 Exocet SSMs, 3×100-mm guns, 4 twin Breda 40-mm L70 guns, 4×533-mm torpedo tubes, 2 Bofors 375-mm A/S mortars and 2 depth charge projectors and depth charge rails
Aircraft: none
Crew: 268

Assessment
Anti-air   ★★
Anti-ship   ★★★
Anti-sub   ★★
Damage capacity ★★★

The 'Hamburg' class were among the first warships built for the West German navy after World War II. This is the **Schleswig-Holstein,** *laid down at Hamburg in 1959 and commissioned in 1964.*

FRIGATES

Over the centuries the frigate has performed a wide variety of tasks, from scouting for Nelson's fleet at Trafalgar to defeating the U-boat menace in World War II. Today, the frigate is the work horse of most navies: still a submarine hunter, but with anti-aircraft and anti-ship weapons as well.

Type 22 'Broadsword' class

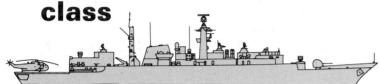

The Type 22 'Broadsword' class frigates were designed for hunting down high-performance nuclear-powered submarines. The primary ASW weapon is the Lynx helicopter. The first four vessels are armed with Exocet SSMs and Seawolf high-performance short-range SAMs, but have no major calibre gun. They were found to be too small to deploy an effective towed array sonar, and the next six vessels, known as Batch 2, were built to a stretched design. The Falklands war showed that guns were still useful and the last four vessels, Batch 3, were changed during production to accommodate a Vickers 4.5-inch gun. They also mounted eight Harpoon anti-ship missiles in place of the less effective Exocets, and the last four Batch 2 vessels have enlarged flight decks. Another Falklands' lesson was the need for effective missile defence, and the Batch 3s are fitted with a 30-mm Goalkeeper close-in weapon system.

Specification
(Type 22 Batch 3)
Dimensions: length 148.1 m (485 ft); beam 14.8 m (48 ft 6 in)
Displacement: 4980 tonnes (4900 tons)
Speed: 30 knots
Armament: 8 Harpoon anti-ship missiles, 2 sextuple Seawolf SAM launchers with 32 missiles, 4.5-in gun, Goalkeeper 30-mm CIWS, 2 Oerlikon/DES 30-mm and 2 triple tubes for lightweight ASW torpedoes
Aircraft: two Lynx or one Sea King or one EH.101 Merlin ASW helicopter
Crew: 250

Assessment
Versatility   ★★★★
Firepower   ★★★
Age   ★★★
Worldwide users   ★

Batch 1 Type 22 frigates were the Royal Navy's first all-missile ships. Later variants carry a heavier armament fit.

Type 23 'Norfolk' class

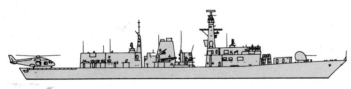

Originally, the Royal Navy wanted 26 'Broadswords' but, due to costs, only 14 were built. The Type 23 'Norfolk' class was promoted to fill the gap and was intended to be a basic ASW frigate. However, the Falklands war taught that cheap ships have limitations, and so the design was upgraded considerably. The Type 23 incorporates a number of stealth features and materials to reduce its radar, acoustic, magnetic and infra-red signatures. It is powered by diesel-electric/gas turbine, which allows it to move quietly up to 10 knots and with jet power to full speed in seconds.

Specification
Dimensions: length 133 m (436 ft); beam 16.1 m (52 ft 10 in)
Displacement: 4270 tonnes (4200 tons)
Speed: 28 knots
Armament: 8 Harpoon SSMs, 32 Seawolf SAMs in a vertical launch system, 4.5-in gun, 2 Oerlikon/DES 30-mm and 2 twin tubes for lightweight ASW torpedoes
Aircraft: one Lynx or one EH.101 Merlin ASW helicopter
Crew: 169

Assessment
Versatility   ★★★
Firepower   ★★★
Age   ★
Worldwide users   ★

The Type 23 ASW frigate is a little smaller and cheaper than the Type 22, but it is a potentially powerful fighting ship.

FFG-7 'Oliver Hazard Perry' class

The 'Oliver Hazard Perry' class was designed in the 1970s to replace the large numbers of US Navy escorts from the 1950s and 1960s, as well as World War II veterans which had been modified in the same period. The older ships were primarily ASW vessels, while the 'Perrys' have much greater all-round fighting capacity, with Harpoon SSMs and Standard SAMs. The primary ASW systems are the frigate's two LAMPS – Light Airborne Multi-Purpose System – helicopters. Built to a modular design, the *Oliver Hazard Perry* was commissioned in 1977. It was followed over the next 12 years by 50 more examples of the type, many of which now operate with the Naval Reserve Force. Spain, Australia and Taiwan operate or are building 20 similar vessels. USS *Stark* was hit 'in error' by Iraqi Exocets in 1987 and the *Samuel B. Roberts* struck an Iranian mine in 1988.

Specification
Dimensions: length 138.1 m (453 ft); beam 13.7 m (45 ft)
Displacement: 4165 tonnes (4100 tons)
Speed: 29 knots
Armament: Mk 13 single-rail launcher with 4 Harpoon SSMs and 36 Standard SM-1MR SAMs, 76-mm gun, Phalanx CIWS and 2 triple tubes for lightweight ASW torpedoes
Aircraft: two Seasprite LAMPS I or two Sea Hawk LAMPS III ASW helicopters
Crew: 206

Assessment
Versatility   ★★★
Firepower   ★★★
Age   ★★
Worldwide users   ★★

With the block obsolescence of many older frigates, the FFG-7 class has become the US Navy's most important escort.

'Rezvyy' class

The first of the 'Krivak' anti-submarine ships appeared in 1970. They were faster and more heavily armed than their Western counterparts, with four large SS-N-14 'Silex' missiles. Twenty-one ships were built before the first of the 11 improved 'Krivak IIs' appeared in 1976. This version had new guns and a larger variable depth sonar. The 'Krivak III', which entered service in the mid-1980s, dropped the 'Silex' launcher for a single gun turret and incorporated a hangar and flight deck instead of the stern gun turrets. The 'Krivak' class has been renamed the 'Rezvyy' and 'Bditelnyy' classes.

Specification
(Krivak III)
Dimensions: length 123.5 m (405 ft); beam 14 m (46 ft)
Displacement: 3660 tonnes (3600 tons)
Speed: 32 knots
Armament: SA-N-4 twin launcher with 40 missiles, 100-mm gun, 2×30-mm CIWS, 2 quad tubes for heavyweight torpedoes and 2 RBU-6000 12-tube ASW mortars
Aircraft: one Ka-25 'Hormone' or one Ka-27 'Helix' ASW helicopter
Crew: 180

Assessment	
Versatility	***
Firepower	***
Age	***
Worldwide users	*

The huge quadruple SS-N-14 launcher dominates the forward end of most of the 'Krivak' class.

'Kortenaer' class

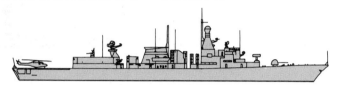

Authorised in the late 1960s, the 'Kortenaer' class was designed to replace 12 older ASW vessels of the Dutch navy. Propulsion and machinery were based on the larger 'Tromp' class, with gas turbines giving the kind of manoeuvrability and acceleration that are vital when hunting fast nuclear-powered submarines. The 'Kortenaer' design was used by the Germans as the basis for eight 'Bremen' or 'Type 122' class ASW frigates, and has been stretched and modified to produce the forthcoming 'Type 123' or 'Deutschland' class. Only seven 'Kortenaer' frigates remain in service.

Specification
('Kortenaer' class)
Dimensions: length 130.5 m (428 ft); beam 14.6 m (48 ft)
Displacement: 3688 tonnes (3630 tons)
Speed: 30 knots
Armament: 8 Harpoon SSMs, octuple Sea Sparrow launcher with 24 missiles, 76-mm gun, Goalkeeper 30-mm CIWS, 2 Oerlikon 20-mm and 2 twin tubes for lightweight ASW torpedoes
Aircraft: two Lynx ASW helicopters
Crew: 176

Assessment	
Versatility	***
Firepower	***
Age	**
Worldwide users	**

The 'Kortenaer' class are very capable ASW frigates. Vessels of similar design are used by the German navy.

'Lupo' class

The 'Lupo' class frigates were designed primarily as convoy escorts, with some surface warfare capability. To reduce the ship's complement, the design's machinery was highly automated, and with a speed of 35 knots it was one of the fastest warships afloat. Although smaller than contemporary American and British designs, the 'Lupos' are heavily armed. The design has been successfully exported: six 'Lupos' are in service with Venezuela and four with Peru. Iraq ordered four 'Lupos', but these were never delivered, having been embargoed during the Iran-Iraq war. Eventually completed, they have since been acquired by the Italian navy.

Specification
Dimensions: length 113.2 m (371 ft); beam 11.3 m (37 ft)
Displacement: 2540 tonnes (2500 tons)
Speed: 35 knots
Armament: 8 Teseo SSMs, octuple Sea Sparrow SAM launcher with 16 missiles, 127-mm gun, 2 twin 40-mm compact, 2 Oerlikon 20-mm and 2 triple tubes for lightweight ASW torpedoes
Aircraft: one AB.212 ASW helicopter
Crew: 185

Assessment	
Versatility	***
Firepower	***
Age	**
Worldwide users	**

'Lupo' class frigates are among the fastest major warships in service.

'Maestrale' class

The 'Lupo' class are primarily escorts and are not really suitable for the fleet ASW role. The eight frigates of the 'Maestrale' class began to enter service in the 1980s to take up the ASW role. The 'Maestrale' design is essentially that of a stretched 'Lupo', with fewer anti-ship weapons and more emphasis on ASW capability. The increase in length and beam has resulted in a vessel with better seaworthiness and habitability, and the extra room allows a second helicopter to be carried along with a variable depth sonar system. The machinery arrangement is similar to that of the 'Lupos', but the extra tonnage knocks three knots off the speed. Even so the 'Maestrales' are still faster than most other frigates.

Specification
Dimensions: length 122.7 m (402 ft); beam 12.9 m (42 ft)
Displacement: 3250 tonnes (3200 tons)
Speed: 32 knots
Armament: 4 Teseo SSMs, octuple Albatros launcher with 16 Aspide missiles, 127-mm gun, 2 twin 40-mm compact, 2 Oerlikon 20-mm, 2 single tubes for heavyweight torpedoes and 2 triple tubes for lightweight ASW torpedoes
Aircraft: two AB.212 ASW helicopters
Crew: 232

Assessment	
Versatility	***
Firepower	***
Age	**
Worldwide users	*

Maestrale is an enlarged 'Lupo'. It is marginally slower, but it has better ASW capability.

Many older frigates remain in service today; some navies have fitted new sensors and weapons to existing hulls, others have sold their frigates to minor navies. The end of the USSR and East Germany has brought a large number of warships on to the potential export market.

Type 21 'Amazon' class

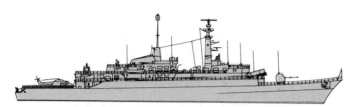

The Royal Navy commissioned eight 'Amazons' in the early 1970s. Although they were popular ships to serve in, they lacked the 'growth' potential to accommodate new weapons and sensors. All but HMS *Amazon* herself served in the Falklands war and two (*Ardent* and *Antelope*) were lost to Argentine attacks. The heavy seas of the South Atlantic caused severe cracking in the upper deck, which led to steel inserts being welded to the hulls after the war. Further work was carried out on the hulls of the surviving Type 21s from 1988–92, but today none remain in service.

Specification
Dimensions: length 117 m (384 ft); beam 12.7 m (41 ft 8 in)
Displacement: 3300 tonnes (3250 tons)
Speed: 32 knots
Armament: 4×MM.38 Exocet SSMs, 1 quadruple Sea Cat SAM launcher, 1×4.5-in gun, 4×20-mm AA guns and 2 triple 324-mm torpedo tubes with Mk 46 or Stingray torpedoes
Crew: 177

Assessment
Anti-surface weapons ★★★
Anti-submarine weapons ★★★★
Anti-aircraft weapons ★★★
Damage capacity ★★★★

Seven out of eight of the Type 21 'Amazon' class served during the Falklands war, including HMS Arrow shown here. However, today they are no longer in service.

A-69 class

Designed for coastal anti-submarine duties, the A-69 'Estienne D'Orves' class frigates were commissioned by the French navy from 1976-84. Seventeen A-69s are currently operated, and three were purchased by Argentina and served in the Falklands war. One, the *Guerrico*, was hit by the Royal Marines on South Georgia with an 84-mm Carl Gustav anti-tank rocket and small-arms fire; she required three days in dry dock to repair. Although not intended for deep-water ASW operations, the A-69s are used for overseas patrols with two or three of the French ships usually stationed in the Pacific.

Specification
Dimensions: length 80 m (262 ft); beam 10.3 m (34 ft)
Displacement: 1118 tonnes (1100 tons)
Speed: 24 knots
Armament: 4×MM.38 Exocet SSMs, 1×100-mm DP gun, 2×20-mm AA guns and 4 torpedo tubes with L3 550-mm anti-submarine or L5 DP 533-mm torpedoes
Crew: 90

Assessment
Anti-surface weapons ★★★
Anti-submarine weapons ★★
Anti-aircraft weapons ★★
Damage capacity ★★

The French A-69 class frigates are built for coastal operations, although they have taken part in overseas deployments. Compare their armament with that of the much larger Type 21 above.

'Leander' class

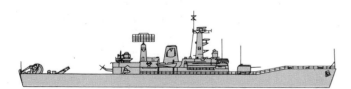

This class of general-purpose frigates has proved enormously successful with 26 'Leanders' commissioned at one time by the Royal Navy. Australia, India and the Netherlands built the type under licence, and Chile and New Zealand have bought some of the 'Leanders' as they were retired from the Royal Navy. Numerous refits created six discrete sub-groups within the Royal Navy and the foreign 'Leanders' tended to acquire better weapons and sensor fits than the British vessels. There are no longer any 'Leanders' in service with the Royal Navy.

Specification
Dimensions: (Batch 3A) length 113 m (370 ft); beam 13.1 m (43 ft)
Displacement: 2540 tonnes (2500 tons)
Speed: 28 knots
Armament: 4×MM.38 Exocet SSMs, 1 six-barrelled Seawolf SAM launcher, 2×20-mm AA guns and 2 triple 324-mm torpedo tubes with Stingray torpedoes
Crew: 260

Assessment
Anti-surface weapons ★★★
Anti-submarine weapons ★★★★
Anti-aircraft weapons ★★★★
Damage capacity ★★★★★

The very successful 'Leander' class frigates were built for several foreign navies as well as the RN, and they have been fitted with an extraordinary variety of weapons and sensors. HMS Ajax, seen here, carried the Ikara anti-submarine system.

'Meko' class

The UK was fortunate that the Argentines attacked the Falklands before the Government's plans for a drastic cut in the Royal Navy took place and before the Argentine fleet completed its modernisation. In 1980 Argentina signed a contract with the German firm Blohm und Voss for three light frigates. The first was launched in 1982 and commissioned in 1985; five more units have followed. The 'Meko' class are a major improvement over the elderly ex-US destroyers operated by the Argentine fleet in 1982.

Specification
Dimensions: length 91 m (298 ft); beam 12.2 m (40 ft)
Displacement: 1494 tonnes (1470 tons)
Speed: 27 knots
Armament: 4×MM.38 Exocet SSMs, 1×76-mm DP gun, 4×40-mm DP guns and 2 triple torpedo tubes with A244 324-mm anti-submarine homing torpedoes
Crew: 93

Assessment
Anti-surface weapons ★★★★
Anti-submarine weapons ★★★★
Anti-aircraft weapons ★★
Damage capacity ★★★★★

After the Falklands war the Argentine navy acquired a powerful squadron of modern German-designed frigates to replace its elderly US warships. One 'Meko' class frigate was deployed to the Gulf in 1991.

'Grisha' class

In 1991 the Russian navy operated over 70 'Grisha' class frigates. The first series of 'Grishas' was built from 1968–74, but successive improvements to the design led to four discrete versions, three for the navy and one sub-class for the KG coastal patrols. Classified by the Russians as 'small anti-submarine ships', the 'Grishas' pack a heavy anti-submarine armament into a relatively small hull. Combined with a respectable anti-aircraft armament, this makes the 'Grishas' much more effective than the profusion of older escort vessels that were retired in the late 1980s.

Specification
('Grisha I')
Dimensions: length 72 m (236 ft); beam 10 m (33 ft)
Displacement: 965 tonnes (950 tons)
Speed: 30 knots
Armament: 1 twin SA-N-4 launcher, 1 twin 57-mm gun turret, 1×30-mm CIWS, 2×RBU 6000 mortars, 2 twin 533-mm torpedo tubes with anti-submarine homing torpedoes and 10 depth charges
Crew: 80

Assessment
Anti-surface weapons ★
Anti-submarine weapons ★★★
Anti-aircraft weapons ★★★
Damage capacity ★★

The 'Grisha' class frigates are dedicated submarine hunters.

'Petya' class

From 1961–69 the former Soviet navy constructed 27 'Petya' class frigates. Shipping a heavy anti-submarine armament that includes homing torpedoes, mortars and depth charges, some of them were modified in the 1970s to carry a variable depth sonar. The 'Petya II' version has a second bank of five torpedo tubes in place of the RBU 2500 anti-submarine mortar. Fourteen 'Petya IIIs' have been exported: ten to India and two each to Syria and Vietnam. 'Petya IIIs' have triple 533-mm torpedo tubes in place of the 406-mm tubes on the Russian frigates.

Specification
('Petya I')
Dimensions: length 81 m (266 ft); beam 9.1 m (30 ft)
Displacement: 965 tonnes (950 tons)
Speed: 33 knots
Armament: 4×76-mm guns, 5×406-mm torpedo tubes with E40 400-mm homing anti-submarine torpedoes, 4×RBU 2500 mortars and 10 depth charges
Crew: 98

Assessment
Anti-surface weapons ★
Anti-submarine weapons ★★
Anti-aircraft weapons ★
Damage capacity ★★

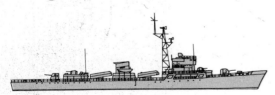

The 'Petya' class are small frigates equipped primarily for anti-submarine warfare. Many 'Petya IIIs' have been exported, but they carry the outdated 533-mm torpedoes.

'Jianghu' class

The first four units of the 'Jianghu' class were laid down in 1973 and the Chinese navy now operates 26 of them. Two were exported to Egypt, two to Bangladesh and four to Thailand. There are three main versions: the 'Jianghu IIs' have a hangar and carry a helicopter; 'Jianghu IIIs' have twin 100-mm gun turrets instead of single weapons. There are reports of severe equipment problems aboard these vessels. The stabilisers do not work, and the air-conditioning must be used sparingly to save the generators. The 100-mm guns are hand-loaded and on the 'Jianghu Is' they have no fire-control radar. Their SSMs are the Chinese copy of the elderly Soviet 'Styx'.

Specification
('Jianghu I')
Dimensions: length 103 m (338 ft); beam 10.2 m (33 ft)
Displacement: 1593 tonnes (1568 tons)
Speed: 26 knots
Armament: 2 twin HY-2 SSM launchers, 2×100-mm guns, up to 12×37-mm AA guns, 2×RBU 1200 mortars and 10 depth charges
Crew: 195

Assessment
Anti-surface weapons ★★
Anti-submarine weapons ★
Anti-aircraft weapons ★
Damage capacity ★★★

The Egyptian frigate Najim al Zaffer during a visit to Portsmouth. The Thai and Bangladeshi navies also operate these Chinese-built warships, armed with guns and obsolescent copies of the Soviet 'Styx' missile.

Modern frigates are capable of carrying a mixed armament able to engage submarines, surface ships or aircraft. However, many navies fit them out primarily for anti-submarine warfare.

'Knox' class

Laid down in 1965, USS *Knox* was the first of 48 'Knox' class frigates. The class was built primarily for an anti-submarine role and had the ASROC missile system as its main armament, which uses a homing anti-submarine torpedo to a maximum range of 10 kilometres. During the 1980s the class was modernised with the addition of Harpoon SSMs in place of the port pair of ASROC launchers, and Phalanx 20-mm CIWS instead of Sea Sparrow missiles as the anti-aircraft/anti-missile system. Thirty-four ships were fitted with towed array sonar. The 'Knox' class of frigates are no longer in service.

Specification
Dimensions: length 134 m (440 ft); beam 14.3 m (47 ft)
Displacement: 3060 tonnes (3011 tons)
Speed: 27 knots
Armament: 8 Harpoon SSMs, 1 octuple ASROC launcher, 1×5-in gun, 1 Vulcan 20-mm CIWS and 4×324-mm torpedo tubes with Mk 46 anti-submarine homing torpedoes
Crew: 283

Assessment
Anti-surface weapons ★★★
Anti-submarine weapons ★★★★
Anti-aircraft weapons ★★★★
Damage capacity ★

USS **Knox** *was the first of a 48-strong class of frigates that is now due to be laid up in reserve as part of the US Navy's 1992 cutbacks.*

'Wielingen' class

The 'Wielingen' class were the first frigates to be built and designed in Belgium, and are the largest ships in the Belgian navy. They are equipped with weapons and sensors from France, Sweden, Canada, the USA and the Netherlands. For surface action they have Exocet missiles and for air defence a Creusot-Loire dual-purpose 100-mm gun and Sea Sparrow SAMs. For ASW they have French L5 homing torpedoes and Bofors anti-submarine rockets. The 'Wielingen' class carries a heavy, well-balance armament in a compact hull. Of the original four ships built, only two remain in service.

Specification
Dimensions: length 106 m (348 ft); beam 12.3 m (40 ft)
Displacement: 1910 tonnes (1880 tons)
Speed: 26 knots
Armament: 4×MM.38 Exocet SSMs, 1 octuple Sea Sparrow launcher with 25 missiles, 1×100-mm DP gun, 2 torpedo tubes and 1 six-barrelled 375-mm anti-submarine mortar
Crew: 159

Assessment
Anti-surface weapons ★★
Anti-submarine weapons ★★★
Anti-aircraft weapons ★★
Damage capacity ★

Westhinder *is one of Belgium's 'Wielingen' class of frigates – the largest ships in their navy. They carry Exocet missiles, Sea Sparrow SAMs and L5 torpedoes.*

'Vosper' Mk 5 class

The Iranian navy currently includes three destroyers: the ex-HMS *Sluys* (a modernised 'Battle' class ship) and two ex-US 'Allen M. Sumner' class vessels. The Iranians' most modern major units are the three British-built frigates, commissioned in 1971-72 and refitted just before the Shah was overthrown. The 'Vosper' Mk 5 is a mid-1960s design equipped with weapons of that period: Sea Killer (an early surface-to-surface missile), good gun armament and a Limbo ASW mortar. Sea Killer is an obsolete system in the 1990s and the Iranians may be short of missiles anyway since *Jane's Fighting Ships* now credits them with rockets taken from BM-21 multiple rocket launchers. There were four ships originally: *Sahand* was sunk by US Navy aircraft in April 1988, and *Sabalan* was crippled by a laser-guided bomb in the same action and spent two years in dock.

Specification
Dimensions: length 94.5 m (310 ft); beam 11.1 m (36 ft)
Displacement: 1118 tonnes (1100 tons)
Speed: 39 knots
Armament: 1 quintuple launcher for Sistel Sea Killer Mk 1 SSM, 1 Vickers 4.5-in DP gun, twin Oerlikon 20-mm cannon and 1 Limbo anti-submarine mortar
Crew: 125

Assessment
Anti-surface weapons ★★
Anti-submarine weapons ★★
Anti-aircraft weapons ★★
Damage capacity ★

The **Saam** *leaves Portsmouth in 1971. Refitted in Britain just before the 1979 revolution, she was renamed* **Alvand**. *Sister-ship* **Sahand** *was sunk by US aircraft.*

'Koni' class

Built by the USSR at the Zelenodolsk shipyard on the Black Sea, the 'Koni' class was widely exported but not operated (other than in the training role) by the Soviet navy. During the 1980s 'Koni' class frigates were supplied to the fleets of Algeria (three), Cuba (two), Libya (two), East Germany (three) and Yugoslavia (four), and in 1990 the Soviets transferred the single 'Koni' they had used for training foreign crews to Bulgaria. The Libyan and Yugoslavian ships were retrofitted with four Styx SSMs and torpedoes: four 406-mm tubes for Soviet Type 40 ASW torpedoes on the former and six 324-mm tubes for the more capable Whitehead anti-submarine torpedoes on the latter. The East German 'Koni' class ships have no future in the navy of reunified Germany and they will be deleted, and the fate of the Yugoslavian frigates remains to be seen.

Specification
Dimensions: length 96.7 m (317 ft); beam 12.8 m (42 ft)
Displacement: 1727 tonnes (1700 tons)
Speed: 27 knots
Armament: 4×SS-N-2 Styx SSMs (Libyan and Yugoslavian only), 1 twin SA-N-4 'Gecko' SAM launcher, 2 twin 76-mm DP guns, torpedoes (see text) and 2×12-barrelled RBU 6000 anti-submarine mortars
Crew: 130

Assessment	
Anti-surface weapons	*
Anti-submarine weapons	*
Age	**
Worldwide users	****

East Germany operated three 'Konis'. Rostock is now F224 of the German navy.

'Mirka' class

Designated as 'small anti-submarine' ships by the Soviet navy, the 'Mirka' class were reclassified as 'escort ships' in the late 1970s. Nine 'Mirka Is' were built between 1964 and 1965, and nine 'Mirka IIs' in the following two years. They are a development of the earlier 'Petya' class. The 'Mirka IIs' were distinguished by the absence of the aft pair of RBU ASW rocket launchers and the addition of a second bank of five 406-mm torpedo tubes loaded with Type 40 homing torpedoes. The ships served with the Black Sea Fleet but today they are no longer in service.

Specification
('Mirka II')
Dimensions: length 82.4 m (270 ft); beam 9.1 m (30 ft)
Displacement: 965 tonnes (950 tons)
Speed: 32 knots
Armament: 2 twin 76-mm guns, 2×RBU 6000 anti-submarine rocket launchers, 2 quintuple 406-mm torpedo tubes with Type 40 homing torpedoes and 1 rack of depth charges
Crew: 96

Assessment	
Anti-surface weapons	*
Anti-submarine weapons	**
Age	*****
Worldwide users	*

A 'Mirka II' under way in the Black Sea during the early 1980s.

'Niteroi' class

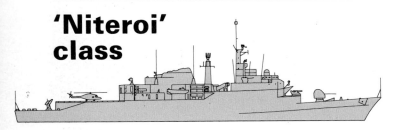

The Brazilian navy ordered six frigates from the British Vosper-Thorneycroft shipyards in 1970. Based on the company's Mk 10 frigate design, four are specialist anti-submarine warfare frigates and two are more general purpose. The ASW frigates have Branik anti-submarine missiles – a development of the Australian Ikara system – whereas Constituicao and Liberal have a second 4.5-inch DP gun turret instead and a rack of depth charges. Most importantly, the latter vessels also have four Exocet missiles, although the Brazilian navy announced in 1991 that the ASW frigates would be receiving Exocet too. Plans to replace the Sea Cat SAMs in favour of Phalanx CIWS have also been mooted; sensors and countermeasures are being upgraded.

Specification
('Niteroi' ASW)
Dimensions: length 129 m (423 ft); beam 13.5 m (44 ft)
Displacement: 3250 tonnes (3200 tons)
Speed: 30 knots
Armament: 2 triple Sea Cat SAM launchers, 1 Branik anti-submarine missile launcher, 1×4.5-in DP gun, 2 Bofors 40-mm guns and 2 triple 324-mm torpedo tubes with Mk 46 homing torpedoes
Crew: 209

Assessment	
Anti-surface weapons	**
Anti-submarine weapons	****
Age	**
Worldwide users	*

Liberal is one of six British-built frigates operated by Brazil.

'Commandant Rivière' class

Classified as 'escorts' by the French navy, the seven 'Commandant Rivière' class frigates are diesel-engined warships designed in the 1950s. The first unit, Victor Schoelcher, was laid down in 1957 and the final one, Enseigne de Vaisseau Henry, was commissioned in 1965. Often deployed to the remnants of the French colonial empire in the Pacific and Indian Oceans, the 'Commandant Rivière' class were eventually fitted with four Exocet missiles, which made them versatile warships given their powerful anti-submarine armament. Commandant Rivière is now a sonar trials ship, stripped of most weapons and fitted with a towed array. Victor Schoelcher was sold to Uruguay in 1988, and two other units followed in 1990. The Exocet missiles and Dagaie decoy launchers were removed before transfer.

Specification
Dimensions: length 102.7 m (337 ft); beam 11.7 m (38 ft)
Displacement: 1778 tonnes (1750 tons)
Speed: 25 knots
Armament: 4 Exocet SSMs, 2×100-mm DP guns, 2×30-mm anti-aircraft guns, 2 triple 550-mm torpedo tubes for L3 anti-submarine homing torpedoes and 1×305-mm four-barrelled anti-submarine mortar
Crew: 159

Assessment	
Anti-surface weapons	**
Anti-submarine weapons	***
Age	*****
Worldwide users	**

Amiral Charner was sold to Uruguay and renamed Montevideo.

Modern amphibious assault ships can land intervention forces ranging in size from small raiding parties to multi-division invasions, and they can do it in any country that has a coastline.

'Tarawa' class

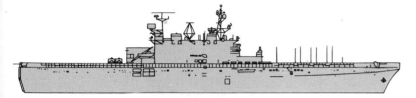

The five ships of the US Navy's 'Tarawa' class were the world's largest amphibious warfare vessels until the arrival of the improved and marginally enlarged 'Wasp' class. Each combines the capabilities of a helicopter assault ship, a dock landing ship, an amphibious cargo vessel and a command ship in a single hull. Each can accommodate a 1,900-man reinforced marine battalion, plus vehicles, freight and fuel. Men and equipment can be landed from the 81-metre floodable docking well, which can hold up to 40 AAV-7 armoured amphibious vehicles or four large utility landing craft. Alternatively, the troops can be landed by the vessel's force of up to 30 embarked helicopters. The 'Wasp' class can operate with air-cushion landing craft, and both types can house AV-8B Harrier aircraft.

Specification
('Tarawa' class)
Type: general-purpose amphibious assault ship (LHA)
Dimensions: length 250 m (820 ft); beam 32.5 m (106 ft)
Displacement: 39,930 tonnes (39,300 tons)
Speed: 24 knots
Armament: 3×5-in guns, 2×20-mm Phalanx CIWS and 2 octuple Sea Sparrow missile launchers
Crew: 937 plus 1900 troops

Assessment
Size	★★★★★
Helicopter capacity	★★★★★
Landing force	★★★★★
Flexibility	★★★★★

The sheer size and capability of the massive general-purpose assault ship the USS Tarawa is bought at great cost. While it has unmatched capabilities, such expensive vessels are beyond the means of all but the US Navy.

'Iwo Jima' class

The ships of the 'Iwo Jima' class have been a most important part of the US Navy's amphibious lift capability for 20 years. They were intended from the outset to land troops by helicopter rather than landing craft, and they resemble a World War II escort carrier in size and general layout. Each can carry a reinforced marine battalion landing team, with vehicles, palletised equipment and stores. The hangar can house 19 out of the typical complement of 24 helicopters. Out of the seven 'Iwo Jimas' that were built, only two remain in service.

Specification
('Iwo Jima' class)
Type: amphibious assault ship helicopter (LHA)
Dimensions: length 180.5 m (592 ft); beam 25.6 m (84 ft)
Displacement: 18,600 tonnes (18,300 tons)
Speed: 23 knots
Armament: 2 twin 3-in guns and 2×20-mm Phalanx CIWS
Crew: 686 plus 1750 troops

Assessment
Size	★★★
Helicopter capacity	★★★★★
Landing force	★★★★★
Flexibility	★★★

The 'Iwo Jima' class LPH was the first vessel designed and constructed specifically to operate helicopters. Each LPH can carry a reinforced helicopter squadron, a marine battalion landing team, together with a wide variety of supporting personnel.

'Whidbey Island' class

Dock landing ships (LSD) were developed during World War II as a means of transporting landing craft across the open sea and launching them in an assault on an enemy coast. A large proportion of the hull of this type of craft is taken up by a floodable docking well. The latest LSDs in US Navy service are the 'Whidbey Island' class. Originally to have been a repeat of earlier LSD designs, the 'Whidbey Islands' were enlarged to enable the vessels to handle four LCAC air-cushion landing craft. The helicopter deck is raised to allow adequate ventilation for the gas-turbine-powered LCACs. There is no hangar, but helicopter and AV-8B refuelling facilities have been fitted. There are two landing spots to allow simultaneous operation of aircraft up to CH-53 size.

Specification
Type: Landing Ship Dock (LSD)
Dimensions: length 185.6 m (609 ft); beam 25.6 m (84 ft)
Displacement: 15,980 tonnes (15,725 tons)
Speed: 22 knots
Armament: 2×20-mm Phalanx CIWS
Crew: 505 plus 504 troops

Assessment
Size	★★★
Helicopter capacity	★
Landing force	★★★
Flexibility	★★★

Dock landing ships were among the most important of the specialised assault vessels developed during World War II, and they are still going strong in the shape of the 'Whidbey Island' class. These vessels are designed to accommodate the latest air-cushion landing craft.

'Newport' class

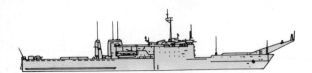

The 20 ships of the 'Newport' class were the last dedicated tank landing ships (LST) built for the US Navy. Instead of bow doors, the 'Newports' are fitted with an aluminium ramp which goes over the bow. In this way, the front of the vessel is not weakened and a higher cruising speed can be maintained. There is also a stern ramp which provides direct access to the water. The main function of the LST is to carry heavy equipment, delivering it directly to the beach. This class can carry several hundred tons of freight, or 20 trucks and 21 Main Battle Tanks, or 25 AAV-7s. Each of the ships has a small helicopter platform aft, but there is no hangar. Four heavy-duty pontoon rafts can also be carried attached to the stern.

Specification
Type: Landing Ship Tank (LST)
Dimensions: length 159 m (521 ft); beam 21.2 m (69 ft)
Displacement: 8585 tonnes (8450 tons)
Speed: 20 knots
Armament: 2×20-mm Phalanx CIWS
Crew: 255 plus 400 troops

Assessment
Size ★★
Helicopter capacity ★
Landing force ★★★★
Flexibility ★★

The 'Newport' class tank landing ships are among those rare major warships that are actually designed to run aground. They deliver heavy equipment directly onto the beach, using a unique ramp which extends 35 metres over the bow.

'Fearless' class

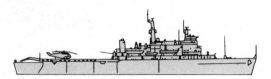

The two vessels of the Royal Navy's 'Fearless' class provide Britain with the bulk of her amphibious capability. Similar in many ways to the American 'Raleigh' and 'Austin' classes, they are designated Landing Platform Dock. LPDs have smaller docking wells but more accommodation than LSDs, and have better aircraft handling facilities. Although now getting on in years, the 'Fearless' class LPDs are tasked with providing command facilities for an amphibious operation, as well as being able to land a light battalion-sized force. A typical load might include 400 troops, 15 Main Battle Tanks, seven medium trucks and 20 Land Rovers. Up to 1,000 troops can be housed for short periods, and four helicopters can also be carried.

Specification
Type: Landing Platform Dock (LPD)
Dimensions: length 152.4 m (500 ft); beam 24.4 m (80 ft)
Displacement: 12,395 tonnes (12,200 tons)
Speed: 21 knots
Armament: 2×40-mm AA guns and 2 Sea Cat SAM launchers
Crew: 617 plus 600 troops (normal maximum)

Assessment
Size ★★★
Helicopter capacity ★★
Landing force ★★★
Flexibility ★★★

Britain's two 'Fearless' class LPDs proved their worth in the South Atlantic in 1982, where they were the heart of the amphibious phase of the successful campaign to retake the Falklands.

'Ivan Rogov' class

The three 'Ivan Rogov' class ships are designated 'Large Landing Ship' by the Russian navy. About the same size as the Western LPDs, the 'Ivan Rogovs' have a similar sized docking well but also include LST features such as a bow ramp. Normally, they have three 'Lebed' class hovercraft, but they can carry six 135-ton 'Ondotra' class landing craft instead. They can ship a reinforced battalion of naval infantry plus their APCs; or the 40 or so vehicles of a naval infantry tank battalion. Each of the 'Ivan Rogovs' has five Kamov Ka-27 'Helix' assault transport helicopters.

Specification
Type: Landing Platform Dock (LPD)
Dimensions: length 159 m (521 ft); beam 24.5 m (80 ft)
Displacement: 14,225 tonnes (14,000 tons)
Speed: 26 knots
Armament: 1 twin 76-mm gun, 4×30-mm CIWS, 1×MLRS and 1 twin SAM
Crew: 250 plus 550 troops

Assessment
Size ★★★
Helicopter capacity ★★
Landing force ★★★
Flexibility ★★★

Ivan Rogov was potentially the most capable amphibious warfare vessel built by the Russians. However, there are indications that the class has had operational problems.

'Ropucha' class

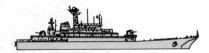

Given the designation 'Large Landing Ship', the 'Ropucha' class of tank landing ship was produced in Poland for the Soviet navy. Designed for roll-on, roll-off operations, the 'Ropucha' design has both bow and stern doors, and the 630 m² vehicle deck stretches the length of the hull. The multi-level superstructure is designed to house two companies of naval infantry for extended periods. This, together with a 450-ton cargo capacity and the ability to carry 24 armoured vehicles, allowed the Soviet navy to employ the vessels on distant ocean operations. The collapse of the Soviet Union means that capability is unlikely to be needed by Russia and the Ukraine, which have inherited most of the 25 ships of this class.

Specification
Type: Landing Ship Tank (LST)
Dimensions: length 113 m (370 ft); beam 14.5 m (48 ft)
Displacement: 4370 tonnes (4300 tons)
Speed: 18 knots
Armament: 1×76-mm gun, 2×30-mm CIWS, 4 quad SA-N-5 'Grail' SAM launchers and 1 or 2 122-mm multiple rocket launchers
Crew: 90 plus 230 troops

Assessment
Size ★
Helicopter capacity –
Landing force ★★
Flexibility ★★

Many of the Soviet navy's amphibious assault vessels were built in Poland, the largest being the 4,300-ton 'Ropuchas'. The class was used in all four Soviet fleets, and will remain in service with the Russian and Ukrainian navies.

ANTI-SHIP MISSILES

The attack on HMS *Sheffield* during the Falklands war made Exocet a household name in 1982. This French missile is one of many such guided weapons that are used by air forces and navies to attack enemy surface warships.

SS-N-2 'Styx'

Specification
(SS-N-2b)
Length: 5.8 m (19 ft)
Diameter: 750 mm (29 in)
Weight: 2300 kg (2 tons 590 lb)
Range: 40 km (25 miles)
Speed: Mach 0.8
Guidance: radio-command/terminal active radar homing
Warhead: 400 kg (880 lb)

Assessment
Range ★
Accuracy ★
Warhead ★★★
Worldwide users ★★★★★

A Russian 'Osa' attack craft fires a SS-N-2 missile. Although an ageing system, the 'Styx' and its copies are still in use, especially with navies supplied by Russia and China.

Introduced over 30 years ago, the Russian SS-N-2 'Styx' was the first surface-to-air missile (SSM) to sink a warship in combat when Egyptian missile boats sank the Israeli destroyer *Eilat* in 1967. The 'Styx' is most widely encountered in 'Osa' or similar missile boats belonging to Russian allies. The missile is configured like a small airoraft, with a wing span of 2.8 metres and a triple tail surface. Iraq fired two 'Silkworm' missiles (Chinese copies of the SS-N-2) at allied warships in the Gulf War; one missed and the other was shot down by a Sea Dart missile launched from HMS *Gloucester*.

SS-N-12 'Sandbox'

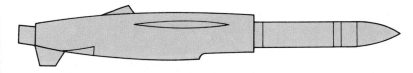

Specification
Length: 11.7 m (38 ft 5 in)
Diameter: unknown
Weight: 5000 kg (4 tons 2060 lb)
Range: 550 km (340 miles)
Speed: Mach 2.5
Guidance: inertial with radio-command and terminal active radar homing
Warhead: 1000 kg (2205 lb)

Assessment
Range ★★★★★
Accuracy ★★★
Warhead ★★★★★
Worldwide users ★

These massive launchers aboard the Russian aircraft carrier Kiev contain a long-range anti-ship missile known to NATO as the SS-N-12 'Sandbox'.

The Russians followed the 'Styx' with the similar and even larger SS-N-3 'Shaddock', which they fitted to submarines intended to attack major surface targets. In the 1970s the Russian navy began to arm its 'Slava' class cruisers and 'Kiev' class aircraft carriers with a new weapon, the SS-N-12 'Sandbox'. Still shrouded in secrecy, the 'Sandbox' is credited with a very long range and a massive warhead. The sheer size of the launchers aboard the *Kiev* give some indication of the missile's dimensions, but all data remains speculative.

Penguin

Specification
Length: 2.96 m (9 ft 5 in)
Diameter: 280 mm (11 in)
Weight: 340 kg (750 lb)
Range: 30 km (19 miles)
Speed: Mach 0.8
Guidance: inertial/terminal infra-red radar homing
Warhead: 113 kg (249 lb)

Assessment
Range ★
Accuracy ★★★
Warhead ★
Worldwide users ★★

The Norwegian Penguin system was designed to inflict crippling damage on an enemy surface ship. For many years the Norwegian naval forces had to be prepared to face a sudden Soviet amphibious attack.

The first SSM to be developed by a Western power, the Norwegian Penguin was designed for land-based coastal defence batteries and small surface ships. Development work began in 1961 and the Penguin was finally accepted by the Royal Norwegian navy in 1972. Further work has made the Penguin a very versatile weapon, with versions available for launch from helicopters and even F-16 fighter aircraft. For a shipboard launch the firing vessel must acquire the target on radar; the fire-control system then calculates the bearing required for interception and the missile is launched. The Penguin follows its pre-programmed trajectory, while its own infra-red homing device searches for the target's exact location and directs it to impact.

Harpoon

Specification
Length: 4.58 m (15 ft)
Diameter: 343 mm (13 in)
Weight: 667 kg (1470 lb)
Range: 110 km (68 miles) (Harpoon 1) to 184 km (114 miles) (Harpoon II)
Speed: Mach 0.85
Guidance: inertial/ terminal active radar homing
Warhead: 227 kg (500 lb)

Assessment
Range   ★★★
Accuracy   ★★★★★
Warhead   ★★
Worldwide users   ★★★★

The sinking of the *Eilat* alerted the US Navy to the potential of SSMs and work began the following year. Operational evaluation was completed by 1977 and US surface ships and submarines began to receive their missiles. The first air-launched Harpoons were in service with US Navy P-3 Orions by 1979. Since then the Harpoon's range and accuracy have increased with three successive versions. All versions except Harpoon IB can execute a 'pop-up' attack; travelling at low altitude, the missile climbs when it nears the target and dives down from above. A radio altimeter keeps Harpoon flying just above the waves, making it hard to detect and shoot down. In the last seconds of flight it uses its own radar to home in on the target.

HMAS Canberra, one of Australia's US-designed FFG-7 class frigates, launches a Harpoon missile. This versatile weapon can be launched from aircraft, ships or submarines.

Otomat

Specification
Length: 4.82 m (15 ft 9 in)
Diameter: 460 mm (18 in)
Weight: 770 kg (1800 lb)
Range: 60 km (37 miles)
Speed: Mach 0.9
Guidance: inertial/ terminal active radar homing
Warhead: 210 kg (462 lb)

Assessment
Range   ★★
Accuracy   ★★★
Warhead   ★★
Worldwide users   ★★★

Given the export sales record of the Otomat, it had just as much chance as the Exocet of becoming a household name. A land- or ship-launched missile developed jointly by Engins Matra of France and OTO-Melara of Italy, Otomat has a longer range and heavier warhead than the MM.38 Exocet made famous in the Falklands. It has been supplied to Algeria, Egypt, Italy, Libya, Nigeria, Kuwait, Peru, Saudi Arabia and Venezuela. Cruising at an altitude of 250 metres, Otomat descends to 50 metres as it nears the target. At about 15 kilometres from the target's anticipated position it switches on its search radar. When it is locked on to the target, Otomat dives to make its final approach just 10 metres above sea level, presenting enemy guns and missiles with a very difficult target.

The Otomat anti-ship missile was developed by French and Italian companies as a joint venture and has been widely exported. It carries a heavier warhead than the famous Exocet missile.

Exocet

Specification
Length: 5.21 m (17 ft)
Diameter: 350 mm (14 in)
Weight: 735 kg (1620 lb)
Range: 42 km (26 miles)
Speed: Mach 0.9
Guidance: inertial/ terminal active radar homing
Warhead: 165 kg (364 lb)

Assessment
Range   ★
Accuracy   ★★★
Warhead   ★★
Worldwide users   ★★★★

Developed for the French navy during the late 1960s, Exocet is in service with the navies and air forces of over 25 nations. The most widely used anti-ship missile in the Western world, its use by the Argentine forces during the Falklands war resulted in the sinking of HMS *Sheffield* and the merchant vessel *Atlantic Conveyor*, and severe damage to HMS *Glamorgan*. Ironically, the Royal Navy was the first customer for Exocet, placing an order for 300 missiles as early as 1970. The French navy uses a submarine-launched variant. Once supplied with the target's range and bearing, Exocet flies at low altitude to intercept, switching on its own radar about 10 kilometres from the target.

Rocketed to fame by the Falklands war, the French-built Exocet missile has been supplied to a large number of Western navies. It has been modernised during the 1980s.

Tomahawk

Specification
Length: 6.4 m (21 ft)
Diameter: 530 mm (21 in)
Weight: 1200 kg (1 ton 405 lb)
Range: 460 km (285 miles)
Speed: Mach 0.7
Guidance: inertial/ terminal active radar homing
Warhead: 454 kg (1000 lb)

Assessment
Range   ★★★★★
Accuracy   ★★★
Warhead   ★★★
Worldwide users   ★

In 1981 a Tomahawk cruise missile was fired from a submarine off the Californian coast and succeeded in hitting its target on a missile range in Nevada. Ten years later the US Navy's submarines repeated the process 'for real', striking Iraqi targets during the Gulf War. However, sea-launched Tomahawks are formidable anti-shipping weapons too and are being carried by several classes of US cruisers and the new 'Arleigh Burke' destroyers, as well as by SSNs. Its long range and large warhead, combined with state-of-the-art guidance systems, make it a very effective naval weapon.

The Tomahawk cruise missile can be fired from submarines and major surface units. In the Gulf War the US Navy launched a hail of cruise missiles from its two 'Iowa' class battleships.

Modern warships of all sizes from missile boats to aircraft carriers have to be able to defend themselves against air attack. The latest generation of naval SAMs can not only shoot down enemy aircraft but can intercept incoming missiles as well.

Albatros

Specification
Type: point defence missile
Dimensions: length 3.7 m (12 ft 2 in); span 0.8 m (31 in)
Weight: 204 kg (450 lb)
Warhead: 33 kg (73 lb)
Performance: maximum speed Mach 2.5; altitude limits 15–5000 m (49–16,400 ft); range 18.5 km (11 miles)

Assessment
Range ★★★
Accuracy ★★★★
Age ★★
Worldwide users ★★★

One of only two Western naval SAMs not to be reloaded by hand, the Italian Aspide system has been widely exported. Radar guided and highly resistant to ECM, it can home in on jamming signals emitted by enemy aircraft.

The Italian Albatros SAM system uses the Aspide missile and Selenia or Marconi radar. Aspide uses the same airframe as the US Sparrow missile but has newer internal equipment that gives it greater resistance to countermeasures. It also has longer endurance and higher speed and is used ashore by the Spada point defence SAM system. Production began in 1977 and some 15 navies have adopted Albatros since then. It can be fitted to NATO Sparrow launchers with only minor modifications, but purpose-built units enjoy a semi-automatic reloader. A lightweight (four tons instead of nine) quadruple launcher is available for warships of under 300 tons displacement.

Sea Cat

Specification
Type: point defence missile
Dimensions: length 1.48 m (4 ft 10 in); span 0.65 m (26 in)
Weight: 68 kg (150 lb)
Warhead: 10 kg (22 lb)
Performance: maximum speed Mach 0.6; altitude limits 15–900 m (49–2950 ft); range 5.5 km (3 miles)

Assessment
Range ★★★
Accuracy ★
Age ★★★★★
Worldwide users ★★★★

Finally used in combat over 20 years after its introduction, the Sea Cat missile showed its age during the Falklands war. While it did disrupt several Argentine attacks, it only scored one confirmed kill.

First trialled at sea in 1961, the Short Brothers Sea Cat was the first naval point defence missile to enter service. Based on the Malkara anti-tank missile, the original version was steered by an operator using a joystick. Flares in the missile's tail helped him gather it into his sights and steer it into the attacking aircraft. Sea Cat was later modified to allow guidance by Contraves Sea Hunter or Signaal M40/44 fire-control systems. The Royal Navy adopted radar-guided versions, which were modified in 1977 to allow the engagement of sea-skimming targets. However, the missile's slow speed and short range makes it unable to deal with supersonic targets. It was used in the Falklands war and is still in service with a dozen or more navies worldwide.

Sea Dart

Specification
Type: medium-range area defence missile
Dimensions: length 4.36 m (14 ft 4 in); span 0.42 m (16 in)
Weight: 550 kg (1212 lb)
Warhead: 24 kg (53 lb)
Performance: maximum speed Mach 3; altitude limits 30–18,000 m (100–60,000 ft); range 65 km (40 miles)

Assessment
Range ★★★★
Accuracy ★★★
Age ★★★
Worldwide users ★

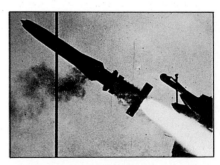

Sea Dart was credited with five kills during the Falklands war. It proved erratic in 1982, shooting down several aircraft outside its theoretical engagement envelope, but proving unreliable aboard Type 42 destroyers.

The British Aerospace Sea Dart is the Royal Navy's standard area defence missile, capable of engaging aircraft at great altitude and long range. However, it is unable to intercept sea-skimming missiles or aircraft flying at extremely low level. Improvements planned in the 1970s fell victim to government defence cuts. The Argentines, themselves users of Sea Dart aboard their Type 42 frigates, exploited this weakness during the Falklands campaign. Nevertheless, Sea Dart did achieve some spectacular kills: HMS *Exeter* shot down a Learjet on 6 June 1982 and a Canberra bomber a week later – both at altitudes of over 12000 metres (39,000 ft). She also brought down two A-4C Skyhawks at very low level, below the missile's official engagement envelope.

Sea Wolf

Developed during the 1960s and first fired in 1973, the British Aerospace Sea Wolf is a fully-automated SAM system capable of formidable accuracy. The entire engagement sequence is automatic, subject to operator veto. In a 1977 test a Sea Wolf missile intercepted a 4.5-in shell in flight, and the Sea Wolf-equipped Type 22 frigates were used as 'goalkeepers' in the Falklands, defending the vital aircraft carriers. On 12 May 1982 HMS *Brilliant* was attacked by four A-4C Skyhawk bombers: two were shot down and one crashed into the sea while trying to evade a missile. However, the system proved temperamental and prone to malfunction at critical moments; the software has since been modified. There have been no exports; an order from Kuwait in 1988 was rejected on security grounds.

Specification
Type: point defence missile
Dimensions: length 1.9 m (6 ft 3 in); span 0.45 m (18 in)
Weight: 82 kg (180 lb)
Warhead: 14 kg (31 lb)
Performance: maximum speed Mach 2; altitude limits 5–3000 m (16–9800 ft); range 6.5 km (4 miles)

Assessment
Range ★★
Accuracy ★★★★★
Age ★★
Worldwide users ★

Sea Wolf is capable of intercepting incoming Exocet missiles and even shells in flight. In the Falklands its software had to be modified to deal with crossing targets, but it remains an excellent point defence system.

Standard SM-1MR

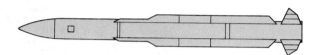

Standard is the US Navy's medium- and long-range area defence SAM and successive versions have provided greater range and greater resistance to enemy countermeasures. The Standard SM-1MR entered service with the US Navy in 1968 and has subsequently been bought by Australia, France, Italy, Japan and the Netherlands. The US Navy has since acquired an extended-range version, twice the weight of the SM-1MR and capable of intercepting enemy aircraft at up to 150 kilometres. The technology of the SM-2ER is deemed too advanced for export, even to NATO countries. The Standard SAM is also used as an anti-ship missile: there are several versions that home in on enemy radar emissions and have a range of some 75 kilometres.

Specification
Type: medium-range area defence missile
Dimensions: length 4.7 m (15 ft 5 in); span 0.9 m (35 in)
Weight: 608 kg (1340 lb)
Warhead: 62 kg (137 lb)
Performance: maximum speed Mach 3.5; altitude limits 30–19,000 m (100–62,300 ft); range 67 km (42 miles)

Assessment
Range ★★★★★
Accuracy ★★★★
Age ★★★
Worldwide users ★★★

Standard is the US Navy's long-range surface-to-air missile system and it has been supplied to many other navies. The export versions are inferior to the very long-range types currently in service with the US Navy.

Sea Sparrow

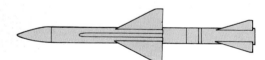

Sea Sparrow is the naval version of the AIM-7 Sparrow air-to-air missile. Adopted during the 1960s as a point defence weapon for the US Navy, successively more capable versions were introduced but none were capable of dealing with sea-skimming targets until the RIM-7M. The system is widely used by NATO navies, but the NATO Sea Sparrow differs from the US Navy version in having fully automated operation. The whole engagement sequence, from target acquisition to launch and impact, can be managed entirely by computer. The NATO Sea Sparrow employs the RIM-7H5 folding-fin version that fits into octuple launchers.

Specification
Type: point defence missile
Dimensions: length 3.98 m (13 ft); span 1.02 m (3 ft 4 in)
Weight: 228 kg (502 lb)
Warhead: 40 kg (88 lb)
Performance: maximum speed Mach 3; altitude limits 8–15,000 m (26–49,200 ft); range 22 km (14 miles)

Assessment
Range ★★★
Accuracy ★★★★★
Age ★★★★
Worldwide users ★★★★

Based on the AIM-7 air-to-air missile, Sea Sparrow dates from the 1960s but has been successively upgraded over the years. Ten NATO navies have Sea Sparrow aboard their warships.

SA-N-3 'Goblet'

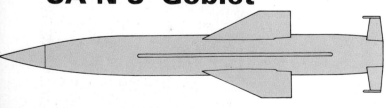

Most Soviet naval SAMs were developed from existing land-based SAMs, but the SA-N-3 appears to have been an original design. It entered service in 1967 and was shipped aboard 'Kresta II' and 'Kara' class missile cruisers, as well as aboard the 'Moskva' and 'Kiev' class helicopter carriers. It had a useful secondary role as a surface-to-surface missile, although its range in this role was limited to the radar horizon. Some were fitted with nuclear warheads. From 1978 the SA-N-3 was replaced by a vertically-launched missile designated SA-N-6 by NATO. This long-range missile is based on the SA-10 SAM and went to sea aboard the 'Kirov' class cruisers.

Specification
Type: medium-range area defence missile
Dimensions: length 6.4 m (21 ft); span 1.7 m (5 ft 8 in)
Weight: 545 kg (1200 lb)
Warhead: 80 kg (176 lb)
Performance: maximum speed Mach 2.5; altitude limits 100–24,000 m (330–78,700 ft); range 55 km (34 miles)

Assessment
Range ★★★★
Accuracy ★★★
Age ★★★★
Worldwide users ★

The large launcher rails on the forward deck of a Soviet 'Kresta' class cruiser fire SA-N-3 SAMs that can also be targeted against enemy ships. Some of the missiles carried 25-kiloton nuclear warheads.

ANTI-SUBMARINE WEAPONS No. 1

As the Soviet navy steadily built up its submarine fleet to menace the North Atlantic sea-lanes, NATO navies developed a plethora of anti-submarine weapons. The Soviets introduced similar systems, but data on many of them remains largely speculative.

SUBROC

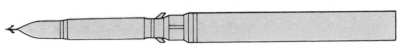

The US Navy introduced the SUBROC submarine rocket from 1965. It was a brutally simple answer to the problem of how a US submarine could exploit its superior sonar to attack an enemy submarine without warning. SUBROC was launched through a submarine's standard 533-mm torpedo tubes and blasted out of the water by its rocket motor. It would follow a pre-programmed path to the target area and then drop a W55 five-kiloton nuclear depth bomb. This would destroy any submarine within about 6000 metres. Providing that the launching submarine had a reasonable idea of the target's course and speed, SUBROC's large killing zone would probably catch the enemy. SUBROC's maximum range of 56 kilometres was about the maximum range at which 1960s US sonar systems might detect a Soviet submarine. Introduced aboard the 'Thresher' class and then the 'Permit' and 'Sturgeon' classes, SUBROC remained in service until 1990.

Specification
Dimensions: length 6.71 m (22 ft); diameter 0.53 m (21 in)
Weight: 1814 kg (1 ton 1770 lb)
Warhead: 295-kg (650-lb) 5-kiloton nuclear depth bomb
Performance: speed Mach 1.5; maximum range 56 km (35 miles)

Assessment
Range ★★★★★
Reliability ★★★★
Age ★★★★
Worldwide users ★★

A SUBROC missile hurtles skyward towards the suspected location of an enemy submarine. SUBROC could afford to miss its target by quite a margin – the nuclear warhead would crush the hull of any submarine within six kilometres.

ASROC

Fitted to many classes of US Navy surface warships, ASROC entered service in 1962. Thirty years later it is still an important ASW weapon, although it has been significantly improved. Like SUBROC, ASROC is a missile that delivers an anti-submarine weapon to the approximate location of the target. It is a more flexible system, delivering either a small nuclear depth bomb or a homing torpedo. The latter was originally the Mk 44, but this was soon replaced by the widely-used Mk 46, which has itself been upgraded several times. The conventionally-armed ASROC is also in service with the navies of Brazil, Canada, Germany, Greece, Italy, Japan, Pakistan, South Korea, Spain, Taiwan and Turkey. ASROC is fired after the launching ship has the range and bearing of the target submarine. The homing torpedo is dropped from the missile and slowed by parachute; the nuclear depth bomb sinks to a pre-set depth before detonation.

Specification
Dimensions: length 4.6 m (15 ft); diameter 0.325 m (13 in); wing span 0.84 m (33 in)
Weight: 434 kg (957 lb) (Mk 44); 487 kg (1074 lb) (Mk 46)
Warhead: 192.8-kg (425-lb) (Mk 44) or 230-kg (500-lb) (Mk 46) torpedoes; 118-kg (260-lb) (Mk 17) 1.5-kiloton nuclear depth bomb
Performance: speed Mach 0.8; maximum range 11 km (7 miles)

Assessment
Range ★★
Reliability ★★★★
Age ★★★★
Worldwide users ★★★

The ASROC missile delivers either a nuclear depth bomb or a homing torpedo to a maximum range of 11 kilometres. The system has been widely exported.

Malafon

Malafon is the standard anti-submarine armament of French navy surface warships. Developed between 1956 and 1965, it consists of a command-guided missile that delivers an L4 acoustic homing torpedo. The missile itself looks like a small aircraft, with its short and unswept wings and a tailplane. Launched from a ramp, Malafon is propelled by two jettisonable solid boosters. A radio altimeter keeps the missile on a flat trajectory, while flares on the wing tips help the launching vessel observe the missile's flight. Course corrections are signalled by radio. Some 800 metres short of the target's estimated position a parachute is deployed, slowing the missile and causing the L4 torpedo inside to be ejected into the sea. The L4 searches in a circular pattern, using active sonar, until it locks on to its target. During the 1980s the L4 was modified to improve its performance in shallow water.

Specification
Dimensions: length 6.15 m (20 ft); diameter 0.65 m (26 in); wing span 3.3 m (10 ft 10 in)
Weight: 1500 kg (1 ton 1075 lb)
Warhead: one L4 electric-powered torpedo
Performance: maximum range 13 km (8 miles)

Assessment
Range ★★
Reliability ★★★★
Age ★★★★★
Worldwide users ★

Malafon is seen here on the midships launcher of the guided missile destroyer Duquesne. It delivers a homing anti-submarine torpedo to a maximum range of 13 kilometres.

Ikara

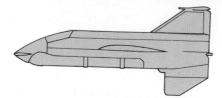

Specification
Dimensions: length
3.42 m (11 ft 3 in); height
1.57 m (5 ft 2 in); wing
span 1.52 m (5 ft)
Weight: depends on the
type of torpedo carried
Warhead: one lightweight
anti-submarine torpedo
Performance: speed
Mach 0.8; maximum range
25 km (15 miles)

Assessment
Range   ★★★
Reliability   ★★★★
Age   ★★★★★
Worldwide users ★★

*Ikara was originally designed in
Australia, and then developed in a
joint Anglo-Australian project.
Widely used by the Royal Navy in
the 1970s and 1980s, it has been
further modified for the Brazilian
navy.*

This is another guided missile that delivers a homing torpedo to attack the
enemy submarine. Initially developed by the Australian government, it attracted
the interest of the Royal Navy and a joint programme with British Aerospace
followed. A third version called Branik was produced for the Brazilian navy's
'Niteroi' class frigates. The Ikara missiles in service today are fitted with Mk 44
or Mk 46 lightweight acoustic homing torpedoes, but since 1982 Ikara has been
compatible with Stingray, A244 and Japanese and Swedish torpedoes. Guided
by radio command to the submarine's estimated position, Ikara ejects its torpedo
and flies on out of the engagement area. The torpedo then descends by
parachute and begins its search pattern.

Limbo

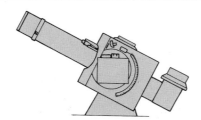

Specification
Dimensions: calibre
305 mm
Weight: 175 kg (386 lb)
Warhead: 92-kg
(203-lb) HE
Performance: maximum
range 900 m (2950 ft);
maximum depth 375 m
(1230 ft)

Assessment
Range   ★
Reliability   ★★★
Age   ★★★★★
Worldwide users ★★★

*The triple-barrelled launcher of the
Royal Navy's Limbo anti-submarine
mortar fires a set pattern of 175-
kilogram depth charges. Reloading
is automatic.*

Air-dropped homing torpedoes are at a disadvantage in shallow waters, where
the poor sonar conditions can prevent them acquiring a target and variations in
temperature and salinity can cause them to strike the bottom and detonate.
Limbo is an anti-submarine mortar developed for the Royal Navy during the
1950s and built on wartime experience of anti-submarine mortars. A three-
barrelled launcher lobs three depth bombs in a set pattern over the submarine's
estimated position. These are detonated either by a pre-set pressure fuse or by
time-delay; for deeper targets there is a version with a proximity fuse. Having
fired a pattern, the barrels are reloaded by pneumatic rammers from a ready-use
magazine alongside.

Bofors anti-submarine rocket

Specification
('Erika' type)
Dimensions: calibre
375 mm; length 2 m
(6 ft 7 in)
Weight: 250 kg (550 lb)
Warhead: 107-kg
(236-lb) HE
Performance: speed
100 m (330 ft) per second;
maximum range 1635 m
(5360 ft)

Assessment
Range   ★
Reliability   ★★★
Age   ★★★★
Worldwide users ★★★

*The Swedish company Bofors has
widely exported its series of anti-
submarine mortars. The Swedish
navy continues to use them against
Soviet/Russian submarines entering
Swedish territorial waters.*

The Swedish navy was one of the few minor navies to have developed its own
torpedoes before World War II, and it continues to rely on an advanced domestic
industry rather than importing weapons from the major powers. The Bofors
375-mm anti-submarine rocket launcher was developed in the 1950s and has
been widely exported. The rockets are launched after the submarine's position
has been plotted by sonar. They are shaped to follow a predictable trajectory
through the water, and a variety of rockets are available with impact or proximity
fuses. The Swedish navy expended a number of 375-mm rockets in anger during
the repeated incursions by Soviet submarines in the early 1980s. The Bofors
rockets are most commonly encountered today fired from a twin-tube launcher,
with 24 rounds loaded by a motor-driven hoist. It is capable of a sustained rate of
fire of two rockets every 45 seconds.

Soviet anti-submarine rockets

Specification
(RBU 6000)
Dimensions: length 1.6 m
(5 ft 3in)
Weight: 70 kg (154 lb)
Warhead: 21-kg
(46-lb) HE
Performance: maximum
range 6 km (4 miles)

Assessment
Range   ★
Reliability   ★★★
Age   ★★★★★
Worldwide users ★★★★★

*Many Russian warships are fitted
with the characteristic rotary
launcher for the RBU series of anti-
submarine rockets. These have also
been widely exported.*

The Russian navy developed a series of anti-submarine rockets fired from
circular multi-barrelled launchers and fitted them to many different classes of
warship. The rockets, with contact or magnetic influence fuses, are fired in
pairs to impact in a pre-set pattern around the estimated position of the
submarine. The most widely used today is the 250-mm calibre RBU 6000,
which first appeared 30 years ago. Twelve rocket launchers are arranged in a
horseshoe shape near the ship's bows and are fired ahead. Reloading is
accomplished one barrel at a time with the launcher in the vertical position.

Index of Weapons by Type

Index of Weapons by Country